Social Work and the Law

A guide for ethical practice

Chris Maylea

macmillan international HIGHER EDUCATION
RED GLOBE PRESS

First published 2020 by

RED GLOBE PRESS

Red Globe Press in the UK is an imprint of Springer Nature Limited, registered in England, company number 785998, of 4 Crinan Street, London, N1 9XW.

Red Globe Press® is a registered trademark in the United States, the United Kingdom, Europe and other countries.

ISBN 978-1-352-00836-4 paperback

This book is printed on paper suitable for recycling and made from fully managed and sustained forest sources. Logging, pulping and manufacturing processes are expected to conform to the environmental regulations of the country of origin.

A catalogue record for this book is available from the British Library.

A catalog record for this book is available from the Library of Congress.

Social Work and the Law

Acknowledgements

To Arif, Susie, Philomela, Charlotte and Nina, thank you for letting me include your stories. The field of social work must keep listening to and learning from you.

Thanks to Peter, Melissa, Megan, Nancy, Kat, Simone, Elena and Eliza for sharing stories, reviewing sections or helping in other ways.

My chapter co-authors, Caroline, Kat, Francis, Meena, Margaret and Asher: this book would not have been possible without your contributions.

Lauren, Indigo, Rosie, Felix, Duglas and Blu, you can have me back now I'm done writing.

CONTENTS

DETAILED TABLE OF CONTENTS

Figures

Tables

Boxes

Chapter 1 INTRODUCTION

One rainy afternoon, Jenny comes into your office. You have been working with Jenny as a social worker for some years, so you are concerned, but not surprised, to see a fresh bruise above her eye. She gives you a document, with 'Summons' written across the top. Reading it, you see that Jenny has been charged with 'Trafficking in a drug of dependence'. This sounds serious. You're not a lawyer, so you give Jenny the phone number of legal aid and move on to things you can help her with – making a payment plan to pay off her fines, finding a new private rental house and providing counselling as she works to leave her partner (who is responsible for the bruising).

As you leave the office that evening, you notice the rain has stopped. You are concerned for Jenny's future but are satisfied that you've done everything you could to help her.

In fact, this social worker did not do everything they could have done to help Jenny. With a better understanding of legal processes and frameworks they could have done a lot more and been a genuinely effective social worker. They might have made a warm referral to the legal aid lawyer, who could have used the contextual information the social worker had about Jenny's history to argue that she should receive a reduced sentence on the basis that she was selling drugs on behalf of her abusive partner. Rather than help Jenny pay off her fines, the social worker should have known that she was eligible to have them revoked under a special circumstances scheme, saving her thousands of dollars. Rather than working to find Jenny a private rental, they might have looked at other legal options to avoid the move. If she was moving to be away from her partner, they might have explored options for keeping him away from her using a family violence order. If she had already got a family violence order but was still moving because she did not feel safe, they might have helped her apply to a victims of crime tribunal to get funding to pay for new locks and a video security system. If she was being evicted from her current place, they might have explored her appeal options to see if the eviction could be avoided. All these responses require a working understanding of the law. Without a good understanding of the law, a social worker will never be as effective as they could be.

In addition to the practical necessity of understanding the law and how to work in legal settings, this knowledge is a key element of what it means to be a social worker. The AASW *Code of Ethics* uses the words law or legal over thirty times and requires that social workers must 'act in accordance with the law'.[1] Social workers cannot act ethically unless they understand the law. Similarly, the AASW Practice Standards specifically require that social workers can 'understand and articulate' the law and can demonstrate an 'understanding of relevant legislation governing practice and the legal frameworks which inform and mandate practice'.[2]

This book has been designed to assist social workers in using the law to support and protect people who use social work services. Social workers can do this in two main ways: by using the law to help people maintain their rights, and by protecting people from the often arbitrary and unfair impacts of the law on members of disadvantaged communities. The book will also help you understand your obligations under the law and explore areas where competing obligations require social workers to act outside the law while working to change it. Reading this book will not make you a lawyer, and non-lawyers are legally barred from providing legal advice (see Box 1.1). As a social worker, you can provide legal information, work with lawyers and other legal professionals, assist people through legal processes, and work to address the oppression and harm often caused by the legal system.

Box 1.1 *Legal advice and information*

Legal information *just explains the law but does not apply it to a particular case.*

Legal advice *applies the law to a particular case, giving recommendations about what to do and what the outcomes might be.*

The relationship between social work and the law has shifted dramatically in recent decades and is now more central to social work practice than ever. Beckett writes that:

> *Where previously social work was located between the state and the poor and needy, in the modern – and postmodern – era, social work has extended into the hitherto private realm of the family ... As a result, social work is not singularly about morals and values, but also about upholding the law.*[3]

This might come as a shock to social workers who have come to the profession to 'help' people, finding that instead the state which employs them expects them to police moral behaviour in families and communities.

Despite the rising importance of the law in social work practice, social workers are not always comfortable with or knowledgeable about the law and how to use it ethically:

> *Newly qualified and more experienced practitioners have reported either little knowledge of legislation or confusion about how to use provisions perceived as complicated, with the result that organisational procedures dominate decision-making and social workers lack confidence in challenging practice within their own and other agencies.*[4]

Social workers have a long history of working in legal settings, applying laws, and working with people who are entangled with the justice system, but they have not always been on the right side of history when doing so. The experience of the Stolen Generation in Australia shows us that doing the *legal* thing is not the same as doing the *right* thing. The vast majority of harm perpetrated by social workers in removing Australian First Nations children was done *legally*, and First Nations children are still removed by social workers from their families at alarming rates today, under perfectly legal processes.[5] Social workers have also been responsible for ethnic cleansing or racial oppression of First Nations communities in New Zealand,[6] Canada,[7] the United States and Apartheid-era South Africa.[8] Social workers have been integral to fascist and other oppressive regimes in Nazi Germany,[9] Greece,[10] Franco era Spain and Argentina,[11] often in actively suppressing or removing the children of left-wing dissidents who fell foul of the authorities. This gives social workers an obligation to study, engage and critique law and legal processes, and to use it as we would any other social work tool, in support of the people we work with and their communities. To help the reader through this process, this book draws on the latest research and incorporates new research, giving social workers the underlying skills, content knowledge and contextual awareness required to be the best social workers they can be.

1.1 Social Work Fields of Practice and the Law

All social workers will work in settings that are influenced, governed and shaped by the law and legal processes. Some of the more obvious settings, such as working in the criminal system, mental health and child protection are dealt with in detail later in the book, but there are many more examples from all practice areas. Figure 1.1 highlights some key areas of practice and some related areas of law:

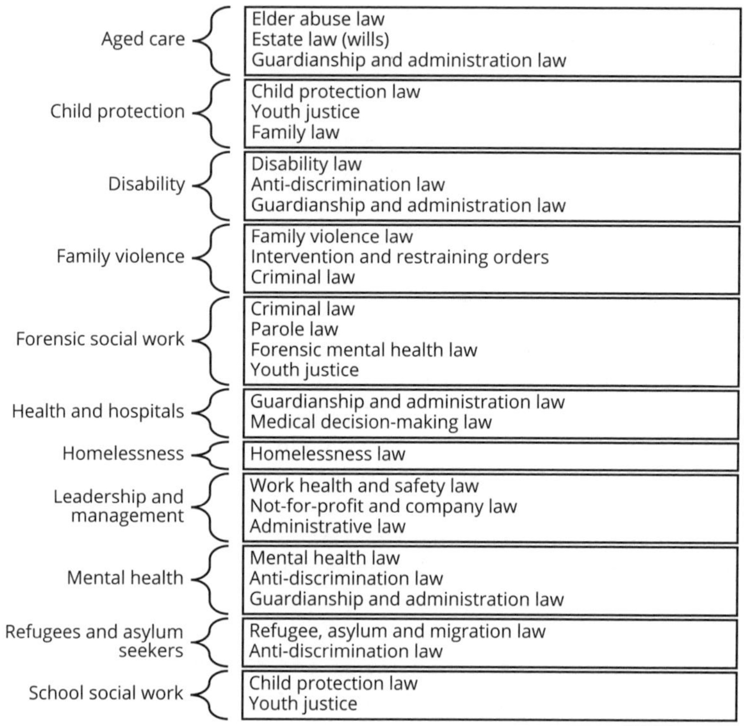

Figure 1.1 *Fields of social work practice and related areas of law*

Many areas of law overlap with many areas of social work practice. For example, social workers in any field may work with people in the criminal legal system, or people who have a family violence order. Social workers will need a general idea of how the law works for these generic areas of law and specialist understanding of the law in their field of practice. Other areas of law, such as the law regarding duty of care, human rights law or mandatory reporting will be present in all fields of practice.

Social workers will also need the ability to find out details of the law in areas they are unfamiliar with to be able to assist their clients or engage in systemic advocacy. This book provides a general overview and provides the first step in developing specialist knowledge in the most common areas of social work practice; but, given the diversity of social work roles and the differences between different states and territories, readers will need to continue their legal education beyond this book. To assist with this, each chapter includes further reading and Chapter 3 includes a section on legal research for social workers.

1.2 Theoretical underpinnings and practice approaches

This book is aimed at helping *all* social workers to understand the law, in multiple legal frameworks guiding diverse practice in a variety of legal settings. The book avoids discussing social work theory and specific practice approaches because as soon as it prioritises one theory or practice approach over another, it will become less relevant for social workers who adopt different approaches.

Take, for example, two social workers working with the same person who is being involuntarily treated in a mental health service. One social worker is the person's case manager, the other their independent advocate. The case manager must use the powers given to them by the *Mental Health Act*, comply with clinical best practice guidelines and be accountable to psychiatrists and nurse unit managers. They will probably use a clinical mental health approach, ideally prioritising recovery but ultimately balancing the person's will and preferences with their best interests and the interests of their community.[12] The independent advocate, conversely, is mainly accountable to the person they work with and the ethics of the advocacy service.[13] They will use a human rights-based approach, ideally prioritising recovery. Both these social workers need to understand the law, but their theoretical basis and practice approaches are fundamentally different. This book is useful for both social workers in this scenario.

Despite this aim, my own preferred theoretical approaches have inevitably influenced the book. From social work, these are primarily critical social work[14] with a preference for anti-oppressive practice.[15] From legal theory, I have drawn heavily on human rights as defined in international human rights law and informed by critical legal studies.[16] This approach is compatible with the Australian Association of Social Workers, (AASW) *Code of Ethics*, but there are many approaches and theories which social workers can bring to legal settings. My co-authors bring their own theoretical approaches by drawing on a mix of legal and social work theories. These co-authors have been chosen intentionally to provide a balance to my own approaches. I have assumed that social workers will bring their own theoretical and practice approaches to this book and have written it to be compatible with as many different ontologies and modalities as possible.

1.3 Terminology

An essential requirement for social workers hoping to act effectively in legal settings is their ability to speak *legalese*, or to use legal terminology correctly. This is a crucial social work skill in many areas, and one of the hallmarks of a good social worker is the ability to switch effortlessly between 'street' and 'office' and to translate between other professional patois, using the language of psychology, community development and medicine on a daily basis. In legal settings, this becomes even more pronounced, as legal terms are often literally in a different language, having come into English from French or Latin. In legal settings, the need to get the terminology correct can be heightened, as the consequences may be significant. For example, if you assist a person in reading a legal document, are they the appellant or the respondent? With legal aid funding limited to only a tiny percentage of people who need it, social workers are often required to help people understand their legal situation and help them understand legal documents. There are many legal dictionaries which can aid readers with this, and most legal terms can be searched for on the internet.

In law, language is usually either *accurate* or *inaccurate*. In social work, language is contested and problematised. In this book, I have tried to write legal terms and phrases as accurately as possible while choosing the least unproblematic language. Sometimes law demands a level of accuracy that can make reading difficult. For example, some laws are criminal – breaking them is a crime. Others are not, and breaking them is not a crime; acting in contravention of them is just 'unlawful' or 'illegal' or 'without legal basis'. These distinctions often mean little to social workers, so in this book I have tried to be as accurate as possible while keeping the language as simple as possible. Social work has the opposite issue, in that words that fairly accurately describe the thing you want to describe are problematised beyond usefulness. When using terms such as 'ethical' or 'unethical' practice in this book, I am doing so in the understanding that these are ambiguous terms which are not universal but must be used to describe a certain thing or relationship.

For example, in law, a *client* is the person who receives legal advice or legal services from a lawyer. In this relationship, *client* is empowering, commanding, in charge of the lawyer. In social work parlance, the word 'client' has become degraded, critiqued by labelling theory as generally problematic. In mental health, for example, the law usually refers to *patients*, while the term preferred by non-clinical services is *consumer*.* Many 'consumers' reject this label, preferring *service user* or *psychiatric survivor*. In family violence, lawyers will refer to the *accused* and the *defendant* whereas social workers might prefer *perpetrator* and *victim* or *survivor*. These words are virtue signals – the use of *accused* and *defendant* signalling that people are innocent until proven guilty, the use of *perpetrator* signalling immediate belief of the victim, distaste for the violent act and an inclination to attribute blame to one party. *Survivor*

* The term 'consumer' has an interesting history, being chosen by the attendees of the *Alternatives Conference* in 1985. This predates the domination of neoliberalism, which saw organisations such as Centrelink refer to welfare recipients as 'customers'. In the context of neoliberalism, consumer can seem a strange choice, but the idea was to project choice and competence, not the passivity implied in terms such as *patient*.

might be preferred over *victim* as it implies less passivity while reminding the audience that many women do not survive family violence.

When referring to Australian First Nations people who identify as Aboriginal and/or Torres Strait Islander, the term First Nations people and communities has been used following guidance from First Nations legal scholars. When referring to specific people, where possible, their tribal or language group has been used. Where people refer to themselves in a certain way, such as having specific heritage, rather than belonging to a specific group, that way has been used instead. This decision has been made in consultation with First Nations scholars with the understanding that not everyone will be satisfied with any one approach.

Where possible, I have referred to *people* as being both accurate and generally unproblematic.

1.4 Using Stories

All the stories in this book are true. I have not fabricated any case studies of people who have worked with social workers on the basis that I should not attempt to portray the voices of people whose experiences I do not share. Susie's, Arif's, Charlotte's, Philomela's and Nina's stories of using social work services were shared with me with explicit permission to use in this book, and they have been paid for their contribution. Other stories of people who have used services which I have included are publicly available, such as those in published law reports or published research, and these have been cited accordingly. I have not used any stories of people who have used social work services in this book unless they are already publicly available or unless they have given explicit permission. I have also used stories about my practice or about other social workers or lawyers where the story is publicly available or if it is about social work practice and not about the person I was working with.

1.5 Overview

This book is structured to build understanding of basic concepts before moving onto more complex aspects of the law. Chapters 2–4 introduce the basic concepts required for understanding the rest of the book. Chapters 5–9 explore the ways social workers work in legal settings or within legal frameworks. Chapters 10–15 each deal with a distinct area of social work practice. The final two chapters bring these together, asking social workers what we can do to progress the profession of social work to be a force for effective change in the law, and how we should act when acting outside the law. As no one person can be expert in the various areas of the law relevant to social workers, this book relies on co-authors in several content chapters. These co-authors are leading experts in their fields.

Chapter 2 provides an introduction to the Australian legal system. This will be particularly relevant for social workers who have come from overseas but will be familiar content to most Australian social workers. Chapter 3 introduces some necessary legal research skills for social workers. Chapter 4 outlines the relationship between ethics, justice and the law, providing an understanding of how these concepts are used throughout the rest of the book. Chapter 5 builds on this to highlight the tensions of adopting a human rights-based approach in involuntary settings. Chapter 6 outlines the legal obligations of social workers with regard to their specific statutory obligations, case notes, information management, duty of care and obligations of silence and compliance. Chapter 7 introduces social workers to the court process and how social workers are involved in this, while Chapter 8 helps social workers understand how they can work with lawyers outside the court environment. Chapter 9 outlines the way human rights work in human rights law and what this can mean for social work practice. This chapter is fundamental to understanding how human rights law influences the law throughout the rest of the book. Chapter 10, co-authored with Katherine Ogilvie and Caroline Lambert, introduces the criminal legal system and how social workers can work with both victims and people who have been accused or convicted of offences. This chapter includes sections on the forensic mental health system and the youth justice system. Chapter 11, co-authored with Francis Zemljak, deals with family law, child protection, family violence and adoption and surrogacy, all areas social workers working with families will need to navigate. Chapter 12, co-authored with Meena Singh, turns to the way social workers can work to uphold the rights of First Nations people and communities both in using the law and in defiance of the law. Chapter 13, co-authored with Margaret Spencer, gives an overview of mental and legal capacity, adult guardianship and the social work role in supporting people who have their rights to make decisions taken away. Chapter 14 builds on this by closely examining the role of social work in mental health law. Chapter 15, co-authored with Asher Hirsch, highlights the human rights issues in refugee and asylum seeker law. Finally, Chapters 16 and 17 help social workers move forward in legal settings, considering how social workers can work outside of or around the law and how they can change the law.

This is a lot for social workers to take in, and tough decisions have been made to provide only the most relevant content and to present a readable and engaging text. This has meant that there is a significant amount which has been left out of this book. Some areas of social work involve the law but are not usefully understood from a legal perspective. For example, discussion of the National Disability Insurance Scheme (NDIS) has not been included in this book even though it was brought to life with the *National Disability Insurance Scheme Act 2013* (Cth). Social workers will have a lot to do with the NDIS, but they will have little to do with the legal side of it.

They must know that there is a legal appeal process and to refer to a lawyer for assistance, but they will usually have little to do with this process. Similarly, social security and Centrelink are bound by law, but social workers are not commonly involved in legal processes in this area. Health, the environment, housing and homelessness are other examples where the law has an impact on practice but does not dominate it. Instead, this book focuses on areas where social workers must understand the law in order to work effectively – where the law forms a regular part of the practice environment or where understanding the law is a necessary precursor to working with specific communities.

1.6 Some caveats

A 'caveat' is a legal word which means a warning or a limitation. This book is full of caveats, but there are four that readers must bear in mind from the beginning:

1. This book is about social work law, not social work practice or theory approaches.
2. The law is continually changing, so some of what is in this book will already be out of date by the time it goes to print. Social workers need excellent legal research skills to keep up to date with the law.
3. The law is complex, too complex to cover everything with total accuracy. This means that I have sometimes chosen simplicity over accuracy so that readers new to the law have some chance of understanding the content. Social workers will soon discover that there are many complexities in even relatively simple legal issues. The important thing is to be able to navigate the process and to know where to go for assistance.
4. The law is not the same everywhere. Australian states and territories each have different laws, and some states seem to like to do things entirely differently for no good reason.* Social workers will need excellent legal research skills to work out what the law is in their state or territory.

This means that this book aims to give readers a research-based overview of the interactions between social work and the law and goes into detail in some common practice areas to illustrate these interactions.

1.7 Referencing

Legal referencing is often difficult for social workers to interpret and in-text referencing of legal sources can make an already complex document

* I'm looking at you, Western Australia.

even more difficult to read. In this book I have used the *Australian Guide to Legal Citation*, but to increase readability all the references are at the end of each chapter. These citations are superscript ([1,2,3, etc.]). Where I have used footnotes, these are indicated with symbols ([*, †]). Legal referencing is discussed in more detail in Chapter 3.

1.8 References

[1] AASW, *Code of Ethics* (Australian Association of Social Workers, 2010) 14.

[2] *Practice Standards* (Australian Association of Social Workers, 2013) 12.

[3] Jonathan P Beckett, 'The Changing Nature of Social Work' (2018) 61(6) *International Social Work* 968, 969.

[4] Michael Preston-Shoot and Judy McKimm, 'Perceptions of Readiness for Legally Literate Practice: A Longitudinal Study of Social Work Student Views' (2012) 31(8) *Social Work Education* 1071, 1085.

[5] Australian Association of Social Workers, 'Acknowledgement Statement to Aboriginal and Torres Strait Islander People' (2004) 14(1) *National Bulletin* 21; Nilan Yu, 'Interrogating Social Work: Australian Social Work and the Stolen Generations' [2018] *Journal of Social Work* 1468017318794230; *The National Apology to the Stolen Generations* (Reconciliation Australia, 2018) <https://www.reconciliation.org.au/wp-content/uploads/2018/02/ra-letstalk_factsheet-apology_v1.pdf>.

[6] Claire Gray, '"You Look a Little Bit Dark for My Liking": Māori and Pasifika Women's Experiences of Welfare Receipt in Aotearoa New Zealand' (2019) 31(1) *Aotearoa New Zealand Social Work* 5.

[7] Karina Czyzewski and Frank Tester, 'Social Work, Colonial History and Engaging Indigenous Self-Determination' (2014) 31(2) *Canadian Social Work Review / Revue canadienne de service social* 211; Raven Sinclair, 'Aboriginal Social Work Education in Canada: Decolonizing Pedagogy for the Seventh Generation' (2004) 1(1) *First Peoples Child & Family Review* 49; Karen McCauley and Duncan Matheson, 'Social Work Practice with Canada's Indigenous People: Teaching a Difficult History' (2018) 30(4) *Practice* 293.

[8] Iain Ferguson, Vasilios Ioakimidis and Michael Lavalette, *Global Social Work in a Political Context: Radical Perspectives* (Policy Press, 2018); Linda Smith, 'Historiography of South African Social Work: Challenging Dominant Discourses' (2014) 50(2) *Social Work/Maatskaplike Werk* <http://socialwork.journals.ac.za/pub/article/view/401>.

[9] Timm Kunstreich, 'Social Welfare in Nazi Germany' (2003) 14(2) *Journal of Progressive Human Services* 23.

[10] Vasilios Ioakimidis, 'Expanding Imperialism, Exporting Expertise: International Social Work and the Greek Project, 1946–74' (2011) 54(4) *International Social Work* 505.

[11] Ferguson, Ioakimidis and Lavalette (n 8).

[12] Gavin Davidson, Lisa Brophy and Jim Campbell, 'Risk, Recovery and Capacity: Competing or Complementary Approaches to Mental Health Social Work' (2016) 69(2) *Australian Social Work* 158.

[13] For a detailed model of independent mental health advocacy, see Chris Maylea et al, *Evaluation of the Independent Mental Health Advocacy Service (IMHA)* (Social and Global Studies Centre, RMIT University, 2019) 56 <sway.office.com/GZJrEJJcVJZlGGvY>.

[14] June Allan, Bob Pease and Linda Briskman, *Critical Social Work: An Introduction to Theories and Practices* (Allen & Unwin, 2003); Bob Pease et al, *Doing Critical Social Work: Transformative Practices for Social Justice* (Allen & Unwin, 2016).

[15] Lena Dominelli, 'Anti-Oppressive Practice' in *Ethics and Value Perspectives in Social Work* (Palgrave Macmillan, 2010); Donna Baines, *Doing Anti-Oppressive Practice: Social Justice Social Work* (Fernwood, 2011).

[16] Trischa Mann (ed), *Australian Law Dictionary* (Oxford University Press, 2015) <http://www.oxfordreference.com/view/10.1093/acref/9780195518511.001.0001/acref-9780195518511>.

Chapter 2 THE AUSTRALIAN LEGAL SYSTEM

Up rode the squatter, mounted on his thoroughbred,
Down came the troopers, one, two, three,
Whose is that jumbuck you've got in your tucker bag?
You'll come a-waltzing Matilda with me.[1]
– Banjo Paterson, lawyer (and poet)

Like much of Australia's colonial history, *Waltzing Matilda* is a political cover-up.[2] The lyrics of a song describe a swagman who steals a sheep and when faced with justice chooses suicide rather than capture. The song is actually about the murder of a man named Samuel 'Frenchy' Hoffmeister, a rebel, unionist and shearer. Hoffmeister and his colleagues were protesting for higher wages during the Great Shearer's Strike in 1894, when they burned down a woolshed full of police (and sheep) during a shootout with the authorities at Dagworth Station near Kyuna, Queensland. Hoffmeister escaped but was later found dead in suspicious circumstances, shot through the mouth near a billabong. The police constable who found him testified that 'there was no sign of a scuffle',[3] and the coroner found that Hoffmeister, presumably 'racked with guilt about the bungled arson'[4] had shot himself. His unionist colleagues quickly agreed that they had no part in the murder, although each with a different version of events, and escaped prosecution. It is still not clear what happened, likely a 'gangland assassination'[5] either by the police or by his fellow unionists as part of a deal to avoid retribution from the police.[6] Hoffmeister's death marked an end to the Great Shearer's Strike, which was a watershed moment in Australia's history, leading to the birth of the Australian Labor Party. Three of the strike's leaders went on to become members of parliament.

The story behind *Waltzing Matilda* illustrates the importance of looking beneath the official history and engaging with both sides of the story in the context in which it occurred. Paterson's antihero is not a jolly swagman or a petty thief with an empty tucker bag. He is, depending on your political persuasion, a freedom fighter or a terrorist, and his murder was either rough but necessary justice or a miscarriage of justice.

Social workers need to grapple with the muddy and sometimes murky context of the legal system, critically engaging with both its history and its myths. The legal system is messy, complex and rich; both a mechanism of oppression and a safeguard for the oppressed. Social workers need a broad understanding of how the legal system works so they can help people through it, protect people from it and work to improve it. Beginning with a brief history of Australian law, this chapter outlines the key elements of the legal system and how they fit together.

2.1 History of Australian law

It can be helpful to understand the history of the law to understand why the law we have now is such a mess. This is mainly because the law we currently have is imported to Australia from England and was already a bit of a mess when it got here (see Figure 2.1). The imported English law displaced a rich, robust and complex framework of First Nations lore, as discussed in Chapter 12. Virtually none of this pre-existing lore has been preserved in contemporary Australian law, and so our law is essentially an inheritance from the English colonial era.

English law that arrived with the colonies derives mainly from a mix of Germanic Anglo-Saxon law and Norman French law, with some Viking influence as well (the word 'law' is of Viking origin). For a while, in the middle ages, England had several different legal systems including one law for the French nobility*; one for the English peasants; and another for the clergy, the monks, nuns and priests of the Church. The king was the ultimate judge, and he delegated judicial decision-making power to stewards or judges. These judges mainly just made decisions according to local customs and tradition. Beginning in the thirteenth century, the 'common law' began to develop, so called because it was 'common' to

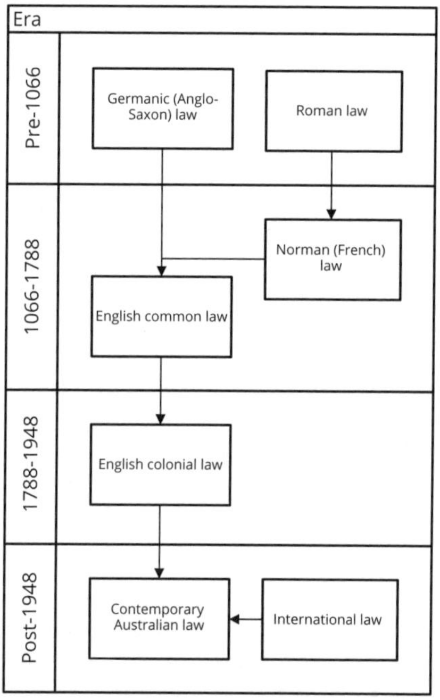

Figure 2.1 *History of Australian law*

* The Norman French invaded England in 1066 and brought many of their laws and customs.

everyone.[*] Judges started writing down their decisions and reading other judges' decisions so that they became more consistent.

A key document in the evolution of rights is the *Magna Carta*, which was passed in England in 1215 and still considered to apply in some Australian jurisdictions.[7] This is one of the first examples of the English government, in this case the king, being required to abide by the law. Before this, the king was the source of the law and was not subject to it. Over time, other aspects of our contemporary system of government developed, including parliaments, constitutional principles, statutes and the separation of powers.

The British colonialists brought this English law with them during the invasion and settlement of Australia. Initially, the colonial law only applied to the white colonialists, but over time came to be enforced against First Nations people and communities as well.[8] Traditional lore and customs were repressed and devalued and are still subject to oppression today.

It is worth noting that while Australia became a new country at Federation in 1901, it was not an independent country, as Australia was no longer a colony but was still a 'dominion' and remained part of the British Empire. It is not until after the Second World War that Australia became functionally independent, and not until 1986 that both the British and Australian parliaments passed the *Australia Acts*,[9] which legally made Australia independent from Britain, although they still share a Queen.

2.2 Federation

Australia is a *Federation,* which means that it has multiple levels of government; Federal/Commonwealth, state/territory and local governments. States and territories each have three arms of government, but local governments do not have a judiciary or legislature and are legally part of the executive branch of the state/territory governments. This divide means that there are Commonwealth laws that apply across the country, state and territory laws that apply only in each state and territory, and local government by-laws that only apply in those local government areas.

---

[*] Some of this early law was quite a bit more exciting than our contemporary legal processes, with penalties including amputation, flagellation and other corporal and capital punishments. Guilt was sometimes determined by 'ordeal', where a person might be thrown in a pond to see if they were guilty or not. As guilty people were thought to float, innocent people often drowned. Other times, a trial might be determined by 'battle', where the two parties might literally fight to see who won the legal case. The idea was that God would not let the wrong person win, so this was a way of letting God decide the outcome of the case. Things have thankfully improved since then, but the legal system can still feel biased and capricious, particularly for people who are socioeconomically less advantaged.

This means that Australia can be divided up into multiple *jurisdictions*. A jurisdiction is the extent of the power to make laws. The Commonwealth is one jurisdiction and each of the states and territories have their own jurisdiction. Each jurisdiction is bound by the physical boundaries of the area covered, but the Commonwealth, states and territories all have different law-making powers. This means that different laws apply in different parts of the country, something we will discuss many times throughout this book.

States have different powers to make laws to the Commonwealth. The Commonwealth government generally only has the power to make laws about specific things, most of which are in section 51 of the *Constitution*. These include the power to provide welfare payments, migration and international relations. The states are left with everything else not given to the Commonwealth, such as health and education. The states can make laws about things to do with Commonwealth powers, but if the Commonwealth makes a conflicting law, the Commonwealth law wins out.

This Federation arrangement means that the Commonwealth might agree to an international convention, but then it is left to the states and territories to decide if they want to follow it or not. The Commonwealth can sometimes force states and territories to abide by international law,[10] but in practice rarely does. The Commonwealth can spend money on whatever it wants to, so we still have federal departments of health and of education, but the Commonwealth cannot make laws about these things. Sometimes, when the Commonwealth does not have the constitutional power to make a law, they just ask all the states to agree to a law, and then each of the states passes an identical version of the same legislation. This happened with the *Health Practitioner Regulation National Law*, which means there is a national scheme for regulating health professionals.*

Territories are different again, in that the Commonwealth is legally responsible for their governance and administration. There are 12 territories in total, with the Northern Territory and the Australian Capital Territory (ACT) operating like states most of the time, with parliament, executive and judiciary, and the other territories having varying levels of self-government. Territories do not have constitutions but do have commonwealth legislation that provides a similar function.[11] The Commonwealth can overrule laws passed by any territory (see Box 2.1).

The way that Australian government is organised as a federation means that the power to make laws is shared between the Commonwealth and the states and territories. This is different from the separation of powers, which divides power up within the different jurisdictions.

---

* Social workers are not included in this national scheme.

Box 2.1 *The Marriage Act*

In 2013, the Australian Capital Territory (ACT) government passed the Marriage Equality (Same Sex) Act 2013 *(ACT) to legalise same-sex marriage. The Abbott government challenged the validity of this legislation in the High Court. The High Court ruled that the Commonwealth government had the power to make laws about marriage and the Commonwealth* Marriage Act 1961 *already defined marriage as 'between a man and a woman'. This meant that the ACT government did not have the power to make laws about marriage, and it was only in 2017 when the Commonwealth changed the wording of the 1961 Act by passing the* Marriage Amendment (Definition and Religious Freedoms) Act 2017 *(Cth) that same sex marriage was legalised.*

2.3 The Separation of Powers

The Australian government, and therefore the Australian legal system, is divided into three main parts; the judiciary, the legislature and the executive (see Figure 2.2). This is called the *separation of powers,* the idea being that the power of government should be spread around so it is more difficult for one person or party to have all the power. In theory, this means that one person or a single group of people cannot dominate the government or the legal system.*

In Australia, there is not a complete separation of powers, as the legislature (the houses of parliament) appoints the executive (the prime minister and cabinet), which in turn appoints the judiciary (the judges). This is established by the *Australian Constitution*, which is the foundation legal document of the Australian government. It cannot be changed by the government but can be changed in a referendum where all Australians get to vote. Each state also has its own constitution.

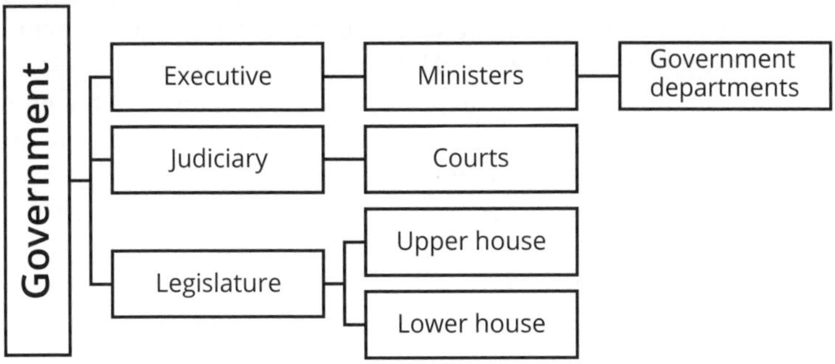

Figure 2.2 *The separation of powers*

* Unless you count rich white men as a single group of people.

Australia is both a parliamentary democracy, in that we have a democratically elected parliament, and a constitutional monarchy, in that we have a monarch, the Queen, as our head of state. The Queen is represented in Australia by the Governor-General, who in theory is the head of the executive branch of government, but in practice this is mostly a ceremonial role.

2.3.1 The executive

In practice, the executive branch of government is led by the prime minister, premier or chief minister and cabinet ministers. These people have responsibility for the day to day running of the country, including the police, the transportation system, and health and welfare services. The executive is responsible for developing government policy and overseeing government departments. Social workers working for government agencies will often be part of this executive branch of government; for example, Centrelink or child protection social workers. This branch of government must follow the law and enforce the law but cannot create new law.

Members of the executive are drawn from the legislature and are usually the leaders of the party that can form a government in the legislature. These are the ministers, who are heads of the departments. These ministers can often delegate powers or authority using legislation. When social workers are exercising powers under legislation, they are acting as part of the executive arm of government.

2.3.2 The judiciary

The judiciary is the court system and is required to enforce the law. It can make law through precedent, which is where a court writes down a decision, and then the reasoning used to make that decision has to be followed by other courts. This is also called the common law. The higher up a court is in the court hierarchy, the more binding its decisions are. Courts are bound by the constitution in the jurisdiction they operate in and by legislation, but also make sure that the other arms of government are complying with the constitution and legislation.

Members of the judiciary are appointed by the executive, although they can usually only be removed by a vote of the legislature and only under certain circumstances. Usually, members of the judiciary have tenure, which means they cannot be removed easily before retirement age. This is done to make them less susceptible to political influence.

Tribunals can sometimes look and feel very similar to courts, but they are part of the executive, not part of the judiciary. Courts and tribunals are discussed in more detail below.

2.3.3 The legislature

The legislature is the parliament, which makes legislation. Legislation is also referred to as 'acts' or 'statutes' or 'statutory law'. Most jurisdictions have two houses of parliament, a lower house and an upper house. Queensland, the Australian Capital Territory and the Northern Territory have just one house of parliament. These houses debate bills, which are voted on by parliament and if passed they are signed by the Governor, Administrator or Governor-General and become acts and become law. At the Commonwealth level, the usual process is that a bill is introduced in the House of Representatives, passes, then is introduced in the Senate, passes, and is signed into law by the Governor-General. Many bills will not pass and will not become law, and others will be changed through the process.

Acts of parliament can overrule common law precedent made by courts, and new acts of parliament can overrule previous acts of parliament. The legislature can also change existing acts by passing amendments. Amendments add, remove or change existing legislation to change the law. Legislation must be consistent with the relevant constitution, both at the state and federal level.

Since Federation in 1901, Australian law has been shaped more by statutory law than common law, so we have gone from a system where the law is made primarily by judges, by precedent, to a system where parliaments drive law reform.

Members of parliament are elected by democratic vote and serve limited terms. Parliament also decides who the ministers in the executive will be, passes laws allowing funds to be spent by the executive and scrutinises the actions of the executive.

2.4 The Rule of Law

The rule of law is a crucial element of the Australian legal system. It states that all people, including the government, should be ruled by and obey the law, and that the law should be able to guide the way people act. This can be broken down to three principles: certainty, generality and equality. Certainty means that the law must be able to be understood, that it is clear, stable and accessible. Generality means it is impartial and impersonal, and not targeted at a particular person or group. Equality before the law means that all people are subject to the same law, the same freedoms and the same protections. Compared with many other countries, Australia has a high adherence to the rule of law, but as Box 2.2 highlights, the rule of law should be viewed more as an aspirational principle than something certain in the Australian justice system.

Box 2.2 *A breach of the rule of law*

For many First Nations people, the rule of law is not consistently applied. First Nations Australians account for more than a quarter (28 per cent) of the Australian prisoner population despite representing 2 per cent of the population.[12] *In the Northern Territory, where First Nations people make up 84 per cent of all prisoners, 60 per cent of First Nations people can speak an Australian First Nations language; one study found that 85 per cent of First Nations people did not have the English literacy skills required to work in a mainstream organisation.*[13] *This means for many prisoners the laws they are convicted under are written in a foreign language: English. In 2007, the Federal government launched the Northern Territory Intervention and introduced the* Northern Territory National Emergency Response Act 2007 *(Cth). Because this legislation discriminated against First Nations people, the government had to suspend the* Racial Discrimination Act 1975 *(Cth) so they could pass it.*

If people cannot read the law, they cannot be expected to be certain of it. If one community is so vastly overrepresented in the prison system over so many years, the law cannot be said to be general to all. If a group needs to be discriminated against for a law to pass, that law cannot said to apply equally to all. This means there is quite a bit of work to do to make sure the rule of law applies to all Australians.

2.5 Types of Law

Law can be categorised in many ways. In this section, we cover four types of law: criminal, civil, administrative and international. These distinctions have been chosen as they are most relevant to how social workers see the law, but there are many other ways of dividing the law. Law can be categorised into subject area: property law, commercial law, consumer law, estate law and so on. It can be divided into public (law that governs interactions between people and governments) and private (law that governs interactions between people). Another way is between substantive law (what the law actually is) and procedural law (how we go about the law).

This section focuses on the distinction between civil, criminal and administrative law, before moving onto international law. Criminal law is the framework the government uses to respond to *crimes* and civil law is the framework used to manage *disputes* between two parties. Administrative law is a part of civil law concerned with controlling the power of the government, and international law is the law that governs relationships between governments and between governments and their citizens.

These distinctions are useful but are sometimes a bit blurry at the edges. For example, family violence protection orders are made under civil law, with the order made by the court between the person who is seeking protection and the person accused of violence.[14] If a person breaches the conditions of that order, that is a criminal offence, where the state can prosecute even if the person seeking protection does not want them to. The way the police can respond is governed by administrative law, which is in turn informed by international law. Making things more complicated is that sometimes the same behaviour will be a criminal act and make someone liable under civil law. An example is that intentionally causing a car collision is a crime, and the owner of the damaged car can sue under civil law to have the damage repaired. The police, acting as the executive arm of government, can prosecute the crime, but suing to get the damage repaired is a legal dispute between the two people involved in the incident. These might be separate cases in separate courts, but about the same incident.

2.5.1 Criminal law

Crimes are best understood as offences against society, even when the actual victim is an individual or when there is no identified victim at all. These are behaviours so serious that they must have a social or community response. Examples include murder, drug trafficking, sexual assault or theft. All crimes have *elements,* which are the things that must be proved to show that someone is guilty of a crime.

For example, in New South Wales sexual assault is a crime. Section 61I of the *Crimes Act 1900* (NSW) reads:

> *Any person who has sexual intercourse with another person without the consent of the other person and who knows that the other person does not consent to the sexual intercourse is liable to imprisonment for 14 years.*

This crime has five different elements:

1. *Any person*
2. *who has sexual intercourse*
3. *with another person*
4. *without the consent of the other person, and*
5. *who knows that the other person does not consent to the sexual intercourse.*

The crime must be committed by a *person* and with another *person*. For example, an animal is not legally a person.* Then there must be *sexual intercourse*, which is defined in section 61HA. This is a broad definition,

* A sexual act with an animal is still a crime, but it is a different crime. Interestingly, in New South Wales the penalty is the same – 14 years imprisonment under the *Crimes Act 1900* (NSW) s 79. For some crimes, a company can be a legal 'person', but not in this case.

including any object or body part, but excludes, for example, 'proper' medical procedures. *Consent* is also defined, in section 61HE. All of these elements must be met for a person to be found guilty of the crime of sexual assault. The *standard of proof* for criminal offences is *beyond a reasonable doubt*. The *onus of proof* is usually on the prosecution, so the prosecution has to prove beyond a reasonable doubt that each element is met. If it cannot be shown beyond a reasonable double, then a person cannot be found guilty.

Criminal offences must be heard in a court, not a tribunal. Criminal trials can only be started by the government and are *prosecuted* by the *prosecution*. In a criminal case, the person being prosecuted is called the *accused* or the *defendant*. If a criminal case is appealed to a higher court, the party who is appealing is usually called the *appellant,* and the other party is the *respondent*.

Criminal law can include punishments including prison, community-based orders or fines. Some crimes are only punishable with prison, some only with fines, some with both. Other outcomes include loss of driver's licence, ban from being a company director or being listed on a sex offenders register. Crimes are either indictable or summary offences. Indictable offences are usually more serious and can be heard by a judge and jury, summary offences are usually less serious and can be heard by a magistrate.

The criminal legal system is covered in detail in Chapter 10.

2.5.2 Civil law

Civil law is about settling legal disputes between two parties. This includes many different areas of law, including property law, negligence law or consumer law. The civil law is much more varied than the criminal law and is most easily understood as everything that is not criminal law. The *burden of proof* for civil law is the *balance of probabilities*. In civil law, the *onus of proof* is usually on the person who starts the legal action. This means the person who starts the legal process needs to prove that it was more likely than not that something happened.

A common example of a civil case is negligence. There are three elements to the tort* of negligence:

1. The negligent party must have owed a duty of care to the other party.
2. They must have somehow breached their duty.
3. The other party must have suffered some harm as a result of the breach of the duty of care.

The duty of care is discussed in detail in Chapter 6, but the process is similar to criminal law. If one party can prove each element on the balance

* A tort is a infringement of a legal right. It is civil, not criminal, but you can 'commit' a tort in the same way that you can 'commit' a crime.

of probabilities, the court can award compensation. Compensation will usually be financial. Under civil law, courts can also order that things be done or not done. For example, they can order protestors not to protest,[15] or that information be taken off the internet.[16] Civil law cannot result in prison as a punishment, but people can be 'administratively detained' under administrative law.

The laws about binding contracts are civil laws. If two people agree to be bound by a contract and one person breaches that contract, the other person might take them to court to have the contract enforced or to get damages* to cover anything they lost as a result of the breach.

The government can also be a party in a civil case. All Australian governments can be sued just like a company or a person. If a government agency is negligent or breaches a contract, they can be sued under civil law, and if a person breaches a contract, the government can sue them under civil law. Just because the government is involved does not mean the case is criminal, although the government is always one 'side' in criminal cases.

2.5.3 Administrative law

Administrative law is the part of civil law concerned with controlling the power of government. This is usually about challenging decisions made by government decision-makers. For example, the executive branch of government has the power to detain people for reasons associated with mental health, migration law or quarantine. Administrative law allows for certain people such as doctors or immigration officials to make decisions about this detention.

This area of law is very relevant to social workers. Social workers will often be empowered by and bound by administrative law, such as when making decisions in child protection, social security or mental health. Social workers will often need to support people to challenge decisions made by decision-makers, for example helping people to appeal decisions made under the National Disability Insurance Scheme (NDIS) at the Administrative Appeals Tribunal. Much of the law covered in this book is administrative law – child protection, disability, mental health and refugee law is all administrative law. All of these areas of the law are also covered by international treaties, so understanding international law is central to understanding administrative law.

2.5.4 International law

International law governs the way nations work with each other and how they treat individuals within their nations. It includes a range of issues relevant to social workers, including human rights, discrimination, refugee

* Damages is a legal word for the money paid to repair the harm done when a person commits the tort.

and asylum seeker processes, migration, the use of force, sustainability, the environment and international development. Social workers need to understand the basic frameworks of international law for three main reasons: international law provides the basis for human rights law as discussed in Chapter 9, because much local law is influenced in some way by international law, and because international law provides additional avenues for advocacy. Social workers working in international conflict zones will also need to understand international humanitarian law – the 'laws of war'.

The key to understanding international law is that it is not really 'law' in the way local law is. It is not readily enforceable and there is no 'international police force' to enforce it. It is better understood as a formalisation of politics and diplomacy in formal agreements between nation states.* In general, nations have first to agree to be bound by international law, and even when they agree they sometimes change their minds later. Countries can be pressured into complying with international law with the threat of economic or other sanctions, or with threats of invasion, but these are applied inconsistently.† This has led to the observation that 'almost all nations observe almost all principles of international law and almost all of their obligations almost all of the time'.[17]

This is not to say that international law has not been incredibly effective. Since the Second World War, when international law has dominated international relations, the world has seen the longest period of peace and prosperity in recorded history. International law has been used to push a neocolonialist agenda and is largely driven by and supported by capitalist and western ideologies.[18]

The United Nations plays a significant role in international law. Set up in 1945 by the adoption of the *Charter of the United Nations,*[19] it is made up of 193 member states, including Australia. The United Nations includes the General Assembly, which is a bit like a parliament, and various bodies and committees. It deals with a range of issues, including managing international peacekeeping, humanitarian aid and sustainable development, but also works to establish international law. This is done partly through various documents, including *declarations*, which are not intended to be binding, and *conventions*, which countries sign and ratify and agree to be bound by. In Australia, the executive of the Commonwealth government (the prime minister and cabinet) can agree to the treaty and sign it, but it does not become enforceable locally until the parliament puts it into local legislation. Courts should make decisions which are consistent with

---

* International law uses the term 'states', 'states parties' or 'nation states' to mean countries. This is confusing because Australia also has 'states' and 'the state' is also used to describe the government as a whole; but don't blame me, this is just the way it is.

† For example, as discussed in Chapter 15, Australia continues to flout its obligations under international refugee law, with little consequence.

international law where it does not conflict with local legislation, but local legislation can always override international law.[20]

2.6 Courts and Tribunals

Social workers will often be required to attend courts and tribunals as part of their practice, either to give evidence or as a support person (see Chapter 7). Courts and tribunals are separated by jurisdiction, with the Commonwealth system at the federal level, and each state and territory having its own system. The state and territory systems are all slightly different but generally have a similar structure. The High Court sits at the top of both systems, hearing appeals* from both the federal courts and from state and territory supreme courts. It also hears cases about disputes about the *Constitution*. Figure 2.3 simplifies the court and tribunal hierarchy.

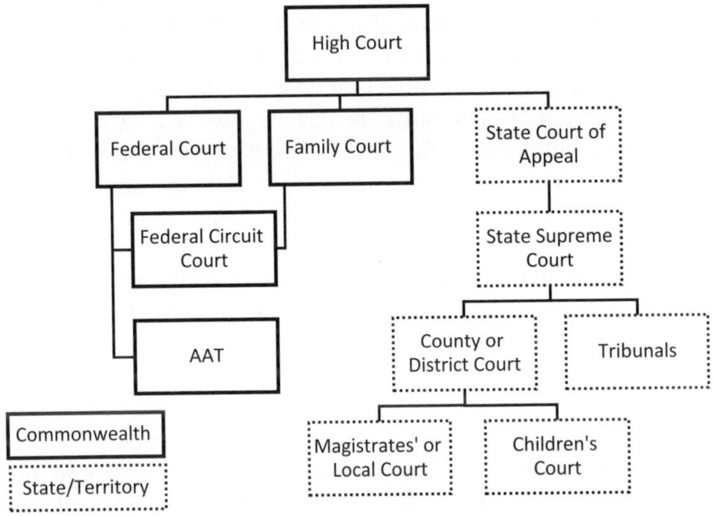

Figure 2.3 *Australia's court and tribunal hierarchy*

Below the High Court sits the Federal Court, which hears industrial disputes, some consumer law and bankruptcy matters, as well as appeals from the Administrative Appeals Tribunal (AAT). Also at this level is the Family Court, which hears matters about divorce and separation, parenting responsibility and parenting orders. Note that this does not include matters about child protection, which fall under state jurisdiction and are heard in the Children's Court or equivalent. The Federal Circuit Court hears less serious Federal matters.

* An appeal is an application to a higher court to reconsider the decision made by the lower court.

In the state or territory court hierarchies the High Court still sits at the top. Beneath that there is a Supreme Court, which includes an appeals division known as the Court of Appeal. In some jurisdictions, there is a County or District Court below that, and below that again is the Local or Magistrates' Court. The higher the court, the more serious the cases. Courts *list* the matters they are going to hear, usually on the court website. In the *criminal lists,* you might find a driving offence heard in the Magistrates' Court, a serious drug or sex offence in the County Court, and a murder charge in the Supreme Court. The same holds the *civil list;* a dispute about paying for minor property damage to a car in the Magistrates' Court, a serious workplace injury matter in the County Court, or a major multimillion-dollar dispute between two banks in the Supreme Court. Each jurisdiction has different rules for which matter will be heard in which court, which relate to the jurisdiction of each court. Cases can also work their way up from the lower courts to the higher courts on appeal.

There are also various specialist courts including development or land and environment courts, coroner's courts, children's courts (see Chapter 11) and courts for First Nations people (see Chapter 12), which are different in each jurisdiction. Western Australia has its own Family Court, which replaces the Commonwealth Family Court in that state. Social workers will become familiar with the specifics of their jurisdiction and their field of practice, but it is essential to be able to see where that fits within the broader context.

Mostly, social work practice is done in magistrates' courts, while working with people who are accused of less serious offences or in the children's courts when working with young people or children. This is partly because the magistrates' courts are so busy – 92 per cent of all criminal cases are finalised in the magistrates' courts.[21] It would be unusual for a social worker to have much contact with the High Court.[*] The lack of legal aid funding means that more and more people are unable to afford a lawyer,[22] particularly at magistrates' courts, which means social workers will often have to do what they can to fill in the gaps. Social workers cannot represent people in court, but they can give evidence to help the court make a decision, as discussed in Chapter 7. This might be as simple as explaining to the court the supports the person has in their life, or it might be a complex and rigorous child protection assessment report.

Each jurisdiction also has a number of tribunals. These are not courts and are actually part of the executive arm of government, but they make decisions where legislation gives them the power to do so. They can often

[*] One notable exception to this is the transcript of *McGarry v The Queen P61/2000* [2001] HCATrans 333, where there was some dispute about whether a report written by a social worker was reliable or not. Justice Gaudron of the High Court casts some aspersions on the social work profession stating 'I do remember a piece of graffiti that I saw some 20 years ago, "Forget police verbals. Worry about the social worker..."'.

feel court-like, but they cannot sentence people to prison. At the federal level is the Administrative Appeals Tribunal, which hears a range of matters relevant to social workers, including:

- Welfare payments including child support, family assistance, paid parental leave, social security and student assistance
- Migration and refugee visas and visa-related decisions
- Veterans' entitlements
- National Disability Insurance Scheme appeals
- Freedom of Information requests.

At the state and territory level, there are big tribunals such as the civil and administrative tribunals, which hear matters including administrative law, equal opportunity, consumer law, commercial disputes, guardianship and professional licensing. There are also specialist tribunals, such as mental health tribunals and victims of crime assistance tribunals. These are arranged differently in each jurisdiction but all aim to provide easier and simpler access to justice than going through the court system. They are less formal, often do not require legal representation and are often much quicker.

Partly because they are designed to not always require legal representation and partly because they deal with lower level issues, social workers will often support people at tribunals. For example, if a person is being evicted from their accommodation, a social worker might help them through the tribunal process, explain to the tribunal member that they need more time to pay and then help the person set up a payment plan. These practical supports can make all the difference to people struggling through the legal system.

2.7 Alternative Dispute Resolution

Sitting alongside and sometimes within the formal court system are a range of alternative dispute resolution approaches. The idea is to prevent people from needing to use the formal court system or to reduce their engagement with it. The earlier in the dispute that the dispute can be settled, the better for everyone. Going to court is expensive and can be traumatic, and often both parties end up with an outcome they did not want. In recognition of this, alternative dispute resolution processes have begun to become more and more popular. They often incorporate aspects of restorative justice discussed in Chapter 4. Common alternatives include negotiation, mediation, conciliation, judicial conferencing and arbitration. Figure 2.4 shows these in order of increasing structure and formality.

Sometimes alternative options are required by law, such as when applying to the Family Court. The *Family Law Act 1975* (Cth) requires people to get a certificate from registered family dispute resolution practitioner. This usually means people have to engage in mediation

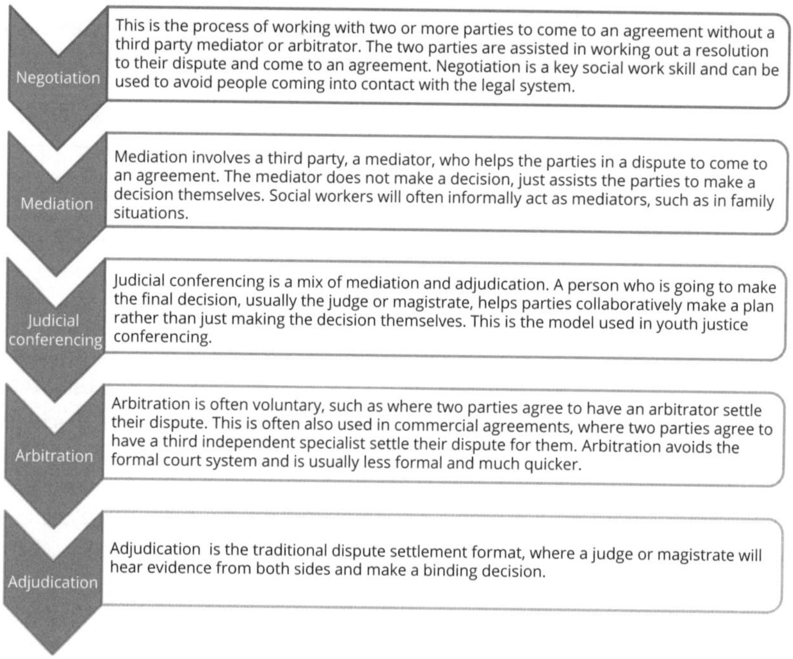

Figure 2.4 *Alternative dispute resolution*

before they can go to court. This is done to prevent people from coming to court unnecessarily, both to reduce load on the court and to ensure people have the best opportunity to work through issues themselves. This is great if it does solve the problem at the mediation stage, but if it fails to find a solution it runs the risk of merely increasing the time the whole process takes. Social workers should be aware that there are exemptions where child abuse or family violence is present, to avoid the mediation becoming another avenue for the perpetration of abuse. Alternative dispute resolution is also legally required in many child protection proceedings. For example, *Children and Young Persons (Care and Protection) Act 1998* (NSW) allows for families to be required to attend a Dispute Resolution Conference, where the family can identify issues and agree on a plan to move forward.

There are many other opportunities for social workers to support alternative dispute resolution. Social workers with high level negotiation skills can ensure people they work with get the best possible outcomes as early as possible. This often overlaps with advocacy, for example when social workers might help a person negotiate better terms on their repayment plan on a loan, avoiding defaulting on the loan. Similarly, social workers can informally mediate between family members, perhaps preventing a young person becoming homeless or ensuring that an older person's preferences are recognised when making later life plans. Social workers are also able to become formally trained mediators, such as the Family Dispute Resolution Practitioners under the *Family Law (Family Dispute Resolution Practitioners) Regulations 2008* (Cth).

Social workers might participate in judicial conferencing in the Koori Court or other problem-solving courts, where they can help people make plans or provide information to the court about services that are available. A typical judicial conferencing plan might include a requirement that a person seeks treatment for drug and alcohol abuse or anger management, and the person providing that treatment could be a social worker. Social workers often also conduct assessments that are submitted to problem solving courts or provide reports about how the plan went. For example, a school social worker might be asked to provide a report to the court detailing how well a young person is engaging with their education.

One of the key skills social workers can bring to alternative dispute resolution is an understanding of the legal and social issues that combine to bring people into contact with the legal system. By sharing this understanding with the people they work with, they can help people make better decisions about how they navigate the justice system, reduce stress for individuals and create more integrated communities.

2.8 Conclusion

This all results in a very messy legal context, but in general the system seems to work. The states balance the power of the Commonwealth, international law influences the Commonwealth and the separation of powers means that none of the different parts of government get out of balance. The whole thing holds itself in tension, like a complex island ecosystem or the strands of a spider's web, each part reliant on others, none able to have too much power. For social workers, this mess is frustrating and clearly in need of improvement as people fall through the gaps, so social workers who want to improve it need to understand what holds it all together. Even social workers who want a fundamentally different system of government need to understand the current system in order to understand how to overthrow it. For those who just seek to make the current system better, understanding it is essential to changing it without accidentally breaking it.

Main points

1. The legal system of Australia is a colonial import of the British legal system. It replaced the existing legal system of First Nations people and communities as it spread across the continent.
2. Australian governments are arranged into three arms: the executive, the judiciary and the legislature.

3. Australia is a federation, with three levels of government: Commonwealth, state and territory, and local government.
4. The rule of law means that all people, including the government, should be ruled by and obey the law, and that the law should be able to guide the way people act. The rule of law can be broken down to three principles; certainty, generality and equality.
5. The rule of law is stronger in Australia than in many other countries, but there are many examples of breaches.
6. There are many ways to divide law, including public and private law, civil and criminal law, substantive and procedural law.
7. The four main types of law most relevant to social workers are criminal, civil, administrative and international law.
8. There is a hierarchy of Australian courts, with the High Court at the top and local and magistrates' courts at the bottom. There are also tribunals, which are a bit like courts but are usually less formal and quicker.
9. Legal disputes were historically settled by courts but are increasingly being settled using alternative dispute resolution techniques.

Discussion questions

1. What breaches of the rule of law can you think of? Is the rule of law always a good thing?
2. How do the judiciary, executive and legislature overlap? What implications does this have for government?
3. What are the courts called in your jurisdiction? How many of them are there? What are the specialist and generalist tribunals?
4. How would you categorise these issues? Are they public or private law, civil or criminal? Can you categorise them in some other way?
    a. Violent assault
    b. A divorce
    c. An application for asylum
    d. A car accident
    e. Street art on a shop window
    f. Not buying a train ticket
    g. A boat runs into another boat in international waters.
5. For each of the issues above, which court or tribunal would these disputes be settled in?
6. How can social workers stop conflict from turning into legal disputes?

Further reading

Robin Creyke, David Hamer, Patrick John O'Mara, Belinda Smith and Tristan Taylor, *Laying Down the Law*, 10th ed (LexisNexis Butterworths, 2017).

'Halsbury's Laws of Australia' (LexisNexis, 2019).

'Encyclopaedic Australian Legal Dictionary' (LexisNexis, 2019).

2.9 REFERENCES

[1] Andrew Barton Paterson, 'Waltzing Matilda' (1895).

[2] The full lyrics are:

Once a jolly swagman camped by a billabong
Under the shade of a coolibah tree,
And he sang as he watched and waited till his billy boiled,
'You'll come a-waltzing Matilda, with me.'

Chorus:
Waltzing Matilda, waltzing Matilda,
You'll come a-waltzing Matilda, with me,
And he sang as he watched and waited till his billy boiled,
'You'll come a-waltzing Matilda, with me.'

Down came a jumbuck to drink at that billabong,
Up jumped the swagman and grabbed him with glee,
And he sang as he shoved that jumbuck in his tucker bag,
'You'll come a-waltzing Matilda, with me.'
(Chorus)

Up rode the squatter, mounted on his thoroughbred.
Down came the troopers, one, two, and three.
'Whose is that jumbuck you've got in your tucker bag?
You'll come a-waltzing Matilda, with me.'
(Chorus)

Up jumped the swagman and sprang into the billabong.
'You'll never catch me alive!' said he
And his ghost may be heard as you pass by that billabong:
'You'll come a-waltzing Matilda, with me.'
(Chorus)

[3] 'The Death of Samuel Hoffmeister: A Magisterial Inquiry', *Morning Bulletin (Rockhampton, Qld. : 1878–1954)* (Rockhampton, Qld, 18 September 1894) 6.

[4] Ian Walker, 'The Matilda Myth', *Background Briefing* (ABC Radio National, 15 February 2011) <https://www.abc.net.au/radionational/programs/backgroundbriefing/the-matilda-myth/2994754>.

[5] ABC News, 'Waltzing Matilda an Old Cold Case' (12 February 2010) <https://www.abc.net.au/news/2010-02-12/waltzing-matilda-an-old-cold-case/329506>.

[6] Dennis O'Keeffe, *Waltzing Matilda: The Secret History of Australia's Favourite Song* (Allen & Unwin, 2012) <http://ebookcentral.proquest.com/lib/rmit/detail.action?docID=876812>.

[7] *PJB v Melbourne Health and Another (Patrick's Case)* [2011] VSC 327 [93].

[8] *R v Murrell and Bummaree* [1836] NSWSupC 35.

[9] *Australia Act 1986* (Cth), *Australia Act 1986* (UK).

[10] *The Commonwealth of Australia v State of Tasmania* [1983] HCA 21.

[11] See, for example, *Australian Capital Territory (Self-Government) Act 1988* (Cth); Northern Territory (Self-Government) Act 1978 (Cth).

[12] Australian Bureau of Statistics, '4517.0 – Prisoners in Australia, 2018' (6 December 2018) <http://www.abs.gov.au/ausstats/abs@.nsf/Lookup/by%20Subject/4517.0~2018~Main %20Features~Prisoner%20characteristics,%20Australia~4>.

[13] Fiona Shalley and Allison Stewart, *Aboriginal Adult English Language Literacy And Numeracy In The Northern Territory* (Office of the Pro Vice Chancellor Indigenous Leadership Charles Darwin University, 11 September 2017) <https://www.cdu.edu.au/sites/default/files/opvcil/55675_wce_statistical_report_lr_fin_r2.pdf>.

[14] *Family Violence Protection Act 2008* (Vic).

[15] *McDonald's Australia Ltd v Watson* [2013] VSC 502.

[16] *Trkulja v Google LLC* [2018] HCA 25.

[17] Louis Henkin, *How Nations Behave* (Columbia University Press, 1979) 47.

[18] Irene Watson, *Aboriginal Peoples, Colonialism and International Law: Raw Law* (Routledge, 2015).

[19] United Nations, *Charter of the United Nations*, 24 October 1945, 1 UNTS XVI.

[20] *Minister of State for Immigration and Ethnic Affairs v Ah Hin Teoh* [1995] HCA 20.

[21] Australian Bureau of Statistics, *4513.0 – Criminal Courts, Australia, 2017–18* (Australian Government, 28 February 2019) <https://www.abs.gov.au/ausstats/abs@.nsf/0/D8D460DDF174BC36CA2582410016B417?Opendocument>.

[22] Law Council of Australia, *The Justice Project* (2018) <https://www.lawcouncil.asn.au/justice-project/final-report>.

Chapter 3 LEGAL RESEARCH

Much of the legal system is based on expert lawyers fighting over what the law is, so it is no surprise that it can be difficult for social workers to follow along. It is also constantly changing, sometimes in conflict with itself and at other times silent on important issues. Take, for example, the very basic question of 'what is a parent?'. As discussed in Chapter 11, this is not always clear. Be prepared for the law not to present a clear answer and to have to work with this ambiguity. This does not mean social workers should give up trying to understand the law, but that they may have to work harder to keep their knowledge current to be as effective as they can be.

A good social worker will have a basic understanding of how the law works in their area of practice, but more importantly they will know how to find out more about the law when they need to. Having good legal research skills is important for being able to advocate at all levels and for supporting people through the legal system. There are two main avenues for doing legal research as a social worker: primary sources and secondary sources.

3.1 PRIMARY SOURCES

Law exists in documents, mainly in legislation and in common law. These documents *are* the law, but there are a lot of them and they can be long and boring and complicated, and even lawyers often do not really understand them unless they specialise in that specific area. This means that for social workers it will usually be easier to find a secondary source that explains the issue. Even when using secondary sources to help explain the law, social workers will need to understand how the primary sources work to understand the secondary source.

3.1.1 Legislation

As discussed above, legislation is laws written down and passed by parliament. Some of these, such as the *Migration Act 1958* (Cth) are notoriously difficult to read and understand, but others, such as the *Family Violence Protection Act 2008* (Vic) are fairly straightforward. Legislation is usually written in italics and (nearly) always has the year it was originally passed by parliament.* Legislation always has the jurisdiction listed, either

* This does not mean it has not been changed since then – legislation is often amended and changed by parliament over time without changing the year in the title.

in the text as in 'the Victorian *Family Violence Protection Act 2008*' or in parentheses as in *Family Violence Protection Act 2008* (Vic). This is important because different jurisdictions might pass two Acts with the same name in the same year, such as the *Mental Health Act 2014* (Vic) and the *Mental Health Act 2014* (WA).*

Legislation is broken up into parts and sections. For example, section 5 of the *Family Violence Protection Act 2008* (Vic) defines family violence:

1) *For the purposes of this Act, family violence is—*
   a) *behaviour by a person towards a family member of that person if that behaviour—*
      i) *is physically or sexually abusive; or*
      ii) *is emotionally or psychologically abusive; or*
      iii) *is economically abusive; or*
      iv) *is threatening; or*
      v) *is coercive; or*
      vi) *in any other way controls or dominates the family member and causes that family member to feel fear for the safety or wellbeing of that family member or another person; or*
   b) *behaviour by a person that causes a child to hear or witness, or otherwise be exposed to the effects of, behaviour referred to in paragraph (a).*

This definition is absolutely essential for social workers to be familiar with, both so they can spot family violence and so they can explain it to people they work with. It is also vital to be able to communicate it simply and in non-legal language.

Remember definitions will be different in each jurisdiction. In the Northern Territory, section 5 of the *Domestic and Family Violence Act 2007* (NT) reads:

Domestic violence is any of the following conduct committed by a person against someone with whom the person is in a domestic relationship:

a) *conduct causing harm;*
b) *damaging property, including the injury or death of an animal;*
c) *intimidation;*
d) *stalking;*
e) *economic abuse;*
f) *attempting or threatening to commit conduct mentioned in paragraphs (a) to (e).*

---

* These simple naming rules are somewhat undermined when parliaments name such legislation as the *Legislation Act 2001* (ACT).

There is clearly a lot of overlap between these two, but they are not the same. The Victorian definition is much broader, including controlling and dominating behaviour and including additional protections for a child exposed to violent behaviour. Social workers will have their own, non-legal definition of family violence, but good social workers will be familiar with both legal and non-legal definitions – which you can usually only find by actually looking at the legislation.

Legislation is often also broken up into different parts dealing with different aspects of the legislation. For example, legislation usually starts with the purpose of the Act, definitions and the key principles which underpin it. It will also outline to whom the Act applies, who has what powers under the act, and how decisions are made and challenged under the act. Legislation can also create *statutory bodies*, which are organisations that are part of government.

The easiest way to find legislation is just to search for it using Google – each of the jurisdictions has a website providing all legislation for that jurisdiction. If this does not work, try the Australasian Legal Information Institute (www.austlii.edu.au). If you have access to a university library website, they will have library guides with links to other databases.

3.1.2 Common law

Case law, also called common law, is created by judges writing down their decisions so that lawyers and other judges can follow them. As with legislation, common law is notoriously difficult to read and is something that many lawyers struggle with. For social workers, reading cases is more of a way to understand the legal system and to read actual experiences of the law, rather than a way of interpreting precedent to determine what the law is. Sometimes, however, when writing an academic essay, policy document or submission, it will be necessary to read and be able to appropriately cite cases.

One of the most famous cases in Australian history is the Mabo case, where the High Court found that Terra Nullius was not applicable in Australia. This paved the way for native title and traditional ownership of the land by Australia's First Nations, as discussed in Chapter 12. The citation for this case is:

Mabo v Queensland (No. 2) ('Mabo case') (1992) 175 CLR 1

That breaks down as:

Mabo	This is the name of the party who started the case. In this case, Eddie Mabo is the plaintiff.
v	This is short for 'versus', but is pronounced as 'and' in civil cases and 'against' in criminal cases. So you say 'Mabo and Queensland' if you are reading this out loud. Sometimes an '&' is used instead.
Queensland	This is the other party – the defendant. In this case, Eddie Mabo took the state of Queensland to court. (And won!)
(No 2)	This means this is the second case related with this name. There is a 'Mabo No 1' as well.
('Mabo case')	This is the short name given to the case. Usually only famous cases have short names.
(1992)	This is the year. If it is in (round brackets) it is the year of the decision, [square brackets] the year the report was published.
175	This is the volume number.
CLR	This is the court or the report series it is in. In this case, the Commonwealth Law Reports. Sometimes this is the court.
1	This is the starting page.
	Sometimes there is a 'pinpoint' here. That is used if referring to a specific page or paragraph in the case. If in [square brackets] it is a paragraph number, if no brackets it is a page number.

Figure 3.1 *Case citation example*

Judgments can be reported in different places and will then have different citations. For example, sometimes the Mabo case is cited as *Mabo v Queensland (No. 2)* [1992] HCA 23. This is the same case but in a different report. For most purposes for social workers it will not usually matter which one you use.

If the name of one or both other parties is just a single letter or an identifier, such as 'PBU' or just 'A', that means the party is anonymous, which is usually the case if the party is a vulnerable person or a child. If it is 'R' or 'The Queen' that means it is a criminal case. 'R' is short for 'Regina' or 'Rex', which is Latin for Queen and King.* This is because it is the state that is the party in a criminal case. This is easily confused when one of the parties is actually a name of a state, such as *Mabo v Queensland.* This is a civil case between Eddie Mabo and the State of Queensland, not a criminal case. Even more confusing, sometimes in a criminal case it will have the name of the state, territory or the Commonwealth, or the government department of prosecutions. The general rule is:

* Her Royal Highness signs all documents 'Elizabeth R' as in 'Elizabeth Regina' – including her first Instagram post: <instagram.com/p/ButJtIMnBrV>.

- If it has R, the Queen or the department of prosecutions then it is a criminal case.
- If it has the name of the state, territory or Commonwealth it could be civil or criminal.
- If it does not have either then it is probably civil.

Overseas cases are different again, and there are exceptions to this general rule in Australia too.

With the internet and internet databases, it is no longer necessary to know the report series to look up the case, but it is still important to cite properly to distinguish this case from other cases with the same name. For example, *Mabo v Queensland* (No. 1) (1988) 166 CLR 186 is a different case to *Mabo v Queensland* (1986) 64 ALR 1.

3.1.3 Other primary sources

In addition to legislation and common law there are a range of other relevant documents. Bills are legislation that have not been 'enacted' by parliament. There are also regulations, which are like legislation but lower level and are usually made to help legislation work. For example, the *Family Law Regulations 1984* (Cth) sit under the *Family Law Act 1975* (Cth).

Another primary source is records of parliamentary debates, sometimes called *Hansard.* This is a record of what the members of parliament said when they were discussing a bill. This gives useful insight into what the parliament wanted a piece of legislation to do. This can be used to compare what parliament intended with what is happening in practice.

Internationally, there are cases, legislation and constitutions in other countries. There are also treaties, conventions and other agreements between countries, and declarations by the United Nations. There are also decisions of international bodies such as the International Court of Justice. There are many legal research texts that can guide social workers in this area.[1]

Cases, legislation and other primary sources are often long and technical. They are meant for lawyers to read, and even if social workers are interested they may not be able to work out what it all means. Luckily, the only thing lawyers like doing more than talking is writing, so there are many fine secondary sources that can help with legal research.

3.2 SECONDARY SOURCES

There is a range of good quality secondary sources and different sources will be more or less useful depending on the application. For academic or policy work, such as making submissions to royal commissions, there are more formal options such as journal articles, books and government publications. Included in these are law reform commission documents, including those from the Australian Law Reform Commission and various state and territory equivalents. They provide detailed and balanced technical analysis of the issues.

Be aware that as with any research the bias of the author or organisation will inform the work, particularly on controversial legal issues. For example, reports published by the Department of Home Affairs will have a very different analysis of refugee law than reports on the same topic published by the Refugee Council of Australia or the Australian Human Rights Commission. Social workers will need to apply critical research skills to negotiate contested issues. On areas of developing or contentious law, there will often be law reform commission reports or senate inquiry reports, which are very useful for understand the broad context of an issue. These reports often contain submissions from people or organisations to intentionally argue one side of the issue, so use these with care and an understanding of the author's agenda. These resources are often created so parliament can made a decision about changing the law, so they can go out of date very quickly if parliament does make changes.

Other great resources are 'bench books'. These are guides written for judges to help them understand the law. They are very legal and technical, but they are published by and for judges so they are very comprehensive and are usually up to date.[2]

Other types of secondary sources will be much more useful when working directly with people who need guidance in the legal system. Victoria has the excellent *Law Handbook*, published by the Fitzroy Legal Service,[3] while New South Wales (NSW) has the 'Find Legal Answers' website hosted by the State Library of NSW.[4] Not all jurisdictions are as well served, but all have legal aid services that have websites with resources available. These sources are especially useful when working with people who cannot afford or who are not eligible for a lawyer. Social workers cannot provide legal advice, but they can provide legal information, which includes providing fact sheets or helping people read from websites.

When a person asks for help with a legal issue, the first step will often be to go online and find out what information is available. This will often be followed by referral to a lawyer – usually legal aid or a community legal centre – but it is an important part of the social work role to help people understand the legal situation and context so they know what to tell the lawyer. Not all lawyers are good at explaining things in ways people can understand, so social workers can assist with this as well.[5] Most people who need legal aid cannot access it, so social workers may need to directly support people who cannot get a lawyer.[6]

3.3 LEGAL REFERENCING

Each of the referencing styles has a specific way of referencing legal documents, so check with the style guide you are using for the rest of the document. In-text citation styles such as American Psychological Association (APA), 6th ed., or *Harvard* are most common in social work academic work, while legal academic work and legal reports tend to use footnotes, often the *Australian Guide to Legal Citation*. This is because citing full cases and legislation in text can get very messy. For example, the following sentence from Chapter 6 can be cited with a footnote or endnote as:

> Mandatory reporting for child abuse is legislated in every state and territory.[7]

Or using in text referencing as:

> Mandatory reporting for child abuse is legislated in every state and territory. (*Children and Young People Act 2008* (ACT) s 356; *Children and Young Persons (Care and Protection) Act 1998* (NSW) ss 23, 27; *Care and Protection of Children Act 2007* (NT) ss 15, 16, 26; *Child Protection Act 1999* (Qld) s 13, *Education (General Provisions) Act 2006* (Qld) s 364, 365, 365A, 366, 366A; *Children's Protection Act 1993* (SA) ss 6, 10, 11; *Children, Young Persons and Their Families Act 1997* (Tas) s 3, 4, 14; *Children, Youth and Families Act 2005* (Vic) ss 182(1)(a)–(e), 184, 162(c)–(d); *Crimes Act 1958* (Vic) s 327; *Children and Community Services Act 2004* (ACT) 124A, 124B; *Family Court Act 1997* (WA) s 5, 160).

This shows why footnotes are often the preferred style for legal referencing.

Most citation styles only provide limited information for citing legal sources, focusing on cases and legislation. For more detailed guidance, such as on citing international agreements, United Nations materials, legislation and cases from other countries, government gazettes, tribunal decisions, unreported judgments and a range of other documents, the *Australian Guide to Legal Citation* can be combined with the required style.

3.4 CONCLUSION

Legal documents have special rules about naming and other conventions that can make the situation confusing for social workers. Once they have mastered those rules, legal research is just like any other kind of research. In many ways, it is easier because there are so many secondary sources that explain the law. The real difficulty is that because law can change so quickly it can be difficult to tell what the situation currently is, or what it was at a certain point in time. The best thing social workers can do to keep up is to develop good legal research skills and always consult with a lawyer if possible.

Main points

1. Legislation and court decisions have special rules for citation.
2. Legal research can be done with primary sources, such as legislation and court reports, or secondary sources, such as books, journal articles or reports.
3. Many legal documents are stored in specific databases. The easiest for social workers is Austlii, which is free online.
4. Social workers can use other published materials to help people they work with. Most states and territories have law handbooks.

Discussion questions

1. What is the definition of family violence in your jurisdiction? How does it differ from the definitions in other jurisdictions?
2. Find the mental health, child protection or other legislation for your jurisdiction. Try and answer each of these questions:
    a. What does the purpose of the act state that it is?
    b. What are the principles that underpin it?
    c. To whom does it apply?
    d. Who has what powers under the act?
    e. How are decisions made under the act?
    f. How can you challenge those decisions?
    g. Does the act set up any statutory bodies?
3. What is a parent in your jurisdiction? How is it different in different legislation?
4. Is the story of French Hoffmeister in Chapter 2 really the inspiration for *Waltzing Matilda*? What evidence is there? What kind of sources can you find that help you understand what really happened?

Further reading

If you have access to a university library, it will probably have a library guide specifically for doing legal research, with links to legal databases. If not, use Austlii.

Jay Sanderson, *A Practical Guide to Legal Research*, 4th ed (Thomson Reuters Professional Australia Ltd, Lawbook Co., 2017).

Robert Watt and Francis Johns, *Concise Legal Research* (Federation Press, 2009).

Melbourne University Law Review Association, *Australian Guide to Legal Citation* (2018).

3.5 References

[1] See, for example, Mandy Burton and Dawn Watkins, *Research Methods in Law* (Routledge, 2013) <http://search.ebscohost.com/login.aspx?direct=true&db=nlebk&AN=611818&site=ehost-live&scope=site>.

[2] See, for example, Court and Tribunal Services, 'Equal Justice Bench Book', *Supreme Court of Western Australia* (2017) <https://www.supremecourt.wa.gov.au/equaljustice/T/the_contents_of_this_bench_book.aspx>; Judicial Commission of New South Wales, 'Bench Books & Handbooks' (2019) <https://www.judcom.nsw.gov.au/category/publications/bench-books/>; *National Domestic and Family Violence Bench Book* (Australasian Institute of Judicial Administration, 2019) <dfvbenchbook.aija.org.au>; Judicial College of Victoria, 'Publications' (Text, 16 April 2019) <http://www.judicialcollege.vic.edu.au/publications>.

[3] Fitzroy Legal Service, 'The Law Handbook', *The Law Handbook* <https://www.lawhandbook.org.au/>.

[4] State Library of NSW, 'Find Legal Answers' <https://legalanswers.sl.nsw.gov.au/>.

[5] Chris Maylea et al., 'Socialising the Law: Multidisciplinary Practice with Lawyers and Social Workers' in Simon Rice, Andrew Day and Linda Briskman (eds), *Social Work in the Shadow of the Law*, 5th ed. (The Federation Press, 2018).

[6] Australia and Productivity Commission, *Access to Justice Arrangements: Inquiry Report* (Productivity Commission, 2014).

[7] *Children and Young People Act 2008* (ACT) s 356; *Children and Young Persons (Care and Protection) Act 1998* (NSW) ss 23, 27; *Care and Protection of Children Act 2007* (NT) ss 15, 16, 26; *Child Protection Act 1999* (Qld) s 13, *Education (General Provisions) Act 2006* (Qld) s 364, 365, 365A, 366, 366A; *Children's Protection Act 1993* (SA) ss 6, 10, 11; *Children, Young Persons and Their Families Act 1997* (Tas) s 3, 4, 14; *Children, Youth and Families Act 2005* (Vic) ss 182(1)(a)–(e), 184, 162(c)–(d); *Crimes Act 1958* (Vic) s 327; *Children and Community Services Act 2004* (ACT) 124A, 124B; *Family Court Act 1997* (WA) s 5, 160.

Chapter 4 ETHICS, JUSTICE AND THE LAW

Law, as we know it today, is a relatively new concept across the scope of human history. While there is evidence of Ancient Egyptian law codes dating back 5000 years, throughout history most humans have lived in small communities without the need for complicated written laws. If you misbehaved, a community elder, who was probably also your mum or your aunty, would give you a stern look or a clip over the ear and you would stop misbehaving. Traditional human societies usually had no way to write down legislation and legal decisions. Instead, they were characterised by rich and complex cultural narratives, better understood as lore rather than law.* Resources in these societies were usually limited and held in common by the community; everyone knew everyone else; and community elders would maintain order through storytelling, role modelling and sometimes punishment or shaming. As discussed in Chapter 12, for pre-invasion First Nations people in Australia the law/lore was integrated into all aspects of society and the land. Traditional societies had and have strong principles of ethics and justice, but it was only with the development of advanced agriculture and the consequential surplus of resources that there was something to fight over and only with the development of writing that rules could be recorded. Populations increased, inequality became entrenched, people travelled more, and so existing social bonds could not maintain social order. Communities needed to formalise rules and decision-making processes to ensure consistency and fairness. These formal rules are called laws.

Laws are about keeping the peace, protecting people, protecting private property and about making people conform to societal norms. They can be seen either as being simply arbitrary rules that are made by people with lawmaking power or as natural necessities inherent to human interaction. Some laws are about how to organise society sensibly and others are about ensuring fundamental rights and responsibilities.

Anyone who has come into contact with a toddler knows that we are born with a finely tuned sense of fairness and are acutely aware of when we are being 'left out' or being oppressed in some way. Toddlers also have extremely well-developed processes for raising complaints about fairness, and many parents find having consistent rules and routines an effective way to establish fairness in the family environment. Societies do the same

* 'Law' comes from an old Norse word meaning 'something laid down or fixed' and 'lore' comes from an old English word meaning 'to learn'. Law is something imposed by authority; lore is something shared in the community.

thing. Humans seem to respond well to rules they see as fair or 'just' and are usually willing to follow them. When laws are perceived as unfair or unjust, or when they are discriminatory or unreasonable or able to be abused by a specific group, humans are remarkably consistent in calling for them to be changed. Humans are also remarkably consistent at testing the law and breaking it, particularly when the laws seem to lack enforceability or appear unfair.

This simplistic overview is troubled by the wide variety in how we understand fairness, which is in turn informed in the way we understand goodness. As social workers, it is vital that we critically engage with the underlying assumptions of what is fair and good that prop up the law, as we would otherwise be guilty of complicity in oppression. A salient example is the role social workers played in the removal of children of the Stolen Generation and perpetrating other harms against First Nations people,[1] most of which was entirely legal, and in many cases *required* by law (see Chapter 12). To avoid such tragedy in the future we must be attentive and engaged in the thinking that underpins the law, not just the law itself. In this chapter, we unpack ethics and justice, as these basic concepts underpin everything else covered in this book.

4.1 Ethics

Ethics is the name we give to thinking about how to do good things and how to do things in a good way. Every time we use a phrase such as a 'good social worker' or say we 'should' do something a certain way we are making a decision about ethics and ethical behaviour. Much ink has been spilled on this topic by social work academics, and the only consensus is that there is no consensus. You can choose between *virtue ethics*, *rule based ethics*, *consequentialism*, *utilitarianism*, or any number of other ways of understanding what is good or what are good behaviours. Even the idea that 'good' or 'not good' exists is up for debate, challenged by *relativism*. My personal preference is *Cyrenaic hedonism*, but as a social worker, I adopt an *ethics of care* within an *anti-oppressive framework*. This section briefly outlines some of these ethics and how they relate to social work practice and the law.

4.1.1 The Australian Association of Social Workers *Code of Ethics*

Whichever approach you adopt, the core document for social work ethics is the Australian Association of Social Workers (AASW) *Code of Ethics*.[2] The *Code of Ethics* is best viewed as a starting point rather than a complete guide to practice. It is fundamentally a consensus document that seeks to find common ground for the broad church of social work practice rather than a coherent ethical model that can be implemented without further consideration. This is because many of the elements of the *Code of Ethics* will conflict with legal obligations or with each other. For example, as discussed in Chapter 5, the *Code* requires social workers to act in the best interests of people they work with and support them in their self-determination. In involuntary settings, the role of the social worker is often to limit the person's ability to make their own choices to further their 'best interests'. Similarly, the requirement that social workers obtain informed consent may also conflict with the person's 'best interests', such as when sharing information might be distressing or harmful to relationships. The obligation to uphold human rights, and to specifically subscribe to the principles of international human rights law, will regularly cause ethical conflict for social workers in legal settings. These tensions are just part of what it means to be a social worker. This means that social workers must be able to identify:

> *... the range of decisions that could be made and the reasoning behind each in terms of ethical theories, codes of ethics, legal and natural justice principles, laws, organisational policies and social work best practice principles.*[3]

The *Code of Ethics* acknowledges that this will result in a range of possible actions or decisions that could be made in a given circumstance:

> *... ethical dilemmas may arise when a social worker must make a choice between alternative courses of action, each of which is supported by moral considerations and each of which may result in an outcome that is, in some way, undesirable.*[4]

The *Code of Ethics* also states that:

> *Tensions may occasionally arise between observing the Code and complying with legal or organisational requirements. Social workers must act in accordance with the law and with organisational directives. If the law or organisational directives conflict with perceived moral obligations, a social worker should seek guidance from competent professionals ...*[5]

This is sound advice but hardly provides concrete guidance. It is, of course, possible to act legally while being unethical and to act ethically while acting outside the law, so the instruction to act in accordance with the law will not always result in an ethical decision. The *Code* implies that such a thing as a 'competent professional' will be handily available when decisions need to be made, which is not always the case. Social workers will often find their direct supervisor instructing them to do something that they feel is unethical or unlawful. The *Code* also assumes that the law is knowable and able to be followed, which again is not always the case, as we will see many times in this book. The reality is that social workers have to make decisions using their own judgment based on the information available to them, and this will mean they will make a variety of decisions: some they will be comfortable with later and others will keep them awake at night for years to come. If an experienced social worker has never made a decision that keeps them awake at night, this does not mean they are a good social worker, just an unreflective one.

The lack of concrete guidance means that social workers must be *ethically literate*. Lawrence writes:

> *Ethics is not just a matter for moral philosophers, or ethicists; it is inescapable for all humans, because of the essential social and cognitive nature of our existence. Because of the nature of their work, social workers are especially embedded in moral reasoning ... The profession has much to offer in the troubling circumstances of our current world.*[6]

As a social worker, you need to be clear about how you construct your ethical worldview or you risk reverse justifying every dodgy decision you make with different ethical reasoning. This is the central problem with ethics in social work – we need ethics but cannot agree on a shared basis for ethical reasoning, what ethical action is, or even if goodness exists.

4.1.2 Relativism versus universalism

Relativism is the idea that there is no absolute or universal objective truth.[7] Universalism is the idea that there is some universal truth, often given by god. Relativism has been discussed for millennia, but often appears in debates about postmodernism. The idea of moral relativism suggests that what with think is 'good' or 'not good' stems from human culture with language and belief systems. This means that not only does 'good' and 'not good' vary from person to person and society to society, but that in a realist sense it does not exist at all. For most social workers, this idea poses a problem because social workers are supposed to make the world better. If there is no such thing as 'good' it undermines our very reason for existing. In legal settings it becomes even more problematic as we try and argue that a law is 'good' or 'not good'.

One way for social workers to resolve this is 'moderate universalism'.[8] If they choose to do this, social workers can use human rights as their 'universal truth' that applies to everyone, but understand that the application of human rights will vary from culture to culture.

Another option is using *hedonism* as a guide to what is good. Hedonism is the theory that something that causes pleasure is good and something that causes pain is bad. By locating goodness in the experience of a person, it attempts to resolve the tension between relativism and universalism. Good is both universal, in that all people can experience pleasure and pain, and relative, in that each person will experience this differently. Various philosophers have argued that some types of pleasure are better than others, for example that excessive sex and drinking alcohol cause more pain than pleasure in the long run.* Some types of hedonism, such as *Cyrenaic hedonism*, argue that immediate gratification should always be pursued at every opportunity, whereas others, such as *Epicureanism*, argue that restraint, moderation and caution will result in the most pleasure overall.

For social workers who want to 'do good', this absence of a clear definition of goodness poses some difficult problems that they will need to grapple with throughout their practice. Once a social worker has decided if they agree that there is such a thing as 'goodness' and that it can be applied to social work, they need to work out what that means. Is goodness a thing that is done, a rule that is followed or something that results from an action? These different perspectives are virtue ethics, rule-based ethics and consequentialism.

4.1.3 Virtue ethics

Virtue ethics is about being a 'good' person. It does not focus on ethical rules or consequences of behaviour, just on having good moral character.[9] This means the focus is on developing a 'good' way of being, of cultivating 'good' emotions and reactions, and acting on them in 'good' ways.

If someone acts according to virtue ethics they do not act in a certain way because the rule tells them to, or because the outcome of the action will be good. They act in a certain way because that is the right way to act. For example, a 'virtuous' person is not faithful to their spouse because they fear being caught or because they want to go to heaven, but because being faithful is the right thing to do. They deeply, inherently, want to be faithful. This is important for social workers and the law because it highlights that just doing the right thing is not sufficient – the person must be doing the right thing for the right reasons, not because they fear the consequences if they do the wrong thing or because they think they should follow the rules.

4.1.4 Rule-based ethics

Rule-based ethics, known as deontology, are about following rules, rather than about the consequences of actions.[10] If the rule is ethical and followed properly, the action is also ethical. This leads to the obvious question about which rules are 'good' and should be followed. These rules might be given by god, professional ethical codes such as the AASW *Code of Ethics*,[11] or a set of laws.

---

* Personally, I think this says more about the sex life of your average ethics philosopher. Epicurus, the father of Epicureanism, famously preferred cheese over sex, which just goes to show how difficult ethical decisions can be.

This can also be applied to human rights, by saying that if an action is consistent with human rights then it is ethical. This has some obvious problems for social workers in legal settings. Sometimes the application of human rights needs additional input, such as balancing one person's right to free speech with another person's right to feel safe. In this example, human rights alone cannot guide action, as a decision must be made as to which right takes precedence. Similarly, some laws might appear to result in 'bad' outcomes, either intentionally or unintentionally. This means that deontology is often contrasted with consequentialism.

4.1.5 Consequentialism

Consequentialism is the ethical approach that suggests something is ethical if the end result, the consequence, is good.[12] This means that following rules, or the reason that an action is taken, is less relevant. One common consequentialist approach is *utilitarianism*.

Utilitarianism argues that the greatest good for the greatest number is the best approach. This is a bit misleading, as really it is about having the total amount of good in society increase. This means that if half of society experiences more good, that cannot cause disproportionate harm for the other half of society. It does mean that if something causes a huge amount of good for one part of society, this can be used to justify causing a just-slightly-less-than-huge amount of harm for another part of society, just so long as the total amount of good goes up slightly.

This causes problems for social workers who might not feel that inequality is justifiable on consequentialist grounds. Utilitarianism does little to account for power, fairness or justice, instead focusing on what happens at the end of the process.

These three ways of understanding what is good – virtue ethics, deontology and consequentialism –are useful for framing ethical decision-making but do little to provide concrete guidance for social workers in practice. Often, ethical dilemmas will be a matter of deciding if a rule should be followed or if the end result justifies breaking the rule, which is a straightforward conflict between deontology and consequentialism. To provide guidance as to what should happen when these conflicts arise, social work has developed a number of ethical approaches that include understandings of power and human relationships. Two key approaches that are particularly relevant to social work in legal settings are ethics of care and anti-oppressive ethics.

4.1.6 Ethics of care

Ethics of care is a feminist informed ethical approach that focuses on the interpersonal relationships between people.[13] An ethics of care promotes well-being through maintaining relationships and social networks. This is closely linked to virtue ethics, as it focuses on 'good' ways of acting, but is different to traditional virtue ethics where the virtue exists within the person, not in relationships between people. This perspective views interdependence, caring, emotional intelligence and empathy as good, and incorporates critiques of sexism, classism and other forms of discrimination. This rejects the idea that good for one person is good for another, and also that one person's pleasure can be compared with another person's pain. Ethics of care addresses the question of 'how do we decide which good is best' by locating good in interactions between people.

The ethics of care resolves many of the ethical dilemmas that arise between rule based ethics and consequentialism because it allows social workers to look to the impact that a decision might have on relationships – between the social worker and the person and the person's family, community and society. This can be particularly useful in critiquing law and social policy and also asking how the law or policy enhances care and promotes human relationships. Many laws, such as those that affect the prison system, cause significant damage to people's relationships. When working in legal spaces, an ethics of care can help social workers reinforce and rebuild these relationships.

Gilligan, an original proponent of ethics of care, observed that for men, ethics is about justice, rights and rules, and for women, ethics is about relationships and responsibilities.[14] When considering the relationship between law, ethics, care and justice, tensions emerge between whether care or justice is more 'good', more ethical. Gray writes:

> *... we might have laws and procedures to ensure a just system wherein people have rights, without compassion, there is no guarantee that these systems will function in a humane way. Neither justice nor care, by itself, is sufficient. Justice says everyone is entitled to the same treatment but an ethics of care may lead to differential treatment, as it may dictate that some people are needier of care than others based on situational and often subjective judgements.*
>
> *Thus, an ethics of care is not necessarily just and a just system is not necessarily caring.*[15]

Ethics of care is very useful for practice and critique, but it gives less guidance for achieving social change. For a more active ethical approach, anti-oppressive practice gives social workers a grounding for ethical social action.

4.1.7 Anti-oppressive ethics

Anti-oppressive ethics locates the 'good' relative to oppression. Oppression is bad; anti-oppressive practice is good. This ethical approach underpins anti-oppressive social work practice, which requires social workers to address organisational, structural and sociocultural oppression. It explicitly requires legal and political action to work towards a world free of oppression, including sexism, racism, ableism and homophobia.[16] In legal settings, anti-oppressive practice is particularly useful as it engages with issues of power and the role of the social worker in perpetuating power dynamics. Dominelli defines anti-oppressive practice as:

> *... a form of social work practice which addresses social divisions and structural inequalities in the work that is done with people whether they be users ('clients') or workers. [Anti-oppressive practice] aims to provide more appropriate and sensitive services by responding to people's needs regardless of their social status. [Anti-oppressive practice] embodies a person centred philosophy; an egalitarian value system concerned with reducing the deleterious effects of structural inequalities upon people's lives; a methodology focusing on both process and outcome; and a way of structuring relationships between individuals that aims to empower users by reducing the negative effects of social hierarchies on their interaction and the work they do together.*[17]

This brings together the process, the outcome, the relationships and the relationships between people into a practice approach that provides ethical guidance. This illustrates the way ethics can be integrated into social work practice, particularly in legal settings. When asking if a law is a 'good' law or a 'bad' law, or if an action is a 'good' act or a 'bad' act, social workers can ask whether it is oppressive or whether it reduces or combats oppression.

Anti-oppressive practice relies on critical reflection and reflexivity to identify and assess oppression. These are not foolproof approaches, so anti-oppressive practice requires empowerment to minimise both intervention and the role of the social workers in the partnership. This sits somewhat uncomfortably with many roles of social workers in legal settings, where social workers are often tasked with taking control of people for their own protection or the protection of others. Social workers will be required to take away people's ability to make decisions for themselves or write objective reports assessing people without their consent. This means that the principle of minimal intervention, so central to anti-oppressive ethics, can be hard to reconcile with the legal or ethical 'responsibility' of social workers to intervene, or at least to make sure supports are available.[18]

Social workers, by their participation in legal settings, will maintain regimes of oppression, be they in prisons, hospitals, refugee processing centres or in the community. This makes practising anti-oppressively very difficult in many social work roles in legal settings, particularly involuntary settings, as discussed in Chapter 5. This will inevitably lead social workers to practise outside the boundaries of the law, and demand change from the law. These topics are discussed in Chapter 16 and Chapter 17.

Anti-oppressive practice, ethics of care and other social work approaches are only two possible ethical frameworks social workers might choose from, and even within these approaches there is ongoing disagreement as to how they should be applied. Despite disagreements, ethics is central to social work. Box 4.1 illustrates how central ethics is to social work practice, and how acting ethically and acting legally can be two different things.

Box 4.1 *An ethical or a legal choice?*

In New South Wales, social workers who work with children are mandatory reporters for child abuse. If a social worker 'has reasonable grounds to suspect that a child is at risk of significant harm' they must legally make a report.[19]

I worked with a Bundjalung man who lived on country in a community based around a former mission. We worked with several people on the old mission and had a good relationship with many community members. The community was proud and strong but living with past trauma and ongoing disadvantage and discrimination.

One night, a child broke in and stole some drugs from the man I was working with. He chased the child down the street, screaming and yelling. The child managed to get away, but only just. I knew the child and knew he was clearly at risk of significant harm, so I was legally required to report.

I knew if I made a report the whole community would know it was me, and I knew that if they knew that, I and the organisation I worked for would lose their trust. I would certainly lose the trust of the person I was supposed to be working with and supporting. I knew that police would get involved, child protection would drop by and that then nothing would happen. The issues facing that community were far beyond anything that could be fixed by a report to child protection. My report would not actually bring better outcomes to anybody.

In the end, I raised it with my supervisor and she instructed me to make an anonymous report to protect myself from legal ramifications. I did, but I have always regretted it. I wish I had made the ethical decision, not the legal one. An ethics of care approach would have led me to sit down with the community elders and asked for their guidance. I should have offered support to the family of the child and worked to make a plan to move forward with the consent and agreement of all involved. Then, with permission, I might have made a report and fulfilled my legal obligation.

This brings us to the key difference between law and ethics. Law should ideally give a black and white, *correct* and final decision. It should be clear what the answer is. In practice, this is not often the case, but it is a fundamental aim of law to provide certainty. Ethics is not concrete, and usually is a matter of picking the *best* or *least worst* option rather than the *correct* one. Law certainly needs to play a part in ethical decision-making but is just one part of the process. Box 4.1 shows how law can present a false dichotomy, a question of 'to report or not report', whereas ethics brings us to a much more messy and nuanced response. This is only made messier when we also want to make decisions that are *just*, or when we want to see *justice* be done.

4.2 JUSTICE

Justice is a concept that is familiar to all of us, and yet very difficult to define. The easiest way is to say, 'justice is fairness', but then we have to define 'fairness', which is even more difficult. We can say that laws *should* be just and that legal processes *should* be just, but we know that this is just not always true. So, to be able to critique the legal system for being 'unjust' we have to try harder to work out what justice is. Bingham identifies 29 different types of justice:

> *a sampling includes corrective, substantive, distributive, social, procedural, organizational, interactional, inter-personal, communicative, communitarian, restorative, and transitional justices. Even within this sampling, there are multiple definitions for a given term.*[20]

Traditionally, justice has been about either punishing a person for some wrongdoing or about settling disputes. This can be seen in the idea of 'an eye for an eye, and a tooth for a tooth', where a person that takes another person's eye should have their own eye taken away from them. This dates back to one of the very earliest recorded laws, the Code of Hammurabi,* roughly 3700 years ago, but it was already being rejected by Jesus in the New Testament 2000 years ago.[21] The problem with this idea of straight-forward punishment is that it does not take into account the context of how people live and interact with each other. Straightforward punishment or restitution is not necessarily ethical. Justice has also evolved to mean something more than just punishment or restitution. Keenan writes that:

> *Justice, then, is not dependent upon the law. That a society does not outlaw an activity does not mean that the activity is just ... The more we act for the common good, by being inclusive and letting others speak for themselves, the more we can learn about the people whom we ought to become.*[22]

To understand how justice can mean different things in different contexts, consider five different types of justice that will be relevant to social workers and people they work with: retributive, distributive, procedural, interactional and informational:

---

* You get the sense that the tooth fairy was not very welcome in Hammurabi's house.

Retributive justice (punishment)

Retributive justice is about punishing a person, making them suffer in the way they made others suffer. This is the old 'eye for an eye, a tooth for a tooth' approach. It does seek to prevent offending by making clear that offenders will be punished, but does not attempt to reintegrate them into society.

Distributive justice (outcomes)

Distributive justice focuses on the outcomes of a dispute or process. For example, if a person has their car stolen, distributive justice is concerned to make sure that they get their car back, plus compensation for the cost of not having a car.

Procedural justice (process)

Procedural justice (also called procedural fairness) ensures that people feel part of the process and are able to participate. The legal process must be free from bias, decisions must be based on evidence, and people who are affected by the decision must be able to present their case. This is often lacking for victims in the criminal legal system, who report feeling left out of the process when the state prosecutes the offender.

Interactional justice (interpersonal)

Interactional justice is present when people felt heard and are treated with dignity and respect throughout the justice process. This is particularly important for ensuring procedural justice as people who are treated disrespectfully or rudely may struggle to be involved in the justice system or to reintegrate into society.

Informational justice (understanding)

Informational justice relates to the way people understand the process. If people can appreciate the reasons decisions are being made and why processes are the way they are. This reduces frustration with the system, and enables people to participate in the system.

Figure 4.1 *Five types of justice*

These understandings of justice are particularly relevant to social workers as they each provide an opportunity for social work practice to support people in the traditional justice system. Social workers are often limited in the way they can impact the punishment people receive, as this is usually determined by the courts, but they can look at and advocate for alternatives that people might find more satisfying, such as *restorative justice*, as discussed later in this chapter. Similarly, social workers would rarely be involved in determining the outcomes of a legal dispute, but they can help people be more involved and support opportunities for *alternative dispute resolution,* discussed in Chapter 2, which may result in better outcomes for all parties.

By expanding or varying how we conceive of justice, social workers can find more opportunities to ensure justice is done. Social workers can provide information to people, which can help them be more involved in the process. This is particularly useful when social workers can act as interpreters, decoding legalese when working with lawyers and legal officials. Similarly, social workers can ensure that the interpersonal experiences of the traditional justice system are as good as they can be. Often, just having a social worker in the room will mean that people get better treatment from authorities. This is so well established that it is common policy for police to be required to have a third person in a police interview where the person has a cognitive impairment or mental illness diagnosis.[23]

To further explore the concept of justice we will consider four more concepts of justice of key relevance to social workers.

4.2.1 Justice as upholding rights

A common way of understanding justice is that justice is achieved when people have their rights maintained and uphold their responsibilities. This is a legalistic way of understanding justice and should be contrasted with the ideas of social, therapeutic and restorative justice discussed later. As already discussed, a rights-based approach to understanding justice has been critiqued as being a particularly masculine understanding and should be contrasted with an ethical approach that prioritises relationships and social integration.[24]

Rights are usually understood as *freedoms* or *entitlements*. These are things that we are allowed to do or are allowed to demand be done. Every right has a corresponding responsibility. If I have a right to walk down the street, everyone else, including the government, has a responsibility to let me walk down the street. These rights can, of course, be reasonably limited, such as when the street is blocked for roadworks. Rights can be individual or held by groups or communities. For example, a group of people might form a nation and have the right to self-determination or have the right to have their culture respected. Individual legal rights might include the right to vote or to sue a person in court.

In Chapter 9 we discuss human rights in more detail, but human rights are just one set of rights that social workers must be attuned to. Rights and their corresponding responsibilities can be legal, social, ethical or moral. They are not necessarily legally enforceable and are often the subject of disagreement. The 'right' to housing is a good example. We can see the right to housing under international law in article 25 of the *Universal Declaration of Human Rights*[25] and article 11(1) of the *International Covenant on Economic, Social and Cultural Rights*.[26] We can see it in local law in section 51(xxxi) of the *Constitution*, which ensures the Commonwealth can only take property 'on just terms', and in common law and legislation that protects private property and governs private rental agreements. These local laws are enforceable but only stop someone taking your housing away – they do nothing to ensure that you are given housing if you do not already have it. For people without access to housing, all states and territories provide social housing programs. These fulfil the responsibility to provide housing but do not provide an enforceable right for individuals to be housed, evidenced by the nearly 200,000 households waiting for public housing.[27] This means you have a legal and enforceable right not to have your house taken away, but a social and unenforceable right to be given housing. Achieving justice in the sense of having your right to housing upheld requires both social programs to provide housing and laws to prevent your housing being taken away.

The work of social workers working in legal settings will often be about supporting people to attain their rights. This might be a human right that is not enforceable under local law, such as the right to dignity,* or it may be a human right that is enforceable under local law such as the right to freedom of religion.[28] It may be a right that is not a human right but is a legal right, such as a person's right to child support or right to 'quiet enjoyment' in their rooming house. Social workers will also help people attain non-legal, non-enforceable rights, such as the right to participate in social and community events. This means that social workers will often also be working to help people, organisations and governments adhere to their responsibilities, so that others can attain their rights. This is particularly relevant when it is the social worker who holds the relevant responsibility.

4.2.2 Social justice

Social justice is what social work is all about. If we could achieve social justice, we could all go home. Social justice sits right in the definition of social work:

> *Social work is a practice-based profession and an academic discipline that promotes social change and development, social cohesion, and the empowerment and liberation of people. Principles of **social justice**, human rights, collective responsibility and respect for diversities are central to social work.*[29]

Social justice is about fairness and justness at a social level, where the distribution of wealth, opportunities and privileges are fairly and equitably distributed. A nice way of thinking about this is supplied by philosopher John Rawls, who asks you to imagine you are an unborn baby circling the earth, about to be born to a random family.[30] He suggests that this unborn baby would see the prospect of being born into our current society as way too risky. The odds of being born into a disadvantaged family far outweigh the chance of being born into a comfortable existence. If this baby were to design society, it would be much more equal – much less risky. Rawls asks us to redesign society from the perspective of this baby. Rawls calls this the 'veil of ignorance', and it helps us put aside our reluctance to relinquish our current privilege and think about the world from a social justice perspective. One question for social workers when thinking about this is how useful the law is when working towards justice.

---

* The right to dignity may be legally enforceable in some jurisdictions, such as in Victoria under the *Charter of Human Rights and Responsibilities*. See Chapter 9 for more on human rights.

Laws are just as often about preserving social inequality as they are about achieving social justice. Inequality in Australia has been rising for decades,[31] meaning our society has become *less* socially just. Property laws prevent those who have little from taking from those who have much. The court system favours those who can afford expensive lawyers, and the prison system is full of people who have experienced social disadvantage. Our immigration legislation is designed to limit the number of people coming into the county who are fleeing persecution, while we enjoy one of the highest standards of living in the world. For social workers, engaging with the law is often about critically engaging with injustice caused by the law.

Take, for example, the *Fair Work Act 2009* (Cth). The object of this Act is to:

> *... provide a balanced framework for cooperative and productive workplace relations that promotes national economic prosperity and social inclusion for all Australians ...*[32]

This piece of legislation is genuinely about protecting the fundamental rights of workers and upholding a minimum wage, but it is not about social justice. It implicitly recognises that some social *injustice* is necessary to the economy and recognises that people will be paid different amounts for the same amount of work, that some people will be paid more and that some people will be paid less. This is not *fair*, and it highlights how Australian society has given up on social justice. We accept that some people will be paid more than others even for the same amount of work and for the same contribution to society. The *Fair Work Act 2009* (Cth) seeks to limit injustice but does not attempt to achieve social justice. If we think about it at all, we probably rationalise it by reflecting on the efficiency of free markets at determining wages. What this means if we think critically is that capitalism requires injustice in order to operate. It requires some to have less so they strive to have more.

Some might not see this as an issue; after all, we need motivation to perform at our best and inequality is a way of motivating people to do better. This argument would be much more sound if the inequality were not so often distributed in a way that meant people could not do anything at an individual level to address it. In 1951 the United Nations' International Labour Organisation introduced the *Equal Remuneration Convention*,[33] requiring equal pay for equal work for women, but it was not until 1973 that women had a legal right to equal pay for equal work,[34] and even then this did not apply to all women. Despite clear legislation requiring equal pay,[35] in 2017–18 men working full time earned $25,717 per year more than women working full time.[36] In the largest 200 Australian companies, there are more chief executive officers (CEOs) named Andrew than there are CEOs who are women.[37] This is hardly an indicator of a socially just society.

As another example, take unemployment. In a socially just society, there would be no unemployment and every person who was eager and willing to work would be able to be employed. Social workers know that unemployment is bad, that it causes poverty and other disadvantage, that it impacts negatively on children in unemployed families and that work can be central to human dignity and self-image. Economists view unemployment more as a 'regrettable necessity'. In economic policy this is widely admitted; as unemployment drops, wages rise because workers are in higher demand, which means inflation rises and the economy suffers. This has led to governments ensuring that unemployment does not drop too low, to keep a big enough pool of available workers.[38] This is partly the responsibility of the Reserve Bank of Australia, which is tasked with Australian payments policy, monetary and banking policy.[39] Hang on, I hear you cry, does not section 10 of the *Reserve Bank Act 1959* (Cth) legally require it to maintain full employment?

Yes it does, but the body legally responsible for ending unemployment quietly ignores this legal obligation because the capitalist economy requires unemployment so it can function. The point is that if social workers hope to work towards social justice, the law is only part of the solution and will in some cases be one of the main barriers which need to be overcome. Achieving social justice will require a fundamental reorganisation of our social, legal and economic systems. Of course, many laws work towards social justice, often by upholding human rights as discussed in Chapter 9, but social justice will prove difficult to legislate. Rather, social workers will have to see the law as one factor in the long march towards social justice. Fenton writes:

> *The value base of social work is characterised by helping people with their problems and by giving attention to social justice issues ... Therefore, social work should be concerned with helping people with their welfare needs and understanding and promoting social justice, such as understanding the effects of social injustice, tackling this where possible, taking cognisance of a person's difficult circumstances (e.g. poverty, lack of opportunity) and working towards an aim of a more just society and positive change for the individual.*[40]

While working towards social justice, there are other things social workers can do to make the justice system more just. One of these is to support therapeutic justice.

4.2.3 Therapeutic justice

Therapeutic justice seeks to harness the power of the justice system to increase individual and community well-being. This approach does not attempt to divert the law away from its function in settling disputes or punishing wrongdoing but seeks to ensure that when it is doing these other things, it is as therapeutic as possible. The Law Council of Australia states that:

> *Therapeutic justice is increasingly being accepted by Australian judicial officers and policymakers as an important and relevant perspective in improving the quality of justice. It aims to improve the administration of justice for both victims and offenders by addressing the issues underlying legal disputes and encouraging all participants to engage in the court process. Therapeutic justice can restore and heal victims and provide opportunities for both victims and offenders to improve their health and wellbeing, which in turn minimises the risk of further harm. Allowing victims to have a voice in proceedings as active participants often enhances their experience of justice.*[41]

Examples of therapeutic justice in practice often focus on 'problem-solving' courts, such as mental health or drug and alcohol courts, or the First Nations courts discussed in Chapter 12. The Alcohol and Other Drug Treatment Court (AODT) in New Zealand is held up as a successful example of this approach. It is designed on the premise that the offending that brings people into the justice system is linked to or caused by their drug and alcohol use. The court uses a case management approach, where people appear before the court and are given an opportunity to engage in treatment before being sentenced. Usually, if they engage in treatment they get a reduced sentence.

> *The AODT Court is seen as giving high-risk and high-needs offenders the opportunity and tools to change their lives through access to, and engagement in, AOD treatment. The consensus amongst stakeholders, participants and whānau*[*] *is that the AODT Court is resulting in transformational change for graduated participants and their whānau. For current participants and some of their whānau members, the court has reduced AOD-related harm. Exited participants also benefited from the AODT Court, in particular understanding the recovery journey and services available like the 12-Step programme.*[42]

Compare this to the traditional approach of imprisoning offenders, which is widely critiqued for both contributing to personal trauma and inhibiting community connections. Note the language changes; 'offender' becomes 'participant'. When people finish the program, they are no longer 'offenders' but become 'graduates'. Furthermore, note the inclusion of

---

[*] *Whānau* is a Māori word meaning extended family but may also include spiritual and tribal links.

whānau in this process. The inclusion of family and key supports for the person sometimes extends to cultural representatives, such as in the Koori Court model, where two elders sit with the judge or magistrate and provide cultural guidance, reinforcing aspects of culture, community and country.

The key to this approach is the wrap-around services that become part of the court. Rather than just the judge, prosecution and defence, the court expands to include case managers, housing workers, peer support workers, drug and alcohol treatment providers and other therapists. Many of these additional staff will be social workers. Madden and Wayne outline several roles social workers can adopt to make the justice system more therapeutic, including mediating, improving communication, working closely with other professionals and advocating for more therapeutic ways of doing justice.[43]

It is important to note that ultimately a judge or magistrate will still sentence a person, often to prison, and that all the additional therapeutic aspects do little to combat broader social issues such as poverty, discrimination or intergenerational trauma. It is focused on 'fixing' a 'broken' individual. Therapeutic justice is not about achieving social justice, but about making the justice system more therapeutic.

4.2.4 Restorative justice

Restorative justice takes a different approach that attempts to bring about both individual and community level change. Rather than viewing a person as evil, restorative justice views the person as not sufficiently integrated into society.* The actions may be evil and should be condemned, and the person must atone for the harm they have caused, but they are supported in this process. Restorative justice describes a process of making *whole* again after a crime has been committed. It is about repairing the damage done by the crime, not just punishing the offender or deterring future offences with punishment. It recognises that crimes cause trauma to the whole community, which requires healing processes, and that these are often neglected in the traditional justice system.

Restorative justice often takes place alongside other approaches to justice. All states and territories have youth restorative justice programs and some also have programs for adults.[44] Usually, in order to participate in restorative justice, a person has to first plead guilty or be found guilty by a court. Sometimes the process involves just the victim and the offender, sometimes a bigger group including family members or other people impacted by the crime.

---

* It needs to be noted that these are not new concepts and represent justice as practised by many traditional communities both in Australia pre-invasion and across the world.

One way of understanding the process of restorative justice is to break it down into four key values, each of which represents something missing in the contemporary justice system.[45]

1. Inclusion
2. Encounter
3. Amends
4. Reintegration.

Restorative justice is not without drawbacks. It can be expensive to run and unpopular with people who want to see a harsh response to criminal behaviour. It has been suggested that the process, which can be very daunting and difficult to navigate, will 'favour middle class, articulate participants' and fail to safeguard offenders' and victims' rights.[46] Most problematically for social workers, it still targets the individual as solely responsible for the crime. The community and society are required to support the reintegration of the offender, but no lens is applied that might address the causal social factors in offending, such as poverty, social exclusion or discriminatory laws. For this reason, neither therapeutic justice nor restorative justice will bring about social justice.

4.3 Nina's story

To think about rights, ethics and justice, consider Nina's story and reflect on how justice has been done. Think about the different ways in which Nina experiences justice and fairness, and what kinds of ethical approaches help you understand her experience.

My name is Nina and I am an addict. I have sole parental responsibility for one child, a beautiful eight-year-old boy. I have a criminal record.

I had a fairly normal childhood. My father suffered from alcoholism but was never sloppy or violent. My mother was very community driven, spiritual, emotionally stable, and strong yet kind, she encouraged us to use our imagination, gave us opportunities to express ourselves, have outings and family holidays. I suffered from anxiety and in primary school I had a lot of trouble making friends. When I started at a new high school, I joined the 'cool' crowd and started to smoke pot and drink, mainly to fit in with my new friends. I was eventually expelled, but in the end, I completed high school, then completed a Certificate III in Children's Services. Around this time, I was involved in a minor incident; a food fight with strangers that escalated to physical violence. Charges were laid, although I never laid a finger on another person. I followed the advice of a lawyer to plead guilty and was told I would not have a conviction recorded. The charge was listed as 'no conviction recorded', but it still showed up on my police check – I could not work in childcare as a result. I was young and devastated and had no idea how to rectify the issue.

My dad employed me in his business; I worked in the office, on-site and in the factory. I then got a second job and got promoted to supervisor. I received an inheritance, bought a house with no mortgage. I was set. Things were looking up until I was badly injured in a car accident. The driver of the other vehicle was speeding; a P plater with a high blood alcohol reading. No charges were laid and he got a payout. This did not feel like justice to me.

Afterwards, my life consisted only of rehabilitation; for a year I had no work. I couldn't drive. I had no social life. Instead; lots of pain, tears, appointments, TV, bed, drugs and depression. I was broken not only physically but mentally.

Toward the end of that year, I met a man who seemed to be everything I'd dreamed of. I gave birth to my son the following year; as a single woman. It had become clear over the months prior that I had in fact deluded myself about the father of my child. My son's father is a sexual predator, ice addict, dangerously manipulative, violent abusive, sick man. He preyed on my younger sister, but the police did not press charges. He broke into my home, he terrorised me and my son. I took out a family violence protection order. He breached it 70 times but was not charged. What did it mean to breach a protection order? I was lost and confused. Again, I felt betrayed by the justice system.

While in this relationship I had also occasionally used ice with him. Afterwards, I began using again. It wasn't long before it had a hold of me, and I was using daily. I thought at the time it was helping me be a better parent; it allowed me to get the housework done, look after my child and be socially involved. For three years I battled drug addiction, but managed to care for my son, attended counselling sessions to assist me with my addiction and trauma. My life was chaotic, my mental state deteriorating. I began selling to close friends to support my habit as I was struggling financially.

My son's father became more violent and I was hospitalised following an attack. Child protection became involved. I could not afford a lawyer but because I owned my house I was not eligible for legal aid. My son's father did have a lawyer. I did everything the court ordered. I got clean and had my son returned. I was awarded victims of crime compensation. With that money, I began the Family Court process to get sole parental responsibility. This took nearly two years and cost tens of thousands of dollars. Throughout this, the perpetrator manipulated the system, lied to me and the court, dragged out the court case and was never held accountable for his behaviour.

For a year I was drug-free, studying, no financial stress, and sole custody of my son. Then my father died. I couldn't cope so went straight back to the very substance that had assisted me for so long; ice. I dived straight in head first. Using more than I ever had and selling immediately because I know how much money was in it. It numbed the pain I felt and filled the hole in my chest; I could deal with life again.

Sometime later the police arrived with a search warrant. They found a substantial amount of ice. I was taken into custody and bailed until my court hearing. A few months later, before my hearing, another search warrant. I was sentenced to 14 days in prison; the magistrate told me to 'dry out'. I had never been on a corrections order, or drug treatment order. This did not feel like justice.

While in prison I was in a holding cell for three days, communal toilet, no natural light, fluorescent lights on day and night, concrete box as a bed, plastic coated mattress, no pillow and a thin cotton blanket. You wouldn't keep your pet there over the weekend.

Not being eligible for legal aid I had no contact with the outside world, no lawyer, no family. At the hearing, the duty solicitor hardly communicated with me before the hearing and I couldn't understand what she told me. I was eventually released on the basis of one letter to the magistrate from a close family friend. She argued that more time in prison would be detrimental to my mental health and keeping me inside would only provide me with relationships that were of a criminal nature. Thanks to her involvement I was released and since then I have been in recovery. I regularly attend Narcotics Anonymous.

Now, I am a paid employee of a community legal centre and a member of a women's leadership group. Our vision is for women to avoid and escape the cycle of imprisonment through access to the community, connection and support. Hopefully, my story gives you some insight as to how the justice system failed me and how a situation can quickly escalate into time being served and having a criminal record, one that will be against my name for life.

It is not difficult to see where social workers might have better supported Nina throughout her engagement with the justice system. This might have included helping her fit in at school or organising a lawyer when she first ran into trouble while studying her Certificate III. A social worker might have helped her in rehab, or in the early years after her child was born, or in the wake of her father's death. A social worker might have worked with her son's father to address his toxic behaviour. Social workers might also have advocated to the government for a fairer test of legal aid so that people like Nina do not have to represent themselves. Social workers who understand the law, and who make good use of the law can help make the legal system more just.

4.4 Conclusion

Social work is an ethical profession that often comes into contact with the law. Social workers must work to uphold people's rights and work for justice, including social justice. As we will see throughout this book, these are difficult things to reconcile. The law is not always just or ethical; rights must be balanced with other rights, responsibilities and interests, and social workers will not be provided with concrete guidance in how to navigate every situation. Social workers can only look to their ethics, know the law and use reflection and reflexivity to guide their practice.

Main points

1. Social work is a profession with a robust ethical focus and a code of ethics, but this will not always provide concrete guidance in all situations. Social workers will need to work out their ethical frameworks to guide their practice.
2. Justice is a complex and disputed concept. There are many different ways of experiencing justice, and different situations will call for different ways of making sure justice is done.
3. Traditionally, justice has focused on punishment and deterrence. Increasingly, social, therapeutic and restorative approaches to justice are gaining traction.
4. Every person has rights; some are legal and enforceable; others are not. Each right has a corresponding responsibility. Rights can be limited, and often are limited by the law.

Discussion questions

1. What is your ethical framework? How will it influence how you interact with people in legal settings? Does it allow you to make decisions for other people?
2. Consider Nina's story. What needs to be done to achieve justice for people in her situation? What could be done to provide justice for Nina now?
3. What approaches to justice have you experienced? Think about the experiences you have had in your practice, in the legal system or any kind of conflict resolution process.
4. What 'lore' exists in your community? Think about what kind of non-legal sanctions you might experience if you breach community standards. Is having your social media account suspended for bad behaviour law, lore or something else?

Further reading

M. Gray, 'Moral Sources and Emergent Ethical Theories in Social Work' (1 September 2010) 40(6) *British Journal of Social Work* 1794–1811.

Ian Freckelton and Kerry Petersen, *Tensions and Traumas in Health Law* (Federation Press, 2017).

John Rawls, *A Theory of Justice* (Oxford: Oxford University Press, 1999).

Daniel W. Van Ness and Karen Heetderks Strong, *Restoring Justice: An Introduction to Restorative Justice* (Routledge, 2013).

Jane Dalrymple and Beverley Burke. *Anti-Oppressive Practice: Social Care and the Law*, 2nd ed. (McGraw-Hill Education, 2006).

4.5 References

[1] Australian Association of Social Workers, 'Acknowledgement Statement to Aboriginal and Torres Strait Islander People' (2004) 14(1) *National Bulletin* 21.
[2] AASW, *Code of Ethics* (Australian Association of Social Workers, 2010).
[3] Ibid, 15.
[4] Ibid, 14.
[5] Ibid.
[6] John Lawrence, 'A Life Worth Living: The Ethical Base for Social Work Education and Practice' (2019) 0(0) *Australian Social Work* 1; ibid.
[7] Maria Baghramian and J. Adam Carter, *Stanford Encyclopedia of Philosophy*, ed. Edward N. Zalta (online at 8 June 2019) 'Relativism'.
[8] Lynne M. Healy, 'Universalism and Cultural Relativism in Social Work Ethics' (2007) 50(1) *International Social Work* 11.
[9] Rosalind Hursthouse and Glen Pettigrove, 'Virtue Ethics' in Edward N. Zalta (ed.), *The Stanford Encyclopedia of Philosophy* (Metaphysics Research Lab, Stanford University, Winter 2018, 2018) <https://plato.stanford.edu/archives/win2018/entries/ethics-virtue/>.
[10] Larry Alexander and Michael Moore, 'Deontological Ethics' in Edward N. Zalta (ed.), *The Stanford Encyclopedia of Philosophy* (Metaphysics Research Lab, Stanford University, 2019) <https://plato.stanford.edu/archives/win2016/entries/ethics-deontological/>.
[11] AASW (n 2).
[12] Walter Sinnott-Armstrong, 'Consequentialism' in Edward N. Zalta (ed.), *The Stanford Encyclopedia of Philosophy* (Metaphysics Research Lab, Stanford University, Summer 2019, 2019) <https://plato.stanford.edu/entries/consequentialism/>.
[13] M. Gray, 'Moral Sources and Emergent Ethical Theories in Social Work' (2010) 40(6) *British Journal of Social Work* 1794; Joan C. Tronto, 'An Ethic of Care' in Ann E. Cudd and Robin O. Andreasen (eds), *Feminist Theory: A Philosophical Anthology* 1st ed. (Blackwell, 2005).
[14] Carol Gilligan, *In a Different Voice* (Harvard University Press, 1982).
[15] Gray (n 13) 1805–6.
[16] Lena Dominelli, 'Anti-Oppressive Practice' in *Ethics and Value Perspectives in Social Work* (Palgrave Macmillan, 2010); Jane Dalrymple and Beverley Burke, *Anti-Oppressive Practice: Social Care and the Law* 2nd ed. (McGraw-Hill Education, 2006) <http://search.ebscohost.com/login.aspx?direct=true&db=nlebk&AN=234192&site=ehost-live&authtype=sso&custid=s5445732>.
[17] Dominelli (n 16) cited in Lena Dominelli, 'Deprofessionalizing Social Work: Anti-Oppressive Practice, Competencies and Postmodernism' (1996) 26(2) *The British Journal of Social Work* 153, 170–1.
[18] Dalrymple and Burke (n 16).

[19] *Children and Young Persons (Care and Protection) Act 1998* (NSW) s27.
[20] Lisa Blomgren Bingham, 'Designing Justice: Legal Institutions and Other Systems for Managing Conflict' (2008) 24 *Ohio State Journal on Dispute Resolution* 1, 28.
[21] Matthew 5: 38–9.
[22] James F. Keenan, *Virtues for Ordinary Christians* (Rowman & Littlefield, 1996) 69.
[23] *Police Interviews with Vulnerable Adult Suspects* (Text No Research in practice No. 21, Australian Institute of Criminology, 2011) <https://aic.gov.au/publications/rip/rip21>.
[24] Gilligan (n 14).
[25] UN General Assembly, *Universal Declaration of Human Rights*, 10 December 1948, 217 A (III).
[26] UN General Assembly, *International Covenant on Economic, Social and Cultural Rights*, 16 December 1966, United Nations, Treaty Series, vol. 993, p. 3.
[27] AIHW, *Housing Assistance in Australia 2018* (Australian Institute of Health and Welfare, 28 June 2018) <https://www.aihw.gov.au/reports/housing-assistance/housing-assistance-in-australia-2018/contents/priority-groups-and-wait-lists>.
[28] *Australian Constitution* s 116.
[29] IFSW, 'Global Definition of Social Work', *International Federation of Social Workers* (2014) <https://www.ifsw.org/what-is-social-work/global-definition-of-social-work/>.
[30] John Rawls, *A Theory of Justice* rev. ed. (Oxford University Press, 1999).
[31] *Inequality in Australia 2018* (Australian Council of Social Service and University of New South Wales, 2018) <https://www.acoss.org.au/wp-content/uploads/2018/07/Inequality-in-Australia-2018_Factsheet.pdf>.
[32] *Fair Work Act 2009* (Cth) s 3.
[33] International Labour Organization (ILO), *Equal Remuneration Convention*, 29 June 1951, C100; Australia did not sign this Convention until 1974.
[34] *Equal Pay Case* (1972) 147 Commonwealth Arbitration Reports 172.
[35] *Workplace Gender Equality Act 2012* (Cth).
[36] Workplace Gender Equality Agency, 'Gender Pay Gap', *Australian Government* (2019) <https://www.wgea.gov.au/topics/gender-pay-gap>.
[37] Conrad Liveris, *Gender Equality at Work 2018* (2018) 23.
[38] Frederic Mishkin, *Strategies for Controlling Inflation* (No w6122, National Bureau of Economic Research, February 1998) <http://www.nber.org/papers/w6122.pdf>.
[39] Tom Cusbert, 'Estimating the NAIRU and the Unemployment Gap' (2017) June Quarter *Reserve Bank of Australia Bulletin* <https://www.rba.gov.au/publications/bulletin/2017/jun/2.html>.
[40] Jane Fenton, 'An Analysis of "Ethical Stress" in Criminal Justice Social Work in Scotland: The Place of Values' (2015) 45(5) *British Journal of Social Work* 1415, 1428.
[41] Law Council of Australia, *The Justice Project* (2018) 43 <https://www.lawcouncil.asn.au/justice-project/final-report>.
[42] Liz Smith, Alison Chetwin and Maria Marama, *Final Process Evaluation for the Alcohol and Other Drug Treatment Court* (Ministry of Justice, 17 August 2016) 5 <https://www.justice.govt.nz/assets/Documents/Publications/FINAL-AODT-Court-final-process-evaluation-20160818.pdf>.
[43] R.G. Madden and R.H. Wayne, 'Social Work and the Law: A Therapeutic Jurisprudence Perspective' (2003) 48(3) *Social Work* 338.
[44] J. Larsen, *Restorative Justice in the Australian Criminal Justice System* (Text, Australian Institute of Criminology, 2014) <https://aic.gov.au/publications/rpp/rpp127>.
[45] Daniel W. Van Ness and Karen Heetderks Strong, *Restoring Justice: An Introduction to Restorative Justice* (Routledge, 2013).
[46] Heather Strang, *Restorative Justice Programs in Australia: A Report to the Criminology Research Council* (Centre for Restorative Justice, Australian National University, 2001) 37 <http://crg.aic.gov.au/reports/strang/index.html>.

Chapter 5 Working in Involuntary Settings

For social workers working in involuntary settings, there is an inevitable ethical tension. The values base of social work requires social workers to empower people, whereas many of the roles social workers work in require social workers to control people. The central question for social workers in involuntary settings is whether they are there to care for a person or to control them. The awkward answer is; 'both'. Social work has always been in tension with itself as its emancipatory theoretical stance grinds against the expectations of society. These tensions, care versus control, best interest versus rights-based, risk management versus emancipation, are everywhere in social work practice. Do social workers 'know better' than the people they work with? This is the central question. Does our professional status allow us to run people's lives better than they can themselves? Ultimately, the law says yes, sometimes it does. The AASW *Code of Ethics* concurs:

> *Social workers will endeavour to minimise the use of legal or other compulsion. Any action which violates or diminishes the civil or legal rights of clients must be ethically, professionally and legally justifiable.*[1]

By virtue of our position as social workers we are empowered, often legally empowered, to interfere with people's parenting, schooling, housing, diet, medication, relationships, finances and a thousand other things. Yes, there are checks and balances, oversight mechanisms and multidisciplinary teams to reduce abuses of this power, but this power exists nonetheless. In order to understand the role of social workers in legal settings, social workers must have some notion of these competing tensions. Hardy points out that although the care and control functions of social work are often positioned as being separate and in conflict, in most social work roles both will be required:

> *The debate between these two camps can be polarised, with advocates of alternatives accusing their opponents of idealism or of oppression. Others point out that it is perfectly possible to conceive of care and control as complementary facets that together comprise the social work role ...*[2]

Social workers will often work with people who are compelled to work with them, either by formal legal orders or by virtue of their situation. This means social workers must constantly bring their ethical literacy to their practice in legal settings.

There are many strategies suggested for social workers working with 'involuntary clients', for which readers are directed to the further reading section at the end of this chapter. Rather than summarise these practice skills, this chapter explores three aspects of this tension so that social workers can better understand the following topic-based chapters. These are the continuum of involuntariness, the tension between best interests and rights-based approaches, and the domination of risk management paradigms.

5.1 All Social Work is Involuntary

It is tempting to see social work in legal settings as more restrictive than other social work practice. This is often true, but in truth nearly all social work practice is at least partially involuntary. Nobody wakes up in the morning, stretches, yawns, and says 'I hope I need to see a social worker today.' Social workers work in spaces with people who do not want to be in those spaces, making all social work settings somewhat involuntary. Even social workers who are in 'voluntary' services will regularly hold some coercive power over people they work with. Mental health residential rehabilitation services, for example, may be theoretically voluntary, but if non-compliance with the rehabilitation program results in eviction and homelessness, the program is not truly voluntary. Similarly, if a women's refuge in a small country town is the only safe accommodation available, women escaping family violence do not have a choice other than to stay in that refuge. Social work services do not usually operate in a free market where people can choose the services they receive. People are forced by circumstance into the service system and once in the system, they are offered limited choices. The *Code of Ethics* uses Trotter's definition of involuntary clients:

> *Involuntary Clients: people who have not chosen to receive services, or who may be actively opposed to receiving services, which are often court-ordered or provided under threat of some other legal sanction.*[3]

There are graduations on the continuum of involuntariness.[4] At one end of this continuum sits private fee-paying counselling services, where people have a genuine choice of social worker even if they would rather not need counselling to begin with. Somewhere in the middle of the continuum of involuntariness is the oversight function of social work practice, particularly where mandatory reporting obligations apply (see Chapter 6). Social workers in the popular imagination are often viewed as being a kind of soft power police force: 'stealing or removing kids', 'do-gooders', 'interfering/busy bodies'.[5] This means that even if people are voluntarily engaging with social workers, they may comply out of fear of unspecified repercussions. For a family in survival mode, the stress of having a social worker 'meddling' with their affairs may be enough to convince them to do what the social worker wants.

At the pointy end of the continuum of involuntariness sits the criminal, child protection, guardianship, involuntary mental health and asylum seeker processing systems. In the most restrictive environments people will be restricted in what they eat, what they wear, whom they speak to and what they say. Often, these restrictions will be dictated by the law, but other times the coercive nature of the restriction will be less clear. For example, many men's behaviour change and drug treatment programs are theoretically voluntary, but people will participate in order to demonstrate to a court that they should have access to their children or to stay out of prison. If the alternative is not seeing their children or going to prison, they cannot be said to be voluntarily participating.

The law both gives the state power to intervene in people's lives and sets limits on that power, but in this murky space between voluntary and involuntary both the power of the state to intervene and the limits become blurry. For example, Centrelink requires people to participate in job seeking to receive Newstart Allowance. Failing to participate will result in the person's payment being cancelled. If this occurs there are clear appeal rights and a structured process. The payment is a legal right that the person has if they meet the requirements. In non-legal setting, for example, a charity which provides free meals, the person receiving the meal has no legal right to it. If the charity decides not to provide meals to that person, they cannot easily appeal; they cannot enforce their right. In this way, the involvement of the law can be *less* restrictive, or at least the law restricts both the provider and the recipient.

This is a common phenomenon across social work. People in mental health settings will be told, 'take your medication or you will be put on a treatment order'. Child protection social workers will say, 'you need to do this parenting program or you risk your children being removed'. When a person is put on a treatment order, or when an application is made to the court, the person has all sorts of rights – rights to a lawyer, rights to appeal, rights to have an independent third party judge the circumstances. Before the law is involved, when just the *threat* of legal involvement exists, the person does not have these rights. It is important for social workers to understand that just because a person is not formally mandated by law to work with them does not mean they are necessarily less restrictive or less involuntary.

Social workers often operate in these settings, where the threat of legal restrictions exists, but they are rarely the decision-makers actually deciding if the restriction should be put in place or what the restriction should be. Most often, it is the role of a judge, magistrate or tribunal member who will make the decision about the restriction, and social workers will be responsible for advising the decision-maker, implementing the restriction and reporting back to the decision-maker. Despite not actually being the decision-maker, social workers still wield a lot of power over people's lives, both in the formal power given by the law and in their role in advising and reporting to the decision-maker.

This means that social workers should never assume that the person they are working with is voluntary just because they are not legally compelled to work with the social worker. It also means that just because a person is legally compelled to work with the social worker the social worker should not substantially change their approach; the same quality of service should be provided, although the coercive nature of the setting must be acknowledged. Social work values of respect for persons, social justice and professional integrity all still apply.[6] Really, the question is what social workers should do with this power they yield – should they use it in the person's best interests or to uphold their rights?

5.2 Best-Interests versus Rights-Based

As discussed in Chapter 9, social work is a human rights-based profession.

> *Social work is also a best-interests profession, as detailed in the AASW Code of Ethics: Social workers will maintain the best interests of clients as a priority, with due regard to the respective interests of others.*[7]

Specifically when working in involuntary settings:

> *Social workers will identify and promote the legitimate interests of involuntary clients, taking into account any conditions that apply to their situation.*[8]

In practice, these two fundamental bases of the profession are often in conflict. This is not confined to Australian social work, with the same tensions between rights-based and best-interests approaches evident in the British professional capabilities framework.[9] It is true that often what the social worker determines is in the best interests of the person is often going to align with that person's rights, but in involuntary settings this is often not going to be the case. There are two main reasons why this is a problem – nobody really knows what 'best interests' are and people often behave in ways that are contrary to their own interests. For decades this has been well understood:

> *Deciding what is best for a child poses a question no less ultimate than the purposes and values of life itself. Should the judge primarily be concerned with the child's happiness? Or with the child's spiritual and religious training? Should the judge be concerned with the*

> *economic productivity of the child when he grows up? ... [I]f the judge looks to society at large, he finds neither a clear consensus as to the best child-rearing strategies nor an appropriate hierarchy of ultimate values.*[10]

A best-interests approach assumes that a person can, at least to some extent, objectively assess what another person's best interests are. The idea of objectivity in law has long been critiqued as merely a stand-in for white male values and continues to be the subject of ongoing debate.[11] The assumption that it is possible to predict future harm accurately has also come under critique, as discussed later in this chapter. Social workers should bear in mind that the social workers who perpetuated the Stolen Generation were working in what they assessed as the best interests of First Nations children,[12] and that First Nations children are still being removed at alarming rates on exactly the same basis.[13]

Even if it were possible to accurately predict the future and to agree on which interest is most important, it is not possible to remove bias from the process:

> *... the diversity of values and circumstances which would affect decisions ... precludes any realistic expectation that decisions would not be made according to the idiosyncratic opinion of individual judges – that, in other words, using a 'principle' like 'best interests' in the exercise of a welfare power would mean there are no rules at all.*[14]

There is also the problem of working out whose interests should be prioritised. In child protection, this is simpler, as the child's interests can be said to need more protection than the parents'. Similarly, in family violence, it seems that the interests of the survivor should generally take priority over those of the perpetrator. When balancing the interests of a carer with the interests of a person with a disability, this is not so clear.

Despite these problems with a best-interests approach, which are well recognised by lawmakers,[15] it is widely used in Australian law and, in regard to children, there does not appear to be an acceptable alternative. A rights-based approach to child protection has the same problems: which rights should be prioritised and so on. In regard to adults, however, a rights-based approach has more applicability.

A rights-based approach to social work in involuntary settings must incorporate three key rights – the individual right to autonomy, the collective right to self-determination and the right to be free from unlawful discrimination. In some cases, people will behave in ways that mean they are deprived of their right to autonomy, such as when people commit crimes and are incarcerated. Human rights law allows for imprisonment so long as it is necessary and proportionate. This is also reflected in the *Code of Ethics*:

> *Social workers will recognise that in some cases their ability to promote self-determination is limited because clients may be involuntary clients or because clients' actions pose a serious threat to themselves or others.*[16]

In other cases, the rights-based approach solves the problems of a best-interests approach. Take, for example, the right of self-determination belonging to Australia's First Nations people.[17] Affording this right to First Nations communities in relation to the care of First Nations children would have avoided the Stolen Generation, and would go a long way in addressing the over-representation of First Nations children in out-of-home care today (see Chapter 12). This is an example where a rights-based approach would likely result in a *better* outcome, but a *better* outcome is not always necessary. A rights-based approach holds that adults should be allowed to make bad decisions if they want to, should be able to accept the consequences, and should be allowed to learn from those consequences.

Added to this is the right that people generally have to make decisions that are not in their best interests. These include the 'rights' to eat unhealthy food, to drink alcohol or to engage in risky behaviours such as unprotected sex or motorcycle racing. It also includes the right to give gifts to charity or to care for a loved one – these are all behaviours that are not objectively in a person's best interests, but it is generally accepted that people have the right to make those decisions themselves.

This is key to understanding the right to be free from discrimination. If a right to make a decision is afforded to others in society, it must not be denied on the basis of sex, gender, race, ethnicity, disability or any other attribute that constitutes unlawful discrimination. The right to live free from unlawful discrimination should be at the heart of human rights-based social work. Children are usually parented from a best-interests perspective (by their parents), and so a best-interests approach is not inherently discriminatory when used in the legal system. When parents stop acting in the best interests of their children, their right to made decisions about their children is limited by the state. Adults, conversely, are usually governed from a rights-based perspective, and so when a certain group is singled out for a best-interests approach, the treatment is different. When people using mental health services, people living with disabilities or First Nations people and communities are subject to best-interests practice, this is not only a deprivation of their rights to autonomy and self-determination but also a breach of their right to not be discriminated against.

This dichotomy will not always be the main tension in involuntary settings. Often the person's human rights and the social worker's assessment of their best interests will be the same. When they do not align, however, social workers must critically and reflexively engage with their practice. If a social worker decides to override a person's human rights in order to further their interests, this decision should not be undertaken lightly.

5.3 RISK MANAGEMENT

It is not possible to consider the role of social work in involuntary settings without regard to the role of social work in managing risk. Hardy writes that:

> *Risk, in one form or another, is arguably the major issue with which contemporary social work is grappling. Not only must social work practitioners work with risk, and assess and intervene to reduce it, but social work agencies must respond to and manage it, while social work research and education must produce and enable development of the knowledge and skills required to do so.*[18]

The rise of risk management in social work is aligned with the rise of neoliberalism in social work,[19] but it is not only a function of neoliberalism. Risk management has become a central part of all government and organisational functioning. In social work, this has stemmed from a number of high-profile incidents, particularly in the United Kingdom but also in Australia, in which social workers have been implicated for failing to act to prevent harm. Social work has not helped this, positioning itself as being able to predict risk despite not always being able to demonstrate an evidence base for its predictions. Davidson, Brophy and Campbell write that:

> *... mental health social work has embraced the professional status that assessing risk bestows while also being criticised for its inability to accurately predict the future and so prevent all harm.*[20]

Grant et al. suggest that social workers use risk to mitigate their own anxiety about what will happen, which can distract from providing appropriate care and support:

> *Regardless of the source of the fear and anxiety, it is important that it is separated from the task of care. The emotional experience of clinicians is not a patient care issue; it should not determine or unduly influence patient care. Clinicians could consider employing emotion regulation strategies to address their own fear and anxiety, before returning focus to the well-being of the person with whom they are working.*[21]

A risk management approach will often, but not always, be aligned with a best-interests approach, such as when detaining a person to limit their risk of suicide. Other times, such as when indefinitely detaining someone seeking asylum to discourage other people from seeking asylum in that country, it might be in direct contravention of their best interests. Risk management may also be consistent with a rights-based approach, such as when helping someone apply for a family violence protection order. Most of the time, helping someone uphold their rights involves allowing them the 'dignity of risk', which means that they are allowed to take risks, allowed to fail, and allowed to come to harm and to learn from that harm.[22]

As with a best-interests approach, risk assessment and risk management assume that the professional is better at assessing the situation than the person being assessed. This might be because they are more objective, have better training or more experience, but often it is just assumed that professionals are able to manage risk because they are professionals. This assumption is not always well borne out by the evidence. Even the best current models at predicting violence in offenders on release from prison might only correctly classify 60 per cent of cases.[23]

For example, we can identify groups of people who are more likely to attempt suicide: people who have made previous attempts, people who express suicidal intent, people with physical health problems and people of male gender, but consistently we are unable to determine which of the people in those groups, or who fit into all those groups, will actually attempt suicide.[24] Meanwhile, as we fail at predicting this accurately, people who *do not* fit into those groups miss out on services because they are 'low risk', which *increases* their risk of attempting suicide. Large et al write:

> *Despite the ubiquity of advice to use suicide risk assessment in clinical practice, there is no evidence that these assessments can usefully guide decision making.*[25]

The same applies to assessing the risk of abuse and neglect of children,[26] sexual offending,[27] and violent offending.[28] The most accurate risk assessment tools are often based on *static* factors – things that a person cannot change about themselves, such as their prior convictions, age, childhood abuse and criminal family background. These provide little guidance for social work intervention, other than to identify people who might be most in need of services and support.

Even when risk assessment tools are able to be shown to be effective at assessing risk, they are often only useful when applied to the populations they were designed with. For example, generic risk assessment tools in child protection can result in oppressive and racist results when used with families of colour and particularly with First Nations families.[29] This is a terrible thing if we are only racistly oppressing one child, but when we also consider that children of First Nations families are nearly ten times more likely to be placed into out-of-home care than children of settler families,[30] we start to see how carefully risk assessment should be used.

This is not to suggest that social workers should abandon risk assessments altogether, but it should certainly abandon a blind adherence to risk management as an exact science. Even if risk assessment could be developed into an exact science, it still poses questions about how this should be brought into practice, particularly in involuntary settings. Take, for example, the risk that a person might harm another person. Social workers may conduct a risk assessment and decide that there is a chance that an event will occur. At what percentage of probability would it be reasonable to detain a person? If we could say the risk is at 100 per cent chance they will seriously harm another person, it may well be justified in detaining them. What if it is a lower chance – say 20 per cent or 10 per cent? Remember, the burden of proof in civil law is *on the balance of probabilities*. That means it has to be *more likely than not* that something happened – 51 per cent likely – and for criminal law it must be *beyond a reasonable doubt*. By this reasoning, we probably should not detain the person unless it is more likely than not that they will harm someone else. This means, in practice, that *half* of the people who are assessed at 50 per cent will go on to harm someone else and yet we have 'failed' to detain any of them. One in ten of those who are assessed at 10 per cent chance of harming someone else will go on to harm someone, but if you detain people who are assessed at 10 per cent risk you have detained nine out of ten people unnecessarily. These are uncomfortable equations. How many people are we willing to detain to prevent one person from causing harm? Nine? Fifty? A hundred?

Social workers should take two things away from this. First, we are not very good at predicting risk, and even when we are we get it wrong. Secondly, even if we were really good at it, we would probably be uncomfortable with the implications for human rights.

Proponents of risk assessment warn against overstating the lack of evidence. They argue that risk assessment may be useful in 'treatment allocation, waiting list prioritisation or referral for more detailed assessments'.[31] These are good arguments and social workers can certainly, carefully, use risk assessment for these purposes. When risk assessment is used to deny people their fundamental human rights, social workers should carefully consider the consequences.

5.4 Conclusion

Working in involuntary settings requires social workers to balance irresolvable tensions. The notion that the social worker is better positioned to make decisions about a person's life should sit uncomfortably with social workers, but this is the central premise of this work. Social workers should approach this carefully, reflectively and reflexively. As will be shown in the following chapters, this is a very difficult balance to get right and social workers in the past have regularly got it very wrong. Moving forward, social workers can do better work by being aware of the law, of their responsibilities and by working alongside people to help them make their own decisions.

Main points

1. Nearly all social work is involuntary, in the sense that people do not want to be in situations that they need a social worker. This means nearly all social work practice sits on a continuum between voluntary and legally mandated engagement.
2. Just because a person is not legally mandated does not mean they are voluntary. Threats of force can be just as persuasive as the force itself, and threats of force do not have the legal limits and oversight mechanisms that define legal force.
3. Much of social work practice will need to balance tensions between best interests and rights-based approaches, usually finding a balance between the two.
4. Risk management has come to define involuntary settings, but this is not without its problems. Social workers should be wary of uncritically accepting risk management narratives and should engage with both the ethical issues and the evidence that underpins them.

Discussion questions

1. Are social workers in involuntary settings there to care for the involuntary person or control them?
2. Do social workers know better what is best for the people they work with? Even if they do, does that give them the right to make decisions about them?
3. Does your practice approach draw more on a human-rights or a best-interest perspective? In which situations and why?
4. What role should social workers play in risk management? What can social workers bring to multidisciplinary teams that are responsible for managing risk?

Further reading

- Chris Trotter, *Working with Involuntary Clients: A Guide to Practice* (SAGE, 2006).
- Ronald H. Rooney and Rebecca Mirick, *Strategies for Work with Involuntary Clients* 3rd ed. (Columbia University Press, 2018).
- Stephen A. Webb, *Social Work in a Risk Society: Social and Political Perspectives* (Palgrave Macmillan, 2006).

- Martin Smith, 'Wounding Healers. Killing with Kindness on the Road to Hell' (2 January 2019) 33(1) *Journal of Social Work Practice* 109–15.

5.5 References

[1] AASW, *Code of Ethics* (Australian Association of Social Workers, 2010) 26.

[2] Mark Hardy, *Governing Risk: Care and Control in Contemporary Social Work* (2015) <http://public.eblib.com/choice/publicfullrecord.aspx?p=1986784>.

[3] Chris Trotter, *Working with Involuntary Clients: A Guide to Practice* (SAGE, 2006) 2; AASW (n 1) 44.

[4] Ronald H. Rooney and Rebecca Mirick, *Strategies for Work with Involuntary Clients* 3rd ed. (Columbia University Press, 2018).

[5] Barbara Staniforth, Kelsey L. Deane and Liz Beddoe, 'Comparing Public Perceptions of Social Work and Social Workers' Expectations of the Public View' (2016) 28(1) *Aotearoa New Zealand Social Work* 13, 18.

[6] AASW (n 1).

[7] Ibid 25.

[8] Ibid 26.

[9] Jonathan P. Beckett, 'The Changing Nature of Social Work' (2018) 61(6) *International Social Work* 968.

[10] Robert Mnookin, 'Child-Custody Adjudication: Judicial Functions in the Face of Indeterminacy' (1975) 39(3) *Law and Contemporary Problems* 226.

[11] Catharine A. MacKinnon, 'Reflections on Sex Equality under Law' (1991) 100(5) *The Yale Law Journal* 1281; Matthew Burch and Katherine Furman, 'Objectivity in Science and Law: A Shared Rescue Strategy' (2019) 64 *International Journal of Law and Psychiatry* 60.

[12] Nilan Yu, 'Interrogating Social Work: Australian Social Work and the Stolen Generations' [2018] *Journal of Social Work* 1468017318794230.

[13] *Child Protection and Aboriginal and Torres Strait Islander Children* (Text, Australian Institute of Family Studies, 31 January 2019) <https://aifs.gov.au/cfca/publications/child-protection-and-aboriginal-and-torres-strait-islander-children>.

[14] M. Rayner, 'Protection and Promotion of the Best Interests of the Child' (1997) 9.

[15] Australian Law Reform Commission, *Seen and Heard: Priority for Children in the Legal Process* (No. 84, Australian Government, 1997) <https://www.alrc.gov.au/publications/16-childrens-involvement-family-law-proceedings/best-interests-principle>.

[16] AASW (n 1) 26.

[17] UN General Assembly, *United Nations Declaration on the Rights of Indigenous Peoples: resolution / adopted by the General Assembly*, 2 October 2007, A/RES/61/295.

[18] Hardy (n 2) 1.

[19] John Wallace and Bob Pease, 'Neoliberalism and Australian Social Work: Accommodation or Resistance?' (2011) 11(2) *Journal of Social Work* 132; June Allan, Bob Pease and Linda Briskman, *Critical Social Work: An Introduction to Theories and Practices* (Allen & Unwin, 2003).

[20] Gavin Davidson, Lisa Brophy and Jim Campbell, 'Risk, Recovery and Capacity: Competing or Complementary Approaches to Mental Health Social Work' (2016) 69(2) *Australian Social Work* 158, 159.

[21] Kellie Grant, Jenny Martin and Jenni White, 'Risk: What Is It, Whom Does It Protect, and What Happened to Care?' in Jennifer M. Martin (ed.), *Mental Health Policy, Practice, and Service Accessibility in Contemporary Society* (IGI Global, 2018) <http://ebookcentral.proquest.com/lib/rmit/detail.action?docID=5516346>.

[22] Pauline Marsh and Lisa Kelly, 'Dignity of Risk in the Community: A Review of and Reflections on the Literature' (2018) 20(5–6) *Health, Risk & Society* 297.

[23] Anthony Costa Constantinou et al, 'Risk Assessment and Risk Management of Violent Reoffending among Prisoners' (2015) 42(21) *Expert Systems with Applications* 7511; Nadine A.C. Troquete et al, 'Predictive Validity of the Short-Term Assessment of Risk and Treatability for Violent Behavior in Outpatient Forensic Psychiatric Patients' (2015) 27(2) *Psychological Assessment* 377.

[24] Melissa K.Y. Chan et al, 'Predicting Suicide Following Self-Harm: Systematic Review of Risk Factors and Risk Scales' (2016) 209(4) *The British Journal of Psychiatry* 277; Matthew Michael Large et al, 'Can We Usefully Stratify Patients According to Suicide Risk?' (2017) 359 *BMJ* j4627; Matthew Michael Large and Nav Kapur, 'Psychiatric Hospitalisation and the Risk of Suicide' (2018) 212(5) *The British Journal of Psychiatry* 269; Christian G. Huber et al, 'Suicide Risk and Absconding in Psychiatric Hospitals With and Without Open Door Policies: A 15 Year, Observational Study' (2016) 3(9) *The Lancet Psychiatry* 842; Jacqui Wise, 'Suicide Prevention Should Focus on First Three Months after Discharge, Study Finds' (2017) 357 *BMJ* j2664.

[25] Large et al (n 24) 359.

[26] Della Knoke and Nico Trocmé, 'Reviewing the Evidence on Assessing Risk for Child Abuse and Neglect' (2005) 5(3) *Brief Treatment and Crisis Intervention* 310.

[27] Anthony R. Beech, Leam A. Craig and Kevin D. Browne, *Assessment and Treatment of Sex Offenders: A Handbook* (John Wiley & Sons, 2009) <http://ebookcentral.proquest.com/lib/rmit/detail.action?docID=428288>.

[28] Constantinou et al. (n 23).

[29] Sohki Aski Esquao and Susan Strega, *Walking This Path Together: Anti-Racist and Anti-Oppressive Child Welfare Practice* (Fernwood Publishing, 2015); Sarah Maiter, 'Using an Anti-Racist Framework for Assessment and Intervention in Clinical Practice with Families from Diverse Ethno-Racial Backgrounds' (2009) 37(4) *Clinical Social Work Journal* 267.

[30] *Child Protection and Aboriginal and Torres Strait Islander Children* (n 13).

[31] Achim Wolf and Seena Fazel, 'Overstating the Lack of Evidence on Suicide Risk Assessment' (2017) 210(5) *The British Journal of Psychiatry* 369, 369.

Chapter 6 THE LEGAL OBLIGATIONS OF SOCIAL WORKERS

Social work practice is bounded on all sides by obligations – ethical, practical, organisational and legal. Usually, these obligations are invisible, only becoming apparent when the boundaries are transgressed or tested. Even when they are visible they are often fuzzy, poorly defined and filtered through the layperson's misguided conviction of the certainty of the law.

The law as it applies to social workers is not clear and is not consistent. This is for two main reasons; social workers are not a registered profession and they are difficult to sue. Unlike medical doctors, psychologists, occupational therapists and nurses, social workers are not governed by the Australian Health Practitioner Regulation Agency (AHPRA) and not regulated by the *Health Practitioner Regulation National Law Act 2009* (Cth).* Social workers in specific roles, such as child protection or mental health, will be subject to legislation as a result of their employment, but this is because of their roles as child protection workers or mental health professionals, not because they are social workers. Similarly, social workers providing a health service in some jurisdictions may be subject to legislation that regulates the provision of health services, but this applies broadly, from cosmetic surgery to drug and alcohol counselling, not specifically to social workers.[1] Without a piece of legislation to clearly state the law as it applies to social workers, they must turn to precedent in the common law for guidance.

Precedent, as discussed in Chapter 2, consists of decisions made by courts on previous cases. This means that social workers could look to other decisions made by courts about similar situations, see what the court said about the similar situation and make a decision about how to act. The problem with this is that social workers are not often the subject of legal action that might generate precedent.

Yes, social workers who behave badly are subject to the same consequences as anyone else, but there are very few cases of social workers who are trying to do the right thing and getting into legal trouble. There are cases of social workers causing car accidents,[2] threatening to kill people,[3] accessing child pornography,[4] and pretending to be psychologists,[5] but in years of searching I have not found a single Australian case where a social worker was found guilty or held liable while doing their job in good

* Although this is set to change in South Australia, with the introduction of the *Social Workers Registration Bill 2018* (SA).

faith.[*] There are a few cases where social workers are subject to legal action but the court ruled in their favour.[6] There are many cases overseas,[7] but none in Australia.[†]

This is not to say that social workers always behave according to the law. There are lots of documented examples of social workers not complying with the law but not being subject to legal sanction, and the lack of court reports does not mean there has not been any legal action because only a small percentage of all cases are published in court reports and many civil cases are settled before they go to trial. What it does mean is that there is no body of common law we can look to for guidance on what the legal obligations of social workers are.

This is the case partly because in Australia social work is difficult to define legally. To argue that a social worker should or should not do a certain thing, we must first be able to define what social work practice is. This is difficult in part because we do so many things; casework, counselling, advocacy, community work, policy work and research; and because when we do those things we do them in such a wide variety of ways, informed by many different theoretical and practice perspectives. Because it is difficult to say what social workers do, it is difficult to say what we should not do.

The other issue is that as a general rule social workers have no money, so suing a social worker is not worth the effort. Social work services are usually delivered via organisations who do have money, such as government departments, so the government department gets sued instead. This means there are laws about how governments and other organisations should operate when providing social services, but not as many laws about social workers specifically. This leads to a third contributing factor, which is that social workers are generally viewed by courts as providing an essential service that should not be interfered with unnecessarily.

This is not to say that the law shows no interest in the practice of social workers. There are nearly 4000 Australian reported legal cases that involve a social worker in some way, usually giving evidence or submitting reports. Justice Bell is damning of the social worker in *Patrick's Case,*[8] where the social worker tries to sell Patrick's house against his will (see Chapter 13). The coroner in the Chloe Valentine Coroner's Inquest slams a number of social workers for ineptitude,[9] saying their failure to comply with their legal

[*] A comprehensive search by an experienced law librarian also uncovered no examples.

[†] In other jurisdictions, such as in England, social workers are registered and can be suspended or banned from social work practice by the Health and Care Professions Tribunal. These are often due to quite serious issues such as rape and child sexual assault, but there are cases where social workers have been suspended or banned for poor case noting and report writing, forging a sick leave doctor's certificate, not providing sufficient managerial support or failing to undertake an assessment.

obligations resulted in Chloe's death. In neither of these cases were legal proceedings commenced against the social workers.

Without legislative registration, regulation of the profession is left to the Australian Association of Social Workers (AASW) and its *Code of Ethics*.[10] Social work students will be familiar with the phrase:

Social workers in Australia are bound by the AASW Code of Ethics.

In reality, only social workers who chose to be members of the AASW are 'bound' by the *Code of Ethics*, and even then the worst that can happen is that they can be kicked out of the AASW. The AASW publishes the names of those who are 'ineligible for membership' on their website,[11] but unless potential employers were to consult this list it is unlikely that ejection from the AASW would lead to any inconvenience to the offending social worker. This means that while social workers may *choose* to be *guided by* the *Code of Ethics*, they are not legally *bound* by it.

There are some clear legal requirements for some social workers in some situations. For example, social workers in health services in New South Wales (NSW) are legally bound by the *Code of Conduct for unregistered health practitioners* under the *Public Health Act 2010* (NSW) and can be investigated by the NSW Health Care Complaints Commission. This is mainly focused on complaints management, rather than legal sanctions, but social workers who breach this Code can be banned from practising and have a public statement posted online that details how they breached the Code. This will not apply to social workers who are working in NSW in services that are not health services, such as welfare or community development services. Similar schemes operate in other jurisdictions.[12]

These complaints processes and possible legal sanctions are important for social workers in health settings to be aware of, but not frightened by. For example, the only two social workers banned by the NSW Health Care Complaints Commission were having sexual relationships with people they were working with.[13] Unprofessional relationships are discussed in detail later in this chapter but this highlights just how serious misconduct must be before social workers are sanctioned by the law.

Social workers should take away two things from this situation. First, social workers should be aware of their legal obligations but not afraid of them. The courts will generally back social workers who are trying to do the right thing. Secondly, the courts and parliaments are generally willing to give social workers a wide discretion on how to practise rather than binding them with legal obligations that will make them less effective.

The remainder of this chapter deals with a range of legal obligations common to social work practice: informed consent, statutory obligations, case notes, confidentiality, privacy and mandatory reporting, the duty of care, and unprofessional relationships.

6.1 Free and Informed Consent

Social workers have an ethical duty to seek informed consent from people they work with,[14] but the legal obligations are a little fuzzier. Informed consent is:

> *... the giving of information to a client in order to gain that client's voluntary agreement to a proposed social worker-client interaction.*[15]

Legally, consent must be free, so people cannot be pressured into a decision, and it must be informed, so people must be given all the relevant information to make a decision. Capacity to give consent is discussed in more detail in Chapter 13, but generally in order to legally give consent people must be able to understand, retain, use and weigh the information about the decision, and communicate their decision.

Usually, anything invasive or physical, such as medical procedures, can only be done with consent. If consent or legal justification is not provided, these acts will be prohibited by civil or criminal law. For actions that are not clearly breaches of the law, such as taking a referral without a person's consent or visiting them at work without consent, social workers must look to their ethics for guidance. Some limits are placed on this by the law of negligence, confidentiality and privacy, as discussed later, but otherwise social workers are *ethically* but not usually *legally* required to get informed consent.

Social workers commonly provide 'consent forms', which purport to give legal consent to share information when signed. These are useful in that they help people understand what might happen with the information they provide but are not a substitute for actually getting consent. Consent is decision specific, so, for example, just because a person says that the social worker can do a referral to one organisation does not mean they can do a referral to another organisation. To be properly informed, a person should have the opportunity to consent to each piece of information that is shared about them. In addition, consent that is conditional on getting access to an essential service is not really free. If a person has to sign a consent form in order to get access to housing, treatment, support, advocacy or any other social work service, they are under some duress to sign the form. This becomes even more difficult when working with people who are mandated by law to work with social workers (see Chapter 5). Just because the legal requirement to seek consent is removed in these circumstances does not mean that the ethical obligation changes. Social workers are ethically obliged to seek consent in all situations even if the legal obligation is removed.

6.2 STATUTORY OBLIGATIONS

Social workers have statutory powers and obligations under a range of legislation owing to the roles they work in. Social workers working for government child protection agencies will have very different legal powers and obligations from social workers working in non-government child counselling roles. Commonly, some social work roles will be given the power to undertake assessments, such as under the *Sentencing Act 1995* (WA) or the *Children and Young People Act 2008* (ACT), which will then be used by a court to make decisions in a case (see Chapter 7 for guidance on writing court reports). Social workers in some roles might be authorised to detain people for assessment under mental health legislation.[16] Less commonly, legislation might allow for a social worker to be appointed as a support person for vulnerable participants in the legal system, such as section 47 of the *Adoption Act 2009* (Qld), which allows for courts to appoint someone to support the child through the adoption process. These are powers given to specific social workers who are working under those pieces of legislation, not to all social workers generally. This is quite different from, for example, lawyers or registered medical practitioners, who get some statutory powers and responsibilities simply because of their profession.

These powers come with a range of obligations. There are general obligations that apply to any person who is given a power, particularly a decision-making power.[17] The obligations include the requirement that decision-makers act with procedural fairness; in other words, people affected by the decision should be given an opportunity to have a hearing and the person making the decision should be impartial. Decisions should be made based on evidence, only relevant considerations should be taken into account and the decision should be made for a 'proper' and 'reasonable' purpose.

Box 6.1 *Acting without procedural fairness*

A newly graduated mental health social worker, Shaun, was instructed by his supervisor to attend to an 'incident' involving a man who was a regular user of the service. Shaun's supervisor instructed him to fill out an 'Assessment Order' – a form authorising compulsory assessment under the Mental Health Act *so that he would not have to worry about doing it when he got there. Shaun attended, and used his powers under the* Mental Health Act *to require the man to go to hospital for assessment.*

Shaun has really acted without procedural fairness in this case. He has not assessed if an Assessment Order needs to be made and has not assessed any evidence. His desire to save time is not relevant to his decision. Instead, Shaun should have attended and then made a decision about whether an assessment order needed to be made or not.

With almost all powers there are also specific obligations in the same legislation that gives the power. If Shaun was practising in Victoria, the Victorian Mental Health Act 2014 *requires that 'there is no less restrictive means reasonably available to enable the person to be assessed,'*[18] *and that people must be supported to make or participate in decisions about their assessments.*[19] *In Victoria, where there is a human rights Charter (see Chapter 9), Shaun is also required to consider the possible impact on his decision on the person's human rights. Shaun has failed to comply with these specific statutory obligations.*

In practice, the sort of behaviour in Box 6.1 happens all the time and there is often little that can legally be done about it, although sometimes decisions are challenged in court or feature in the media. It is up to individual practitioners, supervisors and organisations to work to ensure that decisions made with statutory powers are made in line with the obligations those powers bring. This does not need to be particularly onerous. The Victorian Supreme Court has said that when making decisions that impact on human rights:

> *... it will be sufficient in most circumstances that there is some evidence that shows the decision-maker seriously turned his or her mind to the possible impact of the decision on a person's human rights and the implications thereof for the affected person, and that the countervailing interests or obligations were identified.*[20]

This means that social workers using statutory powers should, in Victoria at least, retain evidence that they thought about the impact of their decision on a person's human rights. One of the most effective ways that this can be done is by ensuring that any decisions that are made are clearly articulated in case notes.

6.3 Case notes

Given that social workers might spend up to half their day writing case notes and reports,[21] it is reasonable to expect clear guidance on the legal requirements of such notes. Unfortunately, for the reasons explained above, this is not always provided. Case notes are not legally required to be written in any particular way – there is no *Case Notes Act*. Instead, case notes are formed by a mix of the preference of the writer, organisational policy and the legislation relevant to that jurisdiction. The AASW states that:

> *Case notes may be subject to a range of legislative processes and requirements during and following the*

> *conclusion of the professional relationship. The nature of these requirements may differ greatly according to the State and nature or context of practice. Statutory bodies, for example, are subject to Freedom of Information legislation, which may differ slightly from State to State. In any context, notes can be subpoenaed for any number of reasons. Processes for responding to a subpoena may differ depending on the Court and similarly organisations may vary in their policy and procedure for doing so.*[22]

There are three legal issues to consider when writing case notes. The first is that the case notes might appear in court. This may be via subpoena, where a party to a case legally requires the case notes to be submitted as evidence. When this occurs, it is vital that the court can clearly see what occurred in each case and why, particularly when social workers are using statutory powers.

The Chloe Valentine Coroner's Inquest is a prime example of poor social work note taking leading to poor social work practice, in this case contributing to Chloe's death. The social workers were accused of deliberately including some information and deliberately excluding others, of not writing notes at the time things happened and generally not taking note taking seriously. The coroner said that:

> *Note taking is intended to record matters factually and accurately. There is, I suppose, a place for social workers to record their opinions of people and their behaviours and motivations in the case notes, but these should be expressly recorded as opinions, and not mixed in with the factual record of the event. I intend to recommend that Families SA train social workers in the art of proper note taking, with emphasis on the need to be factually accurate, and make a clear distinction between the facts of an event and the worker's opinions and judgements about the event and particular individuals.*[23]

Note that the coroner does not say that opinions should not be included, only that they should be clearly labelled as opinions and separated from factual observations. It is important that professional opinions, and the professional reasoning that led to those opinions, be documented.

The second legal issue to consider is that case notes might be used to justify a decision by the social worker. If the social worker or their organisation is sued in court, or if a decision they make is subject to review by an internal investigation, tribunal or court, it is vital that the reasons for that decision are clearly documented.* In general, courts are willing to give health professionals the benefit of the doubt if they can explain why they made a decision. This allows social workers to make decisions that are less restrictive, and potentially more 'risky', if they clearly document that in the case notes. Carroll and McSherry write:

> *Having clarified the rationale for making a decision, the decision needs to be communicated both in writing (documentation) and verbally (with the client, carers, co-workers). Recovery-focussed and legally defensible care, however, requires not only the communication of the clinical decision itself but also communication of its logical basis ... Comprehensive documentation of risk management decisions requires "thinking out loud for the record"...*[24]

The third legal issue is less about the content of the notes and more about how the notes are handled. For example, many social work organisations will be subject to the *Privacy Act 1988* (Cth), the *Freedom of Information Act 1982* (Cth) or similar state and territory legislation. Privacy legislation restricts how information should be kept, while Freedom of Information legislation details when it must be released. Unless social workers are in private practice, how long the case notes are kept for, who they can be shared with and how they should be stored will be a matter for the organisation to deal with, rather than the individual social worker. This is a very good thing as it all gets rather complex,† so the main thing for social workers to do is follow the organisational policy on case note retention, storage and sharing. This also links to social workers' obligations of confidentiality and privacy.

6.4 Confidentiality, Privacy and Mandatory Reporting

Confidentiality and privacy are often used interchangeably, but legally they are two different concepts. Privacy applies to the person, confidentiality applies to the information collected about the person. Confidentiality can be seen as an extension of privacy, as privacy about sharing information.

---

* This will not help very much if they were bad reasons to begin with, as was the case in *Patrick's Case,* where the court found that the social worker's decision-making process had failed to take into account Patrick's human rights.

† As an example of how complex this can be, for social workers in private practice receiving Medicare rebates, just some of the relevant legislation includes the *Human Services (Medicare) Act 1973* (Cth), *Health Insurance Act 1973* (Cth), *Veteran's Entitlement Act 1986* (Cth), *Health and Other Services (compensation) Act 1995* (Cth), *Privacy Act 1988* (Cth), *Privacy Amendment (Enhancing Privacy Protection) Act 2012* (Cth), *Aged Care Act 1997* (Cth), *Private Health Insurance Act 2007* (Cth).

For example, a person might exercise their right to privacy and ask you not to visit them at home, while you uphold their right to confidentiality by not telling anyone else what you see while in their home. Social workers should never invade a person's privacy or breach their confidentiality without good reason. Respecting privacy, including confidentiality, is a core value of social work practice.[25]

Social workers are also bound by law to respect privacy and confidentiality, but for social workers to effectively do their jobs, both privacy and confidentiality must sometimes be limited. For example, in child protection settings, a social worker will infringe on a parent's right to privacy if they do a surprise or unwanted home visit to ensure that the home is an appropriate environment for the child. Similarly, they may pass this information on to relevant authorities, infringing on the parent's right to confidentiality. This has led some to call for social workers to stop pretending that confidentiality is a core value of social work when it is so often breached in practice.[26]

When the need or desire to breach confidentiality arises, social workers must ensure they are familiar with the relevant law to inform their decision-making and to communicate this to the people they work with. The key to navigating this difficult area of social work is to consistently and repeatedly communicate with people; both so that they can decide what they want to share with the social worker and so they are able to make decisions about what happens with their information. It is common practice to say that 'everything we discuss will be confidential except when I need to disclose to prevent harm to you or someone else, or where required by law'. That is a great start but means little to the person whose information is being collected. Rather, social workers must explain what that means in each specific situation to each person they work with.

This section looks first at privacy and confidentiality and when they *may* be limited before moving on to mandatory reporting, which is when confidentiality *must* be broken.

6.4.1 Privacy and confidentiality

Privacy is a fundamental human right in international law (see Chapter 9) featuring in both the *Universal Declaration of Human Rights*,[27] and the *International Covenant on Civil and Political Rights*,[28] as well as local human rights laws. The *Privacy Act 1988* (Cth) is the main Commonwealth law governing privacy, and sets out 13 Privacy Principles as well as creating the *Australian Information Commissioner*. The principles cover:

- *the open and transparent management of personal information including having a privacy policy*
- *an individual having the option of transacting anonymously or using a pseudonym where practicable*
- *the collection of solicited personal information and receipt of un-solicited personal information including giving notice about collection*

- *how personal information can be used and disclosed (including overseas)*
- *maintaining the quality of personal information*
- *keeping personal information secure*
- *right for individuals to access and correct their personal information.*[29]

All states and territories have similar legislation,[30] except South Australia, which has an official policy instead. There are extra rules about 'sensitive' information, which includes information about health, race or ethnicity, sexual orientation, religion, criminal history and political belief. Most social work records will contain some of this information so will have to comply with these additional rules. The main difference between general and sensitive is that sensitive can only be collected with the person's consent. General information can usually be collected without consent but the person must be informed that you are collecting it and how it will be used.

6.4.2 Breaching confidentiality

There are two ways the law deals with breaching confidentiality: first, when social workers are *permitted* to breach, the law says they can if they want to; and secondly; when they are *required* to breach, the law says they have to. The first law to consider is the *Privacy Act 1988* (Cth) or the relevant state or territory equivalent. Section 16A of the *Privacy Act 1988* (Cth) permits the release of information if:

(a) it is unreasonable or impracticable to obtain the individual's consent to the collection, use or disclosure; and
(b) the entity reasonably believes that the collection, use or disclosure is necessary to lessen or prevent a serious threat to the life, health or safety of any individual, or to public health or safety.

Similarly, the Health Privacy Principles in Schedule 1 of the *Health Records Act 2001* (Vic) allows for disclosure of information if there is:

(i) a serious threat to an individual's life, health, safety or welfare; or
(ii) a serious threat to public health, public safety or public welfare—

This is a good example of how difficult it can be to work out if you can disclose or not. What is a 'serious' threat? The Commonwealth Act allows disclosure to protect 'life, health or safety', but the Victorian Act is 'life, health, safety or *welfare'*. This means if your organisation is governed by the Commonwealth Act, you cannot disclose to prevent a threat to welfare, but you can if your organisation is governed by the Victorian Act. Check the wording for your jurisdiction and see how it compares to the Commonwealth.

Working out which Act applies can be difficult, but in general Commonwealth agencies and private sector organisations with an annual turnover of $3 million or more are bound by the Commonwealth legislation and state, while territory or local council agencies are bound by the state or territory legislation. Some organisations will be covered by both, some by neither. If you are not sure, the Office of the Australian Information Commissioner has a hotline that can give advice. Some states and territories also have information commissioners who can give advice.

Box 6.2 *Not Amy's drugs*

Amy is going to be evicted from her community housing property because the police found drugs on the premises. She confides to you, her social worker, that the drugs are not hers but belong to her son. She asks you not to tell anyone as she does not want her son to get into trouble. You know that Amy will become homeless and likely receive a fine, but she still refuses to get her son into trouble.

Are you permitted to disclose this information to Amy's housing worker if doing so would prevent her from being evicted?

Disclosure without consent is also allowed to help find a missing person or to report unlawful activity or serious misconduct to the police or another enforcement body. It is very common for people to disclose unlawful activity to social workers, and in some jurisdictions it is required to report this by law, as discussed later. This reinforces the importance of telling people what your obligations are before they tell you anything you might want or be required to report.

There are also specific exemptions in certain legislation that allow for breaches of confidentiality. For example, section 79 of the *Firearms Act 1996* (NSW) specifically states that social workers can breach confidentiality if they believe a person who is in possession of a firearm poses a threat to themselves or to public safety. There are also specific restrictions in legislation that prevent disclosure of information, such as section 60E(1) of the *Legal Aid Commission Act 1979* (NSW), which prevents information shared in legal aid conferencing sessions being used as evidence. There are also limited protections for sexual assault counselling.[31] Courts may also impose restrictions on publication of identifying information, usually of ongoing cases or cases involving vulnerable people or children.

These are all examples of when social workers are *permitted* or *not permitted* to report or otherwise disclose information. Whether they do or not will largely be an ethical question or decided as a matter of social work practice, but sometimes the law takes this decision away from the practitioner and requires that a report be made.

6.4.3 Mandatory reporting

The main area in which social workers are required to report is child abuse, but there are other broader obligations as well.[32] It is not usually a crime to fail to disclose or fail to report an offence, but there are some exceptions.[*] Failing to report treason, for example, carries a maximum sentence of life imprisonment.[33] In NSW it is an offence to conceal any 'serious indictable offence',[34] but this law does not always apply to certain professionals, including social workers.[35] In the Northern Territory not reporting family violence is a crime.[36]

There are a range of situations where social workers might be legally compelled to disclose information. For example, the *Corrections Act 1986* (Vic) s 22 reads

> *(2) An officer must report immediately to the Governor anything which might reasonably be thought to jeopardize the security of the prison or the welfare of the prisoners.*

For this legislation, an 'officer' is pretty much anyone who is employed by the prison, including health workers, but also includes volunteers and people employed by other organisations that do outreach work in prisons.[37] This is pretty broad and could include failing to report if a prisoner has contraband. This section has no offence or penalty attached to it, so just failing to comply with it might not be a criminal offence but it is still required by law.

In Victoria, it is a crime not to report child sexual assault,[38] although if the disclosure is made to a 'counsellor' then there is no obligation for the counsellor to report. Social workers will sometimes be counsellors when they are 'counselling' but not when they are not.[39] NSW has an even broader offence, introduced in 2018, which makes it a crime for any person not to disclose a 'child abuse offence', which includes a range of violent and sexual offences.[40] These criminal offences for concealing a crime are a bit different from mandatory reporting legislation for child abuse, which does not usually include criminal punishments for failing to comply.

---

[*] In English common law it used to be an offence not to report a felony, which is an old term for a serious crime. In Victoria and South Australia this common law offence, called 'misprision of felony', has been abolished. In the other jurisdictions misprision of felony has not been used for decades and so probably no longer applies, partly because we no longer use the word felony any more – instead we have indictable (more serious) and summary (less serious) offences.

Table 6.1 *Are social workers mandatory reporters?*

Jurisdiction	Are social workers mandatory reporters?
ACT	If they are school counsellors or public servants working in child or family services.
NSW	If they work with children in health care, welfare, education, children's services, residential services, or law enforcement.
NT	Yes – every adult is a mandatory reporter.
Qld	No.
SA	Yes.
Tas.	If they work in government-funded agencies providing health, welfare or education services to children
Vic.	No.
WA	No.
Cth.	Only if they are family consultants, family counsellors or family dispute resolution practitioners working with the Family Court.

Mandatory reporting for child abuse is legislated in every state and territory.[41] This requires specific groups of people to report suspected cases or risks of child abuse and neglect. Generally, the legislation requires professionals who work with children and who form a 'reasonable belief' or 'reasonable suspicion' that abuse is occurring or is likely to occur. What constitutes abuse varies, but generally covers sexual, physical, emotional and psychological abuse. Social workers are only specifically identified as mandatory reporters in South Australia, but often social workers will fit into other groups, such as school counsellors or public servants (Table 6.1).[*] This does not mean that social workers who are not mandatory reporters are restricted from making reports, just that they are not necessarily required to do so by law. People who make reports under mandatory reporting legislation are usually able to have their identities kept secret so that nobody knows who made the report.

The Australian Institute of Family Studies has produced a fact sheet that breaks down the requirements in each jurisdiction.[42]

6.4.4 Other requirements to breach confidentiality

Social workers may also be required to breach confidentiality by direct court order, often via a subpoena. Social work notes are not protected in the way that legal files are by client professional privilege, but there are some protections. The NSW Supreme Court has ruled that there is 'a public interest in preserving the confidentiality of protected confidences between

[*] In what can only be assumed to be an attempt to make life difficult for social workers trying to learn more about the law, in the Victorian *Children, Youth and Families Act 2005*, section 182(g) states that social workers are mandatory reporters 'on and from the relevant date'. This date has never been announced, so social workers are not mandatory reporters in Victoria.

a social worker and client',[43] but in doing so reinforced that this is not complete protection. This means that social workers should assume that anything they write may be used as evidence in court but should seek legal advice if subpoenaed.

Aside from legislation and court orders that require disclosure, social workers will sometimes owe a duty of care to people they work with. This will sometimes include a requirement that they breach confidentiality to prevent harm to a person, as discussed in Section 6.5.

6.5 Duties of Care and Your Duty to Care

Duty of care is a legal term commonly misused in social work parlance. Be very careful if you hear someone telling you that you cannot do something because we have a duty of care – usually what they mean is that 'something bad might happen'. When social workers get this wrong the consequences can be serious. In *Parker v Grams* the Federal Magistrate is scathing of the social worker's interpretation of their duty of care:

> *I am afraid that I have a very different view of the social worker's 'Duty of Care' from that which she holds.*[44]

In this section, we unpack what this duty actually means for social workers.

A duty of care relates to the possibility that a social worker (or another) might be liable for harm that happens to another person. A duty of care is a legal term that means if harm is caused, the person or organisation that owes the duty would have to pay money to compensate the person who is harmed. This is governed by the law of negligence, which is aimed at providing compensation to a person when harm is negligently caused by another person's action. There are three steps the plaintiff must prove in a case of negligence:

1. Duty – the defendant must owe a duty of care to the plaintiff.
2. Breach – the care provided must be lower than the standard of reasonable care.
3. Causation – the defendant must have caused the harm.

Each of these three *elements* must be proved for the defendant to be found negligent. Social workers will not always owe a duty of care. Some relationships, such as doctors to their patients, lawyers to their clients, teachers to their students, will always owe a duty. Social workers and people they work with are not included as one of these predetermined relationships so the question of if a duty is owed will have to be done on a case-by-case basis. This is usually done by determining if the harm was 'reasonably foreseeable'. The court will look at the relationship between the two parties and consider a number of things, including:

- The kind of harm suffered
- The defendant's control over the situation
- The nature of the relationship
- Ethics and human rights
- Other legal principles and relationships.

If a person suffers harm as a result of a relationship where the social worker has a high level of control and the person is very vulnerable, it is more likely that a duty of care will exist. If the social worker has little control over the situation and the person is not vulnerable, a duty is less likely to exist. For example, in a residential rehabilitation facility, where 24-hour care is provided, a social worker (and the whole service) is very likely to owe a duty of care to residents. In a community development facilitation process, where the social worker is helping a group of residents hold a meeting, it is much less likely that a duty of care will exist – although the owner of the building where the meeting is taking place might owe a duty. Some relationships are protected from being sued for negligence; for example, child protection agencies cannot usually be sued for wrongly accusing a person of abusing a child.[45]

Next, the social worker must *breach* the duty of care. This means that they must do something or not do something different from what a reasonable social worker would do. This is easier to demonstrate with doctors and lawyers than it is with social workers. Social workers do so many things and have so many different approaches to things they do that it is really difficult to show that they should have done something a certain way. Despite this difficulty, if it can be shown that the social worker acted 'outside the bounds sanctioned by professional opinion', they will have breached their duty of care.[46] So even if harm is caused by a social worker, and the social worker owed a duty of care, if they acted in a reasonable way for a social worker to act then they will not be liable. This means that social workers must 'exercise professional care and skill' to 'the standard of the ordinary skilled person exercising and professing to have that special skill'.[47]

Finally, it must be shown that the social worker *caused* the harm and that the harm was caused by a breach of the duty. This does not need to be direct but can be indirect. For example, in one case, two sisters, DC and TB had been sexually abused as children by their stepfather.[48] As adults, they sued the State of NSW and the social worker for not protecting them by reporting the matter to police.[*] The sisters claimed that the State of NSW and the social worker owed them a duty of care, which they had breached. This was upheld by the court, which found that a duty existed,

[*] While the High Court can and often does hear appeals from the state and territory supreme courts, it often rejects appeals for various reasons. This case was heard in the NSW Supreme Court, then appealed to the NSW Court of Appeal, then was refused leave to appeal to the High Court.

that the reasonable thing to do was to make a report to police, and that by not reporting to police harm had been caused. The harm was not directly caused by the social worker but by the stepfather, but as a reasonable social worker would have intervened, they were responsible for the harm. This case, of DC and TB, initially included the social worker, but on appeal to the NSW Court of Appeal DC and TB only sued the State of NSW, not the social worker. This means the precedent applies to the state and child protection services generally but gives less guidance for social work practice.

So even this case, in which a social worker was sued for negligence, ended up in the final stage without the social worker involved. There are lots of cases like this, such as *Trevorrow v State of South Australia*,[49] where Bruce Trevorrow, a Ngarrindjeri man and a member of the Stolen Generation, was awarded compensation for the negligent removal from his family. Despite much of the negligence being undertaken by social workers, the defendant in the case was the State of South Australia. In that case, there was clearly a duty of care because the social worker who removed him exercised complete control over his welfare. The social worker breached that duty by not properly assessing if Trevorrow needed to be removed and then by not properly supporting him in the adoptive family. The court found that harm had occurred as a result of this. Note that the issue was not the racist removal, but that the removal had been done without care. This is an important lesson for social workers – it is often not the actual act, but the lack of care taken that makes it negligent.

Any duty imposed on social workers by legislation will generally override a social worker's duty of care – although they should undertake that statutory duty with care. For example, in the case of *McKenna*,[50] a psychiatrist discharged a person from a mental health inpatient unit who then killed his friend. The High Court found that because the *Mental Health Act 1990* (NSW) required 'less restrictive' treatment, the psychiatrist did not owe a duty of care to not discharge the man – but there was a duty to treat him in the least restrictive way. This meant that even though very serious harm resulted from the actions of the psychiatrist because the psychiatrist was acting as required by the statute, he did not breach the duty of care. This is also the case in the case of *Sullivan v Moody*,[51] where the court found that the child protection workers could not be found liable in negligence for wrongly accusing the father of abusing the child. Because the social workers were required by the *Community Welfare Act 1972* (SA) to report and respond to child protection issues they did not breach the duty of care to the father.

Sometimes, even when the court finds that there was negligence, such as in the case of *Presland*,[52] it might not award damages because it might make other decision makers act too defensively. Grant et al point out that the healthcare negligence framework in Australia is often criticised because it is unfairly weighted against people who are injured by healthcare workers.[53] While this is a problem for people who work with social workers, it lends support to the argument that social workers should just focus on providing good services and not being intimidated by legal risks. Note also in both *McKenna* and in *Presland* that it is the health service – the government – who is getting sued, not the psychiatrist who made the decision.

This is important because in Australia, while the organisations social workers work for often get sued, social workers themselves almost never do. This is not to say that it cannot happen, and clearly it is not a great career move to cause your employer to be sued, but the important point is to take care, and not to avoid risk at the expense of failing to provide care. When social workers do owe a duty of care, part of that duty will be to uphold a person's human rights, not to override their rights in an attempt to prevent all risk of harm.[54] For social workers, it is vital that we remember our ethical duty to care for people who come to us for help, and not be fixated on the potential for litigation against us – particularly when that happens so rarely.

6.6 Obligations of Silence and Compliance

Social workers in some roles – usually those who work in government departments – may be bound by specific obligations of silence and compliance.[55] These obligations may be in employment contracts, legislation or in common law.[56] They will only apply to specific roles, not to all social workers, but most social workers will be subject to some obligation to silence. The nature of these obligations vary but two cases illustrate this variety; that of @LaLegale and that of the Save the Children workers on Nauru.

@LaLegale is a Twitter handle run by Michaela Banerji, who worked for the then Department of Immigration and Border Protection. Banerji used the account to criticise government policies anonymously and was subsequently dismissed under the *Public Service Act 1999* (Cth).[57] Banerji claimed this contravened her constitutional right to freedom of political communication. The High Court found in 2019 that Banerji's dismissal was lawful because she breached the requirement for public servants to be apolitical 'at all times' – even when not at work.[58] The High Court found that the right to political communication in the *Constitution* (see Chapter 9) is not 'a personal right of free speech'. For social workers, both inside and outside of the public service, this means that they may be restricted in their ability to communicate about political issues by their employer.

The case of the Save the Children workers on Nauru is a little more hopeful. A number of Save the Children staff, including social workers, publicly raised concerns with harm to children in the Nauru asylum seeker detention facility. Following this, some were fired and referred to police by then Immigration Minister Scott Morrison, accused of 'inciting protest and self-harm' and breaching section 70 of the *Crimes Act 1914* (Cth), which restricted the sharing of information.* A review then found that the social workers' claims were accurate and criticised the government's response,[59] and the government eventually paid over $1 million in compensation.[60] The AASW bravely called for the government to apologise,[61] which it did not do. Despite the final positive outcome, the case highlights the extreme lengths that governments and other organisations will go to in order to enforce employee obligations of silence and compliance. In Chapter 16 we return to this example to discuss what social workers can do to combat or avoid some of these obligations when it is necessary to do so.

6.7 Unprofessional Relationships

Finally, let us turn to the vaguely grubby area of the law concerning unprofessional relationships for social workers. In general, while social workers may be subject to ethical, organisational, professional or moral sanctions for entering into intimate relationships with people they work with, consenting adults are generally legally free to do what they like, but there are some exceptions to this.

In some jurisdictions, the age of consent is higher if one party is the other party's social worker. In South Australia, for example, the age at which a person can legally consent to sex is ordinarily 17 but increases to 18 if the other person is their social worker.[62] There are also criminal consequences in some jurisdictions for workers who both provide treatment or support services to a person with a cognitive impairment or mental illness and have sexual relationships with them.[63] The Victorian legislation, in particular, is very broad and carries a term of five years' imprisonment, up to ten years for multiple offences.

The case of *Kirbach v Health Care Complaints Commission (No. 2)* highlights the risks of such relationships.[64] In this case, Kirbach was a mental health social worker who was in a sexual relationship with an 18-year-old woman who was a client of the mental health service. The relationship itself was not unlawful, although he did also assault the young woman and received a criminal conviction for that. The legal consequences for having the relationship was a five-year ban on providing health services, handed down by the NSW Health Care Complaints Commission, and a public notice that stated that the social worker 'poses a risk to the health or safety of members of the public'. This is publicly available online, so even after the five-year ban has passed it will remain as a barrier to employment, not to mention the public humiliation involved.

---

* This section has been removed by the *National Security Legislation Amendment (Espionage and Foreign Interference) Bill 2018* (Cth) and replaced with a range of other offences.

Outside these legal restrictions, the question of whom social workers should or should not sleep with will largely be an ethical one,[65] but it is certainly considered best practice to look for sexual partners outside professional relationships, as illustrated in Box 6.3.

Box 6.3 *Sarah's eating cornflakes*

Some years ago, I supervised a social work student on placement. Sarah was very energetic, very enthusiastic and very keen to help. She was great one on one and really connected with the people who attended our group activities.

Early one morning I received a call from a colleague who looked after our residential properties. This colleague had been visiting John, who attended our residential rehabilitation program, in one of the service's transitional properties. Sitting in the kitchen with John was Sarah. She was still in her pyjamas eating her cornflakes. Sarah told my colleague that she and John were in love and that she was moving in.

We had a real issue about what to do next. The relationship was clearly consensual. We wanted to support John's choices. John really needed the accommodation and we really did not want him to leave the program but at the same time we could not have a student who had had access to all the residents' files living in the supported accommodation run by the service. In addition, as a student on placement Sarah would have had access to all of John's files – years of psychiatric history.

We terminated Sarah's placement on the basis of her breaching both organisational policy and the Code of Ethics, *but we could not legally require her to move out. If she and John wanted to be together, that was up to them, but we could not have her living in our accommodation and working in the program. We did not report Sarah to the police. Had this incident taken place in NSW, she may have been charged under section 66F of the* Crimes Act 1900 *(NSW) which makes it a crime, punishable by up to ten years in prison, for a person to have sexual intercourse with a person with a cognitive impairment (including severe mental illness) who is provided care by the person. Consent is no defence to this offence.*[*]

---

[*] This is a slightly problematic provision as it assumes that anyone with a diagnosis of severe mental illness is automatically sexually vulnerable and unable to make choices about whom they have relationships with. Readers should make their own assessment of this but note that discriminating against a person on the basis of the diagnosis is a violation of their human rights under the Disability Convention, as discussed in the following chapters. Readers who have strong feelings about this being a crime, for or against, are encouraged to reflect on this while reading Chapters 9, 13 and 14.

Alert readers will note that if this had happened in NSW by not reporting a 'serious indictable offence' I could have been charged under section 316 of the Crimes Act 1900 *(NSW).*

Sarah and John's experience is a difficult one to unpack. Love, sex and relationships are notoriously difficult to legislate against, and the specific ban on having sexual intercourse with a person who has been diagnosed with a mental illness is the kind of paternalism that crosses into discrimination.[66] Conversely, there are many terrible examples of carers, paid and not paid, sexually abusing people they were supposed to be caring for. John is entitled to make his own decisions about who he is intimate with, but Sarah has a responsibility not to use her position in unethical ways. As with many legal obligations, this law is a fairly blunt tool – well meaning but not always resulting in a helpful outcome for everyone.

6.8 Conclusion

Social workers should be aware of their legal obligations. These will be different depending on the statutory powers and obligations they may have, duty of care and contractual obligations. There is no one place that social workers can go to find these out and they will have to look to their organisation for guidance. Social workers rarely face legal consequences, but this should not be seen as an excuse for less than ideal practice. Nearly all legal obligations can be met and exceeded by just doing ethical social work, so social workers should focus on that. This aims social work practice higher than the low bar of just meeting legal obligations. Sometimes, as we see in Chapter 16, social workers' ethical obligations will clash with their legal obligations, and social workers will need to navigate that too.

Main points

- The law as it applies to social workers is not clear and not consistent. This is because social workers are not a registered profession and they are difficult to sue. As a general rule, if a social worker is trying to do the right thing, they are unlikely to get into legal trouble.
- Social workers have statutory powers and obligations under legislation. For example, the *Sentencing Act 1995* (WA) empowers social workers to undertake assessments.
- Social workers are required by law to respect a client's privacy and confidentiality. However, this requirement must be balanced against a social worker's requirement to do their job effectively, as well as navigating circumstances where confidentiality must be broken in instances of mandatory reporting.

- The primary area in which social workers are required to make mandatory reports is in child protection. Every jurisdiction has its own piece of legislation to regulate reporting, where specific groups of people are identified as mandatory reporters.
- Social workers will not always have a duty of care to clients. However, if the social worker has a high level of control over the client, or the client is particularly vulnerable and thus reliant on the social worker, a court may find a duty to be present.

Discussion questions

1. What if a person wants to see what you have written about them in their file? Should you show them? What if it has information given to you in confidence by a family member?
2. Look up section 10D of the *Family Law Act 1975* (Cth). If you are a family counsellor, in what circumstances are you *permitted* to breach confidentiality and in what circumstances are you *required* to breach confidentiality?
3. Look up the Coroner's Report from the Chloe Valentine case. What do you think about the social worker's practice?
4. Research the relevant legislation concerning unprofessional relationships in your jurisdiction. If there are provisions prohibiting relations, what are the legal consequences? Are they reasonable?

Further reading

- Ben Mathews, 'A Taxonomy of Duties to Report Child Sexual Abuse: Legal Developments Offer New Ways to Facilitate Disclosure' (2019) 88 *Child Abuse & Neglect* 337–47.
- Christopher Maylea, 'Minimising Coerciveness in Coercion: A Case Study of Social Work Powers under the Victorian Mental Health Act' (2 October 2017) 70(4) *Australian Social Work* 465–76 <https://doi.org/10.1080/0312407X.2017.1326158>.
- Australian Institute of Family Studies, 'Mandatory Reporting of Child Abuse and Neglect', Child Family Community Australia (1 September 2017) <https://aifs.gov.au/cfca/publications/mandatory-reporting-child-abuse-and-neglect>.
- AASW, 'Professional Boundaries and Dual Relationships' (Australian Association of Social Workers, 2017) <https://www.aasw.asn.au/document/item/2354>.
- Read *Parker v Grams* [2012] FMCAfam 401 for a scathing assessment of a social worker misinterpreting what their duty of care required them to do.

6.9 References

[1] See, for example, *Health Complaints Act 2016* (Vic); *Health and Community Services Complaints Act 2004* (SA); *Health Professionals Act 2004* (ACT); *Health Care Complaints Act 1993* (NSW); *Health and Community Services Complaints Act* (NT); *Health Ombudsman Act 2013* (Qld); *Health Complaints Act 1995* (Tas); *Health and Disability Services (Complaints) Act 1995* (WA) .

[2] *Rubin v State of Western Australia* (2016) 75 MVR 274.

[3] *CEJ v Children's Guardian* [2016] NSWCATAD 164.

[4] *Phillips v Police* [2010] SASC 240; Candice Marcus, 'Child Porn Offender Avoids Jail', *ABC News* (online at 26 September 2012) <https://www.abc.net.au/news/2012-09-26/child-porn-offender-avoids-jail/4281436>.

[5] Psychology Board of Australia, *'No Excuse' Says Board as Court Fines Social Worker for Claiming to Be a Psychologist* (30 November 2016) <https://www.psychologyboard.gov.au/News/2016-11-30-media-release.aspx>.

[6] *DC v New South Wales* [2009] NSWSC 297; *Solomon v Sumner* [2005] WASC 128.

[7] See, for example, *E v K* [1995] 2 NZLR 239.

[8] *PJB v Melbourne Health and Another (Patrick's Case)* [2011] VSC 327.

[9] Mark Johns, *Inquest into the Death of Chloe Lee Valentine* (State Coroner, South Australia, 2015).

[10] AASW, *Code of Ethics* (Australian Association of Social Workers, 2010).

[11] AASW, 'Ineligible for Membership – AASW – Australian Association of Social Workers' <https://www.aasw.asn.au/information-for-the-community/ineligible-for-membership-of-the-aasw>.

[12] See, for example, *Health Complaints Act 2016* (Vic); *Health and Community Services Complaints Act 2004* (SA); *Health Professionals Act 2004* (ACT); *Health Care Complaints Act 1993* (NSW); *Health and Community Services Complaints Act* (NT); *Health Ombudsman Act 2013* (Qld); *Health Complaints Act 1995* (Tas); *Health and Disability Services (Complaints) Act 1995* (WA) .

[13] *Kirbach v Health Care Complaints Commission (No. 2)* [2015] NSWCATAD 234; *Mr Robert Ferguson (Also Known as Bray-Ferguson) – Permanent Prohibition Order* (NSW Health Care Complaints Commission) <http://www.hccc.nsw.gov.au/Publications/Media-releases/2017/Mr-Robert-Ferguson-also-known-as-Bray-Ferguson---Permanent-prohibition-order>.

[14] AASW, 'Code of Ethics' (n 10).

[15] Ellen M Burkemper, 'Informed Consent in Social Work Ethics Education: Guiding Student Education with an Informed Consent Template' (2004) 24(1–2) *Journal of Teaching in Social Work* 141.

[16] Christopher Maylea, 'Minimising Coerciveness in Coercion: A Case Study of Social Work Powers under the Victorian Mental Health Act' (2017) 70(4) *Australian Social Work* 465.

[17] Robin Creyke, John McMillan and Mark Smyth, *Control of Government Action: Text, Cases and Commentary* 3rd ed. (LexisNexis Butterworths, 2012).

[18] *Mental Health Act 2014* (Vic) s 29.

[19] *Mental Health Act 2014* (Vic) s 10.

[20] *Castles v Secretary of the Department of Justice* (2010) 28 VR 141 [186].

[21] Catherine McDonald et al, *Professional Practice in Human Service Organisations: A Practical Guide for Human Service Workers* (Allen & Unwin, 2011).

[22] AASW, *Ethics and Practice Guideline – Case Notes* (Australian Association of Social Workers, July 2016) 3 <https://www.aasw.asn.au/document/item/2356>.

[23] Johns (n 9) 144–5.

[24] Andrew Carroll and Bernadette McSherry, 'Making Defensible Decisions in the Era of Recovery and Rights' [2015] *Australasian Psychiatry* 1039856215614987, 476.
[25] AASW, 'Code of Ethics' (n 10) 27.
[26] Phillip A Swain, 'A Camel's Nose Under the Tent? Some Australian Perspectives on Confidentiality and Social Work Practice' (2006) 36(1) *The British Journal of Social Work* 91.
[27] UN General Assembly, *Universal Declaration of Human Rights*, 10 December 1948, 217 A (III).
[28] UN General Assembly, International Covenant on Civil and Political Rights, 16 December 1966, United Nations, Treaty Series, vol. 999, p. 171.
[29] Office of the Australian Information Commissioner (OAIC), 'Australian Privacy Principles' </privacy-law/privacy-act/australian-privacy-principles>.
[30] *Privacy and Personal Information Protection Act 1998* (NSW); *Information Privacy Act 2009* (Qld); *Premier and Cabinet Circular No 12* (SA); *Personal Information Protection Act 2004* (Tas); *Information Privacy Act 2000* (Vic); *Information Privacy Act 2014* (ACT); *Information Act* (NT).
[31] *Criminal Procedure Act 1986* (NSW) s 296.
[32] Ben Mathews, 'A Taxonomy of Duties to Report Child Sexual Abuse: Legal Developments Offer New Ways to Facilitate Disclosure' (2019) 88 *Child Abuse & Neglect* 337.
[33] *Criminal Code 1995* (Cth) s 80.1(2)(b).
[34] *Crimes Act 1900* (NSW) s 316.
[35] *Crimes Regulation 2015* (NSW) r 4(e).
[36] *Domestic and Family Violence Act* (NT) s 124A.
[37] *Corrections Act 1986* s 14.
[38] *Crimes Act 1958* (Vic) s327.
[39] *Evidence (Miscellaneous Provisions) Act* 1958 (Vic) s 32B.
[40] *Crimes Act 1900* (NSW) s 316A.
[41] *Children and Young People Act 2008* (ACT) s 356; *Children and Young Persons (Care and Protection) Act 1998* (NSW) ss 23, 27; *Care and Protection of Children Act 2007* (NT) ss 15, 16, 26; *Child Protection Act 1999* (Qld) s 13, *Education (General Provisions) Act 2006* (Qld) s 364, 365, 365A, 366, 366A; *Children's Protection Act 1993* (SA) ss 6, 10, 11; *Children, Young Persons and Their Families Act 1997* (Tas) s 3, 4, 14; *Children, Youth and Families Act 2005* (Vic) ss 182(1)(a)–(e), 184, 162(c)–(d); *Crimes Act 1958* (Vic) s 327; *Children and Community Services Act 2004* (ACT) 124A, 124B; *Family Court Act 1997* (WA) s 5, 160.
[42] Australian Institute of Family Studies, 'Mandatory Reporting of Child Abuse and Neglect', *Child Family Community Australia* (Text, 1 September 2017) <https://aifs.gov.au/cfca/publications/mandatory-reporting-child-abuse-and-neglect>.
[43] *Herrick v Knowles* [2014] NSWSC 1223 [60].
[44] *Parker v Grams* [2012] FMCAfam 401.
[45] *Sullivan v Moody* [2001] HCA 59.
[46] *B v Attorney-General* [2004] 3 NZLR 145 [17].
[47] *Rogers v Whitaker* (1992) [483,492].
[48] *DC v New South Wales* [2009] NSWSC 297; *TB v State of New South Wales and Quinn; DC v State of New South Wales and Quinn* [2015] NSWSC 575; *DC v State of New South Wales* [2016] NSWCA 198; *State of New South Wales v DC* [2017] HCATrans 022.
[49] *Trevorrow v State of South Australia* (No 5) (2007) 98 SASR 136.
[50] *Hunter and New England Local Health District v McKenna* [2014] HCA 44.
[51] *Sullivan v Moody* [2001] HCA 59.
[52] *Hunter Area Health Services v Presland* [2005] NSWCA 33.
[53] Kellie Grant, Jenny Martin and Jenni White, 'Risk: What Is It, Whom Does It Protect, and What Happened to Care?' in Jennifer M. Martin (ed.), *Mental Health Policy,*

Practice, and Service Accessibility in Contemporary Society (IGI Global, 2018) <http://ebookcentral.proquest.com/lib/rmit/detail.action?docID=5516346>.

[54] Roger Kline and Michael Preston-Shoot, *Professional Accountability in Social Care and Health: Challenging Unacceptable Practice and Its Management* 1st edition (Learning Matters, 2012).

[55] ALRC, *Secrecy Laws and Open Government in Australia* (No 112, Australian Law Reform Commission, 2009).

[56] See, e.g. *Commonwealth v Fairfax* (1980) 147 CLR 39.

[57] *Banerji v Bowles* [2013] FCCA 1052; *Banerji and Comcare (Compensation)* [2018] AATA 892.

[58] *Comcare v Banerji* [2019] HCA 23.

[59] Philip Moss, *Review into Recent Allegations Relating to Conditions and Circumstances at the Regional Processing Centre in Nauru* (Department of Immigration and Border Protection, 6 February 2015).

[60] Michael Koziol, 'Immigration Department Pays $1 Million Compensation to Save the Children Workers Fired from Nauru', *The Sydney Morning Herald* (online at 31 January 2017) <http://www.smh.com.au/federal-politics/political-news/immigration-department-pays-1-million-compensation-to-save-the-children-workers-fired-from-nauru-20170131-gu27nm.html>.

[61] AASW, *Government Must Apologise to Save the Children Workers and Shut down Nauru* (Australian Association of Social Workers, 6 May 2016) <https://www.aasw.asn.au/news-media/media-releases-2016/government-must-apologise-to-save-the-children-workers-and-shut-down-nauru>.

[62] *Criminal Law Consolidation Act* (SA) 1935 s 49.

[63] *Crimes Act 1958* (Vic) 52B; *Crimes Act 1900* (NSW) 66F.

[64] *Kirbach v Health Care Complaints Commission (No. 2)* [2015] NSWCATAD 234.

[65] AASW, *Professional Boundaries and Dual Relationships* (Australian Association of Social Workers, 2017) <https://www.aasw.asn.au/document/item/2354>.

[66] S. Gascoyne et al, 'The Sexual Health and Relationship Needs of People with Severe Mental Illness' (2016) 23(5) *Journal of Psychiatric and Mental Health Nursing* 338.

Chapter 7 GOING TO COURT AND GIVING EVIDENCE

There are few aspects of legal social work practice as intimidating and important as attending court and giving evidence. Social workers will support people through the court process, attend court as witnesses, and provide other evidence such as court reports that will influence the court process. In this chapter the basic overview of a court case is outlined, followed by a guide for providing support to people in court and suggestions for giving evidence, both in written court reports and in oral evidence.

Courts are intentionally designed to be intimidating, forceful and to remind visitors of the power of the law. This makes them uncomfortable places for people who are not used to this setting. Social workers are usually in court for one of two reasons: providing support to someone they are working with who is a party,* or to give evidence. As discussed in Chapter 6, social workers are rarely parties themselves, and if they are they will usually be represented by a lawyer who can guide them through the process.†

There is different terminology for each party (for each side in the dispute). The first side might be called the prosecution in a criminal case, the applicant or plaintiff in a civil case or the appellant if it is an appeal. The other side will be the defendant or accused in a criminal case or the respondent or defendant in a civil case or appeal. In some situations there will be more than two parties to a case, such as when a person is suing both a doctor and the health service that employs the doctor, or when two people are accused of committing a crime together and are 'co-accused'.

Courts have their own rules and processes. Arrive early as court buildings can often be complex and difficult to navigate. Courts almost always have security with X-ray scanners and similar rules apply as in airports, including the possibility of a delay. Recording devices are usually not allowed, and while mobile phones are usually permitted they are not allowed to be used to record court proceedings. Once in the court, find the court registrar and let them know what case you are there for. Sometimes a hearing might have a specific time, but more often you should plan to be at court for the whole day waiting until the court gets to the case you are

* A 'party' in legal terminology is less fun than it sounds. It just means a person on one side or the other: someone who is suing or being sued, prosecuted or defending, someone who is making an application or contesting an application. Witnesses, observers or supporters are not parties to the case.

† If you are a social worker who is a party in a case and do not have a lawyer, get one.

there for. Bring a book or some work to do. If you have not been to a court before it can be useful to visit before the court date so you are comfortable and familiar with the environment.

On the day there is usually a daily hearing list that details all the cases being heard that day and what court they are in. When entering and leaving the actual courtroom, bow to the judge or magistrate. If addressing the magistrate or judge, stand up, address them as 'Your Honour', 'Sir' or 'Madam' and do not sit down until indicated. Look directly at the magistrate or judge and do not interrupt them. Courts are busy and under a lot of pressure, so it is not uncommon for magistrates and judges to speak harshly or to interrupt. Stay calm and be as prepared as possible, particularly if you are there providing support to another person. Your role as a social worker is to share your calm and project competence.

7.1 The court process

Going to court is sometimes a simple, one off event, such as for a minor traffic offence, or may be a long drawn out process over months or years. Each jurisdiction has a different process, with criminal and civil cases also having different processes and different processes for different types of matters or offences. The criminal process is explored in more detail in Chapter 10.

Figure 7.1 gives an example of a criminal court process for a serious charge – for example, sexual assault. Note that the terminology and process will be different for different offences and in different jurisdictions. This is also not always a linear process, as a person might apply for bail or plead guilty at a number of different points in the process.

As Figure 7.1 shows, after a report is made to the police, they will arrest and charge the person and investigate the alleged offence. For some offences, police can give bail, but for serious offences the police will seek to keep the person in

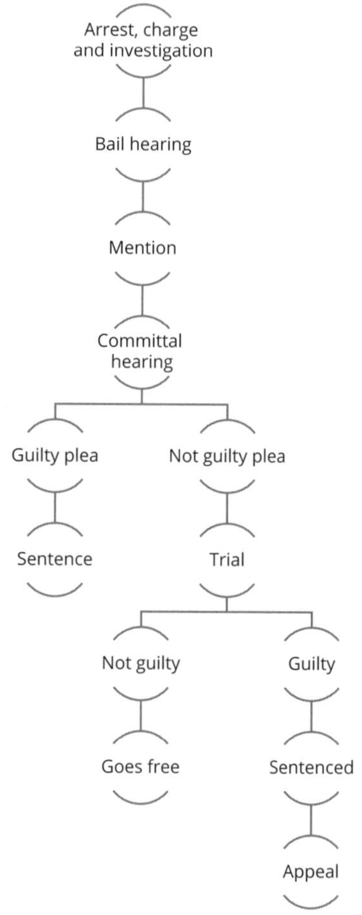

Figure 7.1 *A criminal court process*

custody. If this is the case the matter might go to a lower court (Magistrates' or Local Court) for a bail hearing, where the court will decide if the person can be bailed (released into the community) or remanded (kept in prison until the court date).

Then the lower court will have a mention or filing hearing, which deals with administrative issues and timelines. Following this there will be a committal hearing at the lower court. If the person pleads guilty the sentence may be given in the lower court but more serious offences may have to go to a higher (County, District or Supreme Court) for sentencing. A person can plead guilty at multiple points during the process.

If the person pleads not guilty there might be a contested hearing at a lower court and the matter can be settled there. For more serious offences a case might be 'committed' to the higher court for arraignment, where the charges are read out and dates for the trial and filing of documents are set. Then there will be a trial, which may be days or weeks long, and the judge and/or jury will find the person guilty or not guilty. If not guilty they go free, if guilty they may be sentenced. Only a tiny number of people who plead not guilty are found not guilty – of those who get to this point are 98 per cent of people are proven guilty, although this drops to 93 per cent in the higher courts.[1] Following this, they may either accept their sentence or appeal to a higher court.

As another example, Figure 7.2 illustrates a potential child protection court process. This is civil law, not criminal law, even though the state is one side in the case. Again, this is a general example and processes and terminology vary by jurisdiction, sometimes even by region.[*] Individual cases will also vary greatly, with various interim orders and adjournments, appeals and alternative dispute resolution processes.

In a straightforward child protection case, first the child protection agency investigates and makes an application to the court. Next at a mention hearing information is presented to the court about the case. The court may then make an interim order, for example that the father can only have supervised contact with the child, but the child can live with the mother while the court process is ongoing. The court may at any time adjourn the process, to give parties more time before moving on to the next step, which often happens as parents try to show the court they can address any issues or while the child protection agency gathers more information. Often this is done to allow time for alternative dispute resolution processes, such as family conferencing or dispute resolution conferences.

---

[*] This is often because of pilot programs, such as New South Wales's (NSW's) 'Care Circles', a form of alternative dispute resolution only available to Aboriginal and Torres Strait families in the Nowra region of NSW. Similarly, the Neighbourhood Justice Centre in Collingwood in Victoria is limited to the City of Yarra and is the only neighbourhood justice centre in the country.

If agreement can be reached in the alternative dispute resolution process, the parties will agree on orders which are then reviewed by the court at a directions hearing. If they cannot agree, the directions hearing will be used to provide information to the court and set out relevant dates for the contest or determination hearing. The contest or determination hearing is where the court will decide what orders to make. This might include where the child will live and who will have contact with the child. These orders may be only for a fixed period, such as two years, or may be permanent. These orders may also be appealed to a higher court.

Both these examples highlight how long the process can take, which both sides in a case can find extremely frustrating. Courts must balance the importance of giving both sides enough preparation time and of making sure that justice is done in a timely manner. Some courts work on a 'docket system', which means that a particular judge or magistrate will have responsibility for that case the whole way through the process. Other courts will just assign a judge or magistrate based on availability, which means each hearing might have a different judge or magistrate.

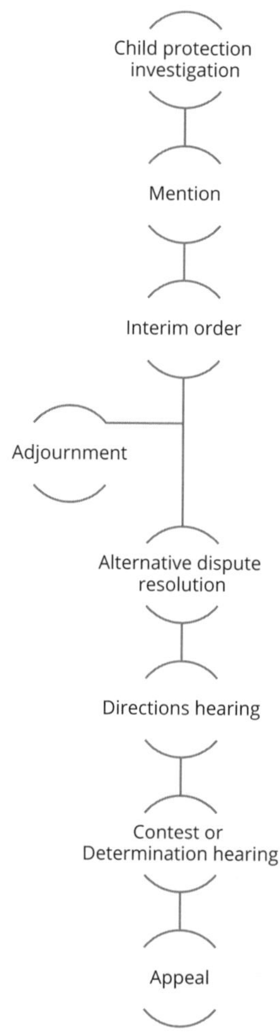

Figure 7.2 *A child protection court process*

There is also a general structure of each court hearing:

1. Hearing opening
2. One side's evidence
3. The other side's evidence
4. Closing addresses.

This general structure applies at all levels and all jurisdictions, but particularly at the lower level courts or at tribunals the structure may be less clear. The process of giving evidence is discussed in more detail later in the chapter.

7.2 PROVIDING SUPPORT

Attending court is often a pivotal point in a person's journey. This is not always the case, for example for traffic fines or procedural matters, but for criminal cases with potential prison time, child protection matters where a child might be removed or where you are supporting a victim who is still processing trauma, court visits can be life-changing events. Social workers should be alert to this and factor this into their practice. In addition to the standard social work responses to any major event, there are a range of considerations specific to the court environment. Providing support to a person in a court setting is particularly important if the person does not have a lawyer. Social workers are not allowed to give legal advice, but they can give legal information, including how courts work. In some courts, there are volunteers who assist people and most courts have guides on their websites.

Find out if the person is eligible for a free lawyer or if they can afford to pay for a lawyer, even if it is just for legal advice and not actual representation. Representation is almost always preferred but is not always freely available. Sometimes there is a 'duty lawyer' at the court who can help on the day. Most legal aid services provide some basic phone advice and many community legal centres have drop-in centres or other assistance. Social workers cannot tell a person what to say in court, but they can help a person get their thoughts clear so long as they do not influence their thinking or what they are going to say. This can be useful even if the person has a lawyer, but make sure to check with the lawyer if they do have one. Social workers can also help organise support letters from employers, teachers or community or religious leaders. Social workers must make sure they are not accidentally giving legal advice or doing legal advocacy – not only is this against the law, they are likely to get it wrong and make things worse for the person they are working with.

Support for a court visit should start long before the court date. Courts are not ideal spaces for children, so organise childcare if necessary. If the person needs an interpreter or hearing-impaired audio loop, you may need to let the court know so they can organise one. Registered psychiatric assistance dogs are usually allowed, but it is a good idea to check with the court and get permission beforehand. Registered guide dogs are always allowed. Organise other supports for the person such as friends and family. If some friends or family members are likely to be unhelpful or disruptive, check with the person you are supporting to see if they should be asked not to come.

Make sure the person you are supporting knows how to act in a court environment. If they have decent clothes, remind them to wear them; if not, get them some. No hats, no sunglasses, no weapons.* A haircut and a shave can change the image a person is projecting from 'clearly criminal' to 'potential for reform'. In less serious criminal cases in particular, the court has some discretion as to sentencing, and appearances can make a big difference. It can be useful to remind people that it is an offence to be in 'contempt of court'. This usually requires seriously bad behaviour and includes abusing or swearing at the magistrate,[2] refusing to answer questions,[3] refusing to leave the court,[4] or disobeying a court order.[5] Magistrates and judges have thick skins but a low tolerance for bad behaviour, so if a social worker can calmly support a person to resist taking their anger out on the court this is almost always a useful contribution.

Just having the social worker in court on the day can influence the outcome. The presence of a social worker gives the court the idea that the person has supports and that they are willing to engage with those supports. In minor criminal cases, this can be an important factor in sentencing as it shows that the person is trying to address the issues that brought them before the court. This will not always have an impact but is worth considering.

Support must continue after the court as well. There are specialist services available, depending on the situation. For family matters, this might include Relationships Australia or for victims of crime there are victim's assistance services. Some jurisdictions have compensation schemes for victims of crime.[6]

7.3 Giving Evidence

The other main reason social workers find themselves in court is when giving evidence. Evidence can be oral or written, and even if it is written the person who wrote it is still likely to be called to give oral evidence to explain it. This can be one of the most stressful professional experiences for social workers, particularly if their practice is being examined. The stakes are often high, with the potential for a person to be imprisoned,

---

* I once represented a person as a lawyer and he turned up with nunchaku (nunchucks), handcuffs and an extendable security baton all attached to his belt. I was able to quietly pop these in my briefcase and leave them outside the building for the duration of the hearing and return them afterward. Had he tried to get these through security it would have been a spectacularly bad look and possibly a criminal offence.

lose their job or have their child removed. A quick search for 'social worker' in the Lexis Advance legal database shows that social workers are most likely to give evidence in criminal cases and family law, but there are also many negligence and social security cases. Social workers might give evidence about a range of issues, but the process is generally the same. The key to successfully giving evidence is preparation.

Social workers should always seek legal advice if they are unsure about giving evidence, particularly if the social worker has been working with the person on a legal issue. Some evidence might be protected from being used in court, and a social worker might cause the person real harm by giving evidence to the other side when they are not legally required to do so. The issues might not be immediately obvious but can have serious ramifications. For example, people in parenting disputes will often try and subpoena clinical notes to use as evidence that the other parent is unfit to parent owing to their seeking treatment for mental health or drug and alcohol use. See Chapter 8 for more on working with lawyers and Chapter 6 on confidentiality.

Witnesses may be called by either side in a case, so a social worker might be called to give evidence in support of the person they work with or against them. All courts and some tribunals can compel or require a witness to give evidence, usually by subpoena. A subpoena is a legal document issued by the court requiring a person to attend court or provide a document. If the social worker is giving evidence in support of the person they work with, a subpoena is not usually necessary and they can give evidence voluntarily. If you are subpoenaed, you or your organisation should seek legal advice before handing over any documents.

Often, the first step is to complete an affidavit. This is a document that details the evidence of the witness. Often other documents including reports or case notes are sometimes attached to the affidavit. This is usually submitted to the court and made available to the other party. It is common for a lawyer to interview the social worker, draft the affidavit, then have the social worker sign to confirm it is correct.

7.3.1 Court reports

Another way social workers give evidence is through written reports. They are sometimes authorised or required to do this under legislation, as discussed in Chapter 6. Usually, a social worker will meet a person or family, conduct an assessment, then write a report based on this assessment. The court then uses this report to make a decision. The key to writing good court reports is to address the decision-making criteria in the legislation that the court will consider. For example, if writing a report for a children's court on a child protection matter, the report will need to take into account what constitutes child abuse in that jurisdiction and detail how that definition of child abuse is met or not met. These reports are often challenging for social workers unused to writing them. They can seem long, repetitive and time-consuming. It is vital that they are completed carefully and accurately, as they may make a significant difference in the outcome of the case.

Reports will often be in a pro forma. The report for the Victorian Mental Health Tribunal has to be signed by an authorised psychiatrist, but in practice, the case manager (often a social worker) will be the one who drafts the report.[7] After covering background information about the person, the questions specifically address the sections of the legislation the Tribunal will consider. The Tribunal has to determine if the treatment criteria apply. One criterion (b) in the legislation reads:

> *b) because the person has mental illness, the person needs immediate treatment to prevent—*
> *(i) serious deterioration in the person's mental or physical health; or*
> *(ii) serious harm to the person or to another person; and*

In the report there is a section that requires the writer to write yes or no:

Table 7.1 *Criterion (b) from MHT 3 Report on Compulsory Treatment*

2.7	**Does the patient need immediate treatment to prevent serious deterioration in their mental health?**
	Does the patient need immediate treatment to prevent serious deterioration in their physical health?
	Does the patient need immediate treatment to prevent serious harm to himself/herself?
	Does the patient need immediate treatment to prevent serious harm to another person?

This shows how closely the report matches the legislation. Report writing should always be done with reference to what the decision-maker – tribunal member, magistrate or judge – will need to know.

Reports also need to be useful for the decision-maker. For example, if you use a phrase such as 'satisfactory', what does this mean? If a person's progress in your drug and alcohol treatment program has been 'satisfactory', does that mean they have completed all the requirements or that they have passed all the drug screening? If so, say so. Be specific.

Sometimes social workers will need access to other material when writing their reports, and sometimes this will require a subpoena. For example, in a child protection proceeding, the child protection worker may work with the lawyer to subpoena school attendance records, medical records or emergency department records both to use as evidence in court and to inform the court report. Get these early, as they can often take time, and translate the key details for the court in your report. The judge or magistrate does not want to have to review pages of medical data or school records, so the social worker's report can help the court make sense of these materials.

The need for specific detail needs to be balanced with the requirement that your report is concise, only saying what needs saying. This takes time, and it is often more difficult to write a long report than a shorter one. Often your reader will only skim the report, so using sub-headings and introductory sentences can help with this. Try and think about which of the decision-making criteria or principles are most relevant. For example, in a criminal case, if the important consideration is focused on a person's rehabilitation prospects, do not spend too much time on the circumstances prior to the offending. Focus instead on what they are going to do next. It will sometimes be appropriate to discuss with a person's lawyer what would be most useful to put into the report, although social workers must use this as advice and not instruction. Many jurisdictions have 'practice directions' available on the court website that can guide report writing.

As with all writing, remember your audience. The decision-maker will read your report, but so will the other people involved, including the parties to the case. Usually, anything provided to the lawyer is also provided to their client, so assume that everyone involved will be able to read your report. This should not change what you put in the report but it may change the tone or language you use, and it may prompt you to explain to the person you are working with what you are going to put in the report before you send it off. People are particularly sensitive to professionals 'cutting and pasting' from prior reports. This does save time, but it makes it look as if the writer has not thought about what they are writing. It also often leads to mistakes when one person's details are copied into another person's report or when circumstances have changed since the last report.

Finally, providing reports on time is essential to the functioning of the court system. Worker unreliability, lateness and poor follow-through have been shown to produce poorer outcomes.[8] Box 7.1 highlights the importance of getting reports completed on time.

Box 7.1 *Report deadlines*

You are a child protection worker working with a family where a child has been removed owing to family violence. You previously applied to the court for an emergency order to have the child removed as the mother was unwilling or unable to protect the child from the violence. The mother, desperate to have her child returned, files a report with the police against the father, who is subsequently arrested. You are now required to write a report for the court to decide if the child should be returned to the mother.

The deadline for the report is Friday, but you think that getting it in first thing Monday will be OK, as the child protection hearing is not until Wednesday. Monday comes, you get busy, and the report is not finished until 5:30 and you have a dinner date. You reread it and send it off Tuesday morning, relieved to have done it with time to spare before the hearing.

The court receives the report Tuesday and you send it to all the parties. The child's mother is staying at a women's refuge that does not publicise its location, so the mail is delayed and the report does not arrive on time for the hearing. The father, who is in prison on remand, does not get the report until right before the hearing. He does not read English well and is on video link from prison to the court, so his lawyer does not have an opportunity to explain what it says.

The child's lawyer gets the report on time but does not have time to make an appropriate time to sit down with the child and explain it. Instead, the lawyer has to phone the child's school. The child is called into the school social worker's office and the child's lawyer asks a series of questions about the report over the speakerphone. Distressed, the child cannot express themselves and returns to class feeling traumatised and frightened about the future.

At the hearing, the magistrate is furious with you for being late. The magistrate has had time to read the report, but the child's mother and father feel excluded and disoriented without all the information. This makes them not want to engage with you in the future and means that you lose the moral high ground. Why should they do the things that you ask them if you are not even bothered to get your reports written on time?

(Thanks to Magistrate Francis Zemljak for this example)

For more detail on court reports read 'Reports and assessments for courts and tribunals' by Swain.[9]

7.3.2 Oral evidence

Social workers are also sometimes required to give verbal or 'oral' evidence in court. This process is governed by complex rules of evidence that social workers do not need to know in detail, but it can help to understand the basic outline of the process. Before giving oral evidence, witnesses will give an oath (swearing by a religious deity or text) or an affirmation (a promise to tell the truth).

Three rules that are useful to be aware of are the hearsay rule, the opinion rule and the relevance rule. There are lots of exceptions to these, but in general:

- Hearsay evidence is a 'second hand' statement, something someone else told you. This is usually not allowed, particularly if the person who told you the statement is able to say that directly to the court. Official documents, such as case notes, are an exception to this rule.
- Opinions are not usually allowed, except for 'lay' opinion and 'expert' opinion. Lay opinion is basic opinions that are based on observation, such as an opinion about a person's age or how fast a car is driving. Expert opinion has to be genuinely expert, and social workers are not usually allowed to give expert opinion – although very senior and qualified social workers have been allowed to give expert opinions in limited situations.[10]
- Evidence must be relevant to the question of law being decided.

If, while you are giving evidence, the other side cries out 'objection, hearsay!' it is because you have included hearsay evidence. Note that rules of evidence apply to affidavits and court reports too, so you may find your reports challenged by the other side. This is why lawyers often draft affidavits rather than letting social workers do it themselves.

After you have been 'sworn in' there are usually three stages of giving evidence; 'examination in chief', 'cross-examination' and 're-examination'.

Examination in chief	What lawyers do to their 'own' witnesses Telling a story No leading questions Open questions No hearsay, no opinions, must be relevant
Cross-examination	What lawyers do to the other side's witnesses Trying to poke holes in the other side's story Leading questions allowed Closed questions No hearsay, no opinions, must be relevant
Re-examination	The first lawyer gets to ask follow-up questions No new topics, only clarification on cross-examination Same rules as examination in chief

Leading questions are questions that have information in the question or that suggest an answer. For example, in examination in chief the lawyer cannot ask 'while you were driving the car, how far over the speed limit were you going?', because this question suggests that the person was both driving a car and going over the speed limit. They have to instead ask, 'how did you get there?' and then they can ask 'how fast were you driving?'

In examination in chief, the lawyers will usually ask open questions, such as 'tell the court what happened on the 16th of May?' because they are not able to ask leading questions and because their witness is usually saying the thing they want them to say. Often this is just a process of the lawyer saying 'and then what happened?' as the witness tells their story to the court. The lawyer will direct this, but it is generally just about hearing the witness's testimony.

In cross-examination, the witness is usually saying something unhelpful to the lawyer's case, so they use closed questions, such as 'you were drinking heavily, weren't you?' or 'so you didn't get a clear look at him, did you?' These are often much more aggressive and can be very uncomfortable for the witness. Cross-examination is often fast, jumping around and disorienting as the lawyer might try and catch the witness off guard. Often, cross-examination is intentionally used to discredit the witness. A lawyer might say 'you have only been a social worker for six months, haven't you?' or might make a big deal of an error in a report to make the social worker look incompetent. Sometimes even judges or magistrates will challenge the social worker giving evidence, particularly if they are not adhering to the rules of evidence. Usually, judges and magistrates will limit aggressive behaviour from lawyers but even low-level aggression or a legitimate challenge can be very disarming (see Box 7.2).

This, as much as anything else, is why it is important to write good notes – the experience of being humiliated in a public setting is very unpleasant. Always remember that the lawyer is just doing their job and testing you as a witness. Try not to take the questioning personally. Often, aggressive or theatrical cross-examination is a sign that the lawyer has a poor case – strong cases speak for themselves and there is no need to discredit a witness.

Box 7.2 *Cross-examination*

One recent unpleasant experience involved a barrister wrongly surmising in her submission that I was both younger than the parents and would in effect struggle to understand parenting. This assumption left me feeling insulted and uncomfortable. – A children's social worker.[11]

In lower level magistrates' or local courts, the process might be less formal and it might be the magistrate asking questions, particularly if there is no 'other side'. Tribunals are not usually bound by the same rules of evidence and are usually less formal, although this varies depending on the tribunal.

In any setting, the key is to be prepared. Re-read all the notes and other documents, practice giving evidence and above all be honest. The whole time the court will be assessing if you are a credible witness and if you are caught in a lie, even a small one, it can be very damaging to your credibility. You can usually ask the court for permission to check your notes if you cannot remember, so you should bring all relevant documents with you on the day.[*] If it is a big and important case, the lawyer calling you as a witness might spend time getting you ready for the hearing, helping you understand the law and the process. They cannot help you decide what to say, but they can tell you what questions they are intending to ask and might be able to warn you of the sorts of questions that might come up in cross-examination.

[*] Avoid the fate of Ms R, the social worker in *Sharpe v Anstey* [2013] FCCA 169 who was described as an 'unimpressive witness' who was 'selective in what she sent to the court'. The Federal Magistrate wrote that 'Ms R arrived for cross-examination at the trial without even bringing her notes or file stating, "No, I just brought with me my report."'

Some other suggestions:

1. Remain calm. It is easy to get flustered when under pressure. Take your time, check your notes and do not let the lawyers rush you.
2. Maintain eye contact with the lawyer on your side. It can be less stressful to not look the lawyer who is cross-examining you in the eye. Always look at the judge or magistrate when addressing them directly.
3. Always answer the question and just the question asked.
4. Keep your answers short and to the point.
5. If you do not understand a question, say so.
6. If you do not know the answer, say so and move on.
7. If you have made a mistake, either in practice or in your report, admit it and move on.
8. If you realise you have said something incorrect, say so before someone else does.

After the process is over it is important to debrief in supervision both for self-care and so to improve your practice in the future. If you worked with a lawyer, ask them how you did and what you can improve on. Giving evidence in court can be challenging but can have a real impact on people's lives, so you need to do your best every time.

7.4 Conclusion

The courtroom can be a difficult environment for social workers and the people they work with. Social workers should ensure that they are able to assist people in this environment by becoming familiar and comfortable with it. When giving evidence, either written or verbal, social workers must conform to the processes. Courts are unforgiving of deviance from their rules, so to be effective social workers must be familiar with them. These are adversarial environments, so social workers should expect to be subject to pressure as the lawyers do their jobs. Outside the courtroom, social workers and lawyers tend to get on a lot better, as discussed in Chapter 8.

Main points

1. It is useful to brush up on courtroom etiquette before entering the courtroom. For example, remembering to address the judge or magistrate as 'Your Honour', 'Sir' or 'Madam' and standing up when they enter the courtroom.
2. The court process is often time consuming, costly and expensive.
3. In circumstances where a person does not have a lawyer, the support of a social worker can be crucial. Remember, social workers cannot give legal advice, but they can give legal information, such as about how the courts work.

4. There are three stages of giving evidence: 'examination in chief', 'cross-examination' and 're-examination'.

Discussion questions

1. Review Figure 7.2 – check to see if the process and terminology is the same in your jurisdiction. Is alternative dispute resolution an option in your jurisdiction?
2. It is important to know if the client you are assisting in court is eligible for a free lawyer or if they have a lawyer. What are the eligibility requirements in your jurisdiction for legal aid?
3. What are the community legal centres and legal aid services available for people in your area?
4. Think about the ways in which collaboration can occur between social workers and lawyers. What are some benefits? What are some challenges or ethical dilemmas that could arise?

Further reading

Phillip A. Swain, '"No Expert Should Cavil at Any Questioning": Reports and Assessments for Courts and Tribunals' (2005) 58(10 *Australian Social Work* 44–57.

Full Care Order, 'Just Another Day in Court as a Social Worker' *The Guardian* (13 January 2012), sec. Social Care Network.

7.5 References

---

[1] In 2017–18 86 per cent of all defendants had their charges proven, but 3 per cent were transferred to other courts and 9 per cent were withdrawn by the prosecution. Only 12,088 of people who went all the way to a finding by the judge were acquitted, compared with 507,169 who were proven guilty. In the higher courts, 1163 were acquitted, compared with 15,348 who were proven guilty: Australian Bureau of Statistics, *4513.0 – Criminal Courts, Australia, 2017–18* (Australian Government, 28 February 2019) <https://www.abs.gov.au/ausstats/abs@.nsf/0/D8D460DDF174BC36CA2582410016B417?Opendocument>.

[2] *Prothonotary of the Supreme Court of New South Wales v Hall* [2008] NSWSC 994.

[3] *Keeley v Brooking* (1979) 143 CLR 162.

[4] *In the matter of Bauskis* [2006] NSWSC 908.

[5] *O'Shane v Channel Seven Sydney Pty Ltd* [2005] NSWSC 1358.

[6] See, for example, *Criminal Injuries Compensation Act 2003* (WA); *Victims of Crime Assistance Act 1996* (Vic); *Victims of Crime Assistance Act* (NT).

[7] https://www.mht.vic.gov.au/forms-and-publication/tribunal-forms/.

[8] Chris Trotter, *Working with Involuntary Clients: A Guide to Practice* (Allen & Unwin, 2015).

[9] Phillip A Swain, '"No Expert Should Cavil at Any Questioning": Reports and Assessments for Courts and Tribunals' (2005) 58(1) *Australian Social Work* 44.

---

[10] Although this is not always the case. See, for example, *Langan & Thurston* [2010] FMCAfam 781.

[11] Andrew Matthews, 'Is the Theatre of the Family Courts – Where Legalese Often Takes over – Really Helpful?', *Community Care* (6 July 2017) <https://www.communitycare.co.uk/2017/07/06/theatre-family-courts-legalese-often-takes-really-helpful/>.

Chapter 8 WORKING WITH LAWYERS

Francis Zemljak, the Children's Court magistrate who co-authored Chapter 11, told me that 'social workers and lawyers make a good salad – they're oil and vinegar'. While this is an excellent line, I think it reflects how things have been rather than the potential. It is true that the professions of social work and law do not have a long history of successful integration, despite there being a significant overlap in the populations they serve. In the United States, there has been much more research on how social workers and lawyers can work together,[1] but this has not been the case in Australia. For many years there have been small numbers of social workers working in the community legal sector,[2] and in recent years there has been increasing integration as social workers have been employed in personal injury law firms,[3] and supporting victims and witnesses to share their experiences in court and in Royal Commissions.[4] There are still many missed opportunities for social workers and lawyers to work together, and while challenges exist they are easily outweighed by the benefits to the people we work with.[5]

8.1 THE LEGAL PROFESSION

Legal training tends to teach lawyers to look at problems as having legal solutions while social workers are trained to look at problems as having social solutions. This leads to a difference in problem-solving techniques. Legal training and practice focus on black and white compliance, whereas social work practice tends to be a bit greyer.[*] There are many exceptions to these generalisations, and there are attempts to introduce interpersonal skills and alternative dispute resolution approaches into legal training. As professional groups, they are also quite demographically different. Social workers are on average ten years older than solicitors, and while solicitors are evenly likely to be male or female, 84 per cent of social workers identify as women.[6]

In New South Wales (NSW), Victoria and Queensland, lawyers are generally either solicitors or barristers. Solicitors are lawyers who generally look after a case outside the courtroom. They will often appear in the local and magistrates' courts and at tribunals, but ordinarily do not appear in the higher courts. Solicitors give legal advice, negotiate on behalf of clients,

* This is actually a very good pun as social workers are on average significantly older than lawyers, although the number of social workers who dye their hair purple probably offsets this to some extent.

gather evidence, draft legal documents and prepare cases for court, but they will often hand a case over to a barrister to be heard in court. Barristers are lawyers who specialise in court advocacy. Most contact that social workers have will be with solicitors as most communication with barristers is done via a solicitor. This means that the solicitor runs the case outside court, getting witnesses and documents organised, and they will 'brief' or 'instruct' a barrister to run the case in court. All judges and magistrates and most tribunal members are also legally trained, but they usually stop being solicitors or barristers when they take on those roles. In jurisdictions outside NSW, Victoria and Queensland there is less or no distinction between barristers and solicitors, although some lawyers may still specialise in court work.

Like social workers, lawyers tend to specialise in a discipline area, such as criminal law, family law or corporate law. Finding the right lawyer for the right issue is an important task for social workers. Usually, the main contacts for social workers are the state or territory legal aid and local community legal centres. Legal aid provides legal services and funding for legal services to people who are disadvantaged, but with limited resources they are not able to provide representation or funding for everyone who needs it. It is easier to get funding for serious criminal offences, for example, than for minor driving offences.

Community legal centres provide free legal services and community legal education, engage in policy advocacy and strategic litigation (see Chapter 17 for more on policy advocacy and strategic litigation). Community legal centres are sometimes generalist, providing generic legal services to disadvantaged groups, but sometimes specialise in specific areas or groups, such as disability law or refugee law. There are also First Nations specific legal services. There is some overlap between legal aid and the community legal centres, so social workers will need to develop an understanding of who can help with what in their region.

Legal aid and community legal centres are also sites of practice for social workers and are key spaces where interdisciplinary practice can make a real difference in the lives of people who use legal and social work services. Community legal centres are increasingly employing social workers to assist legal clients with non-legal issues such as housing and homelessness. In 2016, there were 122 social workers working in legal services, up from 87 in 2011 and 71 in 2006.[7]

8.2 Benefits

Interdisciplinary practice between social workers and lawyers improves both the process of going through the legal system and improving the outcomes at the end of the process. Social workers can improve communication, translating difficult legal concepts into terminology people can understand, and also communicating a person's social context to their lawyer or a court. This facilitates better engagement with legal services and legal processes and providing better integration between services. This also means that social workers and lawyers get a better understanding of the other's speciality – social workers get to understand the law better, and lawyers get to understand the social context better. This means that social workers can identify legal needs early and refer to lawyers before legal issues get out of hand.

Social workers can also assist with practical supports during the legal process. A good example of this is when a person is injured at work they may be entitled to compensation. This can take a long time, and many people settle their claims early, potentially ending up with less compensation than they otherwise might have. With social work support, people can be linked into housing, social security benefits, pain management programs and counselling, which can mean they are more willing to get to the end of the legal process. Personal injury law firms sometimes employ social workers to work with their personal injury teams.[8]

Social workers can also reframe what 'winning' means in the legal system. Lawyers will often work towards a legal win, either in court or an agreed settlement. Social workers are well positioned to challenge this adversarial approach and suggest alternatives that might be more suitable for all parties. Many lawyers have already adopted alternative dispute resolution approaches, but social workers can support this process.

The Women's Homelessness Prevention Project, featured in Box 8.1, shows how social workers and lawyers can work together to get a genuinely good outcome for a person, not just to get a win in court.

Box 8.1 *The Women's Homelessness Prevention Project*

The Women's Homelessness Prevention Project assists women who have received eviction notices from their landlords, such as where they have fallen behind in their rent or it is suggested that they have breached their tenancy agreement (which can be linked to the actions of a perpetrator of violence, children with disabilities or mental illness). The Project has highlighted the role that legal representation, combined with social work support, can play in preventing avoidable evictions into homelessness of women and children. Over a two-year period, 102 women were provided with legal representation and intensive social work support. These women had a total of 157 children in their care, who were also at risk of homelessness. Ninety per cent of the women had experienced family violence in the past ten years, and 84 per cent were suffering from a mental illness. At the end of two years, 83 per cent of finalised matters were successfully resolved, resulting in women maintaining safe and secure housing, or resolving a tenancy legal issue that was a barrier to accessing safe housing. This included directly preventing the eviction of 62 women and their families into homelessness. Using research from the Australian Housing *and Urban Research Institute, this would mean a cost saving of $1,825,900 in health, justice and welfare costs.*

Jia is a woman in her 60s who is from China. Her sole income is the age pension. She has little support after her husband passed away, and her understanding of English is limited. Jia was being chased relentlessly by mail, text messages and phone calls. She didn't understand why. She asked the callers to use an interpreter but they wouldn't. This harassment was having a significant impact on Jia's health: it exacerbated her anxiety and depression, with phone calls leaving her angry and upset; it aggravated her hypertension – contributing to three admissions to emergency in the past – as well as her asthma. A social worker from an outreach team who speaks Mandarin helped discover that Jia was being chased by debt collectors for a utilities bill from a transitional property she had been living in where the electricity hadn't been turned off when she left. With Jia's permission, the social worker contacted the Health Justice Partnership lawyer for assistance. The lawyer was able to stop the debt collectors from contacting Jia. She was very relieved to know that if they did contact her she could tell them to 'call my lawyer'. Jia and the lawyer discussed options. Jia said she was 'not afraid of them any more' and was now ready to try to get the debt waived. After some further help from the lawyer the debt was waived. Jia wrote: You helped me resolve a year's worth of intimidation and dispute. You used the law to uphold the truth. You helped me, a 60-year-old senior widow with high pressure and lots of sickness, finally access justice.

Reproduced with permission from a submission made to the Law Council of Australia by Justice Connect.[9]

See how, in Box 8.1, the variety of skills come into play. The legal skills of the lawyer are essential, but Jia might never have been connected with a lawyer without the social worker being involved. This example is included here both as a great example of multidisciplinary practice, but also as an example of how social workers can document that practice and share it as an advocacy tool. This example was submitted to the Law Council of Australia to try and promote multidisciplinary practice and get governments to fund more multidisciplinary practice models. As discussed in Chapter 17, making submissions are a great way to influence law and policy reform.

8.3 Challenges

The benefits of interdisciplinary practice are clear, but there are some significant challenges. Lawyers and social workers work quite differently and view different issues as more important than others. A key difference between the professions is that nearly always lawyers work on *instructions.* This means they do, and only do, what they have been *instructed* to do by the client. They cannot tell the client what to do; they can only give *advice* to a client. There are limits to how far lawyers can follow instructions. Lawyers cannot do anything illegal or mislead the court, and there are limited situations where a person might not be able to give instructions, such as when they are unconscious or in the case of children (see Chapter 13 for a discussion of legal capacity). Social workers do not have such a clear relationship when working with people. Sometimes they will work on instruction, but often they will decide what is in the best interests of the person and balance that with what the person wants and other factors such as the broader community or interests of family members. This fundamental difference in the way lawyers and social workers work can lead to disagreements when working together.

This is complicated by the fact that lawyers do not always have a good understanding of what social workers do, which can sometimes lead to lawyers devaluing social work practice.[10] Social workers are usually trained to work collaboratively in teams, whereas lawyers are often trained to work in a hierarchy, where it is clear who is in charge. In interdisciplinary practice, this is not usually clear, so working in teams can require extra support and planning.[11]

Other challenges are more difficult to overcome and will only be resolved over time. A major issue for social workers and lawyers is how they handle and share information. As discussed in Chapter 7, social work records are usually able to be subpoenaed or required to be submitted as evidence in court. Lawyers' records are not usually able to be subpoenaed as evidence as they are subject to *legal professional privilege*.[12] This makes the simple act of sitting down together and discussing a person's situation quite difficult. Is information they share with both a social worker and a lawyer protected by legal professional privilege? Is information the lawyer shares with the social worker still protected? What if the social worker and the lawyer share the same file? Unfortunately, we do not know the answer to these questions, as no court has yet ruled on the issue of interdisciplinary practice and there is no legislation that clearly provides guidance. In the meantime, it is up to individual practitioners and organisations to work out a strategy that works for them.

Read Simone's story, and reflect on how the fields of social work and law can learn from each other.

8.4 Simone's story

My name is Simone. In my personal life, I am a sister, partner and daughter. In my professional life, I am a lawyer and I have worked for legal aid, a community legal centre and the government.

In all of these roles I have worked with social workers. Social workers are absolutely invaluable to lawyers working with people in community settings. When I look back on my first job as a criminal lawyer at legal aid, I just wish I knew then what I have learnt from working with social workers over the years. As a lawyer, I have been taught to focus on the individual client in front of me and their legal problem in isolation. On the other hand, social workers see clients as involved in and impacted by broader systems and structures, many of which are oppressive and unfair. This perspective has been particularly useful in my current role, which involves managing a project where lawyers and social workers collaborate closely to support women coming out of prison. By talking to social workers, I now really get the way that sexist and racist power structures drive women's incarceration.

In legal matters, the involvement of a good social worker can make a huge difference to a person's outcome. There have been plenty of times when I have relied heavily on the support available from a particular worker or support service in order to keep a client out of prison or get them bail. It's so great when social workers and lawyers have close and robust professional relationships and work together as equals. I know that lawyers don't always approach working with social workers this way. I know that some lawyers undervalue and under-acknowledge the work that social workers do. I think that is wrong and it needs to change, which requires a big shift in the culture of the legal profession. In the meantime, my advice to social workers is to reach out to lawyers who are working with your clients and share your knowledge with them.

I'll never forget one interaction I had with a colleague who was a social worker. I was caught up in the 'strategy' of the case, and how to negotiate with the other lawyer. My colleague just cut straight through it all and said to me 'it doesn't matter – what matters is when this child will get to see their parents'. She was totally right.

Not all lawyers undervalue social work practice, but many do, and many more do not really understand it. Simone's experience highlights how great it can be for both professionals when they do connect. Social workers have to work to educate lawyers of the value of social work, and this often requires understanding what it is that lawyers will value about social work. The instructions-based approach that lawyers take means that they will often criticise social workers who think they know best for people they work with. By being alert to the sorts of things lawyers value, social workers can show their value to lawyers. One of the things lawyers value most highly is human rights, which are covered in Chapter 9.

8.5 Conclusion

Social workers and lawyers can make a great salad, but both need to work differently to how they are used to working. While social workers have a tradition of multidisciplinary practice, this has historically been focused working with other allied health, health and welfare professionals. To work with lawyers, social workers need to understand them, how they work from different and often unspoken principles. To lawyers, these principles are often ethically more important than individual outcomes, which can confuse social workers who might be inclined to overlook a principle to reduce suffering or alleviate oppression. Social workers who hope to be effective in legal settings must learn the law and legal principles so they can relate to and communicate with lawyers. As allies, social workers and lawyers can do more to support the people they work with than they can achieve alone.

Main points

1. Social workers will likely come into contact with lawyers and legal settings in the course of their practice.
2. Social workers and lawyers are the essential oil and vinegar to a perfect salad: each profession has much to offer and learn from the other.
3. The benefits from working together flow to all parties; the people they work with as well as to both professionals.
4. The challenges of working together are largely due to the legal issues around confidentiality and other differing work practices. Over time the law will evolve to provide more guidance and in the meantime, interdisciplinary practice must proceed with care.

Discussion questions

1. Think about the lawyers you know. Do they have certain ways of working or thinking? Compare them to the social workers you know.
2. Should social workers have the same confidentiality requirements as lawyers? What about the way lawyers work on instructions? How would that work for social workers?
3. Re-read Box 8.1. What roles did the social worker and lawyer play? Could just the social worker or just the lawyer have achieved the same result?

Further reading

Chris Maylea, Nareeda Lewers, Elissa Scott, Penelope Weller, and Stan Winford, 'Socialising the Law: Multidisciplinary Practice with Lawyers and Social Workers', in *Social Work in the Shadow of the Law*, edited by Simon

Rice, Andrew Day and Linda Briskman, 5th ed. (The Federation Press, 2018).

Tamara Walsh, 'Lawyers and Social Workers Working Together: Ethic of Care and Feminist Legal Practice in Community Law' (2012) 21(3) *Griffith Law Review* 752.

Stephanie K. Boys, Stephanie Q. Quiring, Evan Harris and Carrie A. Hagan. 'Social Work and Law Interdisciplinary Service Learning: Increasing Future Lawyers' Interpersonal Skills' (8 August 2015) 35(4) *Journal of Teaching in Social Work* 410–24.

Richard Foster, 'Multi-Disciplinary Practice in a Community Law Environment: Clinical Legal Education Combined with Holistic Service Provision' (1 January 2014) 23(1) *Journal of Law and Social Policy* 169–74.

8.6 References

---

[1] Brigid Coleman, 'Lawyers Who Are Also Social Workers: How to Effectively Combine Two Different Disciplines to Better Serve Clients' (2001) 7(1) *Washington University Journal of Law & Policy* 131; Heather B Craige and William G Saur, 'The Contribution of Social Workers to Legal Services Programs Management of Legal Services' (1980) 14 *Clearinghouse Review* 1267.

[2] Richard Foster, 'Multi-Disciplinary Practice in a Community Law Environment: Clinical Legal Education Combined with Holistic Service Provision' (2014) 23(1) *Journal of Law and Social Policy* 169; Mary Anne Noone, *Integrated Legal Services: Lessons from West Heidelberg CLS* (SSRN Scholarly Paper No ID 2030556, Social Science Research Network, 29 March 2012) <https://papers.ssrn.com/abstract=2030556>; Tamara Walsh, 'Lawyers and Social Workers Working Together: Ethic of Care and Feminist Legal Practice in Community Law' (2012) 21(3) *Griffith Law Review* 752.

[3] Leah du Plooy, Fran Sarrell and Rhys Chamberlin, 'Maurice Blackburn's Outreach Model of Care Providing Social Work Support to Rural Communities' (Conference Presentation at the 12th Biennial National Rural Remote Social Work Conference, Shepparton, July 2015) <https://www.aasw.asn.au/document/item/7882>; Slater & Gordon, 'Social Work Services' (2017) <https://www.slatergordon.com.au/more-services/social-work-services>.

[4] Office of Public Prosecutions, 'Witness Assistance Service' (2017) <http://www.opp.vic.gov.au/Witnesses-and-Victims/Getting-Help-from-the-Witness-Assistsnce-Service>; knowmore, 'Our People', *knowmore* (2017) <http://knowmore.org.au/about/our_people/>.

[5] Chris Maylea et al, 'Socialising the Law: Multidisciplinary Practice with Lawyers and Social Workers' in Simon Rice, Andrew Day and Linda Briskman (eds), *Social Work in the Shadow of the Law* 5th ed. (The Federation Press, 2018).

[6] These statistics are not ideal – this only counts people who put 'social worker' as their profession on the census, and excludes people with social work qualifications in related roles such as policy, management or support work: Australian Bureau of Statistics, *2016 Census – Counting Employed Persons* (Australian Government, 2016). No reliable data is available on the number of trans- or other gendered social workers or lawyers.

[7] Australian Bureau of Statistics, *2016 Census – Counting Employed Persons* (Australian Government, 2016).
[8] Slater & Gordon (n 3).
[9] Law Council of Australia, *The Justice Project* (2018) 93 <https://www.lawcouncil.asn.au/justice-project/final-report>.
[10] Walsh (n 2).
[11] Ross Hyams, *Multidisciplinary Clinical Legal Education the Future of the Profession* (SSRN Scholarly Paper No ID 2215262, Social Science Research Network, 11 February 2012) <https://papers.ssrn.com/abstract=2215262>.
[12] *Legal Profession Uniform Law Australian Solicitors' Conduct Rules 2015* r 9.2. Note that not all jurisdictions have adopted this exact set of rules, but the same principle applies in all jurisdictions.

Chapter 9 HUMAN RIGHTS AND ANTI-DISCRIMINATION LAW

Human rights are central to social work and feature heavily in social work literature and discussions about social work. Tom Calma, the former Aboriginal and Torres Strait Islander Social Justice Commissioner at the Australian Human Rights and Equal Opportunity Commission, said that:

> *Social workers by very definition are human rights workers. Social workers help individuals realise their rights everyday and are ideally placed to help communities claim their collective rights.*[1]

The term 'human rights' features in the very definition of social work:

> *Social work is a practice-based profession and an academic discipline that promotes social change and development, social cohesion, and the empowerment and liberation of people. Principles of social justice, human rights, collective responsibility and respect for diversities are central to social work.*[2]

This is also reflected in the Australian Association of Social Workers (AASW) *Code of Ethics*, which mentions human rights 16 times and explicitly requires social workers to comply with international human rights law, citing 29 international human rights documents.[3] The *Code of Ethics* uses Ife's definition of human rights:

> *Human rights refer to the basic rights and freedoms to which all humans are entitled. They are socially sanctioned entitlements to the goods and services that are necessary to develop human potential and well-being.*[4]

This sounds great, and is something that everyone can get behind, but it should be noted that the concept of human rights has faced fierce critique from many fronts. A Marxist critique views human rights as just another example of bourgeois ideology, protecting individuals and their individual property rather than encouraging communities to come together in solidarity. The word 'human' in 'human rights' seems to exclude the non-human world and the importance of ecology, climate and the inherent value of non-human animals. As discussed in this chapter, a human rights approach can come into significant conflict with a 'best-interest' approach in social work practice, particularly in relation to disability and mental implemented predominantly by privileged white people, resulting in some problematic applications.* It is no surprise, then, that social workers tend to find the concept of human rights 'complex, contested and challenging'.[6] While acknowledging these and many more critiques, human rights are a fundamental part of social work practice, and good social workers will have a well-developed and critical understanding of human rights.

Ife's definition also belies the complexity of what this means in practice, and human rights law is only one part of this puzzle. Nipperess argues that to implement human rights into social work practice properly we need to begin with the lived experiences of the people we work with, then explore the ethical, legal, historical, political, organisational, theoretical and practice contexts (see Figure 9.1).[7] If If this sounds difficult, it is because it is. Embedding human rights-oriented practice in social work requires high-level social work skills that apply reflection and reflexivity as well as an understanding of all these contexts. Human rights law is mainly focused on preventing breaches of human rights, whereas social workers also need to focus on the positive and look at how human rights can be used to create more supportive and engaged communities. Human rights law is important for setting the lowest bar, but social workers should always strive for more than this.

Figure 9.1 *Law is just one part of the human rights puzzle*

Human rights are closely linked to anti-discrimination laws. Often, a person who is discriminated against, on the basis of sex or gender, sexual orientation, race or ethnicity, disability, age or some other attribute will have their human rights breached. It is, of course, fine to treat people differently for a good reason; for example, when one job applicant is chosen over another it is because a person has more experience than another. It is only a problem if they are discriminated against because of their background or personal characteristics. When this happens, it will

* For example, have a look at the picture gallery of all the cases before the International Criminal Court and see if you notice anything about the defendants: <www.icc-cpi.int/cases>.

their background or personal characteristics. When this happens, it will usually also be a breach of international human rights laws, but, as discussed in Chapter 2, international law is not easily enforceable in Australia unless it is brought in by legislation. Many human rights protections in Australia are actually contained in anti-discrimination legislation, as discussed later in this chapter.

Human rights are different from but overlapping with legal rights. A human right may exist in legislation, such as the right of a person not to be discriminated against in the workplace because of their gender. This is a human right in international law,[8] and a legal right, in section 14 of the *Sex Discrimination Act 1984* (Cth). Other rights, such as the right to housing, are in international law,[9] but are not legal rights in Australia. A person cannot sue the government for failing to provide them with housing, although the government would point to public housing programs as evidence of working to meet its obligations in this regard. Other legal rights are in Australian law but are not human rights. A mining company might have a legal right to mine a certain piece of land, but this is not a human right.

Human rights are usually grouped into three generations.[10] The first generation are civil and political, including voting, freedom from discrimination and participation in government. They are 'liberty' rights focusing on freedoms. They are most often negative rights, meaning they stop someone doing something rather than requiring someone to do something. As such they mainly serve to protect the individual from the state.

Second generation human rights are economic, social and cultural, and include work rights, housing, religion and welfare. These are 'equality' rights and are generally positive rights, in that they require someone to do something. They often impose a requirement on the state to provide a service but can also require the state or a person to not do something, such as impose on someone's right to practise their religion.

Third generation rights are collective rights and include the rights of communities to self-determination and to development. They are 'fraternity' rights, which are about interrelationships and community connection. These rights are generally both negative and positive, such as the right to a healthy environment. This requires both action to preserve a healthy environment and prevents individuals, organisations, communities or the state from despoiling the environment. These rights tend to be less clearly articulated in law and can be more difficult to enforce than first generation rights.

One misconception about human rights is that they cannot legally be overridden. This is true of a small number of rights, such as the right to be free from torture or slavery, but most rights can be limited in some way. For example, you have your right to liberty limited by committing a crime and being put in prison or your right to freedom of speech limited by saying something defamatory. Human rights law provides a framework for finding a balance between the competing rights of people, communities and the power of government. Justice Bell, of the Victorian Supreme Court, writes about 'engaging' rights, as something different to 'violating' rights.[11] This is an important distinction, as many areas of law engage with a person's human rights by limiting them without violating them. Under Victorian human rights law, for example, the government cannot breach a person's rights unless the contrary is *demonstrably justified* and *legally demanded*.[12] This means that human rights law does not attempt to prevent all limitations on a person's right; it just attempts to make sure that these limitations are necessary and legal.

Rights must also be balanced when they are in conflict. A person's right to free speech must be balanced with another person's right to be free from harassment and the right to liberty must be balanced with the community's right to safety. This is particularly important for social workers when they are required to do something that engages a person's human rights. For example, a social worker making a report to child protection is engaging a person's right to privacy. If the report is either demonstrably justified or legally demanded, then the person's human right is not breached or violated, only limited. Other times, social workers might engage a person's right to liberty by detaining them for mental health assessment, or their right to bodily integrity, privacy and dignity by subjecting them to involuntary mental health treatment. This underlines the importance of understanding human rights law both to ensure good social work practice and to be an effective advocate against laws or actions that unreasonably or illegally limit human rights.

Often, the question of whether a human right has been *unreasonably* limited will often be a matter of opinion, balancing risks with responsibilities, local law and professional judgment. The best way for social workers to limit violations of human rights is not just to fight each breach as they occur, but also to work towards a society where human rights breaches are less likely to occur in the first place. Box 9.1 highlights this potential:

Box 9.1 *Human rights in action*

Human rights – as a body of law, a set of principles and a way of seeing the world – are animated by one central concern: the protection of individual dignity. The idea of dignity can appear clinical and abstract. But it needn't be.

We know what it looks like when a person's dignity is threatened. As a lawyer, one of the most heart-breaking cases I participated in was an inquest into the death of a man by the name of Stephen Holcroft.

Stephen was a minimum-security prisoner who was being transported from one prison in regional New South Wales to another. While he was being transported in a prison van, Stephen started having a heart attack. Notwithstanding Stephen's increasingly desperate screams and those of the other prisoners in the back of the van, the prison officers felt bound to follow protocol and they did not stop to seek medical attention. Even when the officers stopped – at a hospital – to ask for directions, they did not seek medical attention. When they reached their destination, Stephen was dead.

For the majority of our lives, most of us need little help to protect our dignity. But there are times when we all do. If you have ever seen a parent or other loved one desperately ill in hospital, reliant on others for their most basic functions, you will know how even the dignity of a strong person can come under threat.

A human-rights-centred approach puts protecting and preserving people's dignity at the absolute centre.

The AASW's Code of Ethics *describes the social work profession as 'committed to the pursuit of and maintenance of human wellbeing. Social work aims to maximise the development of human potential and the fulfilment of human needs'. This highlights that respect for human dignity and diversity are values at the core of social work and human rights.*

Social workers are at the coalface of human rights. You bear witness to the experiences of people whose rights have been violated and you work to prevent abuses, and to protect and empower your clients.

Social workers also have an advocacy role, not only in relation to the needs of individual clients but also with respect to systemic problems that you encounter, so that you can promote broader social change.

Edward Santow, Australian Human Rights Commissioner[13]

9.1 LEGAL FRAMEWORKS

The law is both a source of human rights protections and human rights violations. In some areas of the law, such as anti-discrimination law, human rights are woven into its fabric. Others are being slowly reformed to reduce discrimination, such as the changes to the *Marriage Act 1961* (Cth) to allow same-sex marriage and the introduction of the *Same Sex Relationships (Equal Treatment in Commonwealth Laws – Superannuation Act) 2008* (Cth) and the *Same Sex Relationships (Equal Treatment in Commonwealth Laws – General Law Reform Act) 2008* (Cth).* These changes have seen the *legal* discrimination and human rights violations against same-sex couples significantly reduced. Many areas have seen

* This was something of an 'own goal' in the push to end discrimination against same-sex couples, in that it meant that couples receiving Centrelink payments would now be assessed as a couple, not two single people living together, drastically reducing their payments.

some legal reform but no revolution in practice, such as restrictive practices and coercion in disability, mental health and aged care. In other areas of law there are increasing concerns about human rights violations, such as refugee law, anti-terrorism law and cybersecurity.[14] Social workers who adopt a human rights perspective must understand this shifting landscape to be able to work effectively within it.

The legal context of human rights is a complex interplay between international and local law. As discussed in Chapter 2, international law is not directly enforceable in Australia. Australian governments can choose how and when to apply international law. This means that in practice international human rights law only influences local law.

An example of this is the Tasmanian *Children, Young Persons and Their Families Act 1997*, which the Tasmanian government says 'is strongly based on the United Nations Convention on the Rights of the Child.'[15] Under international human rights law, found in article 3 of the *Convention on the Rights of the Child*,[16] in all actions undertaken concerning children the 'best interests of the child shall be a primary consideration'. This is not by itself legally enforceable, but it has *influenced* the Tasmanian Act, which states that with everything done under that Act 'the best interests of the child must be the paramount consideration'. The phrase 'best interests of the child' appears in 76 pieces of Australian legislation, highlighting the wide-ranging influence of the *Convention on the Rights of the Child*. This is one way in which international human rights law is brought into local law.

Another way is when local law just gives power to international human rights documents. To use the same example of Tasmanian child protection legislation, s 8 of the *Children, Young Persons and Their Families Act 1997* states that 'any international convention relating to children to which Australia is a signatory' can be used in interpreting that Act. This example doesn't mean that the international convention, such as the *Convention on the Rights of the Child,* is enforceable under Tasmanian law, but it does mean that it should be taken into account when making decisions.

Sometimes, local law brings the whole international human rights law document into the local legislation. For example, the full text of the *Convention on the Elimination of all Forms of Discrimination Against Women* is actually part of the *Sex Discrimination Act 1984* (Cth).[17] This gives the international law document the same force as legislation and makes the international law legally binding. It is important to understand that while this can make international human rights law enforceable in Australia, the government can at any time repeal the legislation, and then it is no longer legally enforceable. The government does not even have to make new legislation that is compatible with it, as new legislation automatically overrides existing legislation.

Another way in which international human rights law can be used in Australia is when legislation or the common law is not clear on an issue and a court has to make a decision. In these situations, when the court is faced with a number of choices it should adopt the choice that is most consistent with international human rights law.[18] This does not apply if the law is clear, but in circumstances when it is not clear it can be part of the court's decision making process.

All this means that to understand how human rights law is applied in Australia, it is necessary to understand international human rights law before considering local human rights law. As we will see throughout the rest of this book, all areas of social work practice are influenced by United Nations human rights documents.

9.1.1 United Nations human rights documents

International human rights law is generally found in United Nations human rights documents. These documents are all post-Second World War, and while human rights as a concept has a history going back much further, international human rights law is really a phenomenon of the second half of the twentieth century. For social workers, the key documents are:

- *Charter of the United Nations*[19]
- *Universal Declaration of Human Rights* (UDHR)[20]
- *International Covenant on Civil and Political Rights* (ICCPR)[21]
- *International Covenant on Economic, Social and Cultural Rights* (ICESCR)[22]
- *International Convention on the Elimination of All Forms of Racial Discrimination* (ICERD)[23]
- *Convention on the Elimination of All Forms of Discrimination against Women* (CEDAW)[24]
- *Convention Against Torture and Other Cruel, Inhuman or Degrading Treatment or Punishment* (UNCAT)[25]
- *Convention on the Rights of the Child* [26]
- *Convention on the Rights of Persons with Disabilities* (Disability Convention)[27]
- *Convention Relating to the Status of Refugees* (Refugee Convention)[28]
- *Declaration on the Rights of Indigenous Peoples* (UNDRIP).[29]

A key theme of these documents and a core principle of human rights law is 'non-discrimination'. This reinforces the link between anti-discrimination law and human rights. Specific areas of social work practice clearly align with different documents; the *Disability Convention* and disability and mental health, UNDRIP and working with First Nations people and communities, the *Convention on the Rights of the Child* and child protection, the *Refugee Convention* with working with people seeking asylum and people of refugee background. Others, such as the UDHR, ICCPR and ICESCR contain rights that are important in all aspects of social work practice.

Declarations are, even by the loose standards of international law, not enforceable. Conventions, on the other hand, are signed and ratified so countries *agree* to be bound by them – although there is little that can be done if they find complying inconvenient. A contemporary example of this is Australia's continued breach of the *Refugee Convention*, discussed in Chapter 15. Increasingly, Australian courts are *influenced* by international human rights documents when making decisions,[30] but in practice local Australian law and policy is almost always able to override international law.*

There are very limited ways in which social workers might directly use international human rights law. For example, Australia has signed the United Nations *Optional Protocol to the Convention on the Rights of Persons with Disabilities*,[31] which allows people to appeal to the United Nations Committee on the Rights of Persons with Disabilities if their rights under the *Disability Convention* have been violated.[32] It is not impossible for a social worker to support a person to make a complaint using this process, but it does not happen very often, if ever, and would usually require legal expertise. Instead, as discussed later, social workers are able to use the framework of international human rights law to assess and inform their own practice and as an advocacy tool to hold governments to account. Local human rights law, on the other hand, presents many direct and practical opportunities for social workers.

9.1.2 Local human rights and anti-discrimination law

As mentioned above, much local human rights law is influenced by international human rights law. This is particularly the case for legislation but is not the case for the *Australian Constitution* or the common law, which took their shape before contemporary international human rights law existed. This means that local human rights law is a mix of constitutional rights, the common law and statutes. The Commonwealth and every state and territory have anti-discrimination legislation, and some jurisdictions also have human rights legislation.

The constitution

Some countries, including Ireland, the United States and South Africa, have Bills of Rights in their constitutions, which locks in specific human rights and makes it difficult for governments to alter.† Australia does not have a

---

* This language is a source of some contention amongst international human rights law nerds such as myself. For most practical purposes, it is accurate to say that international human rights law is 'not binding', but it is probably more correct to say 'regularly violated' and 'difficult to enforce'. The government has agreed to be bound by it, so it is binding in that sense, but then they just decide not to follow it, so it is not really binding in *that* sense.

† There is an ongoing debate around the value of constitutional rights, and while there are many examples of good outcomes, the 'right to bear arms' in the United States *Constitution* is an example of a problematic and unintended outcome. The wide-ranging and ongoing breaches of human rights by countries including the United States also indicates that a constitutional bill of rights is not in itself a solution to human rights violations.

bill of rights in the *Constitution*, so human rights law is mostly governed by legislation and common law as discussed below. The *Australian Constitution* does include five explicit rights:

- The right to vote (s 41)
- Protection against acquisition of property on unjust terms (s 51(xxxi))
- The right to a trial by jury (s 80)
- Freedom of religion (s 116)
- Prohibition of discrimination on the basis of state of residency (s 117)

The High Court has added one more to this list, which is that people have the right to discuss political issues. The *Constitution* does not explicitly state this, but the High Court found that it implies it because the *Constitution* would not work if people could not meet and discuss political issues.[33] Note that this implied right is not universal, as shown in *Comcare v Banerji*,[*] where the High Court found that public servants can be prohibited from posting political messages on social media as they are required to be apolitical.

These constitutional rights cannot be overridden by legislation, and while they are not wide-ranging, they are important protections, as can be seen in the case of *Roach v Electoral Commissioner*.[34] In this case, the Commonwealth government had introduced legislation to prevent prisoners from voting. Vicki Lee Roach, a Yuin woman from Victoria who was serving a prison sentence for robbing a milk bar, challenged the legislation. The High Court found that a blanket ban on prisoners voting was unconstitutional but found that prisoners serving a sentence of three years or longer are not entitled to vote. This is a good example of human rights law in action because while the right to vote is not an absolute right, this case shows the court interpreting the right in the Constitution to balance with the right of the parliament to make laws governing Australians.

Common law

There are some rights which exist in the common law, which can be overridden by parliament creating legislation. For example, three common law rights are:

- Courts are obliged to refuse to allow an unfair trial to go ahead.[35]
- Police have no power to detain someone just for questioning.[36]
- When courts interpret legislation, they should interpret it in line with human rights.[37]

This last one does not mean that legislation cannot override human rights, just that when it does it needs to be really clear that it is doing so.

---

[*] *Comcare v Banerji* [2019] HCA 23.

Human rights legislation

Without a constitutional Bill of Rights, most human rights law in Australia stems from legislation. Any legislation can give a human right, but there are a number of key pieces of anti-discrimination legislation that are relevant. These include, at the Commonwealth level:

- *Age Discrimination Act 2004* (Cth)
- *Disability Discrimination Act 1992* (Cth)
- *Racial Discrimination Act 1975* (Cth)
- *Sex Discrimination Act 1984* (Cth)
- *Workplace Gender Equality Act 2012* (Cth)

States and territories also have their own anti-discrimination legislation:

Table 9.1 *State and territory anti-discrimination legislation*

Jurisdiction	Relevant legislation
ACT	*Discrimination Act 1991* (ACT)
NSW	*Anti-Discrimination Act 1977* (NSW)
NT	*Anti-Discrimination Act 1992* (NT)
Qld	*Anti-Discrimination Act 1991* (Qld)
SA	*Equal Opportunity Act 1984* (SA)
Tas	*Anti-Discrimination Act 1998* (Tas)
Vic	*Equal Opportunity Act 2010* (Vic)
WA	*Equal Opportunity Act 1984* (WA)

Some jurisdictions also have specific legislation in addition to these broad anti-discrimination acts, such as the *Racial and Religious Tolerance Act 2001* (Vic). These statutes provide social workers with a reasonably easy and effective way of responding when supporting a person who is discriminated against. This legislation is very important and very useful for social workers, who will often find their clients are discriminated against, but this is a good example of how human rights law sets a low bar rather than working towards a more inclusive society. The case of *Haraksin v Murrays Australia Limited* illustrates this problem.[38] In this case, Julia Haraksin tried to book a bus ticket so she could attend a conference, but was told she could not because the buses could not accommodate wheelchairs. She complained to the Australian Human Rights Commission but ultimately had to take the case to the Federal Court. Three-and-a-half years after the incident, the judge found that the bus company had breached the *Disability Discrimination Act 1992* (Cth).* From a legal

* It is also worth noting that the judge in this case made no reference to the *Disability Convention*, only considering local legalisation and standards. This is not a criticism of the judge but highlights how international human rights law is not directly considered even in local human rights decisions.

perspective, this is a clear win – the legislation works. From a social work perspective, this is deeply unsatisfactory – three and a half years is too long to wait for a bus. If a person who uses a wheelchair needs to use a bus, they should not have to go to court to do so. Instead, people should be provided with the services they require when they require them, and it should not be up to the people who need the services to enforce compliance with legislation.

This highlights another key issue with human rights legislation. The legislation does not say 'every person in a wheelchair has a legal right to catch any bus'. It is peppered with words such as 'reasonableness' and 'unreasonableness' and 'unjustifiable hardship', which allow arguments about if it is 'reasonable' or not that the bus is not wheelchair accessible. Social workers need to be aware of this when advocating for people to have their human rights protected, as often the very legislation designed to uphold them can contain allowances for them to be violated when it is convenient to do so. Social workers can advocate for clear and explicit protections of human rights in legislation to avoid this in the future.

It is important to remember that legislation that limits human rights usually also contains protections against human rights violations. Mental health, child protection, disability and migration legislation all exist so that people's rights and responsibilities can be balanced. A good example of this can be seen in *Patrick's Case,*[39] where a social worker organised for Patrick's house to be sold against his will so that he would be forced to stay in supported accommodation. In that case the judge found that the social worker had not acted consistently with Patrick's human rights and overturned the decision.[*] Another case that illustrates this is *PBU & NJE v Mental Health Tribunal,*[40] which is a case about the way in which a person's human right to bodily integrity can be limited to give them electroconvulsive therapy (ECT) against their will but only under very specific circumstances and conditions. These cases do not mean that someone's house can never be sold against their will, or that a person can never be given ECT again; they just mean that the people who made those decisions violated, rather than legally limited, the human rights of the people concerned. Both of these cases consider the relevant legislation, the *Mental Health Act 2014* (Vic), but also the *Disability Convention* and Victoria's human rights *Charter*.[41]

[*] This case also involved the Victorian *Charter of Human Rights and Responsibilities*. *Patrick's* Case is discussed in more detail in Chapter 13, and a role play based on this case is available on the resources website.

Three jurisdictions have introduced specific human rights legislation:

Table 9.2 *Human rights legislation*

Jurisdiction	Human rights legislation
ACT	*Human Rights Act 2004* (ACT)
Qld	*Human Rights Act 2019* (Qld)
Vic	*Charter of Human Rights and Responsibilities Act 2006* (Vic)

The Australian Capital Territory (ACT) Act is the oldest of these, dating to 2004, with Queensland's only introduced in 2019. For lawyers, these offer a whole new set of arguments and principles on which to argue in court, but this is of little use for social workers – for whom they are useful tools for reminding government agencies of their obligations. For example, if a social worker is working with a person who is being evicted by a public housing authority, the social worker can point to their right to a fair hearing,[42] and ensure that information is provided in a way they can easily understand. Alternatively, social workers might be reminded of the limits of their authority and respect a person's request not to come to their house so as to respect their right to privacy.[43] These might also lend strength to less definite rights. For example, the preamble to the Victorian *Charter* recognises that 'all people are born free and equal in dignity and rights'. This is probably not legally enforceable, but it is reassuring for social workers to see governments taking human rights seriously.

9.2 Social work practice

For social workers, it can sometimes feel as if the most effective use of human rights law might be to physically knock someone over the head with it, but with the UDHR only running to about eight pages, this is not always the best option.* Instead, social workers can use human rights law to bolster their existing human rights oriented practice, ensure their colleagues act consistently with human rights, and as a lever or platform for advocacy.

Before discussing the way human rights law can be used in social work settings, it is important to note that practising human rights-based social work is not without controversy.[44] Simply upholding human rights will not achieve social justice, so social workers need to see human rights as just one part of the puzzle. This can get really tricky in practice, where human rights might seem a distraction from the main task – for example, finding someone a house to live in or keeping a child safe. It might seem reasonable to suspend a person's right to privacy in order to protect a

* For those of you who prefer this practice modality, I suggest the *Corporations Act 2001* (Cth) – at 3359 pages and six volumes it is ideal for weaponisation.

child, for example. It might even be in their 'best interests' to violate their right, or there might be a clash between two rights, such as the right to free speech and the right to be free from discrimination. There is no good answer which resolves this tension, other than that reflection and reflexivity can assist in navigating it.

At the micro-level of social work practice, social workers work with people right at the point at which their human rights are violated and are as such well positioned to both notice when this occurs and use the law to address it. This might include examples identified above, such as making a complaint to a human rights body or referring a person to a lawyer who can better assist them. Social workers can also help each other by reminding colleagues of their obligations under human rights law, as a way of grounding their practice in human rights. Social workers and other health professionals often feel entitled to interfere with or intrude on people's lives and reminding them about their legal obligations under privacy legislation can be a good way to limit this.

At the meso-level, social workers can work with their colleagues and organisations to ensure that their policies and practices are human rights compliant. For example, if a drug and alcohol rehabilitation facility has a no drugs policy, what happens if a person is found to have breached that policy? Are they entitled to a fair hearing or to an appeal? These are human rights. It might also include smaller, everyday actions, such as reminding a housing or health provider of their obligations under human rights legislation.

At the macro-level, social workers must also work towards ensuring human rights are maintained at systems and societal levels. This may involve policy advocacy, law reform or some other macro-intervention, or it can be embedded in everyday face-to-face practice. It might include supporting a person to give evidence at a Royal Commission so they can share their experience of having their rights breached. The challenge for social workers is keeping human rights at the forefront of their practice while working towards social justice, and not losing sight of that ultimate goal.

Main points

1. As highlighted in the AASW definition of social work, human rights are at the very core of what we do.
2. Human rights are closely linked to anti-discrimination. As social workers, we are often working alongside people who have been discriminated against on the basis of their gender, sex, race, age or other personal attributes.
3. Human rights are generally considered in three generations: civil and political; economic, social and cultural; and collective rights.
4. International human rights laws are not directly enforceable in Australia unless they are legislated into domestic law, although they

are very influential. For example, the UN Convention on the Rights of the Child is directly reflected in *Children, Young Persons and Their Families Act 1997* (Tas).

5. The *Australian Constitution* establishes five explicit rights: the right to vote; protection against acquisition of property on unjust terms; the right to a trial by jury; freedom of religion; and prohibition of discrimination on the basis of state of residency. There is also an 'implied right' to freedom of communication on political issues.

Discussion questions

1. Does your jurisdiction have a human rights charter? What difference would it make if it did, or did not?
2. Think of an instance where a woman confides in you about her abusive relationship but begs you not to tell anyone. How can we, as human rights workers, attempt to balance rights that are in conflict – such as an individual's right to privacy with their right to live a life free from violence and harm?
3. International declarations and conventions are generally not enforceable. So what is the point? Consider the benefits and obstacles faced with regards to international law.
4. Are the few rights set out in the *Australian Constitution* adequate? What would be the benefits of Australia creating a Bill of Rights? Look internationally at how other countries implement a Bill of Rights.

Further reading

- Tom Calma, 'The Role of Social Workers as Human Rights Workers with Indigenous People and Communities' (12 February 2008) <https://www.humanrights.gov.au/news/speeches/role-social-workers-human-rights-workers-indigenous-people-and-communities>.
- Sharlene Nipperess, 'Towards a Critical Human Rights-Based Approach to Social Work Practice', in Bob Pease et al (eds) *Doing Critical Social Work: Transformative Practices for Social Justice* (Allen & Unwin, 2016) 73.

9.3 References

[1] Tom Calma, 'The Role of Social Workers as Human Rights Workers with Indigenous People and Communities' (12 February 2008) <https://www.humanrights.gov.au/news/speeches/role-social-workers-human-rights-workers-indigenous-people-and-communities>.
[2] IFSW, 'Global Definition of Social Work', International Federation of Social Workers (2014) <https://www.ifsw.org/what-is-social-work/global-definition-of-social-work/>.
[3] AASW, *Code of Ethics* (Australian Association of Social Workers, 2010).
[4] Jim Ife, 'Human Rights and Social Justice' in M. Gray and S. Webb (eds), *Ethics and Value Perspectives in Social Work* (Palgrave Macmillan, 2010) 148, 148.

[5] Christopher Maylea, 'A Rejection of Involuntary Treatment in Mental Health Social Work' [2016] *Ethics and Social Welfare*.
[6] Sharlene Nipperess, 'Towards a Critical Human Rights-Based Approach to Social Work Practice' in Bob Pease et al (eds), *Doing Critical Social Work: Transformative Practices for Social Justice* (Allen & Unwin, 2016) 73, 73.
[7] Nipperess (n 6).
[8] UN General Assembly, Convention on the Elimination of All Forms of Discrimination Against Women, 18 December 1979, United Nations, Treaty Series, vol. 1249, p. 13, art 11(1).
[9] UN General Assembly, International Covenant on Economic, Social and Cultural Rights, 16 December 1966, United Nations, Treaty Series, vol. 993, p. 3, art 11(1).
[10] This idea of having three generations dates to an article written in 1977. It is not the only way of understanding or grouping human rights but it is the most common one: Karel Vasak, 'Human Rights: A Thirty-Year Struggle: The Sustained Efforts to Give Force of Law to the Universal Declaration of Human Rights' (1977) 30(11) *UNESCO Courier* 28.
[11] *PBU & NJE v Mental Health Tribunal* [2018] VSC 564.
[12] *Charter of Human Rights and Responsibilities Act 2006* (Vic) ss 7(2), 38(1).
[13] Edward Santow, 'Human Rights in Action: The Role of Social Workers in Detention – Speech to Australian Association of Social Workers (AASW) Queensland State Social Work Conference', *Australian Human Rights Commission* (2016) <https://www.humanrights.gov.au/news/speeches/human-rights-action-role-social-workers-detention>.
[14] Human Rights Watch, 'World Report 2019: Rights Trends in Australia', *Human Rights Watch* (20 December 2018) <https://www.hrw.org/world-report/2019/country-chapters/australia>.
[15] Tasmanian Department of Health and Human Services, 'Children, Young Persons and Their Families Act 1997' <https://www.dhhs.tas.gov.au/children/child_protection_services/children,_young_persons_and_their_families>.
[16] UN General Assembly, Convention on the Rights of the Child, 20 November 1989, United Nations, Treaty Series, vol. 1577, p. 3.
[17] UN General Assembly, Convention on the Elimination of All Forms of Discrimination Against Women, 18 December 1979, United Nations, Treaty Series, vol. 1249, p. 13.
[18] *Minister of State for Immigration and Ethnic Affairs v Ah Hin Teoh* [1995] HCA 20.
[19] United Nations, Charter of the United Nations, 24 October 1945, 1 UNTS XVI.
[20] UN General Assembly, Universal Declaration of Human Rights, 10 December 1948, 217 A (III).
[21] UN General Assembly, International Covenant on Civil and Political Rights, 16 December 1966, United Nations, Treaty Series, vol. 999, p. 171.
[22] UN General Assembly, International Covenant on Economic, Social and Cultural Rights, 16 December 1966, United Nations, Treaty Series, vol. 993, p. 3.
[23] UN General Assembly, International Convention on the Elimination of All Forms of Racial Discrimination, 21 December 1965, United Nations, Treaty Series, vol. 660, p. 195.
[24] UN General Assembly, Convention on the Elimination of All Forms of Discrimination Against Women, 18 December 1979, United Nations, Treaty Series, vol. 1249, p. 13.
[25] UN General Assembly, Convention Against Torture and Other Cruel, Inhuman or Degrading Treatment or Punishment, 10 December 1984, United Nations, Treaty Series, vol. 1465, p. 85.
[26] UN General Assembly, Convention on the Rights of the Child, 20 November 1989, United Nations, Treaty Series, vol. 1577, p. 3.
[27] UN General Assembly, Convention on the Rights of Persons with Disabilities: resolution/adopted by the General Assembly, 24 January 2007, A/RES/61/106.

[28] UN General Assembly, Convention Relating to the Status of Refugees, 28 July 1951, United Nations, Treaty Series, vol. 189, p. 137.
[29] UN General Assembly, United Nations Declaration on the Rights of Indigenous Peoples: resolution/adopted by the General Assembly, 2 October 2007, A/RES/61/295.
[30] *Tomasevic v Travaglini* [2007] VSC 337.
[31] UN General Assembly, Optional Protocol to the Convention on the Rights of Persons with Disabilities, 13 December 2006, A/RES/61/106, Annex II.
[32] The ICCPR, ICERD, CEDAW, UNCAT and ICESCR all also have 'optional protocols' that allow for similar complaints processes.
[33] *Australian Capital Television Pty Ltd v Commonwealth* (1992) 177 CLR 106.
[34] *Roach v Electoral Commissioner* [2007] HCA 43.
[35] *Dietrich v R* (1992) 177 CLR 292.
[36] *R v Lemsatef* [1977] 2 All ER 835.
[37] *Coco v The Queen* (1994) 179 CLR 427.
[38] *Haraksin v Murrays Australia Limited (No 2)* [2013] FCA 217.
[39] *PJB v Melbourne Health and Another (Patrick's Case)* [2011] VSC 327.
[40] *PBU & NJE v Mental Health Tribunal* [2018] VSC 564.
[41] Charter of Human Rights and Responsibilities Act 2006 (Vic).
[42] Charter of Human Rights and Responsibilities Act 2006 (Vic) s 24.
[43] Charter of Human Rights and Responsibilities Act 2006 (Vic) s 13.
[44] See: Tom Grimwood, *Key Debates in Social Work and Philosophy* (Routledge, 2015) <http://ebookcentral.proquest.com/lib/rmit/detail.action?docID=4015703>.

Chapter 10 SOCIAL WORK IN THE CRIMINAL LEGAL SYSTEM

Katherine Ogilvie, Caroline Lambert and Chris Maylea

Katherine Ogilvie is a social worker with extensive experience across the areas of service delivery, program management, policy development and tertiary student supervision. Katherine has worked in Queensland and Victoria across the justice, mental health, disability, asylum seeker, youth homelessness, community development, tenancy/housing and integrated practice sectors. She has worked within government departments, universities, small community agencies and larger non-government organisations and has a long-held passion for social justice and smarter ways of improving complex support systems. Katherine's current role is Social Work and Integrated Practice Manager for RMIT University's Centre for Innovative Justice.

Dr Caroline Lambert is an Industry Fellow & Lecturer at RMIT University and the Social Work and Lived Experience Clinical Educator at Forensicare, the state-wide specialist provider of forensic mental health services in Victoria.

Social workers work with people throughout the criminal legal system in a variety of roles. This may be entirely incidental, such as when working with someone on an unrelated matter and they come into contact with the police, or it may be essential to the social work role, such as working in post-release reintegration programs or supporting witnesses providing evidence. There are relatively few social workers working within the corrections system itself, but many areas of social work practice will include people involved with the criminal legal system. To work effectively across different areas of practice, social workers will need to understand how the criminal legal system works.

The criminal legal system is a multidisciplinary sector, bringing together a variety of disciplines including lawyers (solicitors, barristers, judges and magistrates), corrections officers, paralegals, forensic medical experts, psychologists and social workers. Social workers are not at the top of the pecking order in this system and can sometimes feel their values are compromised as politicians and policy-makers construct a system that tries to punish people rather than rehabilitate them.[1] Despite this feeling of powerlessness, social workers who understand the system can bring much to it, for example by ensuring that social context is included in assessments and in decision-making, by bringing a human rights approach to practice and by working for social justice.

The ICCPR,[2] *Convention on the Rights of the Child* ,[3] UNCAT[4] and *Disability Convention*[5] all specifically reference the human rights of people in detention. Other documents include:

- *Standard Minimum Rules for the Treatment of Prisoners*[6]
- *Body of Principles for the Protection of All Persons Under Any Form of Detention or Imprisonment*[7]
- *Basic Principles for the Treatment of Prisoners*[8]
- *Standard Minimum Rules for Non-Custodial Measures 1990* (the Tokyo Rules)[9]

Criminal law is mainly overseen at the state and territory level, with some at the Commonwealth level.

Table 10.1 *Criminal legislation*

Jurisdiction	Relevant legislation
ACT	*Crimes Act 1900* (ACT)
NSW	*Crimes Act 1900* (NSW)
NT	*Criminal Code Act 1983* (NT)
Qld	*Criminal Code Act 1899* (Qld)
SA	*Criminal Law Consolidation Act 1935* (SA)
Tas	*Criminal Code Act 1924* (Tas)
Vic	*Crimes Act 1958* (Vic)
WA	*Criminal Code Compilation Act 1913* (WA)
Cth	*Crimes Act 1914* (Cth)

This chapter outlines the ways social workers can support people through the criminal legal system, both people who are victims of crime and people who have been accused of crimes. Each of the steps through the system is detailed, with specific focus given to the forensic mental health system and the youth justice system.

10.1 Pathways through the criminal legal system

Figure 10.1 shows how the two main parties could move through the criminal legal system. This is dramatically oversimplified; however, it outlines some basic paths people might follow. The pathway might end at any point, and it commonly does, if the police or prosecution decide not to proceed or if the person is found not guilty. The binary narrative of 'victim' and 'perpetrator' is narrow and unhelpful, as many people who are labelled as offenders have also been victims of offences themselves, and many will have repeated encounters with the criminal legal system from a number of perspectives.

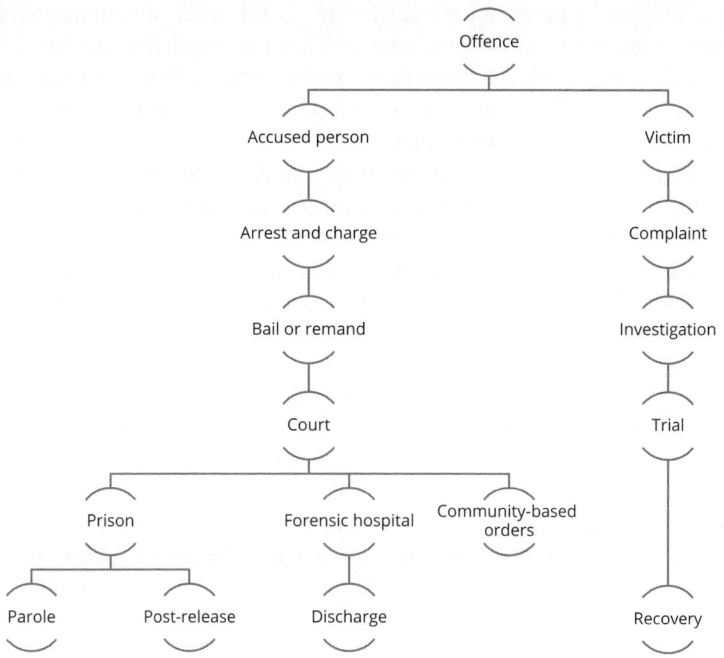

Figure 10.1 *Accused person and victim pathways through the criminal legal system*

Depending on the circumstances and the type of offence, legal processes can take a long time. For sexual assault cases, the median time for a matter to be finalised in court is 31 weeks.[10] Social workers can be involved with assisting all parties along their pathways to minimise the potential trauma of a drawn-out court process.

10.2 Working with victims

Victims of crime extend beyond the person or people who was or were directly implicated. Serious crimes can cause vicarious trauma through family and community networks. Mostly, social work responses to trauma by criminal acts will be similar to any traumatic event, but there are some legal aspects that will only apply when a crime has been committed.

The experience of victims in the criminal legal system is often quite disempowering. Criminal proceedings are run by the state, not by the person who is harmed. This means that victims can feel excluded and unheard throughout some or all parts of the process. There are some opportunities to participate. Victims can make the initial police reports, provide evidence both in and out of court, and in some cases, a 'victim impact statement' can be provided to the court. Victim impact statements are used after a person has already been convicted, when the magistrate or judge is deciding what sentence the person should receive. These opportunities to meaningfully participate in the legal process are limited. Victims play no or very little part in deciding what the person will be charged with or what sentence they receive, which can often leave victims unsatisfied with the process. Often, victims are looking for an apology or reparation, but the criminal legal system is not designed to provide this. The criminal legal system has more of a focus on punishing people who offend, not assisting victims in their recovery. Social workers must be aware of this and take steps to include victims as much as possible, while advocating for options such as restorative justice to provide more actual justice for victims. Social workers can also provide essential information to victims about legal processes and manage expectations throughout often lengthy proceedings.

Social workers can also provide an important link in helping people report crime, particularly for people who might not trust the police or who may be intimidated by the justice system. This is a consideration for survivors of sexual assault or family violence, or First Nations or refugee communities who might have a justified cultural mistrust of the police. Social workers may also support victims while the investigation and trial are ongoing, for example, while giving evidence. As an example, social workers working in the Witness Assistance Service in South Australia will assist people with a range of supports including:

- Information and education regarding court procedures and victims' rights and responsibilities
- Liaising between lawyers and victims
- Undertaking social work assessments and writing reports for the court
- Helping people to write victim impact statements
- Support in court or in meetings about the case
- Referral and liaison with other legal and welfare agencies.[11]

Social workers in other roles may also assist victims in applying for compensation after a crime has been committed. This may be through civil law, by suing someone in a court case; however, this is not an option if the person who caused the harm has no money or if they cannot be found. It might also not be legally possible, depending on the kind of offence committed and the jurisdiction. To address this, all jurisdictions also have victims' compensation schemes. These are not aimed at providing full compensation, instead attempting to provide resources to aid victims' recovery. Victims might apply for funding for assistance such as counselling, having locks changed or more sophisticated security at their house, or for reconstructive surgery. In some cases the person who was accused of the crime does not have to have been convicted. It can be enough that there is evidence that a crime was committed and some harm was done. Victim compensation schemes operate on the balance of probabilities, so it is sometimes possible for a person to get compensation even if the person accused of the crime was found not guilty beyond a reasonable doubt in the criminal system.

Sometimes people who are victims of crime are also charged with or convicted of committing crimes. For example, studies with women in prison indicate that between 57 per cent and 98 per cent of women in prison had experienced physical or sexual abuse. For First Nations women in prison, the intersectional and systemic oppression can be even more complex.[12] This should give social workers pause for thought – if our prisons are full of victims of crime, is incarceration the best possible response to crime? If there is such an overlap between people who are convicted of crime and people who experience crime, why do we treat them so differently?

10.3 People with Specific Needs in the Criminal Legal System

The role of social work in any setting is to offer support and advocacy for people who are vulnerable and disadvantaged, as well as to maximise the development of human potential and the fulfilment of human needs while also identifying and advocating for structural reform.[13] As with many areas of social work practice, people who have been accused of or sentenced for crimes often have multiple and intersecting experiences of trauma, oppression and discrimination. Of Australian prisoners, 1 in 3 have a chronic health condition, 2 in 3 used illicit drugs in the 12 months prior to prison, 1 in 2 had been diagnosed with a mental illness, 2 in 3 had not studied past year 10 and 1 in 2 were unemployed in the 30 days prior to entering prison.[14] A Victorian study found that 42 per cent of male prisoners and 33 per cent of female prisoners had an acquired brain injury, compared with 2 per cent in the broader population.[15]

First Nations people are also vastly overrepresented in Australia's prisons, being 28 per cent of the prison population despite being 2 per cent of the general population.[16] In the Northern Territory, 84 per cent of prisoners identify as First Nations people, despite constituting 30 per cent of the population. This is discussed in more detail in Chapter 12 but is particularly problematic in light of other cultural groups being much less likely to be in prison – people born in a country other than Australia account for 17 per cent of all prisoners, despite making up 35 per cent of the general population. It is crucial for social workers to have a strong cultural lens and provide culturally sensitive responses to First Nations people. Part of this is for social workers to recognise there is no homogeneous best practice, but the importance of being guided by members of that community.

Social workers must be alert to the gendered experiences of women in the criminal legal system, both as people who are accused or sentenced and as victims and survivors of crime. Overwhelmingly, women in prison have histories of physical and sexual abuse and are more likely to be imprisoned for less serious and non-violent offences.[17]

Another group with specific needs is parents, both because of the inherent goal to keep families together where safe and possible, and because there is a clear link between a parent's offending and their children's offending as adults.[18] There are also complex interactions between child protection and young people's offending.[19] Social workers can play a key role in supporting children of people in the criminal legal system, as well as their parents.

That certain challenges or experiences are overrepresented in the criminal legal system is no coincidence, but it is not always clear how the different influences on a person's life will interact in ways that lead to contact with the criminal legal system. Exposure to lead as a child, for example, is strongly linked to violent crime but not property crime.[20] Physical abuse and neglect are strongly linked to youth offending, but sexual and emotional abuse are not.[21] Data shows that 25 per cent of people entering prison were homeless in the four weeks immediately prior to their imprisonment and 31 per cent expect to be homeless when they are released,[22] but other studies show that this relationship is not causal.[23] This suggests that the same things that cause people to commit crimes also cause them to be homeless, but it is not clear that homelessness causes crime, although it does appear that incarceration can lead to homelessness. Factors such as visibility to police also play a role. These complex social and economic factors are important for social workers to grasp, as much of the work that social workers can do in the criminal legal system is to bring social context, both to people accused of or sentenced for crimes and to those negatively impacted by crime. By understanding these links, and helping other disciplines to understand them, social workers can have a real impact in this sector.

10.4 Working with people who have been accused and sentenced

There is a growing understanding that the criminal legal system does little to reduce reoffending or to reintegrate people who pass through it. More than half of people who exit prison return to corrective services within two years.[24] The growing focus on diversion and early intervention hold some promise, and social workers can play a key role in both supporting people to stay out of the criminal legal system and in helping people to reintegrate into society. This section outlines the processes experienced by people who have been accused and sentenced in the criminal legal system.

10.4.1 Infringements

Sometimes people are issued with an *infringement*. The infringement system is for minor crimes – for example, littering, drinking in a public place or travelling on public transit without a ticket. Infringements are often on the spot fines. If people are not in a position to pay the fine, or they dispute the fine, they may challenge it. One example of this is the 'special circumstances' scheme in Victoria, which applies to people who are diagnosed with mental illness or intellectual disability; who have a serious drug and alcohol addiction; who are experiencing family violence; or who are homeless. If people get an infringement because of one of these experiences, they can have the fine withdrawn.[25] If people do not pay or address their fines, there can be serious consequences including imprisonment.[26] Social workers can link people with their local community legal centre to get advice about infringements. Unless people want to challenge their infringements, they do not need to go to court. The rest of this section concerns more serious offences that must be heard by a court.

10.4.2 Pre-trial

Pre-contact

Social workers can be involved with integral services to help prevent or limit contact with the criminal legal system; for example, by providing support with housing, tenancy, employment or with families. Social workers can also assist people in navigating any processes they are part of, such as having conversations about conditions of an intervention order or making referrals to agencies for early legal advice. Social workers can also stand with and advocate for groups when they are not being treated equitably by authorities.

Arrest and charge

Police can arrest a person if they have a warrant for their arrest, or if they have 'reasonable suspicion' or 'reasonable belief' that they have committed a crime. The terminology differs across jurisdictions. Most jurisdictions have specific limits on how long people can be held before they are charged. Police can also search and detain people under certain circumstances.

People who are arrested have a right to silence and the right to a lawyer, although the law around this is complex.[27] This is not a right for a lawyer to be provided – just a right for the person to access a lawyer, which can often be very expensive. Some people are supposed to have additional rights – for example, First Nations people in Queensland accessing lawyers,[28] and in Victoria people living with an intellectual disability, mental illness, acquired brain injury or dementia are supposed to have an Independent Third Person present in police interviews.[29]

People can be charged without being arrested, but often a person is arrested and then charged. The charge is the start of the legal process and details the crime or crimes that the person has been accused of. Usually, the police or the prosecution will charge the person and then the person will either be bailed or remanded until a future court date.

Bail and remand

If people are granted bail, it means they can be released from custody if they agree to attend court as ordered. Bail can include extra conditions, such as residing at a particular address or not contacting certain people or surrendering their passport or regularly reporting to police. Breaching bail conditions can be a criminal offence. If they are able to, sometimes people may leave a 'surety' of money as a guarantee that they will attend court. If they do not attend court, they may not get this money back.

Bail can be granted by courts or police, depending on the kind of offence. Sometimes the police or prosecution will oppose bail if they think the person is a risk to the community or will breach their bail conditions, or not turn up to court. If a person can identify a place they are going to stay, for example, they are much more likely to be bailed than if they cannot. Social workers can play an important role in this process, by working to find housing services or liaise with family members who might be able to provide support. If bail is refused or the person is unable to pay the surety, the person is placed on remand.

People on remand are detained in prison to ensure that they turn up for their court hearing. Usually, time spent on remand will be taken into account in sentencing and sometimes the time spent on remand can be longer than a prison sentence would have been. In theory, people on remand should usually be kept separately from sentenced prisoners and offered programs, as they have not been found guilty of any crime. However, this does not always occur, particularly for women.

10.4.3 Court process

The process of going to court either as a support person or a witness is covered in Chapter 7. For criminal courts, the same process applies. Most criminal charges are settled at magistrates' or local courts, but more serious charges or complex trials are heard in the higher courts and can take weeks or months.

If the person pleads guilty, the process moves on to sentencing. If the person pleads not guilty, the matter will go to a contested hearing or trial. There may be a pre-trial conference, where the parties work out what facts or legal issues are disputed, how long the trial might go for and what witnesses are going to be called. There may also be legal processes such as mentions or committal hearings, and the matter can also be transferred to a higher court.

Trials can take various forms, but to get a simplified idea, proceedings may go as follows:

1. The charge is read out.
2. The prosecution does an opening speech and presents the witnesses for the prosecution.
3. The defence cross-examines the prosecution witnesses.
4. The defence presents their witnesses.
5. The prosecution cross-examines the defence witnesses.
6. If there is a jury, the jury decides if the person is guilty or not. If there is no jury, the judge or magistrate decides.
7. If the person is guilty, magistrate or judge will sentence the person. If not guilty, they may be free to go.

Specialist courts

Many jurisdictions also have specialist courts, such as drug courts, mental health courts, family violence courts, sexual assault courts or courts specifically for First Nations people (see Chapter 12). These courts are all designed to achieve better outcomes by acknowledging the support needs of that group of people and how their circumstances may impact differently on them. These specialist courts often show lower reoffending rates, but they can be politically unpopular as they can appear to be 'soft on crime', which is not the case. They often incorporate elements of therapeutic and restorative justice (see Chapter 4) and seek to address the underlying factors that led to the person being in the legal system. These courts will often include social workers as case managers or as providers of therapeutic services such as drug treatment. Social workers may also be involved in supporting victims in these settings.

The New South Wales (NSW) Drug Court is a good example of a specialist court, discussed in Box 10.1. Despite their success, drug courts are viewed as not being 'tough on crime' and are politically unpopular.

Box 10.1 *NSW Drug Court*

The NSW Drug Court was established in 1999. This court involves close supervision, mandatory drug treatment and drug testing, and rewards and sanctions to ensure compliance. People are eligible if they have been charged with a less serious offence, are facing prison time, have plead guilty and use drugs.

An evaluation found that:

> *... participants in the NSW Drug Court were less likely to be reconvicted than offenders given conventional sanctions (mostly imprisonment). Compared with those in the Comparison Group, Drug Court participants in the present study were 17 per cent less likely to be reconvicted for any offence, 30 per cent less likely to be reconvicted for a violent offence and 38 per cent less likely to be*

reconvicted for a drug offence at any point during the follow-up period.[30]

Sentencing

When a court is considering sentencing options, it will contemplate a number of factors and be guided by the sentencing legislation for that jurisdiction. Social workers generally have little to do with the actual sentencing process, but it is important to understand how courts think about sentencing. When the court is deciding what sentence, it has to have regard to the purpose of the sentence.[31] These are laid out in Figure 10.2.

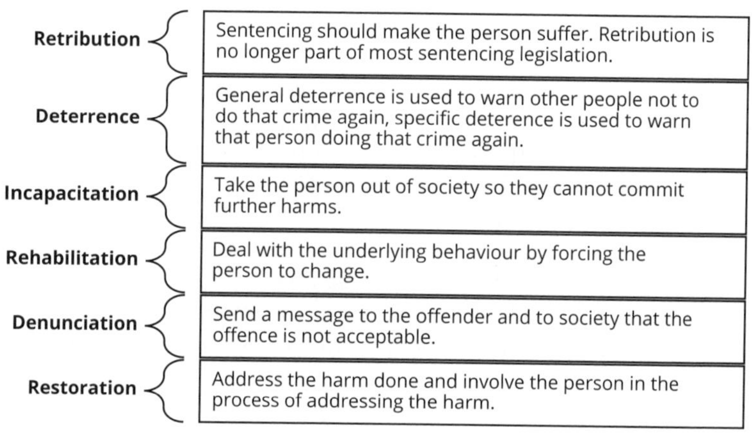

Figure 10.2 *Sentencing purposes*

Sentencing is a process of balancing the relevant legislation for that jurisdiction, understanding the context and comparing the offence and the person with previous sentencing decisions. This means it can be difficult to predict what sentence a person will get for a specific offence. For example, for a person with a long criminal record the court may impose a harsher penalty on the basis of specific deterrence, on the basis that previous punishments were not sufficiently severe to stop them committing the offence again. Social workers will often give evidence as to a person's situation, such as their progress in a drug treatment or anger management program, which may influence the sentence the court imposes.

Sentencing can include fines, imprisonment, community sentences, bonds, deferred or suspended sentences. The most common sentence imposed is a fine, followed by a community-based order then imprisonment, but there are other possible outcomes.[32] A person may have their driver's licence suspended or cancelled, or they be directed into a diversion program. A person may also have to pay compensation to the wronged party or pay court costs or legal costs.

Once the sentence has been decided, there is usually an opportunity to appeal the outcome to a higher court. This may include appealing the conviction or the sentence. There are specific legal rules that determine when an appeal may be made – sometimes there is an automatic right to appeal and other times there must be specific circumstances.

Table 10.2 *Sentencing legislation*

State or territory	**Criminal legislation**
ACT	*Crimes (Sentencing) Act 2005* (ACT)
NSW	*Crimes (Sentencing Procedure) Act 1999* (NSW)
NT	*Sentencing Act 1995* (NT)
Qld	*Penalties and Sentences Act 1992* (Qld)
SA	*Sentencing Act 2017* (SA)
Tas	*Sentencing Act 1997* (Tas)
Vic	*Sentencing Act 1991* (Vic)
WA	*Sentencing Act 1995* (WA)

10.4.4 Prisons

Social workers can also work within the prison system, providing therapeutic interventions to people in prison, both as individuals and in groups, and assisting with reintegration into the community. Some roles for social workers may include a function of reporting the progress or compliance with court orders back to the court or to prison authorities.

Australia only has state and territory prisons. There is no federal prison system. People found guilty of federal crimes are imprisoned in the state or territory prison systems. The number of people in prison in Australia is growing, sitting at around 40,000 people in 2019.[33] There are a range of different types of prisons in Australia, from minimum security prisons where people can access day leave or employment, to supermaximum security where in some sections people might spend almost all of their time confined to a cell.

Australian prisons were historically run directly by the government, but in recent years some jurisdictions have followed the trend from overseas to privatise prisons and have private companies run them or provide services in them. There are many well-documented problems with this,[34] but for social workers the reality is that they may work in a setting in which they are employed by a for-profit company to provide social work services. This gives rise to some conflicts of interest, as the company relies on more people in prison to turn more profit, while the social worker will be guided by social justice and human rights. Increasingly, private prisons are being paid based on reoffending reduction, rather than just the number of prisoners they house, which provides a different incentive structure. In Queensland, the state government has taken back control of two private prisons after a range of issues such as an increase in staff assaults.[35]

As the rising imprisonment rate and the high rates of reoffending indicate,[36] prison does not reduce crime, and prisons are expensive – about ten times more per person than a community-based order.[37] Social workers should critically engage with the assumptions society has made about prisons and people in the criminal legal system and consider if or how they can work either within corrections or outside it to improve the responses to unlawful acts. Many suggest that prisons are unnecessary, countertherapeutic and should be abolished.[38] One response that may hold promise is that of community-based orders.

10.4.5 Community-based orders

All states and territories have sentencing options that allow people to serve their sentence in the community and either avoid imprisonment or reduce the time they would otherwise spend in prison. The court can only make a community-based order if the nature of the offence allows. There are more people on community-based orders than in prison, roughly 70,000 across the country.[39]

Community-based orders may be bonds, such as a good behaviour bond, where people pledge not to offend again for a period of time, or they may be more severe and can include mandatory drug treatment, home detention or requirements not to associate with a certain person or certain place.[40] People may have to plead guilty or agree to certain conditions to be eligible. Often the threat of imprisonment exists for people who do not comply with the conditions of a community-based order. Research shows that community-based orders are more effective at reducing reoffending than short prison sentences.[41]

Community-based orders are different from parole, which follows a time in prison. The experience may be similar, in that if a person breached their parole conditions they may find themselves in prison, but they are legally different things. Community-based orders are usually focused on helping people stay out of prison, whereas parole is meant to be focused on helping people transition into the community after a period of imprisonment.

Although community-based orders better suit some people, some people find them challenging, such as people with caring duties, medical conditions that affect access to the community, or people in regional areas without a driver licence who need to attend regular appointments.

Box 10.2 *What do social workers do in corrections?*

What a social worker does

Social workers are employed in both our prisons and in our Community Correctional Centres. Social workers work with offenders on an individual or group basis.

The role is a challenging one and involves complex case work. However, this is a role that provides professional development opportunities and skills within a unique setting.

Prison

Social workers provide assessment and intervention services for prisoners. They conduct individual counselling, provide treatment assessments for appropriate programs, assess at-risk prisoners and facilitate group programs – all designed to enhance and support rehabilitation.

Social workers address the factors associated with offending behaviour and assist with daily life especially within prison environments.

Community

Social workers within community corrections are responsible for:

- *identifying offender social development needs and providing appropriate referrals*
- *monitoring the response of offenders to conditions of court and implementing measures to ensure they comply with community based sanctions*
- *preparing comprehensive written reports in order to facilitate offenders' release plans, set appropriate parole conditions and to advise of their progress.*

We employ social workers with a strong belief in offender rehabilitation.

To be able to work as a social worker with us you'll need to have appropriate degree or equivalent qualification which gives eligibility for full membership of the Australian Association of Social Workers.

South Australian Department for Correctional Services[42]

Box 10.2 is an extract from the South Australian Department for Correctional Services. It is included here to illustrate what social workers might be *expected* to do in corrections, but of course they will need to do much more. They will advocate for the rights of people in corrections, they will work to empower people they work with and they will stay true to the social justice and human rights basis of social work as required by the Australian Association of Social Workers *Code of Ethics*. Corrections is a good example of a legal system that might expect social workers to do one thing – assessment, case management, referrals, supervision and report writing – while social workers will be required by their ethical framework to do much more.

10.4.6 Parole

If a person is sentenced to a term of imprisonment, they will often be given two time frames by the court – the time of the total sentence and the time at which they may be eligible for parole. People on parole are still technically serving their sentence of imprisonment, just serving it in the community. Parole is not automatic – in most jurisdictions there is a parole board that decides when a person should be released on parole. This serves two functions: it can provide people with an earlier date to work towards and therefore could encourage attendance at therapeutic programs, as well as providing some structure in the community for people upon release. As with community-based orders, some people can find parole really challenging owing to social or economic factors, and some people choose not to apply for parole as they are aware the services they need are not yet set up for them in the community. If a person breaches the conditions of their parole or commits an offence while on parole, they may find themselves serving both the original sentence as well as additional time for breaching the conditions of the parole.

10.4.7 Post-release transition

A final stage of the criminal legal system is the process of post-release transition back to the community. For some, this could be simply walking out of court after paying a fine. For people who have experienced long periods of incarceration, this process can be much more complex.

Just as social workers can work with people to avoid contact with the criminal legal system, they can also support people to stay out of the system on release. The importance of wraparound supports in the community is well documented; however, there is widespread community opposition to resourcing supports for people exiting prison.[43] Social workers can provide essential supports ensuring that people who are exiting corrections are not discriminated against and that people are supported to obtain appropriate housing, family reconnection, psychosocial support, employment and other assistance to transition to the community.

For some groups of people, finishing their sentenced time does not indicate the end of their contact with corrections. Increasingly, governments are enacting legislation that allows for the control of people after they have served their sentence but who are viewed as being too dangerous to live unmonitored in society.[44] This is often focused on people who have been convicted of sexual offences but is increasingly including people convicted of very violent or terrorist offences. Examples of this include sex offender registration programs, where people can live in the community, and post-sentence detention schemes, where people can be detained indefinitely in prison-like environments.

Read Charlotte's story and reflect on her journey into and out of the criminal legal system.

10.5 Charlotte's Story

I grew up in a very sheltered family. My parents had high expectations. I struggled a lot in primary school trying to fit in. I used to get bullied on a daily basis as I was the only Asian looking child at school and wore glasses. I struggled with my identity.

When I went to high school there was more Asians, so I started hanging around with them. Finally, I found a group of people who looked the same as me and obviously I was drawn to them. There were two types of Asians, the cool kids and the geeks. I was drawn to the bad crowd and was drawn to an older guy. I didn't know at the time that he was using heroin.

I got together with him and within a few weeks he used in front of me. I was curious, I had no idea what it was about. That's when he offered to shoot me up. I accepted. Soon he was shooting me up daily. I feel like he got me addicted to drugs because I was able to get money from my parents. He depended on me financially to maintain his drug use. The relationship became abusive and I eventually left him, although I kept using. By the time I was in year 11 my addiction was so bad that I left school and started selling drugs in the city.

I was arrested and was sentenced to a community-based order. My worker was really cold. He didn't really care. He asked if I was still using or using methadone. It felt like he had a checklist and was just working through it. I just felt like another number. Unimportant. Insignificant. I decided not to see him again which meant I breached the court order.

I was on the run for a while but was arrested for shop theft. Because I had breached the community-based order, I was remanded straight away. I was really scared. I was sent to a women's prison for two months on remand. I thought I might get sentenced in the youth system, but then the magistrate said, 'if you want to act like an adult I'm going to sentence you like an adult'. I was sentenced to 12 months without parole for shop theft, breaching the community order and the original drug charges.

I walked out after 12 months more of a criminal than when I went inside. I looked up to women in there who had major trafficking charges. I wanted to live the luxurious life they had, the lifestyle they had. I didn't consider their prison sentences. Prison made we want to do bigger things. I wanted to make money, to keep using.

Because I had no parole, there was no support at the end of my sentence. My mum sent me overseas to keep me clean, but I was bored. When I came back I started seeking out people I knew from gaol. I had a connection with them. But people are different when they use than when they are clean, and it was pretty inevitable that I was going to relapse.

Back to old habits, I got remanded again for shop theft and was put on a drug treatment order. I only agreed to the drug treatment order to stay out of prison, but the worker I got was really good. She showed a lot of empathy, a lot of care, a lot of concern. She took me out for coffee, for lunch. She was really interested in what was going on for me. Sometimes she took notes, but when we went out she didn't write things down. I was complying with the appointments, although because I was still using I was sent to prison seven times for two weeks at a time. Eventually, they cancelled my drug treatment order and I went back inside for another five months. I really appreciated her being there, but she couldn't really help me because I didn't want to help myself.

My charges increased each time I was imprisoned. From shop theft, to possession, to trafficking. I spent the next nine years in and out of prison repeating the same cycle. It is a bit of a blur.

Eventually, I got bailed to a residential rehab. I only did it to get out of jail. I didn't know anything about it, but one of the other girls in the prison got bailed there before I did. It was really hard to work out how to get in as there were no supports in the prison. Recovery was never part of my plan. The first opportunity I had I was going to abscond.

But I didn't. I had some freedom there. I could smoke, I could do trips to places. I had a friend in the rehab who was in the program ahead of me, who managed to graduate from the program. If she could do it, I thought, I can do this. I've been there 16 months now. With the time in custody before I got bailed, I've been clean for two years. I'm right at the end of the program, about two months from graduating. I'm looking for my own place when I move out. I've got connection with my family, friends I never thought I'd have.

I'm not going to lie. It is really hard. I think about using all the time. For me, I just remember the bad times and that's what keeps me on the straight and narrow. I'm finding me again.

There are many things social workers can take away from Charlotte's story. Note how it starts and ends with identity, how she was looking for somewhere to belong and she found that in prison. Now she has to find who she is again. Note also the difference the first worker *could* have made, and how the connection Charlotte found with the second worker provided her with hope, but she feels she was not yet ready for change. The difficulty Charlotte had getting the support she needed and the way the system contributed to her offending highlight the importance of both providing the support, care and compassion people need, and in changing the system itself. In addition, consider the role of peer support and the importance of role modelling, as Charlotte's friend graduated from the program and showed her it was possible.

10.6 Forensic mental health

Forensic mental health sits in a grey area between the mental health system and the criminal legal system. The main aim of the forensic mental health system is to provide a response to people who are accused of crimes where their mental health causes them to commit crimes or makes it impossible or difficult for them to know that what they were doing was wrong. People in the forensic mental health system often do not have a set release date but are instead released when they are assessed as ready to be released – sometimes this is years after they would have been released if they had gone through the mainstream justice system.

Technically, forensic mental health settings are hospitals, not prisons, although this line is blurred in some cases. In most cases, people cannot be forced to take medication while in mainstream prison and need to be transferred to a forensic mental health hospital or special mental health unit in the prison to be forced to take medication. Forensic mental health is a growth area for social workers as policy-makers grapple with the overrepresentation of people who have been diagnosed with mental illnesses in the criminal legal system. As with the broader population, people in the forensic mental health system are ageing. Women are also a growing cohort.

In general, people in the forensic mental health system are those who were found by a court 'unfit to plead' because of their diagnosis, found by a court 'not guilty by reason of mental impairment' or who are in the general prison system and are transferred to a forensic mental health facility because their mental health has deteriorated. Social workers who work in the forensic mental health system will develop a high-level understanding of forensic mental health law, but for the majority of social workers it is enough to know that the system exists.

Forensic mental health social work is quite distinct from other areas of social work by virtue of its context. Forensic mental health social workers may be trained in physical restraint and be required to participate in 'take down' procedures. This may seem, and is, at odds with social work values of 'respect for the person'[45]. Social workers in forensic mental health systems are often required to grapple with the tension between individual rights and perceived community interest. Social workers should reflect on what they can bring to these roles in coercive environments.

10.7 Youth Justice

Youth justice concerns laws, regulations and policies that respond to criminal offending by young people – usually people aged 10–17.* Youth justice is the responsibility of each individual state and territory and is more a separate justice system than it is a subset of the criminal legal system. The youth justice system is designed to be significantly different from the adult criminal legal system in that it is meant to be focused on rehabilitation and reintegration. The idea is to have a set of systems that prioritise community-based supervision over detention, diversion away from the system, and the integration of family and community. The language used is also different, with the term 'supervision' used to describe young people subject to youth justice orders, and 'youth detention' rather than 'imprisonment'. Young people can be made subject to supervision orders even before they are sentenced, unlike in the adult criminal legal system. One reason that the youth system is so different is that it is supposed to be based on doing what is in the 'best interests' of the child, something hardly considered in the adult justice system. This notion of best interests of the child is discussed in more detail in Chapter 11 but stems from the *Convention on the Rights of the Child*.

Social workers are involved throughout the youth justice systems. This might be running diversionary programs including restorative justice or youth conferencing, working with young people on court orders as youth justice workers, or running programs in youth detention facilities. Social workers will often work with young people who are in contact with the youth justice system in child protection, schools or other youth-focused roles.

Other aspects of youth justice are very similar to the adult justice system. It is still concerned with making people responsible for their behaviour, deterring future offending and community protection.[46] As with the adult system, the population of young people in the youth justice system is disproportionately male and socioeconomically disadvantaged.[47] First Nations people are overrepresented – for most of 2018, *every single child* in youth detention in the Northern Territory was a First Nations child.[48] The main offences are similar to the adult system too – theft, assaults and drug offences – although young people are more likely to be charged for theft, breaking and entering and property damage.[49]

In addition to the *Convention on the Rights of the Child*, there are other United Nations agreements relevant to youth justice legislation and administration:

---

* This is only recently the case in Queensland, which passed the *Youth Justice and Other Legislation (Inclusion of 17-year-old Persons) Amendment Act 2016* (Qld) to raise the age to 17 from 16.

- *Standard Minimum Rules for the Administration of Juvenile Justice 1985* (the Beijing Rules)[50]
- *Guidelines for the Prevention of Juvenile Delinquency 1990* (the Riyadh Guidelines)[51]
- *Standard Minimum Rules for Non-custodial Measures 1990* (the Tokyo Rules)[52]
- *Rules for the Protection of Juveniles Deprived of their Liberty 1990* (the Havana Rules).[53]

The influence of international human rights law can be seen in the focus on rehabilitation in youth justice, which is required by the *Convention on the Rights of the Child* and the *Beijing Rules*. In states or territories with human rights acts these also impact on the functioning of the youth justice system. The influence of international human rights law can also be seen in other protections for children and young people, such as the right not be housed with adult prisoners or the right to have an adult present while being interviewed by the police. Usually, offences committed by a child or young person will not be included on their criminal record as an adult.

There is considerable variation in youth justice systems across Australia, both in the way the law is designed and how it is applied (Table 10.3). For example, in 2016–17, the rate of youth supervision in the Northern Territory was five times higher than in Victoria.[54] Victoria also has a 'dual track' system which means that people who are aged 18–20 can be sentenced to detention in a youth facility rather than an adult prison.

Table 10.3 *Youth justice legislation*

State or territory	**Relevant legislation**
ACT	*Children and Young People Act 2008* (ACT)
NSW	*Young Offenders Act 1997* (NSW)
NT	*Youth Justice Act 2005* (NT)
Qld	*Youth Justice Act 1992* (Qld)
SA	*Young Offenders Act 1993* (SA)
Tas	*Youth Justice Act 1997* (Tas)
Vic	*Children, Youth and Families Act 2005* (Vic)
WA	*Young Offenders Act 1994* (WA)

Generally, youth justice has three main approaches, depending on the seriousness of the offence: diversion, youth justice conferencing and court.

10.7.1 Diversion

Diversion is the process of redirecting young people away from the youth justice system. It can happen at any point in the youth justice system, from the initial contact with police, to pre-plea (before the young person pleads guilty), to post-plea but pre-sentence and post-sentence. For social workers, much of youth justice work is about keeping young people out of the criminal legal system.

The most common form of diversion is when the police give a formal or informal warning or caution. In Queensland, for example, the *Youth Justice Act 1992* authorises police to give a formal caution for some offences. Section 15 reads:

> *(1) A police officer instead of bringing a child before a court for an offence may administer a caution to the child.*
> *(2) The child is then not liable to be prosecuted for the offence.*
> *(3) The caution is not part of the child's criminal history.*

Under this scheme, the child must admit to the offence, consent to being cautioned and may have to write an apology to the victim. A formal caution notice is provided to the child. For First Nations children, a respected person from the community can give the caution instead of the police.

It is important for social workers to understand what police are able to do or required to do in their jurisdiction. Police often have wide jurisdiction in deciding whether to caution or charge a young person, so a social worker who knows the law can apply pressure to police in favour of the person they are working with, keeping them out of the justice system altogether, or refer to legal advice when necessary.

There are also more structured diversionary programs, where young people might be required to engage in drug and alcohol programs or restorative justice. Restorative justice is discussed in Chapter 4. Youth justice conferencing is one of the most common approaches, which sits somewhere between diversion and a formal court process.

10.7.2 Youth justice conferencing

Youth justice conferencing is usually used for offences that are too serious for a warning or caution. Young people may be referred by police or by courts but usually the young person has to agree to participate, and if they do participate they usually receive a lower penalty than otherwise. Usually, the young person has to admit to the offence – if they wish to plead not guilty then the matter must go to court.

A conference will be led by a convenor and can include the young person, their family or support person, the young person's lawyer, the victim, their family or support person and a police officer. In some circumstances it may also include an Elder from the young person's First Nation's, religious or cultural community. In the conference they will talk about what happened, how it impacted the victim, and what can be done to repair the harm done to the victim. Together, they will make a plan including actions which address the offending behaviour and the harm caused by the offending.

Usually, if the conference convenor assesses that the conference has been successful they will then make a report back to the court and the judge or magistrate may impose a less severe penalty than would otherwise have been imposed. If the child or young person does not complete the plan there may be consequences, depending on the jurisdiction.

10.7.3 Children's Courts

Criminal charges concerning young people are usually heard in a specialist children's court, although for serious offences they can sometimes be heard in a higher court before a judge and jury. Children's courts are usually less formal than adult courts but otherwise are similar to other courts. Children's courts generally have a broader range of sentencing options, and in some jurisdictions courts are restricted from imposing harsher sentences where a less harsh sentence is appropriate.[55] Victoria, for example, has a 'sentencing hierarchy' that is illustrated in Figure 10.3:

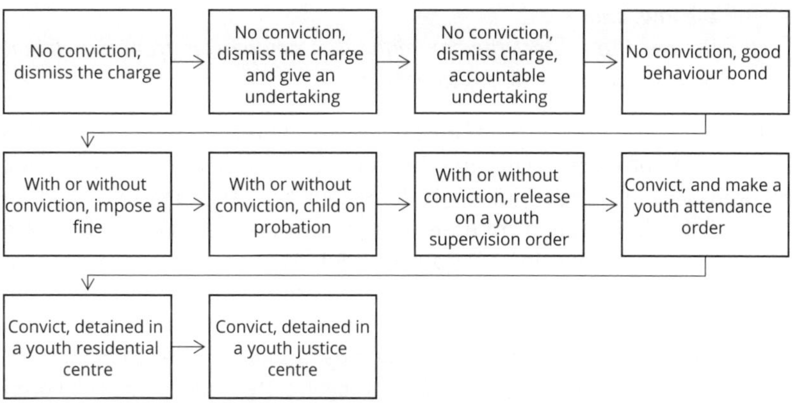

Figure 10.3 *Victoria's youth justice sentencing hierarchy*

This approach is quite different from the approach taken in the adult system. Not all jurisdictions have the same approach, but Victoria's approach to sentencing is a good illustration of how youth justice can be done differently from adult justice. When an adult is sentenced in Victoria, the court must consider the sentencing principles in section 5(1) of the *Sentencing Act 1991* (Vic):

a) to punish the offender to an extent and in a manner which is just in all of the circumstances; or
b) to deter the offender or other persons from committing offences of the same or a similar character; or
c) to establish conditions within which it is considered by the court that the rehabilitation of the offender may be facilitated; or

d) *to manifest the denunciation by the court of the type of conduct in which the offender engaged; or*
e) *to protect the community from the offender.*

Compare this to matters to be taken into account for youth justice sentencing, in section 362(1) of the *Children, Youth and Families Act 2005* (Vic):

a) *the need to strengthen and preserve the relationship between the child and the child's family; and*
b) *the desirability of allowing the child to live at home; and*
c) *the desirability of allowing the education, training or employment of the child to continue without interruption or disturbance; and*
d) *the need to minimise the stigma to the child resulting from a court determination; and*
e) *the suitability of the sentence to the child; and*
f) *if appropriate, the need to ensure that the child is aware that he or she must bear a responsibility for any action by him or her against the law; and*
g) *the need to protect the community, or any person, from the violent or other wrongful acts of the child.*

Compare these two. There are similarities, with community protection featuring in both, but significant differences in the way the law tries to link children back into their families and communities. The idea that children can and should be rehabilitated is also seen in the way the youth justice system prioritises diversion over punishment. As social workers, we should consider why we think that this approach is used with children and young people and not with adults. The level of community understanding and acceptance of children who commit crimes is much higher than that for adults, yet many adults in the criminal legal system were once children who were not given every advantage in life. Social workers should reflect on why it is seen as fair and just to treat a child as needing reintegration and not punishment, and why for adults who commit certain crimes we are far less sympathetic.

10.8 Conclusion

The criminal legal system can be a complex space for a social worker to operate within. The criminal legal system is mainly experienced by disadvantaged and oppressed people who may also have been the victims of crime, as well as people with mental health issues or cognitive disabilities. Social workers have an opportunity to respectfully engage with people in the criminal legal system, to assist people to access community supports and to stay out of this system, as well as work towards systemic reform to provide therapeutic rather than punitive responses to vulnerable people.

Main points

1. Supporting victims can include: working with families and other persons impacted by the harm; helping victims who feel intimidated by the justice system; and assisting victims who feel unsatisfied with the justice process.
2. The court process is designed to respond to offenders, not help victims in their recovery. A social worker working in this setting can work to create space for the victim to be heard and advocated for.
3. Many people who have been accused and convicted of crimes have overlapping layers of oppression, trauma and discrimination that may have led to coming into contact with the criminal legal system.
4. Social workers have a role to play at most stages of the criminal legal system: pre-contact; arrest and charge; bail and remand; the court process; prisons; parole; and post-release reintegration. All stages are with a view to provide therapeutic and culturally sensitive responses.
5. Social workers play an important role within the prison setting by helping people in prison to prepare for reintegration into the community.
6. All states and territories have sentencing options that allow people to serve their sentence in the community rather than in prison.
7. Social workers may work in forensic mental health, which is a system designed to respond to people accused of crimes where their mental health causes them to commit the crime or prevents them from identifying that what they were doing was wrong.
8. The focus in youth justice is on rehabilitation and reintegration, rather than punishment, which significantly impacts the type of sentences given to young offenders.
9. Generally, youth justice has three approaches to offending: diversion; youth justice conferencing; and children's courts.

Discussion questions

1. Find the relevant legislation on sentencing in your jurisdiction and locate the provision that discusses the 'purposes of sentencing'. Should sentencing favour retribution? Deterrence? Rehabilitation? Restoration? Or should sentencing be a balancing act of all 'purposes'? How is it different for young people?
2. What rights do children and young people have in the criminal legal system that are not given to adults? Where are these rights found in your jurisdiction? Look in the state or territory youth justice

legislation, in the local human rights act (if one exists in your jurisdiction) and in common law.

3. What can social workers do to respond to the growing numbers of people in prisons and what other ways are there of thinking about this issue?
4. How can social workers utilise a critical or structural lens for looking at the criminal legal system?

Further reading

Brian Stout, *Community Justice in Australia: Developing Knowledge, Skills and Values for Working with Offenders in the Community* (Allen & Unwin, 2016).

Australian Institute of Health and Welfare, *The Health of Australia's Prisoners 2015* (Australian Institute of Health and Welfare, 2015).

Chris Cunneen, 'Young People and Juvenile Justice', in Lisa Young, Mary Anne Kenny and Geoff Monahan (eds) *Children and the Law in Australia*, 2nd ed. (LexisNexis Butterworths, 2016).

10.9 References

---

[1] Jane Fenton, 'An Analysis of "Ethical Stress" in Criminal Justice Social Work in Scotland: The Place of Values' (2015) 45(5) *British Journal of Social Work* 1415.

[2] UN General Assembly, *International Covenant on Civil and Political Rights*, 16 December 1966, United Nations, Treaty Series, vol. 999, p. 171.

[3] UN General Assembly, *Convention on the Rights of the Child*, 20 November 1989, United Nations, Treaty Series, vol. 1577, p. 3.

[4] UN General Assembly, *Convention Against Torture and Other Cruel, Inhuman or Degrading Treatment or Punishment*, 10 December 1984, United Nations, Treaty Series, vol. 1465, p. 85.

[5] UN General Assembly, *Convention on the Rights of Persons with Disabilities: resolution/adopted by the General Assembly*, 24 January 2007, A/RES/61/106.

[6] United Nations, *Standard Minimum Rules for the Treatment of Prisoners*, 30 August 1955.

[7] UN Commission on Human Rights, *Body of Principles for the Protection of all Persons Under any Form of Detention or Imprisonment*, 7 March 1978, E/CN.4/RES/19(XXXIV).

[8] UN General Assembly, *Basic Principles for the Treatment of Prisoners: resolution/ adopted by the General Assembly*, 28 March 1991, A/RES/45/111.

[9] UN General Assembly, *United Nations Standard Minimum Rules for Non-Custodial Measures (The Tokyo Rules): resolution/adopted by the General Assembly*, 2 April 1991, A/RES/45/110.

[10] *Crime Statistics Australia* (Australian Institute of Criminology, 2019) <http: //crimestats.aic.gov.au/facts_figures>.

[11] 'Witness Assistance Service', *Office of the Director of Public Prosecutions* (2011) <https://www.dpp.sa.gov.au/was/witnesses/witness-assistance-service/>.

[12] Mandy Wilson et al, 'Violence in the Lives of Incarcerated Aboriginal Mothers in Western Australia' (2017) 7(1) *SAGE Open* 215824401668681.
[13] AASW, *Code of Ethics* (Australian Association of Social Workers, 2010).
[14] Australian Institute of Health and Welfare, *The Health of Australia's Prisoners 2015* (Australian Institute of Health and Welfare, 2015) <http://www.aihw.gov.au/publication-detail/?id=60129553527>.
[15] Martin Jackson et al, *Acquired Brain Injury in the Victorian Prison System* (No 04, Corrections Victoria, 2011).
[16] Australian Bureau of Statistics, '4517.0 – Prisoners in Australia, 2018' (6 December 2018) <http://www.abs.gov.au/ausstats/abs@.nsf/Lookup/by%20Subject/4517.0~2018~Main%20Features~Prisoner%20characteristics,%20Australia~4>.
[17] Bree Carlton, *Women Exiting Prison: Critical Essays on Gender, Post-Release Support and Survival* (Routledge, 2013).
[18] Stacy Tzoumakis, Melanie Burton and Vaughan J Carr, 'Parental Offending and Children's Conduct Problems' 13.
[19] *Young People in Child Protection and under Youth Justice Supervision 2015–16* (Australian Institute of Health and Welfare, 2017) <https://www.aihw.gov.au/reports/youth-justice/young-people-in-youth-justice-supervision-2015-16/contents/table-of-contents>.
[20] Jessica Wolpaw Reyes, 'Environmental Policy as Social Policy? The Impact of Childhood Lead Exposure on Crime' 43; Anna Aizer and Janet Currie, *Lead and Juvenile Delinquency: New Evidence from Linked Birth, School and Juvenile Detention Records* (Working Paper No 23392, National Bureau of Economic Research, 2017) 61.
[21] Anna Stewart, Susan Dennison and Elissa Waterson, *Pathways from Child Maltreatment to Juvenile Offending* (Australian Institute of Criminology, 3 November 2017) <https://aic.gov.au/publications/tandi/tandi241>.
[22] Australian Institute of Health and Welfare (n 14).
[23] Julie Moschion and Guy Johnson, 'Homelessness and Incarceration: A Reciprocal Relationship?' [2019] *Journal of Quantitative Criminology* <http://link.springer.com/10.1007/s10940-019-09407-y>.
[24] *Report on Government Services 2018* (Productivity Commission, 25 January 2018) 20 <https://www.pc.gov.au/research/ongoing/report-on-government-services/2018/justice>.
[25] *Infringements Act 2006* (Vic) s22.
[26] *Pathways to Justice – an Inquiry into the Incarceration Rate of Aboriginal and Torres Strait Islander Peoples: Final Report* (Australian Law Reform Commission, 2017).
[27] See, for example, *Evidence Act 1995* (NSW) s 89A.
[28] *Police Powers and Responsibilities Act 2000* (Qld) s 431.
[29] Victoria Police Operating Procedure 4.6.3.2.
[30] Don Weatherburn et al, 'The NSW Drug Court: A Re-Evaluation of Its Effectiveness' (2008) 121 *Crime and Justice Bulletin* 16.
[31] *Sentencing of Federal Offenders* (Discussion Paper No 70, Australian Law Reform Commission, 2005) <http://www.austlii.edu.au/au/other/lawreform/ALRCDP/2005/70.html>.
[32] *Crime Statistics Australia* (n 10).
[33] Australian Bureau of Statistics (n 16).
[34] J. Rynne and R. Harding, 'Private Prisons' (Taylor and Francis Inc, 2016).
[35] Australian Associated Press, 'Queensland to End Private Jails Experiment after Scathing Report', *The Guardian* (online at 25 March 2019) <https://www.theguardian.com/australia-news/2019/mar/26/queensland-to-end-private-jails-experiment-after-scathing-report>.
[36] *Crime Statistics Australia* (n 10).
[37] Anthony Morgan, 'How Much Does Prison Really Cost?' 84.
[38] There is a lot of academic literature on this topic, but for an easy to read overview see Rachel Kushner, 'Is Prison Necessary? Ruth Wilson Gilmore Might Change Your Mind',

The New York Times (online at 17 April 2019) <https://www.nytimes.com/2019/04/17/magazine/prison-abolition-ruth-wilson-gilmore.html>.

[39] *Crime Statistics Australia* (n 10).

[40] *Pathways to Justice – an Inquiry into the Incarceration Rate of Aboriginal and Torres Strait Islander Peoples: Final Report* (n 26).

[41] Joanna J.J. Wang and Suzanne Poynton, *Intensive Correction Orders versus Short Prison Sentence: A Comparison of Re-Offending* (New South Wales, Bureau of Crime Statistics, October 2017) 1 <https://search.proquest.com/docview/1960971755/abstract/8D8671CD26814B45PQ/1>.

[42] Department for Correctional Services, 'What a Social Worker Does', *Government of South Australia* <https://www.corrections.sa.gov.au/careers/Working-with-prisoners-and-offenders/social-workers>.

[43] Matthew Willis, 'Supported Housing for Prisoners Returning to the Community' 51.

[44] Tamara Tulich, *Post-Sentence Preventative Detention and Extended Supervision of High Risk Offenders in New South Wales* (SSRN Scholarly Paper No ID 2660057, Social Science Research Network, 2015) <https://papers.ssrn.com/abstract=2660057>.

[45] AASW (n 13).

[46] Chris Cunneen, 'Young People and Juvenile Justice' in Lisa Young, Mary Anne Kenny and Geoff Monahan (eds), *Children and the Law in Australia* 2nd ed. (LexisNexis Butterworths, 2016).

[47] *Youth Justice in Australia 2016–17* (Australian Institute of Health and Welfare, 2018) 54.

[48] Territory Families, *Youth Detention Census* (Northern Territory Government, 2018).

[49] *Youth Justice in Australia 2016–17* (n 47).

[50] UN General Assembly, United Nations Standard Minimum Rules for the Administration of Juvenile Justice ('The Beijing Rules'): resolution/adopted by the General Assembly, 29 November 1985, A/RES/40/33.

[51] UN General Assembly, United Nations Guidelines for the Prevention of Juvenile Delinquency ('The Riyadh Guidelines'): resolution/adopted by the General Assembly, 14 December 1990, A/RES/45/112.

[52] UN General Assembly, United Nations Standard Minimum Rules for Non-Custodial Measures (The Tokyo Rules): resolution/adopted by the General Assembly, 2 April 1991, A/RES/45/110.

[53] UN General Assembly, United Nations Rules for the Protection of Juveniles Deprived of Their Liberty: resolution/adopted by the General Assembly, 2 April 1991, A/RES/45/113.

[54] *Youth Justice in Australia 2016–17* (n 47).

[55] See, for example, *Children (Criminal Proceedings) Act 1987* (NSW) s33 or *Children, Youth and Families Act 2005* (Vic) s 361.

Chapter 11 FAMILIES, CHILDREN AND YOUNG PEOPLE

Francis Zemljak and Chris Maylea

Magistrate Zemljak was appointed in July 2008 and has been at the Children's Court of Victoria since then. Prior to his appointment he specialised in family law and held a number of part time appointments including to the Guardianship and Administration Board, VCAT, the Victorian Child Death Review Committee and the Medical Practitioners Board. He was accredited by the Law Institute of Victoria as both a Specialist in Family Law and as a Specialist in Children's Law.

Families, children and young people can come into contact with the law in many ways, but the areas most relevant to social workers are family law (regarding divorce, property and parenting orders), usually heard in the Family Court or the Federal Circuit Court, family violence and child abuse, which is mainly dealt with in the criminal legal system, and child protection, which is usually heard in state and territory children's courts.[*] Despite the difference in jurisdictions, these issues will often overlap in practice. For example; family violence will sometimes constitute child abuse, which will trigger child protection involvement and may lead to separation and divorce. There is also overlap with youth justice; children who are in child protection are 12 times more likely to be under youth justice supervision than the general population, and children under youth justice supervision are 12 times more likely to be involved in the child protection system.[1] Social workers will be involved in every step of the process, as counsellors helping couples navigate relationship challenges, as family violence workers helping survivors rebuild their lives, as child protection practitioners investigating child abuse and as youth workers helping young people make good choices.

There are fundamental differences in the way these laws operate. Family law is private law; it governs the relationships between two or more parties. Child protection is public law; it governs the relationship between the person and the state. This is important to understand because if a person breaches a family law order, it is up to the other party to point out

[*] This is the case because, as discussed in Chapter 2, the Commonwealth has the power under section 51(xxi) of the *Constitution* to make laws about marriage, but does not have the power to make laws about child protection.

this breach and use the legal system to uphold their own rights. If a person breaches a child protection order, it is the responsibility of the state to step in and correct the breach.

Another difference in the different areas of law is how the different concepts are defined. For example, a 'child' or 'young person' can differ significantly by jurisdiction and by legislation. The 'age of majority' or the age a person is an adult is 18 years, but different age limits govern the age at which children and young people can open a bank account, consent to medical treatment, have sex or learn to drive. Even in one area of law, such as the law to consent to sex, the age can vary depending on who is doing what with whom. For example, in Tasmania, the age of consent to sex is 17 years, but for people aged 12–14 it is not a crime if that person has sex with a person three years older, or if a person is aged 15 or 16 it is not a crime if that person has sex with a person five years older, so long as both parties consent.[2] Similarly, it is not always clear what a 'parent' is. In 2019 the High Court ruled that sometimes, but not always, sperm donors may be legal parents.[3] Social workers need to be aware of the relevant definitions and how they apply to the areas they work in.

There are some commonalities across these areas of law, the most obvious being that the aims of most of these areas of law are to promote the 'best interests of the child'. This phrase comes from the *Convention on the Rights of the Child*.[4] Article 3 states that:

> *In all actions concerning children, whether undertaken by public or private social welfare institutions, courts of law, administrative authorities or legislative bodies, the best interests of the child shall be a primary consideration.*

The phrase 'best interests of the child' appears in 76 pieces of Australian legislation, in relation to topics including child protection, youth justice, parenting, divorce, adoption, surrogacy, family violence, corrections, education, anti-discrimination, citizenship, guardianship, disability, mental health and criminal law.[*] This principle of the best interests of the child is actually a relatively new idea and not without controversy. Historically, children were seen as the property of the father,[5] and still today there is a tension between 'parental rights' and the 'best interests' of the child. There is also the question of which of the interests should be prioritised – should the focus be on the child's immediate happiness or immediate safety, their long-term success or some other priority, such as their religious or moral education? Critics sometimes argue that the wide discretion this principle affords allows decision makers, including judges, magistrates and social workers, to impose their

[*] You can see where it appears in legislation in your jurisdiction by searching for 'best interests of the child' on austlii.edu.au.

own idea of what 'best interests' should be.[6] Despite this criticism, the principle does allow for both community standards and contemporary understandings of development, such as attachment theory, to be considered when making decisions about children. All decision-makers, judges, magistrates and social workers alike, bring their own worldview to the decisions they make, but most professionals will strive to be guided by the evidence before them rather than their own personal views on what is 'best'. The multiple checks and balances of the legal system also protect families from having one single person dictate outcomes, with oversight processes built into government decision-making processes, appeals to higher courts and the opportunity to revisit matters multiple times. Ultimately, for children, the best-interests principle seems to be the best possible approach we have available, and it is required by international law.

The other key documents of international law are:

- *International Covenant on Civil and Political Rights* (ICCPR)[7]
- *International Covenant on Economic, Social and Cultural Rights* (ICESCR)[8]
- *Convention on the Elimination of All Forms of Discrimination against Women* (CEDAW)[9]
- *Hague Convention on the Protection of Children and Co-operation in Respect of Intercountry Adoption (Child Protection Convention).*[10]

These documents all cover the rights of families, women and children. International legal documents are rarely referred to in the day-to-day running of families and young people's legal processes, but their influence can be seen in the relevant legislation.

In the rest of this chapter, we examine three of these key areas of law concerning families, children and young people: family law, child protection and family violence. At the time of writing (2019), there are several proposals under consideration for reform of the family law, family violence and child protection legal systems, so social workers must use the legal research skills from Chapter 3 to ensure their knowledge is current.

11.1 Family law

The term 'family law', when used in the Australian context, refers to the laws governing marriage, divorce, parenting orders, property settlement and spousal maintenance. It is mostly governed by the *Family Law Act 1975* (Cth) (*Family Law Act)*. Cases under the *Family Law Act* are mostly heard by the Family Court or the Federal Circuit Court, but in Western Australia there is a separate Family Court of Western Australia.*

* This section will not address the Western Australian context although many characteristics are the same and the Family Court of Western Australia still uses the

The *Family Law Act* applies to both legally married and de facto relationships, and to parents who have never been in a family relationship.[*] Polygamous marriages entered into overseas are also included, although polygamy is not permitted under Australian law.[11] Marriages are governed by the *Marriage Act 1961* (Cth) but separation and divorce are governed by the *Family Law Act*. Australia has 'no-fault' divorce, which means either party in a couple can get a divorce if they want to. The only requirement is that the two people are 'separated' for at least 12 months and that there is no reasonable likelihood of resuming married life.[12] A couple may be 'separated' and still live together.[13]

For many divorcing couples, this is the extent to which they engage with the law. They will separate for 12 months then apply to the court for a divorce. If there are no children or property, or if they can agree on what to do with their children or property, no further legal processes are required. Family law is required when divorcing couples cannot agree about children or property.

11.1.1 Family dispute resolution

The *Family Law Act 1975* (Cth) has a focus on resolving disputes before the matter gets to court. This is based on the idea that involving children and families in litigation can be harmful, costly and in many cases make the conflict worse. Social workers can play a key role in mediating disputes both formally and informally, reducing the harm that can result in drawn out and expensive litigation.

Much family dispute resolution is undertaken by *family counsellors* or *family dispute resolution practitioners* in Family Relationship Services or similar services outside the court. Matters can usually only progress to court if families have already undergone family dispute resolution. When matters do progress to court, the judges are assisted by *family consultants* who work with families to resolve their disputes. Family consultants also conduct assessments and write reports for the court and provide information to the court. Social workers can become family counsellors, family dispute resolution practitioners or family consultants if they meet the requirements as defined by the *Family Law Act* and relevant regulations.

Family Law Act 1975 (Cth). For detail on the situation in Western Australia and on the *Family Court Act 1997* (WA) go to: <https://www.familycourt.wa.gov.au/F/family_court_legislation.aspx>.

[*] This might include brief sexual encounters, sperm donor arrangements, surrogacy arrangements. There is an ongoing debate about what exactly constitutes a 'parent', as discussed at the end of this chapter.

***Box 11.1** Litigation guardians*

Sometimes the family law or child protection intervention results from a person being admitted to a mental health service. When a person 'lacks capacity' (see Chapter 13) courts can sometimes appoint a litigation guardian. *The litigation guardian can represent the person. This is different to just getting a lawyer to represent the person, as the litigation guardian does not require instructions on what to do. Social workers should be aware of this so a person's rights can be upheld in legal proceedings.*

11.1.2 Children

Legally, when parents can make decisions about their children, they are said to have 'parental responsibility'.[14] Unless there is a court order to the contrary, parental responsibility is shared between both parents.[15] In some cases, such as when parents separate or divorce, there are sometimes disputes about who will have parental responsibility and other decisions about children, such as how much time they spend with each parent or where they will live. If parents agree on what should happen with the children the court does not need to get involved. If they want to, they can complete a parenting plan, which is not legally binding, or they can apply for 'consent orders'. Consent orders are used where parents agree on what should happen, but might not trust each other to do what they have agreed to do. The court will assess them, and if the plans are in the best interests of the child the court can approve them, making them legally binding.

If parents cannot agree they will be directed into family dispute resolution. If dispute resolution fails, the court can make parenting orders about parental responsibility. Either of the child's parents, the child, grandparents or any other person concerned with the care, welfare or development of the child can apply for a parenting order.[16]

These orders can cover anything to do with the care, welfare and development of the children, including whom children will live with, how much time they have with various people, including parents and grandparents, and who will have parental responsibility for the children. When making a parenting order the court must have the child's best interests as the paramount consideration.[17] Section 60CC of the *Family Law Act* outlines all of the different things which the court should consider when determining a child's best interests, including:

> *a. the benefit to the child of having a meaningful relationship with both of the child's parents; and*
>
> *b. the need to protect the child from physical or psychological harm from being subjected to, or exposed to, abuse, neglect or family violence.*

There are additional considerations in section 60CC, too many to list here, but they include the views of the child, parents and other relevant people, how much the parents have participated in the child's life and any lifestyle, culture and traditions the court thinks are relevant. The court can appoint an independent children's lawyer to represent the child's best interests to the court.

Once a parenting order is in place it is legally binding. Circumstances can change over time and it is not unusual for parents to apply to the court for changes in parenting orders. Orders can also be appealed in some circumstances. Social workers can play a key role in helping people understand this and manage their expectations, for example by helping them plan what they need to do to have parental responsibility restored. This might include seeking mental health support, engaging in drug and alcohol treatment or men's behaviour change programs. Social workers can turn a 'bad result' for a person into a catalyst for change and support them to achieve the result they had hoped for.

If a party breaches an order the court may impose a range of penalties ranging from changing the original order to fines and imprisonment. Parents sometimes try to take children away, either so the court cannot make an order or in breach of an existing order. If this happens the other parent can apply for a location or recovery order. A location order requires people or organisations to provide information to locate the child and a recovery order allows police to find and recover the child. If there is a parenting order in place it may be an offence to take or send a child out of Australia if the other party does not agree.

11.1.3 Property

As with children, if a couple can agree on how to share their property in a divorce or separation then the court does not need to be involved. Similarly, if they can come to an agreement in dispute resolution they can get consent orders about property. The court will only make consent orders if it is convinced the orders are fair.

If a couple cannot agree, the court can make orders about how property is shared, including real estate, bank accounts, businesses, superannuation and spousal maintenance. Social workers tend to have more to do with children in the family law process, rather than property disputes, but it is important that they are able to access information about it and refer to a lawyer as appropriate, particularly if one party might be taking advantage of the other. It is not unheard of for perpetrators of family violence to use the court process to continue their abuse, which can make it hard for survivors to get what they are entitled to. Social workers should make sure that people they work with get their fair share in this process.

11.1.4 Child support

As with parenting orders and property orders, if parents can agree about child support the court does not need to be involved. If the parents disagree, the Commonwealth Department of Human Services have a formula that is used to determine which parent should pay and how much they should pay. This is all governed by the *Child Support (Registration and Collection) Act 1988* (Cth) and the *Child Support (Assessment) Act 1989* (Cth). Some children, such as those with a disability who are over 18 or stepchildren, may not be covered by this legislation and instead, the Federal Circuit Court or Family Court may make a child maintenance order in these situations. Decisions made by the Department of Human Services about child support can be reviewed internally by the department or in some cases by the Administrative Appeals Tribunal.

Child support can be collected privately or through the Department of Human Services. If the person who is required to pay stops paying, it is usually easier to enforce the collection of child support if it is done through the Department of Human Services than if it is done privately. For social workers working with people receiving child support it can be useful to double check how this has been arranged, as they may be entitled to more than they are receiving or may be able to enforce collection for unpaid amounts.

11.2 CHILD PROTECTION

There is a lot of overlap between the family law and the child protection system. Despite this, family law is nearly all Commonwealth legislation, while child protection is the responsibility of each state and territory.* Each state and territory has a different legislative framework for child protection and each piece of child protection legislation interlinks with other legislative frameworks, including youth justice, adoption, family violence and mandatory reporting.[18] Generally, child protection orders will take priority over family law orders, although social workers should direct the person to a lawyer if they have both orders as the legislation is complex.[19] The Australian Institute of Family Studies lists 90 distinct pieces of legislation relevant to child protection across Australia.[20] Each jurisdiction is a bit different, but all require that the 'best interests of the child' are paramount in all decision-making.[21]

Below the overarching 'best-interests' principle, the aims of the law in each jurisdiction are the same; to protect children from harm, to keep children with their families where possible and to provide care for them

---

* As noted above, this is because section 51(xxi) of the *Constitution* gives the Commonwealth the power to make laws about marriage, but not the power to make laws about child protection.

when it is not possible. All jurisdictions have three main stages: a preventative stage where services try and address any issues with the family, an intervention stage where the courts may make orders while the issues are being sorted out, and a final stage where the child is placed long term. These stages do not always happen in this order as sometimes emergency legal intervention is required and often long-term placements break down. The Australian Institutes of Family Studies has produced a resource that breaks down the law in each jurisdiction.[22]

Social workers are involved throughout these stages. As discussed in Chapter 6, social workers will often facilitate the first involvement a child has with the child protection system if they report voluntarily or under a mandatory reporting scheme.* Often social workers will work in early intervention programs, helping families to overcome obstacles that would otherwise result in child protection involvement. Social workers will often work as child protection workers who investigate child protection incidents, provide support to families, take matters to a children's court if necessary, supervise children on court orders and organise accommodation, specialist supports, adoption and permanent care. In contrast with England and Canada, in Australia not all child protection workers are social workers, with many psychologists or human services workers working as child protection workers.[23]

11.2.1 'Early' intervention

Removing children from their families should be something that is done only as a last resort, so all states and territories have agreed to provide early intervention services to prevent children coming into contact with child protection systems.[24] These are generally outside the legal system but become part of the experience of the child protection system as families are often required to work with early intervention services under the threat of involving statutory child protection services if they refuse.

Early intervention really includes the whole health and welfare system, including housing and homelessness, mental health, disability, family violence and education. As Figure 11.1 shows, the statutory end of the child protection system is only a small portion of the service system.

Some risks to children are easier to intervene early than others. Neglect in the context of poverty or homelessness, for example, may be easier to highlight earlier than later. Other risks, such as sexual abuse, may not become apparent until long after the abuse has been perpetrated, and no amount of social services intervention may be sufficient to protect children.

---

* Mandatory reporting is covered in detail in Chapter 6 as mandatory reporting requirements are not limited to child protection.

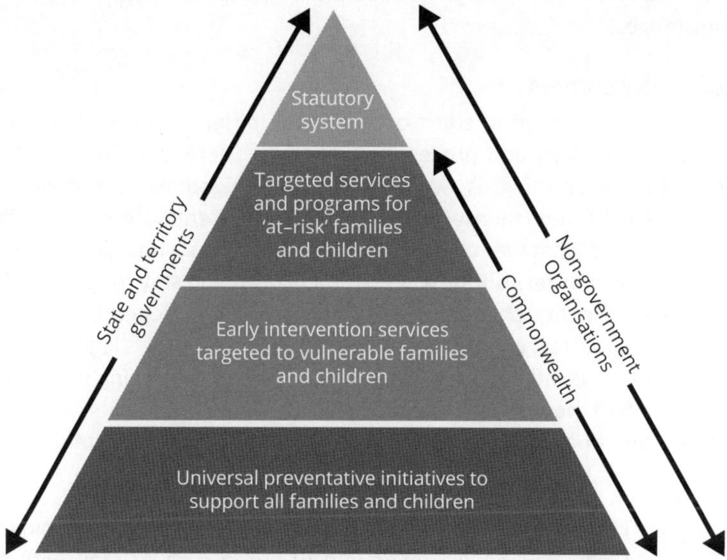

Figure 11.1 *A system for protecting children*[25]

11.2.2 When is a child in need of protection?

Ordinarily, health, welfare and other support services can only be provided with the agreement of the parents or primary caregiver of a child. Child protection law provides a way for those services to be provided without the agreement of the parents and for children to be removed as a last resort. If a child is abandoned or their carers die, the state must ensure that they are cared for. This becomes more difficult to navigate if the parents or primary carers are still present and do not agree that the child is in need of protection. In these cases, the law provides a process for intervention and a threshold test for determining if a child is in need of protection.

The different jurisdictions have different ways of framing when child protection services can legally intervene in the life of a child or young person. This is variously written in the legislation as 'in need of care', 'in need of protection', 'in need of care and protection', 'at risk' or 'at risk of harm'. What this means in practice is slightly different too. For example, in New South Wales (NSW) or Tasmania, a child is automatically 'at risk' or 'at 'at risk of significant harm' in an environment where 'domestic violence' is present. In other jurisdictions, the child must be shown to have been at risk of or experienced some other kind of harm as a result of violence.

In the event that a child is found to be in need of protection, they are not necessarily immediately removed from the family. Courts will only remove children when it is necessary to do so and in the best interests of the child. Courts have a range of orders they can make depending on the circumstances.

11.2.3 Court orders

There are a wide range of court orders in the different jurisdictions, with different terminology and processes. Generally, there is an initial holding phase while everything is worked out, investigations are done and evidence is collected, then a phase where the parents are given a 'final chance' to make whatever changes are required, then a final period where the court makes orders about where the children will stay long term. This process can repeat, change or stop at any time depending on the circumstances. Often child protection is linked into other legal matters, and the process is influenced by those, such as a parent being imprisoned or admitted to a mental health service.

Child protection orders can be grouped into four main types of orders[26]:

- Interim and temporary orders
    - Usually used while a court process or investigation is ongoing
    - Child may be placed in out-of-home care or stay with the parents
- Finalised supervisory orders
    - The child is supervised by the state or territory department and the department can make decisions about the child
    - The child usually stays with the parents
    - Guardianship of the child is unaffected
- Finalised guardianship or custody orders
    - Transfer legal guardianship to the state or territory department or non-government agency
    - Can be short term (less than two years) or long term (more than two years)
- Finalised third-party parental responsibility orders
    - Transfer legal guardianship to a third party, such as a relative
    - Can be short term (less than two years) or long-term (more than two years).

A court may make a number of different orders over the course of a child's engagement with the child protection system. This might start with a temporary order that requires one parent to have no contact with the child while the department investigates claims of abuse, then change to a supervisory order to give the parents a chance to demonstrate they are able to care for the child. This might include a requirement that they are drug-free for a certain period, and they may be required to provide drug test results to the court. If they are not able to demonstrate this, the court may make a finalised third-party order for the child to live with a grandparent. At the end of this order, if the parents are still not able to demonstrate they can care for the child, the court may make a long-term order for the child to stay with the grandparent until they are 18.

Social workers often play a role in this process by writing reports for the court. This might be an assessment of the parent's parenting skills, of risks to the child from other family members or a report on a parent's progression through a drug treatment program. These reports form a vital part of the court's decision-making and are a key skill for social workers in many areas of practice. Writing court reports is discussed in more detail in Chapter 7.

Remember, the court is always trying to determine what is in the best interests of the child. This requires finding a balance between keeping the child with the parents and finding a permanent home for the child. Sometimes the court will order that these reports are done, other times reports are requested by one of the parties to the case (the parent or one of the parents) to support their side of the case. Social workers are crucial to providing the court with the information it needs to make this decision.

First Nations children are significantly overrepresented in the child protection system and are nearly ten times more likely to be placed into out-of-home care than children of settler families.[27] Social workers have a key role to play in addressing the poverty, intergenerational trauma, discrimination and cultural misunderstandings that have led to this situation. One way in which the law attempts to address this issue is with the Aboriginal and Torres Strait Islander Child Placement Principle. This seeks to place First Nations children in First Nations families wherever possible. This is discussed in detail in Chapter 12.

11.3 Family violence

More than half of women killed worldwide in 2017 died at the hands of a partner or relative[28] and one in six Australian women over the age of 15 have experienced physical and/or sexual violence by a current or previous partner.[29] Men also experience family violence, but at much lower rates. It is generally accepted that while the law has a role to play, ending family violence will require a shift in social attitudes, not just better legislation or more policing. Despite this, social workers will often work with people who require the protection of the law and with people who perpetrate family violence. Assisting people to navigate this legal system is a common social work task.

Often, family violence will also involve criminal offending, for example in cases of physical or sexual assault. Other times it may not be criminal offending, for example in cases of psychological or financial abuse. Sometimes there will be insufficient evidence of family violence for a criminal conviction (which requires proof *beyond a reasonable doubt*) but sufficient evidence for a court to decide that a person should not be allowed contact with a child or another person (which is civil law and can be decided on the *balance of probabilities*). Criminal law, family law and child protection all respond *after* an incident has occurred and do little to prevent the incident occurring in the first place. This has led to the development of family violence protection orders specifically aimed at addressing and preventing family violence.

Supporting survivors of family violence is as much about understanding the legal system as it is about understanding the law. For example, most courts have safe rooms where people can wait so they do not see their perpetrator prior to the hearing. In some cases they may be able to appear via video link. If social workers know about these protections, they will be better placed to help people feel safe about going court and escaping the cycle of violence.

11.3.1 What is family violence?

There is no standard definition of family violence under Australian law and any definition is open to some level of interpretation. Not all conflict in intimate or family relationships is family violence, so the law needs to draw the line at some point. There is a long list of things that *might* be included in definitions of family violence, but the definition in each jurisdiction varies:

- Physical violence or abuse
- Sexual abuse
- Reproductive abuse
- Economic and financial abuse
- Emotional abuse
- Psychological abuse
- Cultural abuse
- Spiritual abuse
- Social abuse
- Technology abuse
- Stalking
- Harassment
- Exposing children to family violence
- Damaging property
- Animal abuse
- Forced marriage

The definition of 'family' can also vary, but generally includes immediate and extended family, de-facto and former partners. It will usually include elder abuse perpetrated by a family member.

11.3.2 Family violence orders

People affected by family violence can apply to a court for an order to protect them from family violence.* In some circumstances, police might apply for a family violence order, which means it is not always up to the person affected by violence to decide if an order is put in place or not. If a

* There are also other violence protection orders that are not family violence protection orders, which are not covered here. They include orders that may be used in cases of stalking, neighbour disputes, school bullying or violence in the workplace.

person wants to apply for an order or is made subject to an order it is always a good idea to assist them in getting legal advice. In some jurisdictions, people can apply online rather than applying in person at the court, although they will usually have to go to court for a hearing anyway. These are civil orders – the burden of proof is the balance of probabilities (more likely than not). These orders are called different things in different jurisdictions:

- Apprehended Domestic Violence Orders (NSW)
- Domestic Violence Orders (ACT & NT)
- Family Violence Orders (Tas)
- Intervention Orders (Vic & SA)
- Protection Orders (Qld)
- Violence Restraining Orders (WA).

These orders can include a range of conditions, which vary by jurisdiction (Table 11.1). They can require a person to stop doing family violence, to contact or stalk or go near a person, to stay away from certain places or to prevent a person from damaging property. They can include 'exclusion orders' so that the perpetrator is required to stay away from the shared residence, allowing the victim to stay at home. These orders are designed to be flexible to meet the needs of different circumstances, and so can include restrictions regarding children or pets. They can also be changed or revoked, although usually this will require going back to court. These are civil law orders and so do not by themselves result in a criminal record, but if a person breaches the conditions in a family violence order this may be a criminal offence. Social workers can assist people in complying with these orders and staying clear of the criminal legal system. Be aware that it may be a criminal offence for *either* party to breach the conditions – even for the person who applied for the order. Criminal offences must be proven *beyond a reasonable doubt.* This means a court may find it is more likely than not that the violence occurred and make a family violence order, but another court may still find the person not guilty of a crime.

Table 11.1 *Family violence legislation*

Jurisdiction	**Relevant legislation**
ACT	*Domestic Violence and Protection Orders Act 2008* (ACT)
NSW	*Crimes (Domestic and Personal Violence) Act 2007* (NSW)
NT	*Domestic and Family Violence Act 2007* (NT)
Qld	*Domestic and Family Violence Protection Act 2012* (Qld)
SA	*Intervention Orders (Prevention of Abuse) Act 2009* (SA)
Tas	*Family Violence Act 2004* (Tas)
Vic	*Family Violence Protection Act 2008* (Vic)
WA	*Restraining Orders Act 1997* (WA)

Family violence orders only work if they are enforced.[30] Police sometimes decide that there is insufficient evidence or that minor breaches should not result in arrest. Social workers can play a key role in this, by advocating to police and assisting police by collecting evidence of a breach, for example by saving text messages or photos or by documenting incidents in file notes. Social workers may also be called to give evidence in court if they witness a breach.

Social workers must also engage with the problematic implementation of family violence law, which is fraught with tension on both sides. Family violence protection orders work better in cases where the parties are not required to have contact, such as when there are no shared children or property.[31] They may be less effective in preventing violence for people of colour[32] and people of colour are disproportionately arrested for breaching family violence orders.[33] The court environment is not always the ideal place to resolve disputes, and it can be difficult for court orders to reflect the complexity of human relationships in families, resulting in some issues that might have been solved amicably ending up in the court system.

Despite these issues, family violence law can play a key role in protecting survivors of family violence. Survivors report feeling more empowered by having an order and more confident to contact police.[34] They are also an important symbolic statement, clearly indicating that such behaviour is no longer tolerated by the community or by the government. Ultimately, as with all social issues, the law is only going to be one part of the solution. As Box 11.2 shows, they can make a real difference in people's lives.

Box 11.2 *What use are family violence protection orders?*

Scenario 1: You are a social worker in a homelessness case management role, working with Faith. Faith has two children, a 13-year-old girl and a 17-year-old boy, and an elderly cat. She came to your service looking for emergency accommodation so she could leave her violent partner. You tell her that while she is welcome at a local family refuge, her son would not be able to stay there as they do not allow males over 16 years. You offer her emergency accommodation in a local hostel, but she knows that her daughter would not be safe there. In either case, she would have to leave her cat behind and she is fearful of what her partner might do. Disheartened and defeated, she returns to her partner. You do not see her again.

Scenario 2: You are a social worker in a homelessness case management role, working with Faith. Faith has two children, a 13-year-old girl and a 17-year-old boy, and an elderly cat. She came to your service looking for emergency accommodation so she could leave her violent partner. You call your contact at the local Community Legal Centre, who helps Faith file a family violence protection order application. While she is doing that, you record the abusive and threatening text messages on Faith's phone. Together with the lawyer, you go to the police station, where you show the police the text messages. The police can see that Faith's partner has a history of convictions for violence against women, so they make a temporary family violence order, attend Faith's house and remove her partner so Faith can go home. The lawyer you referred Faith to will represent her at court for the family violence order hearing. Faith is fearful that her partner will return to their house, but the police promise to come immediately if she calls them. Faith has a long and difficult journey ahead of her, but you have helped her use the law to take the first step.

Box 11.2 illustrates the way that social workers who understand how to work with the law and in legal systems can be so much more effective. This social worker understands what family violence is, how family violence orders can be used and what their limitations are. The law has not fixed the immediate issue – Faith still feels unsafe – but it has made a significant difference to her situation.

11.3.3 Elder abuse in families

Elder abuse is an aspect of family violence but does not fit easily with the understanding of family violence as men's violence against women and children. Not all elder abuse is family violence, such as abuse by staff in aged care facilities, and there is much less data available than for men's intimate partner violence against women.[35] Men are more likely to commit elder abuse than women and women are more likely to be victims, but the split is much more even than with intimate partner violence, with sons and daughters being the most common perpetrators. Elder abuse is very likely to be financial but is also commonly physical, sexual, emotional or neglectful.[36] Social workers must be particularly alert to elder abuse in guardianship and administration matters (see Chapter 13) or they risk becoming unwitting perpetrators and assisting in elder abuse themselves.

11.4 Interactions between family law, child protection and family violence

In recent years the law regarding family law, family violence and child protection has undergone significant reform.[37] This process of law reform is still ongoing, and it is not difficult to see why. For some families, the magistrates' or local court may make a family violence protection order, the children's court may make a child protection order and the family court may make an order about parental responsibility. Aside from the bureaucratic issues this presents, it may mean that courts are working at cross purposes and that people find complying with court orders difficult.

Sometimes family violence orders will be inconsistent with family law parenting orders,[38] for example by prohibiting contact between two parents when they are required to deliver or collect a child they have shared care for. When this happens, seek legal advice to make sure that everyone is clear on what is required as it is easy to get it wrong.

Family violence is often raised in family law or child protection matters as a reason why children are in need of protection or should not have access to a parent. Where there is a risk of family violence, families may not have to attend family dispute resolution before applying to a court,[39] and the matter may be able to be fast-tracked through the Family Court.[40] There are also specialist supports available for people in this situation. Social workers should also be alert to the potential that perpetrators of family violence will attempt to use the legal system, particularly the family law system, to continue family violence.

11.5 THE CHANGING NATURE OF FAMILIES AND THE LAW

The law concerning children and families is evolving to keep up with changing ideas of family. The law is designed to manage blended and stepfamilies, with these family formulations becoming increasingly common in the last century, but developments in assisted reproductive technology and the law concerned same-sex marriage were not envisaged by the current legal frameworks. A number of cases have tested the law in this area,[41] which is still evolving. It is not always clear, for example, what rights a same-sex couple have if they use a sperm donor father.[42]

The law is also changing in relation to trans-people and their families. Historically, people were stuck with the gender they were assigned at birth. In recent years *legal* gender has been increasingly based on physical sex and able to be changed if people have undergone gender transition surgery or hormone treatment. Both of these approaches caused havoc for people who transitioned while married, who would sometimes have to divorce to legally change their sex. The *Marriage Amendment (Definition and Religious Freedoms) Act 2017* (Cth) has addressed that to some extent, so now trans-people can usually change their *legal* gender without being required to divorce, but the focus on surgery remains in some jurisdictions. In *AB v Western Australia* (2011) 244 CLR 390, the High Court indicated a move away from linking physical sex to gender, focusing on social acceptance of gender. In most Australian jurisdictions, surgery is still required to change *legal* gender, but this is changing. In some jurisdictions, it is also possible to have no legal gender recorded. Social workers should be familiar with the rules in their jurisdiction so as to be able to support people with their gender identity.

For some groups, particularly same-sex or other 'rainbow' families, adoption and surrogacy law has historically been discriminatory, although this has changed dramatically in recent years, with only Western Australia still prohibiting same-sex couples having a child via a surrogate. Even this is likely to change with the *Human Reproductive Technology and Surrogacy Legislation Amendment Bill 2018* (WA) before the Western Australian Parliament at the time of writing.

Adoption law is becoming less relevant to social workers in Australia as the rate of adoptions has plummeted since the 1970s. In 2017–18 there were only 330 adoptions in the entire country, 233 of which were instances where the child already knew the adoptive parent – for example, grandparents or foster carers.[43] For social workers, especially those working overseas or in community development contexts, it is important to note that there is a strict legal framework governing both local and intercountry adoptions. Each state and territory has adoption legislation and the Commonwealth has legislation regarding intercountry adoption (Table 11.2). Given the rarity with which social workers need to navigate this topic, it is enough to be aware that there is adoption law and to be able to find how it applies in your jurisdiction should you need to support someone going through this process.

Table 11.2 *Adoption legislation*

Jurisdiction	**Relevant legislation**
ACT	*Adoption Act 1993* (ACT)
NSW	*Adoption Act 2000* (NSW)
NT	*Adoption of Children Act 2007* (NT)
Qld	*Adoption Act 2009* (Qld)
SA	*Adoption Act 1988* (SA)
Tas	*Adoption Act 1988* (Tas)
Vic	*Adoption Act 1984* (Vic)
WA	*Adoption Act 1994* (WA)

Similarly, surrogacy law has changed in recent decades to reflect changing family norms. Surrogacy is when a woman has another person or couple's baby and gives the other person or couple all parental rights to the baby. This is usually done because the couple is unable to conceive themselves. This can be unpaid or unpaid. Paid surrogacy is prohibited in all Australian jurisdictions except the Northern Territory, while the Australian Capital Territory, Queensland and NSW also prohibit people from paying for an overseas surrogate.[44] Unpaid surrogacy is legal but regulated in most states except the Northern Territory, where there are no laws about surrogacy (Table 11.3). As with adoption, social workers are unlikely to need to be intimately familiar with surrogacy law other than to be able to find out the law if necessary.

Table 11.3 *Surrogacy legislation*

Jurisdiction	Relevant legislation
ACT	*Parentage Act 2004* (ACT)
NSW	*Surrogacy Act 2010* (NSW)
NT	No legislation governing surrogacy
Qld	*Surrogacy Act 2010* (Qld)
SA	*Family Relationships Act 1975* (SA)
Tas	*Surrogacy Act 2012* (Tas)
Vic	*Assisted Reproductive Treatment Act 2008* (Vic)
WA	*Surrogacy Act 2008* (WA)

11.6 Conclusion

All social workers will work with families, children and young people and those people will inevitably come into contact with the law. Many social workers, particularly those who work in child protection, will have to make decisions using the law, or help judges and magistrates make decisions using the law. This will almost always involve the best interests of the child as a central decision-making principle. Social workers must bring their training, understanding of social issues and their interpersonal skills to bear to help this happen in practice.

Main points

1. In nearly all decisions regarding children under the law, the 'best interests of the child' should be the paramount consideration.
2. Family law is private law; child protection and family violence is public law.
3. Family law in Australia is primarily governed by the *Family Law Act 1975* (Cth), where matters are mostly heard by the Family Court or the Federal Circuit Court. Matters will come before the court where parents cannot agree about children or property.
4. Child protection, unlike family law, is the responsibility of each state and territory.
5. Social workers will often work as child protection workers by investigating child protection incidents, providing support to families, supervising children on court orders, specialist supports, adoption and permanent care.
6. A child should only be removed as a last resort. The law provides a process for intervention, as well as a threshold test for determining when intervention is necessary.
7. Child protection orders can be grouped into four categories: finalised guardianship or custody orders; finalised third-party parental responsibility orders; finalised supervisory orders; interim and temporary orders.

8. Social workers often work with both victims and perpetrators of family violence.
9. While definitions of family violence differ in each jurisdiction, legislation generally includes physical violence or abuse; sexual abuse; emotional abuse; psychological abuse; economic and financial abuse; stalking; harassment; exposing children to family violence; and damaging property.

Discussion questions

1. How is 'family' defined in your jurisdiction in the different areas of law? Does it include non-nuclear family types? Is it inclusive of rainbow families, blended and separated families?
2. What constitutes the best interests of the child in your jurisdiction? Is it the same for family law and child protection? What is different?
3. Under the *Family Law Act 1975* (Cth), where children are involved, divorcing parties are legally required to undergo family dispute resolution. If family dispute resolution is unsuccessful, they must obtain a Section 60I certificate to prove attempts at settling matters outside court. What are the five types of Section 60I certificates a family dispute resolution practitioner can issue? How could this certificate affect the rest of the court process for divorcing parties?
4. What type of child protection orders are found in your jurisdiction's relevant legislation? How are these different from other jurisdictions?
5. Look up how family violence is defined in your jurisdiction's legislation. What types of abuse are identified? Is there anything missing? Who is encompassed in the definition of 'family'? Who is left out?

Further reading

Family Law Council, *Family Law Council Report to the Attorney-General on Families with Complex Needs and the Intersection of the Family Law and Child Protection Systems* (Attorney-General's Department, 2016).

Lisa Young and Geoffrey Monahan, *Children and the Law in Australia* 2nd ed. (LexisNexis Butterworths, 2016).

Council of Australian Governments, 'National Framework for Protecting Australia's Children 2009–2020' (Australian Government Department of Social Services, 2009).

Gary Dumbrill, 'Emic and Alliance; Anti-Oppressive Social Work in Child Protection', in Donna Baines, *Doing Anti-Oppressive Practice: Social Justice Social Work* 3rd ed. (Fernwood Publishing, 2017).

11.7 References

[1] Australian Institute of Family Studies, *The Intersection between the Child Protection and Youth Justice Systems* (Text, Australian Government, July 2018) <https://aifs.gov.au/cfca/publications/intersection-between-child-protection-and-youth-justice-systems/overlap-between-child>.

[2] *Criminal Code Act 1924* (Tas) s 124.

[3] *Masson v Parsons* [2019] HCA 21.

[4] Lisa Young and Geoffrey Monahan, *Children and the Law in Australia* 2nd ed. (LexisNexis Butterworths, 2016).

[5] *Re Agar-Ellis* [1883] 24 Ch D, 336.

[6] Australian Law Reform Commission, *Seen and Heard: Priority for Children in the Legal Process* (No 84, Australian Government, 1997) <https://www.alrc.gov.au/publications/16-childrens-involvement-family-law-proceedings/best-interests-principle>.

[7] UN General Assembly, International Covenant on Civil and Political Rights, 16 December 1966, United Nations, Treaty Series, vol. 999, p. 171.

[8] UN General Assembly, International Covenant on Economic, Social and Cultural Rights, 16 December 1966, United Nations, Treaty Series, vol. 993, p. 3.

[9] UN General Assembly, Convention on the Elimination of All Forms of Discrimination Against Women, 18 December 1979, United Nations, Treaty Series, vol. 1249, p. 13.

[10] Hague Conference on Private International Law, Hague Convention on the Protection of Children and Co-operation in Respect of Intercountry Adoption, 29 May 1993, 33.

[11] *Family Law Act 1975* (Cth) s 6; *Marriage Act 1961* (Cth) s 5.

[12] *Family Law Act 1975* (Cth) s 48.

[13] *Family Law Act 1975* (Cth) s 49.

[14] *Family Law Act 1975* (Cth) s 61B to 61DB.

[15] *Family Law Act 1975* (Cth) s 65C.

[16] *Family Law Act 1975* (Cth) s 65A to 65ZD.

[17] *Family Law Act 1975* (Cth) s 60CA.

[18] The main legislation is *Children and Young People Act 2008* (ACT); *Children and Young Persons (Care and Protection) Act 1998* (NSW); *Care and Protection of Children Act 2007* (NT); *Child Protection Act 1999* (Qld); *Children's Protection Act 1993* (SA); *Children, Young Persons and their Families Act 1997* (Tas); *Children, Youth and Families Act 2005* (Vic); *Children and Community Services Act 2004* (WA).

[19] *Family Law Act 1975* (Cth) s 69ZK.

[20] Australian Institutes of Family Studies, 'Australian Child Protection Legislation', *Child Family Community Australia* (Text, 27 March 2018) <https://aifs.gov.au/cfca/publications/australian-child-protection-legislation>.

[21] Young and Monahan (n 4).

[22] Australian Institutes of Family Studies (n 20).

[23] Philip Gillingham, 'Social Work and Child Protection in Australia: Whose Job Is It Anyway?' (2016) 28(2) *Practice* 83.

[24] Council of Australian Governments, *National Framework for Protecting Australia's Children 2009–2020* (Australian Government Department of Social Services, 2009) <https://www.dss.gov.au/our-responsibilities/families-and-children/publications-articles/protecting-children-is-everyones-business>.

[25] Ibid 4.

[26] *Child Protection Australia 2017–18* (Australian Institute of Health and Welfare, 2019) 37 <https://www.aihw.gov.au/reports/child-protection/child-protection-australia-2017-18/contents/summary>.

[27] *Child Protection and Aboriginal and Torres Strait Islander Children* (Text, Australian Institute of Family Studies, 31 January 2019) <https://aifs.gov.au/cfca/publications/child-protection-and-aboriginal-and-torres-strait-islander-children>.
[28] *Global Study on Homicide 2018: Gender-Related Killing of Women and Girls* (United Nations Office on Drugs and Crime, 2018) <https://www.unodc.org/documents/data-and-analysis/GSH2018/GSH18_Gender-related_killing_of_women_and_girls.pdf>.
[29] *Family, Domestic and Sexual Violence in Australia 2018* (Australian Institute of Health and Welfare, 2018) <https://www.aihw.gov.au/reports/domestic-violence/family-domestic-sexual-violence-in-australia-2018>.
[30] Christopher Dowling et al, *Protection Orders for Domestic Violence: A Systematic Review* (No 551, Australian Institute of Criminology, June 2018).
[31] Ibid.
[32] Ibid.
[33] Lesley Laing, *Social Work & Domestic Violence: Developing Critical & Reflective Practice* (SAGE Publications, 2013).
[34] Christopher Dowling et al (n 30).
[35] Rae Kaspiew, Rachel Carson and Helen Rhoades, *Elder Abuse: Understanding Issues, Frameworks and Responses* (Australian Institute of Family Studies, 2016).
[36] *Elder Abuse* (Australian Law Reform Commission, 2016) <https://www.alrc.gov.au/publications/elder-abuse-dp83>.
[37] Family Law Council, *Family Law Council Report to the Attorney-General on Families with Complex Needs and the Intersection of the Family Law and Child Protection Systems: Final Report – June 2016* (Attorney-General's Dept., 2016) <https://www.ag.gov.au/FamiliesAndMarriage/FamilyLawCouncil/Documents/Family-with-Complex-Needs-Intersection-of-Family-Law-and-Child-Protection-Systems-Final-Report-Terms-3-4-5.PDF>.
[38] *Family Law Act 1975* (Cth) ss 68P, 68Q.
[39] *Family Law Act 1975* (Cth) s 60J.
[40] Daryl J Higgins, *Cooperation and Coordination: An Evaluation of the Family Court of Australia's Magellan Case-Management Model* (Family Court of Australia, 2007).
[41] See, for example, *Groth & Banks* [2013] FamCA 430 and *Re Patrick* (2002) 28 Fam LR 579.
[42] The High Court has ruled on this issue, giving some guidance: *Masson v Parsons* [2019] HCA 21.
[43] Australian Institute of Health and Welfare, *Adoptions Australia 2017–18* (Australian Government, 2018) <https://www.aihw.gov.au/getmedia/6d9374b3-974c-4ba3-8134-d59979733c87/aihw-cws-66.pdf.aspx?inline=true>.
[44] House of Representatives Standing Committee on Social Policy and Legal Affairs, *Surrogacy Matters- Inquiry into the Regulatory and Legislative Aspects of International and Domestic Surrogacy Arrangements* (Commonwealth of Australia, 2016) <https://www.aph.gov.au/Parliamentary_Business/Committees/House/Social_Policy_and_Legal_Affairs/Inquiry_into_surrogacy/Report>.

Chapter 12 FIRST NATIONS PEOPLE AND COMMUNITIES AND THE LAW

Meena Singh and Chris Maylea

Meena Singh is a Yorta Yorta woman who has previously worked as the Director of Client and Legal Services at the Victorian Aboriginal Legal Service and Associate Director, Aboriginal Services at Victoria Legal Aid. She is an experienced lawyer and currently works as a consultant and trainer.

Acknowledgement and thanks to Professor Irene Watson for her guidance on themes to include in this chapter.

As Bundjalung woman Ruby Langford Ginibi writes, the interaction of Australia's First Nations law and the Australian colonial law has been one of oppression, colonisation, assimilation and genocide:

> *One country two laws. Aboriginal laws, traditional and customary laws, have never been acknowledged by the colonial invaders of Aboriginal people. They came with their godly marriages and paternalistic ways, and we were forced to assimilate, and give up our languages, and deny our culture and heritage because our traditional practices were classified as 'heathen' and 'vermin' to be cleared off the face of the earth. Three hundred Aboriginal nations were wiped out by the colonising of our lands, and we were forced by governments to become like white people. We were always the ones who had to conform to white ways and white ideas, because we were never allowed to be our selves.*[1]

The history of social work practice with Australia's First Nations people and communities has been at best problematic and at worst horrendous. The legacy of social work's participation in the Stolen Generations and the continued role of social workers in contributing to the overrepresentation of First Nations' children in child protection attaches to every social worker by association. Social work is still grappling with its Whiteness,[2] struggling to decolonise,[3] and the ongoing role social workers play in legal systems that oppress First Nations people and communities exacerbates this strained relationship.[4] First Nations people are overrepresented in nearly every statutory system that social workers work in – including criminal, mental health and child protection. In this chapter we attempt to provide an introduction to the basic concepts and issues in the law in relation to

First Nations people and communities so that social workers can work towards the decolonisation of the law and reconciliation in partnership with First Nations people and communities.

Readers may wonder why understanding the history and context is so important. They may be thinking 'I don't see colour, I will just treat First Nations people like anyone else' or 'I'm not racist, I don't need to know about other things racist people did.' We are sorry to be the ones to break it to those readers, but these are racist sentiments. Working with First Nations people and their communities without special attention to their history and current context denies both the centuries of oppression and the reality that the solution to contemporary issues lies in listening to First Nations communities and responding to their strengths.

For example, it is unlikely that social workers will be lodging land title claims to the National Native Title Tribunal, so why should they need to know anything about it? The answer lies in the need to appreciate the relationship many First Nations people have with the land and country, and the way law is tied to culture and land in a completely different way to Australian colonial law and culture.[5] It is only through listening and accepting First Nations voices that we can decolonise and progress toward Reconciliation together.

In this chapter, we briefly outline the nature of First Nations law, then examine the impact of colonial law on First Nations people and communities with particular reference to land and country, policing and prisons, and family and community. Following this, we highlight the importance of self-determination and the opportunity for social work to play a role in decolonising the law. This is an inadequate introduction to any of these topics and should be seen only as a starting point for further learning. Learning about First Nations history, experiences and culture should be seen as an ongoing practice essential not only to the profession of social work but to our understanding of the history and contemporary society of Australia.

12.1 First Nations law and lore

To try and discuss the 'law' of First Nations people and communities is in itself a process of colonisation. The topic of 'law' as something that is written down and kept distinct from other aspects of society is a fundamentally White and colonialist notion. Colonialist law is presented as a specialist area, only accessible to a privileged few, after years of training, and practised only by an elite profession. Prior to colonisation, First Nations people and communities certainly had ways of regulating society, but they are not directly comparable to colonialist law. The Pitjantjatara word *tjukurrpa* means something like 'doing things the right way', but also means 'the Dreaming' and the foundation of the world.[6] Irene Watson, a Tanganekald and Meintangk-Bunganditj woman, explains how for many

First Nations people and communities the law is indistinguishable from the larger fabric of society, the land and country, and universe:

> *Many of our First Nations legal systems are embodied in stories and songs. Our ancient laws were not written down; knowledge of law came through living, singing and storytelling. Law is lived, sung, danced, painted, eaten and in the walking of ruwe.* * *Law inheres in all things and is alive in all things, but these days it is an ongoing struggle to keep many things alive in the face of the attempts to bury our law ways as a part of the ongoing colonial project.*
>
> *First Nations laws are still in conflict with the imposed colonial legal system; in the past our old people struggled and many of our people today continue to struggle against colonialism. In particular we struggle to keep the body of First Nations law alive for future generations. We keep a view of law, which lives in all things and emanates love, caring and sharing, and respect for all things in the natural world. It is a view of the world that supports the capacity of peoples to care for country and all our relations, including those we have with the animal, plant and broader natural world. In pre-colonial times the natural world was 'undeveloped', not because of an inability to transform the* ruwe, *but because of a relationship of connectedness with all things in the natural world. Those safe and harmonious relationships were maintained by, for example, fire management, fish farming and other sustainable practices that worked with the natural world rather than changing and fundamentally altering that natural world order.*[7]

Where the colonial law is written on paper and signed by the Governor or Governor-General, Australian First Nations law is written on the landscape and in the sky, in the songs and stories – in the lore. This is both figurative and literal. Christine Black, a Kombumerri and Munaljahlai woman, highlights how a story about respecting a hunter's dogs is embedded into the landscape. In the story, lazy fellas eat a magical hunter's dogs rather than doing their own hunting:

---

* *Ruwe* is a Ngarrindjeri word that means land or country.

> *So he went looking for those dogs and found them. He found all those bones those lazy fellas had left in the campfire. He took those bones and made a special place for them up in the mountains. You can see that special place for miles all around. I like looking up to that place where those two rocks poke up looking like dogs watching me down on the coast. Makes me feel special.*
>
> *But what about those fellas that killed those dogs? Oh that was bad and that hunter made sure they were dead. Then he did something that killed all the people. He changed that land with his magic – he made it all change, just in one day. With his magic he flattened that place out real flat and made that land real hard and black. That's now Munaljahlai country. That story reminds my Grandad's mob to be careful and follow the Law, otherwise the land might suddenly change overnight. A wipeout can happen any time. It happened before and can happen again. That's why we tell this story. To remind people, stay straight with the Law.*[8]

This story reinforces the importance of hunting dogs and the breach of law in taking of another clan's dogs. The law is not just in the story, but the story relates to features of the land. Only in walking the land and telling the story is law translated, and in dispossessing people of their land they risk being dispossessed of their law. Bruce Pascoe, who has Yuin, Bunurong and Tasmanian heritage, reinforces this point, that law is embedded in agriculture, religion and song:

> *There is no separation between a sacred and non-sacred, as all actions are steeped in religious purpose. The mere act of burning grass has a specific story attached to it, a story that directs the need and benefits of the action in law.*[9]

This means that to try and write about the law in relation to First Nations is to try and write about the whole of First Nations culture, history and country, a task well beyond the scope of this chapter. Added to this is the variety and diversity of Australian First Nations culture and society. Prior to colonisation, there were over 250 Australian languages including 800 distinct dialects, all with varying legal (social, cultural) practices. Just as to speak of 'law' in this context is colonising, so speaking of 'First Nations laws' wipes a continent of diversity into a single concept. For comparison, contemporary Europe has around 24 official languages and perhaps 100–150 dialects, and the variation in legal systems there makes it impossible to speak of 'European law' as a single thing.

Perhaps one of the biggest challenges of understanding First Nations law is attempting to understand it in the same way we understand the colonial law. Colonial law is often kept separate from the rest of society, accessible only after years of training and steeped in rituals that can seem archaic and detached from society. By contrast, for First Nations people and culture, the law is everywhere, accessible to everyone, treating us all as equals and reflecting the community's needs and circumstances.

Box 12.1 *Lore and law*

In thinking about law, it can be useful to distinguish between 'law', which comes from an old Norse word meaning 'something laid down or fixed' and 'lore', which comes from an old English word meaning 'to learn'. 'Lore' might better characterise First Nations people and communities' legal systems prior to colonisation.

It is impossible to detail the rich and varied legal systems of Australia's First Nations people and communities,* but there are some themes that are common to many First Nations communities. These include:

- Dreaming, song and storytelling
- Integration of law, culture, practices, land and country
- Embedding law in ceremonial traditions and rituals
- Prioritisation of knowledge and experience of elders

Some readers will question why this is important given the almost total dominance of colonial legal systems. Even laws relating directly to and only to First Nations people and communities are passed in legislation by parliaments. One reason is that the law is still there. Watson explains:

> *What happened to the law? It appears to have disappeared and yet the law is all around us as it has always been; it is still being sung, it lives and breathes in the life force that surrounds us. However, our perceptions of it have changed. Our ability to see and hear songs has changed. The natural world is still singing even though the greater part of humanity has disconnected itself from song.*[10]

Communities in places of first contact with colonial law, such as on the East Coast and Tasmania, have reacted differently to colonisation than communities on other parts of the continent, such as the Central Desert or

---

* Readers from settler backgrounds might start with the further reading at the end of this chapter to continue their journey of understanding and decolonisation.

Kimberly. First Nations cultures and societies have continued to evolve and adapt since colonial contact. In some communities, First Nations law and culture is still the primary way of organising the community and relationships between community members, and in others, it has been influenced or superseded by colonial law and culture, particularly where children were removed and placed with mainstream families. For some First Nations people, their experience will be of living between two worlds, coming into the colonial world to engage with social workers and other services and retreating to the world of community and family. First Nations people may have family from across the country, and as a result may move between different First Nations cultures, compounding the experience of multiple worlds. Social workers must understand this tension when working with people, particularly in legal settings, where misunderstanding can quickly lead to discrimination and oppression.

Another reason to take note of pre-colonial law, suggested by Pascoe, is that First Nations law was effective beyond the comprehension of the settlers, and remains so today. He acknowledges that violence existed, but that it was tightly controlled. He points to the complete absence of imperial violence in pre-colonial Australia as evidence of the effectiveness of the legal (social, cultural) system.

> *This absence demands respect, and the skills employed to bring about the longest lasting pan-continental stability that the world has known must be investigated, because they might become Australia's greatest export.*[11]

Viewed from this perspective, First Nations laws and lore may hold the key to resolving many of the issues of the colonial era described in the rest of this chapter. For social workers who will work with First Nations people and communities, there is an additional need to understand both the experience of where First Nations people and communities come from and where they are going. This is a rich and varied experience, but with the common thread of racism throughout.

12.2 Racism and the colonial law

To speak of the interaction between Australian colonial law and Australian First Nations people and communities without speaking of racism would be in itself a racist act. The colonial law is in whatever form it takes – criminal, child protection, welfarism – based on racist assumptions, and to pretend otherwise is inherently racist. There are, of course, mainstream laws that do protect and maintain some rights of First Nations people, such as laws enabling treaty processes. When developed in conjunction with First Nations people and communities and with a view to decolonisation, these laws represent the potential for a post-colonial legal system. When we refer to the colonial law we mean laws that have not been decolonised, that do not account for the experience of First Nations people and have been passed without the assent of First Nations communities. Just as First Nations laws (societies, cultures) have evolved, so has mainstream law evolved to become less colonial, although there is still much work to do.

At the heart of this racism sits the uncomfortable convergence of benevolence, paternalism and disrespect. Much of the harm committed against First Nations people and communities was perfectly legal, based on or cloaked in the premise that First Nations people and communities needed to be controlled for their own good, because they were incapable of looking after themselves.

This theme of harmful and degrading benevolence can be seen right through the story of the colonial law, from reserves and missions, through the Stolen Generation and to the Intervention. As a result, social workers engaging with First Nations people and communities may find their benevolence is not well received. This history, context and cultural experience will need to be navigated in order to do good social work. In this section we examine two examples of racism in law; that of the wages stolen from First Nations people and the Northern Territory Intervention.

12.2.1 Stolen wages

As the colonists advanced across the continent, they displaced the people who occupied the land. European diseases ravaged First Nations communities, with the frontier wars[12] and massacres[13] of First Nations people accounting for many more deaths. Those who survived were commonly moved onto reserves, stations or missions, where their rights were severely limited, as shown in the example of the *Aborigine Protection Act 1909* (NSW). First Nations people were regularly forbidden from consuming alcohol, marrying, leaving the reserve or working, unless they could get permission. In many cases, First Nations languages and practices were forbidden.

For an example of this legalised racism, consider section 7(e) of the *Aborigine Protection Act 1909* (NSW), which required the 'Board for Protection of Aborigines'

> *... to exercise a general supervision and care over all matters affecting the interests and welfare of aborigines, and to protect them against injustice, imposition, and fraud.*

This benevolent intention is undermined by section 11 of the same Act, which allowed for the Board to enslave First Nations children and collect any money they earned for this work:

> *The board may ... bind or cause to be bound the child of any aborigine, or the neglected child of any person apparently having an admixture of aboriginal blood in his*

> *veins, to be apprenticed to any master, and may collect and institute proceedings for the recovery of any wages payable under such indenture, and may expend the same as the board may think fit in the interest of the child.*

This kind of benevolence was not accorded to the mainstream population, whose children were not legally enslaved. Nor was it small scale. In Queensland alone, it has been estimated that $500 million was owed in unpaid wages, with estimates in other jurisdictions difficult to come by.[14] This money has not yet been repaid and although there are some redress schemes, they are entirely inadequate.[15] The parsimonious and begrudging paternalism can be seen in many different ways, with First Nations people not trusted to own land or other items. In a display of incredible pettiness, section 15 of the same Act states that:

> *Every blanket or other article issued by the Government or by the board to any aborigine shall be considered to be on loan only, and to be the property of the board ...*

The *Aborigine Protection Act 1909* (NSW) was repealed in 1969, the year of the moon landing. This is not ancient history, and social workers must be awake to the rawness of the hurt. Social workers must ask why First Nations people might view, for example, work-for-the-dole schemes with suspicion, when their experience was for so long one of getting ripped off by governments. Similarly, when the damage of these laws is now so evident, social workers should critically analyse contemporary laws with a view to historical mistakes.

12.2.2 The Intervention

In 2007, the Northern Territory Board of Inquiry into the Protection of Aboriginal Children from Sexual Abuse released the Ampe Akelyernemane Meke Mekarle (Little Children are Sacred) Report.[16] This report highlighted widespread sexual abuse of First Nations children in the Northern Territory and sparked national outrage. In response, the Howard government announced the Northern Territory National Emergency Response. This included a range of legislation and increased funding but did little to address the recommendations of the Ampe Akelyernemane Meke Mekarle Report. Critics questioned the timing of the response, which was coincidentally in the lead up to a federal election, following decades of government inaction. Critics also pointed to the way the process was lacking consultation with local communities and criticised the implementation, which involved 600 Australian Defence Force personnel.*

---

* In an astounding illustration of how poorly understood this issue is, declassified documents from the Joint Operations Command show that the Australian Defence Force

The Intervention can be seen as eerily similar to past legislation governing First Nations people. The *Northern Territory National Emergency Response Act 2007* (Cth), along with other legislation, regulated the movement of people and things in 'prescribed areas', restricted the consumption of alcohol and pornography, imposed restrictions on the management of communities, forcibly leased First Nations owned land and imposed controls over First Nations families' money. This Act was overtly and unapologetically racist – the federal government had to legislate to suspend the *Racial Discrimination Act 1975* (Cth) in order to pass it and the United Nations Special Rapporteur found that it 'discriminates on the basis of race, thereby raising serious human rights concerns'.[17]

The Intervention continues to exist, albeit in a less extreme form, now named 'Stronger Futures'. This serves as a salient example of a situation where all parties agree that something needs to be done but where a lack of understanding of history and context led to a highly problematic response. A 2015 study by the Castan Centre for Human Rights Law found that there has either been little progress made or mixed results in areas of employment and economic participation, education, health and life expectancy since the Intervention.[18] The number of children in child protection has increased, reports of self-harm by children are up by 500 per cent, and family violence cases have increased. It is difficult to tell how much of this is because of more services and more reporting, but there is, in any case, no evidence that the Intervention was substantially successful in addressing child sexual assault. The Intervention was not built on solid consultation with First Nations people and communities, and while there are some tangible benefits, it is difficult to see how this kind of response, patronising and controlling imbued with symbolic violence, does anything to address the underlying issues. One of those underlying issues is the dispossession of land and country, and the process of native title reclamation.

12.3 Land and Country

Central to the topic of Australia's First Nations is the systematic dispossession of their land and the ongoing saga of attempts to assert some rights of ownership to some territory. As discussed earlier, Australian First Nations law, culture and society are inseparable from land and country, so understanding all other interactions between First Nations and colonial Australia relies on understanding this relationship.

---

saw this as a way to 'Maintain the reputation of the ADF as a compassionate and capable organisation' and 'Widen the recruiting base for aboriginal soldiers'.
See <www.defence.gov.au/FOI/Docs/Disclosures/015_1718_Documents.pdf>.

The occupation of Australia was entirely legal under British colonial law, as Australia was considered '*terra nullius*'. *Terra nullius* is a legal term that means 'land belonging to no one'. Because the colonists could not (or decided not to) appreciate the relationship of the people to the land, they decided that the land was uninhabited and could be claimed by the British Crown.* The Mabo decision in 1992 meant that the doctrine of *terra nullius* was overturned. In that case, Eddie Mabo, a Meriam man from the Torres Strait, took the State of Queensland and the Commonwealth of Australia to the High Court to claim 'native title' to the Murray Islands. The High Court found that where traditional owners could show they had exercised rights over land since before colonisation, the law would uphold those traditional rights. On land where the traditional owners had been pushed off by the settler societies, they could not claim native title. Following Mabo, the Commonwealth government introduced the *Native Title Act 1993* (Cth), which regulated native title claims. This set up the National Native Title Tribunal, which hears native title claims.

This was progressed by the High Court in the Wik Decision,[19] which found that native title could coexist with pastoral leases. *Akiba v Commonwealth* found that native title could extend out to sea.[20] The Wik Decision and subsequent decisions caused some controversy, with fears that much of the country could become native title. Indeed much of the country has been claimed as native title, with nearly 40 per cent determined to be native title and another quarter of the country subject to native title applications.[21] This has led to some restrictions both on what was eligible and what it could be used for. Generally, native title holders cannot use the land for any 'non-traditional purpose'. This can make it difficult for native title holders to make the most of their land – for example, by selling mining rights. It also means that there are restrictions on how communities can care for their land, particularly when that land is shared with other interests, such as when it is a national or state park. Fundamentally, native title provides title, not sovereignty.

Social workers need to be aware of native title if they are to work effectively with First Nations people, but they are unlikely to have much to do with the legal process behind it. The important lesson for social workers is the way the land, dispossession from the land and access to land must be part of any reconciliation process. Mabo overturned the legal doctrine of *terra nullius*, but the idea that the continent of Australia now belongs to the colonisers lives on in the collective attitude, policy and laws of the settler society. This is particularly present in the way First Nations people and communities are policed and imprisoned.

* In this case meaning first the British Empire and later the Australian government.

12.4 Policing and Prisons

The application of the colonial criminal law to First Nations people and communities is one of Australia's greatest shames and greatest failures. The colonialist law has imprisoned First Nations people at such a rate that they are now 'the most incarcerated people on the planet Earth'.[22] First Nations people constitute 28 per cent of the Australian prison population, despite making up only 2 per cent of the general population.[23] In the Northern Territory 84 per cent of prisoners identify as First Nations, despite constituting only 30 per cent of the population. At the time of writing (2019), every single child in youth detention in the Northern Territory is a First Nations child.[24]

We do not deny that criminal behaviour poses a major challenge for many First Nations communities, although we do suggest that the causative factors are complex and poorly addressed by the colonialist legal system. First Nations people are *less* likely to be imprisoned for homicide, sexual assault or drug offences, but much *more* likely to be imprisoned for assault and unlawful entry.[25] This immediately discounts any suggestion that First Nations people are somehow more criminal, as Hogg writes:

> *The crimes committed by Aboriginal offenders are overwhelmingly crimes of poverty, despair and defiance. Enormous numbers are drawn into the criminal justice net for crimes like public drunkenness, swearing, damage to property, fighting and theft … High recurrent contact, as much as offence gravity, contributes to high incarceration rates.*[26]

The denial of First Nations' ways of doing justice has been a significant contributor to this issue. In First Nations communities where pre-colonial culture is still dominant, customary law is still practised, but not acknowledged by the colonial authorities. Practices such as ritual spearing as punishment for wrongdoing are viewed as criminal acts, and First Nations people may be punished twice, once in the colonial legal system and once in the First Nations justice system.[27]

Lateral violence, the idea that people who are oppressed by violence will express violence towards others, rather than at their oppressors, may also contribute to the issue. It is not surprising that having been taught by colonialist history that violence is superior to lawful behaviour First Nations people might internalise this lesson. To the extent that this is the case, it seems unlikely that further violence, in the form of the criminal legal system, is likely to fix the issue. Indeed, the statistics clearly show that mass incarceration has not led to reduced convictions of First Nations people.

A critical view of the criminal legal system's response to First Nations people views this as an extension of the process of dispossession, based on an assumption of *terra nullius*:

> *The criminal justice system not only punishes Indigenous people but strives to delegitimize Indigenous sovereignty through the practice of jurisdiction and authority.*[28]

This needs also to be viewed in the context of the experience of First Nations people and communities beyond Australia. Incarceration rates for First Nations people and communities in Canada, New Zealand and the United States are also disproportionately high,[29] although not as high as for Australian First Nations people.* This suggests that the common denominator is colonialism and that the issue can only be addressed by decolonisation and reconciliation.

Finally, something must be said about First Nations deaths in custody. In 1991, the Royal Commission into Aboriginal Deaths in Custody documented the appalling number of First Nations people dying in police custody and in prisons.[30] There are too many examples to list here, but First Nations people are still dying in Australia's prisons across the country.[31] There is some inkling of light on the horizon – since 2003 the rate of First Nations people dying in custody has actually been lower than the rate of the general prison population,[32] but given the massive overrepresentation of First Nations people in prisons this is at best a silver lining. Mass incarceration is extremely damaging to the social fabric of First Nations communities, taking people off country and away from their culture, family and community.

12.5 Family and Community

The nature of First Nations family and community is fundamentally distinct from the colonial notion of the nuclear family. Ruby Langford Ginibi, a Bundjalung woman, writes that:

> *Kinship network was law! Aboriginal man was a social father to all the children of the clan, and Aboriginal woman was a social mother to all the children of the clan. Everyone had a place, no one was excluded or left out: this was our democracy at work.*[33]

In Central Australia, for example, there exists a kinship system for organising social and family relationships, dictating who can marry whom and designating 'avoidance relationships' where some relationships (particularly mother-in-law and son-in-law) cannot be in the same room, or same car.[34] Of course, kinship systems and family relationships vary across the continent, but the one consistent factor is the disregard the colonial law had for these relationships.

---

* It is worth noting that in these jurisdictions colonial authorities made treaties with First Nations communities, which has not yet occurred in Australia.

Across the country, First Nations children were taken from their families and placed in institutions or with settler families.[35] Many of these children were removed by social workers.[36] This has left a mark on the relationship between social work and First Nations families. While the Australian Association of Social Workers has acknowledged the role of social workers in this process,[37] there is still much to be done both in the profession of social work and in the larger child protection system.

The 1997 Bringing them Home Report brought national attention to the laws, policies and practices that resulted in the Stolen Generation and recommended that all governments work towards healing and reconciliation. More than 20 years later, in 2019, children of First Nations families are still nearly ten times more likely to be placed into out-of-home care than children of settler families.[38] The reasons for this are complex and interconnected.[39] The dislocation of First Nations families from country and the breakdown in culture have led to disruptions in role modelling and cultural narratives necessary for preserving positive parenting practices. Where community parenting practices have survived, social workers have failed to understand them and misinterpreted them as abuse and neglect. In communities where parenting is shared amongst the adults, it may appear as if a child's biological parent is not engaged, leading social workers to intervene inappropriately. First Nations families may also be less likely to seek help owing to the fear of their children being removed, leading to issues escalating and accusations of neglect and abuse. High rates of transience and homelessness, mass incarceration, lack of culturally appropriate services, language barriers and geographical isolation all contribute to the issue to varying degrees. In some communities, there may be a perceived need to protect perpetrators from colonial justice or oppression within communities preventing help-seeking.

There is a very troubling intersection with family violence in First Nations communities, where women are 32 times more likely to be hospitalised for family violence and twice as likely to be killed by their partner.[40] This is both a cause and a consequence of social disadvantage and intergenerational trauma, and demands a response that addresses both the apparent causes and the underlying structural issues.

There are many attempts to address this issue, ranging from the symbolic Apology to Australia's Indigenous Peoples,[41] to the adoption of the 'Aboriginal and Torres Strait Islander Child Placement Principle'. The Child Placement Principle sets out the preferred order of placement when a First Nations child is removed from their family by child protection:

1. The child's own extended family (kin)
2. The child's First Nations community (kith)
3. Other First Nations families
4. With settler families.[42]

Despite all jurisdictions adopting this principle either in policy or law, over 30 per cent of First Nations children who are removed by the state are still placed with settler families or institutions. There is, clearly, much work left to do.

We are not suggesting that the safety and care of children is not a major challenge for some First Nations families and communities; however, it seems unlikely that the policy of continuing high rates of removal will address the underlying issues of disrupted families and dislocation from country and culture. We suggest that legal reform that supports self-determination, allowing First Nations communities to respond to and regulate themselves, may be a more successful approach.

Read Philomela's story and reflect on how her experiences might influence how she works with social workers and how they should work with her.

12.6 Philomela's story

I am an Indigenous woman who is a mother of two children who are not currently living with me. My daughter is in foster care with a non-Indigenous family and my son is with my sister. I can be really detached from myself and my emotions. This can make it seem easy to talk about things but that doesn't mean that it is. I don't tell my workers this stuff. I don't trust them so I don't tell them.

My first memory is of my mum screaming. I lost my dad when I was three. He was murdered. I remember the moment. Someone knocking at the door, this horrible scream coming from my mum. Violence has always been a big part of my life. Violence has been normal for me. This meant that when I went through family violence I didn't know what it was. I thought violence was only physical, but it can be all kinds of things.

I haven't had a massive connection with community or culture but there is a spiritual thing, a part of me, being spiritual – a connection to the land, our people. People that we've lost and people that are here. I've come from a place of not knowing who I am. I didn't know there were black people and white people. My brother's skin is black, mine is white. If he hadn't been teased about it all through school I never would have known the difference. He got his leg broken and we moved to different places because of that. The great thing about being Indigenous you're welcomed by community wherever you go.

Growing up in the criminal world you don't get connection to culture. I grew up in a criminal world. It taught me determination, resourcefulness and to never give up. Honour. What not to do. I was raised like that. I wanted to be different things. I was taught that good manners was not talking to the police. At the start I hated social workers. I called them 'textbook warriors' because they didn't have any life experience. My teachers said things to me you should never say to a child. One day I climbed the fence and ran home to mum. My mum went and beat up the teacher.

My first experience of being involved with the police, aside from when they'd arrest my mum and take us away, was when I was involved with a group of adults writing fake cheques. I had no idea what was going on. After the case, a couple of the police officers said to me, 'if we can't get to your mum we'll get to you'. I've never got on well with the police since then.

When I was younger I wanted to be an armed robber, the best there was. When I was 18 I ended up in gaol for armed robbery. I was raised around drug dealers but we were raised not to do drugs. I ended up in drugs after family violence.

When I needed a family violence protection order it was hard to get one. I couldn't trust the police. I'm still going through the process of escaping family violence. My son's dad, who was out on parole for attempted murder, had custody. My friend who happens to be a lawyer came with me to the police to get a family violence protection order. As a mother, and as someone who is trying to do something different I wanted to, but my values from my upbringing kept me away. In the end, I did go to the police. We waited for two hours and they rejected my application. I get a different response from police and family violence workers and other services because I've been in prison and because I'm Indigenous. That really pissed me off.

Aboriginal organisations can really suck. The government puts them into place so they can look like they're doing something for Aboriginal people. It just makes it look like we get more, but I can't tell you what the extras are. The things that we get were a battle to get those things. It took me six months to get a book in prison.

When I was a kid I didn't know it was possible for me to go to uni. I studied social work in prison. My brother was in prison at the same time and he was studying sociology. He encouraged me to study otherwise I wouldn't have. Later I switched to law. I had good experiences with lawyers growing up because they were the ones that gave me back to my mum. Lawyers fought for us in court. Social workers were the ones that took us away from my mum.

If a social worker wanted to get change, they need to get that connection to the criminal world and reconnect the person back to community and culture. I don't want to leave that whole world behind and I feel guilty leaving people behind. I know how difficult it is coming out of that world and coming into a completely different world. Unless you experience life in that way you won't get it.

Social workers are here to help change the course of people's lives. They have the opportunity to do that at different times in a person's life. When they're a child, or a teenager, or an adult. The experience I had with people supporting me, when they believed in me even when I didn't believe in myself. They helped me believe the power is with me. I'm still trying to get where I'm going, but the experience I had in that criminal world made me. It is like work experience.

Social workers need to be able to admit that they don't have this experience in life, but they need to sit with us and say that we can both use both of our skills to move forward.

Philomela's story speaks for itself. We encourage readers to re-read it and reflect on the way she frames her identity, as coming from a criminal world, of being Indigenous, of studying and of violence. This is not a traditional narrative of redemption and rehabilitation, as she values her experience and her roots, and is unlikely to work with any social worker who does not respect this. Philomela is not conforming to what society wants her to be; she is establishing who she is. There are strength and power in her voice and experience, something that threatens the cosy notions of rehabilitation and whiteness central to social work. Philomela's narrative demands that social workers accept her for who she is and who she has been and demands that social workers get on board to move forward – but only on her terms.

12.7 Self-determination in the law

The right to self-determination is enshrined in the 2007 Declaration on the Rights of Indigenous Peoples (UNDRIP).[43] This Declaration reads:

> *Article 3*
> *Indigenous peoples have the right of self-determination. By virtue of that right they freely determine their political status and freely pursue their economic, social and cultural development.*
>
> *Article 4*
> *Indigenous peoples, in exercising their right to self-determination, have the right to autonomy or self-government in matters relating to their internal and local affairs, as well as ways and means for financing their autonomous functions.*
>
> *Article 5*
> *Indigenous peoples have the right to maintain and strengthen their distinct political, legal, economic, social and cultural institutions, while retaining their rights to participate fully, if they so choose, in the political, economic, social and cultural life of the State.*

Note that this is a Declaration, not a Convention, which means it was adopted by the United Nations General Assembly , not signed or ratified by member states. It passed with overwhelming support – 144 votes to 4. These four voting against were Australia, Canada, New Zealand and the United States. In 2009, Australia formally endorsed the Declaration, but the right to 'maintain and strengthen their distinct political, legal, economic, social and cultural institutions' has not been upheld in Australia. There is no constitutionally recognised First Nations authority, nor recognition of the validity of First Nations law.[44] There is no treaty between the colonial authorities and First Nations, nor was the land ever ceded.

There are some legal institutions that hint at self-determination, albeit always limited and overseen by colonial authority. Victoria, New South Wales, South Australia and Queensland all have some kind of Koori, Circle Sentencing, Nunga or Murri court, where First Nations communities are involved in the court process.[45] These are not courts that practise First Nations law – they still enforce the colonial law – however, they involve First Nations people in the legal process. They attempt to embed therapeutic jurisprudence and restorative justice into the criminal legal system in a culturally relevant way. This is not true self-determination, but it is participation, which is a step in the right direction.

A necessary legal step towards self-determination is a treaty. Australia is the only Commonwealth country not to have a treaty with its First Nations, although some jurisdictions are further along this journey than others. In 2018 the Victorian Parliament passed the *Advancing the Treaty Process with Aboriginal Victorians Act 2018* (Vic). This is not a treaty, but a process to work towards a treaty. The Northern Territory and Western Australia have both indicated they will work towards a treaty, but the Commonwealth has so far resisted calls, including from the National Constitutional Convention.

Box 12.2 *The Uluru Statement from the Heart*

We, gathered at the 2017 National Constitutional Convention, coming from all points of the southern sky, make this statement from the heart: Our Aboriginal and Torres Strait Islander tribes were the first sovereign Nations of the Australian continent and its adjacent islands, and possessed it under our own laws and customs. This our ancestors did, according to the reckoning of our culture, from the Creation, according to the common law from 'time immemorial', and according to science more than 60,000 years ago. This sovereignty is a spiritual notion: the ancestral tie between the land, or 'mother nature', and the Aboriginal and Torres Strait Islander peoples who were born therefrom, remain attached thereto, and must one day return thither to be united with our ancestors. This link is the basis of the ownership of the soil, or better, of sovereignty. It has never been ceded or extinguished and co-exists with the sovereignty of the Crown. How could it be otherwise? That peoples possessed a land for sixty millennia and this sacred link disappears from world history in merely the last two hundred years? With substantive constitutional change and structural reform, we believe this ancient sovereignty can shine through as a fuller expression of Australia's nationhood. Proportionally, we are the most incarcerated people on the planet. We are not an innately criminal people. Our children are aliened from their families at unprecedented rates. This cannot be because we have no love for them. And our youth languish in detention in obscene numbers. They should be our hope for the future. These dimensions of our crisis tell plainly the structural nature of our problem. This is the torment of our powerlessness. We seek constitutional reforms to empower our people and take a rightful place in our own country. When we have power over our destiny our children will flourish. They will walk in two worlds and their culture will be a gift to their country. We call for the establishment of a First Nations Voice enshrined in the Constitution. Makarrata is the culmination of our agenda: the coming together after a struggle. It captures our aspirations for a fair and truthful relationship with the people of Australia and a better future for our children based on justice and self-determination. We seek a Makarrata Commission to supervise a process of agreement-making between governments and First Nations and truth-telling about our history. In 1967 we were counted, in 2017 we seek to be heard. We leave base camp and start our trek across this vast country. We invite you to walk with us in a movement of the Australian people for a better future.

The Uluru Statement from the Heart, in Box 12.2, was developed by the National Constitutional Convention in 2017. This document demands constitutional recognition, a 'Voice to Parliament' and a 'Makarrata Commission to supervise a process of agreement-making between governments and First Nations and truth-telling about our history.' Megan Davis, a Cobble Cobble woman from the Barrungam nation, writes of the Voice to Parliament:

> *The voice is about active participation in the democratic life of the state, whereby Indige nous viewpoints and opinions on policies and laws that affect them are not filtered through bureaucrats or peak bodies, but directly delivered to parliament through a process that is Aboriginal-led and Aboriginal designed.*[46]

The demand for representation, for a treaty and for truth-telling indicate how far Australia must travel to reach reconciliation. These are necessary ingredients for Reconciliation as a step on the journey of decolonisation but fall far short of full self-determination.

12.8 Social work's role in decolonising the law

Much in the way that First Nations law cannot be understood as distinct from First Nations culture, land and society, decolonising law cannot be done without decolonising all other interactions between settler and First Nations people and communities. For social workers, the first step in decolonisation and Reconciliation is to understand the history and context of First Nations people and communities. This must be paired with recognition of the diversity of experiences.

Scholars have pointed out the problems with using the colonialist law to decolonise, critiquing the push for mere recognition of First Nations people in the Constitution as insufficiently radical.[47] Maddison argues that 'White Australia can't solve black problems. White Australia is the problem'.[48] Social workers must instead look to First Nations communities for leadership:

> *... many First Nations in Australia are taking back control, turning away from the state as a solution to their challenges and doing more and more for themselves. Look at the Yawuru in Broome, the Ngarrindjeri in South Australia, the Yorta Yorta in Victoria. The successes of rebuilding Indigenous nations are becoming evident here as well, and yet Australian governments resist supporting these successes at every turn.*[49]

Rowe, Baldry and Earles also advocate decolonising social work by learning from First Nations approaches.[50] In legal settings, this has particular relevance, as so much of the oppression of First Nations people and communities has been enforced by the colonial law. First Nations law, its focus on caring for land and community, its integration into society and ritual may hold answers to many contemporary issues beyond the relationship between First Nations and settler people and communities. This requires social workers to be guided by First Nations thinkers, so we turn to Watson for guidance:

> *How might decolonisation occur and what is the decolonisation of the mind? Perhaps one example to consider is how we might think about the condition of dispossession outside of the 'logic of possession (as a hallmark of modernity, liberalism, and humanism)' and to enable instead a First Nations' standpoint. The challenge would be to think outside of the colonial matrix of power, thinking in terms of a new international law, which is 'disconnected from its own imperial sources and history'. It would challenge the imperial connections that have shaped the foundations of international law and, if effected, would enable us to move away from its colonial*

> *origins and foundations. However, it requires transformative renewal to begin again and move away from what is still considered a 'normal' way of being.*[51]

Social workers can do this – social work training primes social workers to consider new ways of being – but this process will be a long one, a long journey in partnership.

Main points

1. The history of social work participation in the Stolen Generations and the continued overrepresentation of First Nations' children in the child protection system is highly problematic.
2. There is a difference between 'law', which means 'something laid down or fixed' and is fundamentally a colonialist notion, and 'lore', used by First Nations people to mean 'to learn', which is guidance written in the landscape, in the sky, songs and stories. The history of law in relation to First Nations people was based on the premise that First Nation people needed to be 'controlled' and 'protected', as they were incapable of looking after themselves. The Stolen Generations and Intervention are just two examples of paternalistic policies that attempted to regulate and control First Nations people.
3. Customary law, which is still practised in First Nations communities where pre-colonial culture is dominant, is not recognised by colonial authorities and has not been reconciled within Australia's legal system.
4. The right to self-determination is enshrined in the Declaration on the Rights of Indigenous Peoples 2007, formally endorsed by Australia in 2009. Self-determination for First Nations people has not been achieved in Australia.
5. Social workers must look towards First Nations communities for leadership and guidance on decolonisation and reconciliation.

Discussion questions

1. Research the Aboriginal and Torres Strait Islander Child Placement Principle. Upon removal, how often are First Nations children placed in the first preference for placement (the child's own extended family)? What about placement preference two, three or four – with settler families?
2. Does your jurisdiction have a Koori, Circle Sentencing, Nunga or Murri court? How does it work and what are the eligibility requirements to have a matter heard in this court?
3. How have restorative justice and therapeutic jurisprudence been incorporated into these courts?

4. Australia does not have a treaty with its First Nations people. Which countries have made treaties and what would be the benefits of Australia creating a treaty?

Further reading

Irene Watson, *Aboriginal Peoples, Colonialism and International Law: Raw Law, Indigenous Peoples and the Law* (Routledge, 2015).

Bruce Pascoe, *Dark Emu: Aboriginal Australia and the Birth of Agriculture* (Scribe Publications UK Ltd, 2018).

Bill Gammage, *The Biggest Estate on Earth: How Aborigines Made Australia* (Allen & Unwin, 2011).

Noel Pearson and Shireen Morris, *A Rightful Place: A Road Map to Recognition* (Schwartz Publishing Pty. Ltd, 2017).

Thalia Anthony, Indigenous People, Crime and Punishment (Routledge, 2013).

Sarah Maddison, *The Colonial Fantasy: Why White Australia Can't Solve Black Problems* (Allen & Unwin, 2019).

Tom Calma, 'The Role of Social Workers as Human Rights Workers with Indigenous People and Communities' (12 February 2008) <https://www.humanrights.gov.au/news/speeches/role-social-workers-human-rights-workers-indigenous-people-and-communities>.

Bonnie Freeman, 'Soup Days and Decolonisation: Indigenous Pathways to Anti-Oppressive Practice' in Donna Baines, *Doing Anti-Oppressive Practice: Social Justice Social Work* 3rd ed. (Fernwood Publishing, 2017).

Larissa Behrendt, *Indigenous Legal Relations in Australia* (Oxford University Press, 2009).

Bindi Bennett, Sue Green, Stephanie Gilbert and Dawn Bessarab, *Our Voices: Aboriginal and Torres Strait Islander Social Work* (Palgrave Macmillan, 2013).

John Coates and Mel Gray, *Indigenous Social Work around the World: Towards Culturally Relevant Education and Practice* (Taylor and Francis), 23.

12.9 References

[1] Ruby Langford Ginibi, 'Aboriginal Traditional and Customary Law' (1994) 1 *Law Text Culture* 7, 11.
[2] Maggie Walter, Sandra Taylor and Daphne Habibis, 'How White Is Social Work in Australia?' (2011) 64(1) *Australian Social Work* 6.
[3] Sharlene Nipperess and Charlotte Williams, *Critical Multicultural Practice in Social Work: New Perspectives and Practices* (Allen & Unwin, 2019).
[4] John Coates et al, *Decolonizing Social Work* (Routledge, 2016) <http://ebookcentral.proquest.com/lib/rmit/detail.action?docID=1182736>.
[5] Kingsley Palmer, *Noongar People, Noongar Land: The Resilience of Aboriginal Culture in the South West of Western Australia* (Aboriginal Studies Press, 2016).
[6] Ian Keen, *Aboriginal Economy & Society: Australia at the Threshold of Colonisation* (Oxford University Press, 2004) 212, 251.
[7] Irene Watson, *Aboriginal Peoples, Colonialism and International Law : Raw Law* (Routledge, 2015).
[8] C.F. Black, *The Land Is the Source of the Law: A Dialogic Encounter with Indigenous Jurisprudence* (Routledge, 2010) 3.
[9] Bruce Pascoe, *Dark Emu: Aboriginal Australia and the Birth of Agriculture.* (Magabala Books Aboriginal Corporation, 2018) 180.
[10] Watson (n 7).
[11] Bruce Pascoe (n 9) 185.
[12] John Connor, *The Australian Frontier Wars, 1788–1838* (UNSW Press, 2002).
[13] Bruce Elder, *Blood on the Wattle: Massacres and Maltreatment of Aboriginal Australians Since 1788* expanded ed. (New Holland Books, 1999).
[14] Senate Standing Committees on Legal and Constitutional Affairs, *Unfinished Business: Indigenous Stolen Wages* (text, Commonwealth of Australia, 2006) <https://www.aph.gov.au/Parliamentary_Business/Committees/Senate/Legal_and_Constitutional_Affairs/Completed_inquiries/2004-07/stolen_wages/report/index>.
[15] See, for example, Aileen Teo, 'Stolen Wages Update: Establishment of the NSW Aboriginal Trust Fund Repayment Scheme' (2005) 6(9) *Indigenous Law Bulletin* 12; Thalia Anthony, 'Indigenous Stolen Wages: Historical Exploitation and Contemporary Injustice' [2013] (118) *Precedent (Sydney, N.S.W.)* 42.
[16] Pat Anderson, *Report of the Northern Territory Board of Inquiry into the Protection of Aboriginal Children from Sexual Abuse* (Board of Inquiry into the Protection of Aboriginal Children from Sexual Abuse, 2007).
[17] James Anaya, *Report by the Special Rapporteur on the Situation of Human Rights and Fundamental Freedoms of Indigenous People* (No A/HRC/15/37/Add.4, United Nations Human Rights Council) 25.
[18] Dr Stephen Gray, *The Northern Territory Intervention – An Evaluation* (Castan Centre for Human Rights Law, Monash University, 2015) 45.
[19] *Wik Peoples v The State of Queensland* [1996] HCA 40.
[20] *Akiba v Commonwealth* [2013] HCA 33.
[21] Richard H. Bartlett, *Native Title in Australia* 3rd ed. (LexisNexis Butterworths, 2015).
[22] Thalia Anthony, 'FactCheck Q&A: Are Indigenous Australians the Most Incarcerated People on Earth?', *The Conversation* <http://theconversation.com/factcheck-qanda-are-indigenous-australians-the-most-incarcerated-people-on-earth-78528>.
[23] Australian Bureau of Statistics, '4517.0 – Prisoners in Australia, 2018' (6 December 2018) <http://www.abs.gov.au/ausstats/abs@.nsf/Lookup/by%20Subject/4517.0~2018~Main%20Features~Prisoner%20characteristics,%20Australia~4>.
[24] *Youth Justice in Australia 2016–17* (Australian Institute of Health and Welfare, 2018) 54.
[25] Australian Bureau of Statistics (n 23).

[26] Russell Hogg, 'Penality and Modes of Regulating Indigenous Peoples in Australia' (2001) 3(3) *Punishment & Society* 355, 368.
[27] Thalia Anthony, *Indigenous People, Crime and Punishment* (Routledge, 2013) <http://ebookcentral.proquest.com/lib/rmit/detail.action?docID=1323316>.
[28] Ibid 32.
[29] Anthony (n 22).
[30] *Royal Commission into Aboriginal Deaths in Custody* (Australian Government Publishing Service, 1991) <http://www.austlii.edu.au/au/other/IndigLRes/rciadic/>.
[31] Nick Evershed et al, 'Deaths inside: Every Indigenous Death in Custody since 2008 Tracked', *the Guardian* <http://www.theguardian.com/australia-news/ng-interactive/2018/aug/28/deaths-inside-indigenous-australian-deaths-in-custody>.
[32] Alexandra Gannoni and Samantha Bricknell, *National Deaths in Custody Program: Deaths in Custody in Australia 2016–17* (Text, Australian Institute of Criminology, 21 February 2019) <https://aic.gov.au/publications/sr/sr13>.
[33] Ginibi (n 1) 11.
[34] Central Land Council, 'Kinship and Skin Names' <https://www.clc.org.au/index.php?/articles/info/aboriginal-kinship>.
[35] Lana Quall, Diwurruwurru-jaru Aboriginal Corporation and Katherine Region Stolen Generations Families Committee, *So Far from Home: Oral Histories of the Stolen Generations* (Diwurruwurru-jaru Aboriginal Corp, 2002).
[36] Nilan Yu, 'Interrogating Social Work: Australian Social Work and the Stolen Generations' [2018] *Journal of Social Work* 1468017318794230.
[37] Australian Association of Social Workers, 'Acknowledgement Statement to Aboriginal and Torres Strait Islander People' (2004) 14(1) *National Bulletin* 21.
[38] *Child Protection and Aboriginal and Torres Strait Islander Children* (Text, Australian Institute of Family Studies, 31 January 2019) <https://aifs.gov.au/cfca/publications/child-protection-and-aboriginal-and-torres-strait-islander-children>.
[39] Ibid.
[40] *Family, Domestic and Sexual Violence in Australia 2018* (Australian Institute of Health and Welfare, 2018) <https://www.aihw.gov.au/reports/domestic-violence/family-domestic-sexual-violence-in-australia-2018>.
[41] *The National Apology to the Stolen Generations* (Reconciliation Australia, 2018) <https://www.reconciliation.org.au/wp-content/uploads/2018/02/ra-letstalk_factsheet-apology_v1.pdf>.
[42] *Child Protection and Aboriginal and Torres Strait Islander Children* (n 38).
[43] UN General Assembly, United Nations Declaration on the Rights of Indigenous Peoples: resolution/adopted by the General Assembly, 2 October 2007, A/RES/61/295.
[44] Megan Davis, 'Self-Determination and the Right to Be Heard' in Noel Pearson and Shireen Morris (eds), *A Rightful Place: A Road Map to Recognition* (Schwartz Publishing Pty. Ltd, 2017) 62.
[45] *Incarceration Rates of Aboriginal and Torres Strait Islander Peoples (DP 84)* (Australian Law Reform Commission, 19 July 2017) <https://www.alrc.gov.au/publications/specialist-courts-and-diversion-programs>.
[46] Megan Davis (n 44) 67.
[47] Sarah Maddison, 'Recognise What? The Limitations of Settler Colonial Constitutional Reform' (2017) 52(1) *Australian Journal of Political Science* 3.
[48] Sarah Maddison, 'White Australia Can't Solve Black Problems. White Australia Is the Problem', *The Guardian*, 6 April 2019, sec. Australia news, <https://www.theguardian.com/australia-news/2019/apr/07/white-australia-cant-solve-black-problems-white-australia-is-the-problem>.
[49] Ibid.

[50] Simone Rowe, Eileen Baldry and Wendy Earles, 'Decolonising Social Work Research: Learning from Critical Indigenous Approaches' (2015) 68(3) *Australian Social Work* 296.
[51] Watson (n 7).

Chapter 13 ADULT GUARDIANSHIP LAW

Margaret Spencer and Chris Maylea

Dr Margaret Spencer started her career as a nurse before requalifying as a social worker. Margaret has nearly 40 years' experience working with persons with a range of cognitive disabilities and deemed to have complex care needs. For 29 years she worked in the inner city of Sydney supporting persons with cognitive disabilities who were homeless or at risk of homelessness, as well as working with families 'at-risk'. In 2007, she was awarded a doctorate from the University of Sydney. Her research interest is in the area of reproductive justice for persons with cognitive disabilities, with a particular focus on parenting with intellectual disability. She currently lectures in social work in the School of Education and Social Work at the University of Sydney. Since 2009, Margaret has been a tribunal member in the Guardianship Division of the NSW Civil and Administrative Tribunal.

All adults have the right to make their own decisions, including people with disabilities. For most decisions, from choosing what home to live in or choosing what to have for dinner, people will consult with, seek support or share the decision with others. When a person cannot make decisions independently or with the support of others, there are legal provisions that allow others to be appointed to make decisions on their behalf. A person can plan ahead and 'draw up' legal instruments appointing someone to make decisions on their behalf in the case of them losing capacity. Alternatively, orders can be made by a tribunal or court appointing a subsite decision maker for a person deemed to lack the capacity to make important life decisions or to manage their financial affairs. When this is done voluntarily it is often done using 'powers of attorney', when involuntary it is usually called 'guardianship'.[*] This approach is referred to as *substituted decision-making.*

Over the last 15 years, the issue of substitute decision-making, particularly where it is imposed by the state, has come under increased critique. Since the introduction of the *Convention on the Rights of Persons with Disabilities*[1] (*Disability Convention*) the approach of taking away the

[*] These are different to mental health treatment orders, which are discussed in Chapter 14.

right to make decisions has begun to be questioned.[2] The *Disability Convention* requires that people are supported to make their own decisions, and not to have their rights to make decisions taken away from them on the basis of disability or diagnosis. The approach required by the *Disability Convention* is called *supported decision-making.*[3]

Despite these challenges to the established order, the established order is still very well established and social workers will have to work within it. In Australia, adult guardianship laws are made by the states and territories none of which are compliant with the *Disability Convention*.[4] In recent years, there has been and continues to be significant law reform occurring in this space as states and territories grapple with how to make legislative change in order to comply with the *Disability Convention*.[5*] Generally, this means only allowing substituted decision-making as a last resort, with substitute decision-makers being required to act in the least restrictive manner, giving preference to the person's will and preferences while acting in their best interests.

This chapter explains the concepts of capacity and supported decision-making before outlining the legal frameworks that enable voluntary instruments and involuntary orders. It concludes with an overview of supported decision making in the law and guidance for social workers working in adult guardianship law.

Consider *Patrick's Case*, in Box 13.1, as an example of the way the law can be used both to take away Patrick's right to make decisions, and to limit the extent to which his right to make decisions can be taken away.

Box 13.1 *Patrick's Case*

Patrick's Case is a Victorian Supreme Court case about an administration order made by the Victorian Civil and Administrative Tribunal.[6] *Patrick had been living in a mental health inpatient unit as an involuntary patient and the hospital wanted to transfer him to a supported residential service. When they tried to move him to the residential service he returned to his home, which he owned. The hospital social worker applied to the tribunal to appoint an administrator who would sell his house. Patrick's lawyers claimed that the hospital wanted the administrator to sell Patrick's house to force him to move into the supported residential service. The hospital social worker was clear that this would be in Patrick's best interests. The tribunal approved this application and Patrick's house was sold, so Patrick appealed this decision to the Supreme Court of Victoria.*

The Supreme Court found that the tribunal had made the wrong decision because the decision to appoint an administrator was not based on Patrick's ability to manage his finances. Patrick had demonstrated he could

---

* See Chapter 17 for an example of a law reform process reviewing adult guardianship law.

manage his finances. The tribunal decision was made based on what would be in Patrick's 'best interests', not based on Patrick's rights. The Supreme Court found this was a breach of the Victorian Charter of Human Rights and Responsibilities. The judge who made this decision, Justice Bell, later said that without the Charter Patrick's Case would not have succeeded.[7]

Patrick's Case highlights three things: how best interests approaches conflict with rights-based approaches, the importance of understanding the law, and the usefulness of human rights charters. Note that the court did not say that Patrick could never have his right to make decisions taken away, but that the ability of the law to take away Patrick's right to make decisions was limited. Social workers cannot just do what is in Patrick's 'best interests' – they can only do what the law allows them to do. It is worth reading the full text of *Patrick's Case*, as Justice Bell takes the time to explain the full background of the issue and how human rights should be considered when the law allows for substitute decision-making.

13.1 Capacity

Central to understanding this area of law is the question of capacity. This is a bit confusing as there are really two different meanings of capacity and they are often used interchangeably. *Legal capacity* is the legal ability to do legal things, such as sign a contract, get married, sue someone, make a will and vote. Young children, for example, do not have legal capacity. Legal capacity is different from *decision-making capacity* or *mental capacity*, which is the ability to make decisions. This is defined in a number of different ways, but one main way is that a person must be able to do the following things:

1. **Understand** the information about the decision and how it will affect them
2. **Retain** the information about the decision
3. **Use** and/or **weigh** the information about the decision
4. **Communicate** the decision.

Mental capacity is decision-specific, so just because a person might lack the capacity to make financial decisions, for example, does not mean they will automatically lack the capacity to make decisions about where they live or whom they marry. It cannot be assumed that a person lacks capacity just because of their diagnosis. For example, it is quite possible that a person can hear voices or have to spend a really long time thinking about a decision and still have the capacity to make that decision.

This means that a functional assessment is required to determine a person's mental capacity. A functional assessment will specifically focus on the area where decisions are required, for example, lifestyle or financial interests. The assessment will evaluate the person's capacity to understand the information related to the decision that needs to be made, retain and weigh up the information, understand the consequences of potential decisions, make and communicate that decision.

It is also important that the test of capacity does not relate to the nature of the decision – people have a right to make bad decisions. It must be their capacity to make the decision that is assessed, not the decision itself. Mental capacity can also change over time, so a person might be able to make a decision one day and not be able to do so the next.

Traditionally legal and mental capacity have been linked. This has meant that if a person was assessed as lacking mental capacity they would have their legal capacity taken away. For example, a person who is assessed as lacking capacity to make financial decisions would have someone else appointed to administer their finances. The *Disability Convention* requires a different way of thinking about this. It requires that legal capacity is not linked to mental capacity. Instead, the *Disability Convention* requires that countries:

> *... take appropriate measures to provide access by persons with disabilities to the support they may require in exercising their legal capacity.*[8]

This means that rather than assessing a person's ability to make decisions, people must be supported to make decisions. They must be supported to have the mental capacity to exercise their legal capacity. In some cases, this will be quite straightforward. For example, it is no longer accepted that just because a person is non-verbal that they cannot communicate their decision. People who are non-verbal are instead supported to communicate non-verbally, through actions or assistive technology. It is less straightforward when there are questions about a person's ability to remember or retain information, or when their mental distress might interfere with their ability to use information. Strategies for addressing this are explored later in this chapter.

Under the current law, the *Disability Convention* approach has had some influence on Australian adult guardianship law, but most arrangements are still based on assessing a person's mental capacity and denying them legal capacity based on that assessment. This is true across a number of areas of law, including mental health law, criminal law and medical decision-making. Often the substitute decision-making will require the substitute decision-maker to include or involve the person in making the decision, but ultimately the final say remains with the substitute decision-maker.

People can also have a *litigation guardian* appointed for them if they are assessed as lacking capacity to uphold their rights in legal processes.[9] Depending on how these processes are implemented, they can bring

Australian law closer to the *Disability Convention*. Other practices are not compatible with the *Disability Convention*, such as restrictive practices for people with disabilities in schools, hospitals, residential facilitates and prisons. Increasingly, substituted decision-making is used more as a last resort, but it is still widely used. Supported decision-making is often proposed as an alternative to substituted decision-making.

13.2 SUPPORTED DECISION-MAKING

Supported decision-making sits on a continuum of decision-making approaches, between autonomous and substitute.

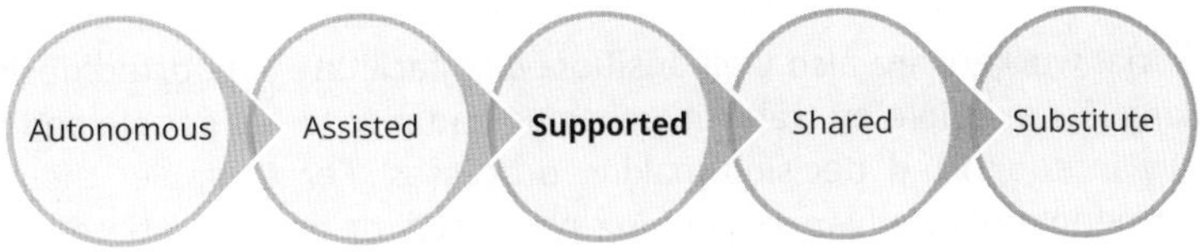

Figure 13.1 *A continuum of decision-making approaches*[10]

Few major decisions will be autonomous for any person making a decision. For decisions such as buying a car or renting a house, people will often seek out assistance both on the process and implementation, if not the decision itself. This level of assistance is different to supported decision-making, which is a much more structured process. Shared decision-making is very similar to supported decision-making, but in a supported decision-making approach the person retains the final say over what happens.[11] In a substituted decision-making approach the person's right to make decisions is taken away, although they may still be consulted on the decision.

Supported decision-making is based on the idea that everyone has the right to make their own decisions and that everyone can exercise this right if they have the right support. It allows people to change their minds, make risky or unpopular decisions and learn by experience. There are five steps to the supported decision-making process:

1. Finding the options and getting information
2. Weighing up choices
3. Deciding
4. Acting on the decision
5. Reflecting.

People have the right to make decisions about the supported decision-making process. This means they get to choose which decisions they want support with, whom they want to support them and what parts of the decision making-process they want support with. This means that social workers may be *decision supporters*, but only if the person agrees for them to play that role. Social workers are well positioned to play this role in some circumstances, as they are trained in reflexive practice and reflective techniques that can help make sure they are not taking over the process. Social workers cannot impose themselves as decision supporters – this would be to substitute the decision about who gets to provide the support. Examples of support include:

- Formal or informal support networks
- Advance planning
- Peer support
- Legally nominated support persons.[12]

Social workers are also well positioned to facilitate supported decision-making, for example by training, coaching and mentoring people and their family in supported decision-making processes. For example, they may assist people with advance planning processes, or help negotiate conflict when supported-decision making gets difficult in practice. There are also a range of different laws which can aid supported-decision making, discussed later in the chapter.

Social workers can also support decision-making by helping people with advance care planning, either through helping people formalise a decision supporter or substitute decision-maker or by documenting their preferences. If a person is likely to need help making decisions in the future, such as people who experience regular episodes of mental distress or who have a degenerative condition, social workers can help them plan for that and assist them in creating voluntary instruments.

13.3 VOLUNTARY INSTRUMENTS

There are a range of legal ways people can hand over decision-making power to another person, called different things in different jurisdictions for different decisions. These can include powers of attorney, advanced medical treatment plans, advanced care plans, advanced statements, psychiatric advance directives, living wills and Ulysses agreements.[13] This section introduces readers to powers of attorney, which are a very common instrument, but social workers should ensure they understand the various options available in their jurisdiction.

A power of attorney is a legal document that a person makes voluntarily. The right to make a power of attorney is an example of legal capacity – children and people who are assessed as not having mental capacity are not legally allowed to grant a power of attorney. Powers of attorney can be *enduring* or *non-enduring*. A non-enduring power of attorney stops having effect if a person loses mental capacity. This might be used if a person wants to give someone else control of their business while they are overseas or to sell their house for them. Enduring powers of attorney stay in effect when a person loses mental capacity. An enduring power of attorney can also be a *sleeping* power of attorney and only comes into effect when the person lacks capacity.

A power of attorney gives certain *authorities* to a nominated person or persons. The authorities given under an enduring power of attorney vary from state to state. In New South Wales, South Australia, Tasmania and Western Australia enduring power of attorney is limited to financial decision-making powers. In Victoria and Queensland, enduring power of attorney instruments may include the authority to make lifestyle decision-making powers as well as financial decision-making powers. In some jurisdictions, there is specific legislation for medical decisions to appoint a medical decision maker.[14] Victoria has also introduced a *supportive* power of attorney, which is discussed later in this chapter.

There are some restrictions on who can be granted powers of attorney; usually, they must be an adult and have mental and legal capacity themselves. Often, they will be a lawyer, a financial manager, a family member or trusted friend, but there are also independent state or public trustees who can be appointed. People can appoint more than one person as an alternative power of attorney in case the first one is not able to take up the role. People who are granted powers of attorney must act in good faith and not abuse their power. This usually means not acting in their own interest, such as giving themselves gifts of money or using the other person's money to invest in their own business.

So long as a person is assessed as having mental capacity they can change or revoke their power of attorney. If there are disputes about a person having mental capacity, or if there are issues with the way a person is using the power, there are oversight bodies that can intervene. This will usually be a tribunal or a court, although state or public trustees will usually have internal dispute resolution and complaints processes.

Social workers should be very alert to elder abuse and other abuses of power, where people may have been pressured into making powers of attorney or where a power of attorney is being abused. Financial abuse is the most common type of elder abuse,[15] and there are criminal penalties for people who abuse these powers.[16]

Powers of attorney are not entirely compliant with the *Disability Convention* because the *Disability Convention* requires that people be able to change their minds at any time, retaining legal capacity irrespective of assessments of their mental capacity. Despite this, they do provide an opportunity for people to make their own decisions about who will make decisions for them, which is not the case with guardianship or financial orders made by a court or tribunal.

Table 13.1 *Powers of attorney legislation*

Jurisdiction	Relevant legislation
ACT	*Powers of Attorney Act 2006* (ACT)
NSW	*Powers of Attorney Act 2003* (NSW)
NT	*Powers of Attorney Act 1980* (NT)
Qld	*Powers of Attorney Act 1998* (Qld)
SA	*Powers of Attorney and Agency Act 1984* (SA)
Tas	*Powers of Attorney Act 2000* (Tas)
Vic	*Powers of Attorney Act 2014* (Vic)
WA	*Guardianship and Administration Act 1990* (WA)

13.4 INVOLUNTARY ORDERS

When people are assessed as not having decision making-capacity, they cannot make voluntary orders such as powers of attorney. In these situations, people with an interest in the welfare and well-being of a person can apply to a tribunal for an order to appoint another person as a decision-maker called a guardian or financial manager.[*]

These orders are only made *when* the person is assessed as lacking mental capacity, not before. There are also additional requirements that the person must have a cognitive disability,[†] and need a decision or decisions made for them. There are generally no restrictions on who can apply for these orders, but it is generally family, friends or health and welfare workers, including social workers. In some roles, such as in hospitals or aged care, a main part of the social worker's role is to apply for these orders.

A guardianship order appoints a guardian who makes decisions to do with a person's lifestyle and well-being. The types of decision-making functions a guardian may be authorised to make include decisions about accommodation, healthcare services and medical and dental treatments. Depending on the jurisdictions, a guardian may also be authorised with coercive powers such as to authorise the police or ambulance to take, keep or return a person to a health or residential facility, to override a person's objections to medical treatment, to approve restrictive practices, to control passport and travel arrangements or to decide access arrangements and approve legal services.

[*] These are different to mental health treatment orders, which are covered in Chapter 14.

[†] A cognitive disability is an umbrella term for conditions that affect a person's thinking and reasoning; cognitive disabilities including neurodegenerative conditions, neuro-atypical conditions such as autism, intellectual disability, acquired brain injury, and mental illness.

The tribunal can appoint a private person such as a family member or friend as a guardian. If there is no suitable private person to fulfil this role, the tribunal can appoint a guardian from the Office of the Public Advocate (Vic, SA and WA) or the Office of the Public Guardian (NSW, ACT, Qld, Tas and NT). Social workers are commonly employed as advocates or guardians within such statutory authorities.

A financial administration order or a financial management order authorises an administrator or financial manager to make decisions about the person's property and finances. A financial manager can be a friend or family member or public or state trustee. Financial orders can be plenary, meaning they can be inclusive of all a person's assets and for an unspecified length of time, or non-plenary, meaning they will be reviewed within a stated period and may include exclusion clauses. A person appointed as a private financial manager by a tribunal is subject to government oversight and has annual financial reporting responsibilities.

Generally, the process for a guardianship order is begun with an application to a civil and administrative tribunal. Social workers, particularly those in hospitals, elder care and disability, will often write these reports. Social workers can help people participate in this process by providing them and their supporters with copies of the report before it is sent. As with any court or tribunal reports (discussed in Chapter 7), social workers need to write the report with an understanding of what the tribunal is trying to do. The criteria for determining if a guardianship order should be made is different in different jurisdictions, so the report needs to respond to the right criteria.

There will usually be a tribunal hearing where the tribunal will make a decision about the application. Social workers should ensure that the person is as involved as possible, ideally being able to participate in the hearing itself and share their will and preferences. These decisions can usually be appealed to a court or an application can be made back to the tribunal to revoke the order.

At the tribunal, guardianship and financial orders will be determined on a threshold test. This means that it cannot just be a 'good idea' to make an order. For example, in NSW, the NSW Civil and Administrative Tribunal can make a guardianship order if the person has a disability that means they are 'totally or partially incapable of managing his or her person' and if the person is 'in need of a guardian'.[17] The tribunal must decide if the person meets this test in relation to the principles in section 4 of the *Guardianship Act 1987* (NSW). These principles include, among others, that the 'welfare and interests' of the person are the paramount considerations, but that the freedom of decision and freedom of action of the person be restricted as little as possible.

This characterises guardianship and administration law in NSW as clearly best interests in nature. Compare this with the South Australian approach, which requires the paramount consideration to be given to 'what would, in the opinion of the decision maker, be the wishes of the person in the matter if he or she were not mentally incapacitated'.[18] This locates the decision in the context of the person, not in the context of some decision-maker's idea of what is good or bad. In addition, the present wishes of the person must be considered, alongside existing arrangements and the requirement that decisions are least restrictive. This is not quite rights-based and is not compliant with the *Disability Convention*, but it is a step in the rights-based direction, as it does not seek to presume what is in a person's best interests, instead looking to work out what the person would have wanted and incorporating that with what they are communicating that they currently want. This is different than supported decision-making, which requires that people are always allowed and supported to make their own decisions.

Box 13.2 *J's boat*

In J v Guardianship and Administration Board,[19] *J wanted to live on his boat. J had been living on his boat prior to having his leg amputated and wanted to return to it. In a very similar set of circumstances to Patrick's Case (see Box 13.1), J's social worker did not think that it would be safe for J to live on the boat. The social worker wrote that J had:*

> *... been assessed as lacking the capacity to decide about his accommodation and as such a Guardian is required to decide about his discharge location.*

The Tasmanian Supreme Court found that there were clear risks in J going back to live on his boat, and intensive support was necessary, but that J did not meet the criteria in the Guardianship and Administration Act 1995 (Tas). It may have been a bad decision for J to live on his boat, but it was his right to make that decision. This meant that a guardian could not be appointed.

J's case, in Box 13.2, highlights a key lesson for social workers. There may well be a very good reason to provide support, which may require intensive and expensive services, but this does not mean a person should have their ability to make decisions taken away from them. The law should not be used to make delivering services easier. Instead, wherever possible, the law should be used to support people to make their own decisions.

Table 13.2 *Guardianship legislation*

Jurisdiction	Relevant legislation
ACT	*Guardianship and Management of Property Act 1991* (ACT)
NSW	*Guardianship Act 1987* (NSW)
NT	*Guardianship of Adults Act 2016* (NT)
Qld	*Guardianship and Administration Act 2012* (Qld)
SA	*Guardianship and Administration Act 1993* (SA)
Tas	*Guardianship and Administration Act 1995* (Tas)
Vic	*Guardianship and Administration Act 2019* (Vic)
WA	*Guardianship and Administration Act 1990* (WA)

13.4.1 Informal guardianship

Aside from the legal frameworks that govern guardianship, much substitute decision-making occurs informally, outside legal frameworks, within families or other relationships. Sometimes this will be voluntary, where a person simply allows someone else to take control of their affairs, and sometimes this will be involuntary, where a person uses coercion or force to gain control. Often, it will be difficult for social workers to tell if an informal arrangement is based on informed consent or if there is coercion or abuse present. These informal arrangements might suit people who want to avoid the processes of the voluntary or involuntary legal systems, but it also means that they will lack the protections from abuse that those systems offer. Social workers may find themselves in situations where they decide to apply for guardianship orders not as a way to take a person's decision-making power away from them, but to protect them from a person who is abusing them.

In these cases, social workers need to work through the ethical and legal issues and apply their own reflexive processes. Questions of capacity and discrimination get very difficult in these situations. If we accept that a person who is assessed as having capacity has the 'right' to stay in an abusive relationship, should we deny this right to someone on the basis that they can be assessed as not having capacity? Is replacing one form of substituted decision-making for another the best way to address issues of power and control in relationships?

13.5 Supported Decision-Making in Law

Victoria has made the most progress in embedding supported decision-making in legal frameworks, but other jurisdictions are also doing work in this area, such as Tasmania and Queensland's review of their guardianship legislation.[20] All jurisdictions, including Victoria, still allow substituted decision-making.

In Victoria, people can make *supportive powers of attorney* under the *Powers of Attorney Act 2014* (Vic), which allow people to appoint someone to assist them to make decisions. This person cannot *make* those decisions – it is not a substitute decision-making process – but they are empowered to assist in the decision-making process and to act on the decision. For example, they may have the power to access banking documents or hospital records. The person can revoke the appointment of a supportive attorney at any point, and the appointment stops having effect if the person who made the appointment is assessed as not having mental capacity.[21] Supportive powers of attorney may help people maintain legal capacity in circumstances where they might otherwise be assessed as lacking mental capacity. Social workers cannot be supportive attorneys for people they work with because care workers, health providers and accommodation providers are excluded from this scheme.[22]

There are other legislative supports for supportive decision-making in Victoria, including the role of the 'support person' in the *Medical Treatment Planning and Decisions Act 2016* (Vic) and the 'nominated person' in the *Mental Health Act 2014* (Vic). Victoria also has practical supports that enable supported decision-making in practice. These include Independent Mental Health Advocacy, which explicitly uses a combination of social work advocacy and a supported decision-making model to help people in involuntary mental health settings.[23] A similar service, Mental Health Advocacy Service, exists in Western Australia.[24]

Other jurisdictions have some embedded supported decision-making to varying extents. At the Commonwealth level, the *National Disability Insurance Scheme Act 2013* (Cth) allows for decision supporters and the *Social Security (Administration) Act 1999* (Cth) allows for both a 'correspondence nominee' and a 'payment nominee' for Centrelink. These are not really guardianship or formalised supported decision-making roles but provide an opportunity for decision supporters to be formally recognised in the system.

13.6 Social Workers in Adult Guardianship

Embedding supported decision-making is not as simple as changing the law. The reality is there are some situations where family, friends and professionals, including social workers, are not able to adequately support people to make their own decisions. There are many situations where social workers are not able to provide adequate housing or food, both of which are prerequisites to the supports people will need to make decisions. There will be situations where people are being taken advantage of by their family and the state has an obligation to protect them, or while people are in a comatose state. Debate is ongoing as to whether supported decision-making can be used in crisis situations or when a person is in extreme mental distress. Until adequate support services can be provided to support people to make decisions, there will remain laws that allow for substituted decision-making.

Social workers will work in substituted decision-making environments and with persons for whom substitute decision making will have been assessed as necessary. Working in such environments, social workers need to be mindful of the power they hold and that in applying for guardianship and financial orders they are effectively seeking the removal of a person's human rights. As discussed in Chapter 16, social workers risk *moral distress* if they base their values on human rights and they are required to act in ways that are incompatible with them. What, then, can social workers do to stay true to their social work values?

First, social workers must not simply accept the status quo. They must continuously use their privileged position to advocate for a community in which people can be supported to make their own decisions. While doing that, they can work to ensure that wherever possible they support people to make their own decisions so that substituted decision-making is not required. This requires forward planning, with advance care planning, including support people and always examining the alternatives before resorting to substituted decision-making. Social workers must be honest with people, explaining to them why they are taking the course of action they have decided and accepting that if they are going to violate people's rights, people will be legitimately angry and upset with them.

When making a guardianship application, social workers should first ensure that an application is necessary and that there are no other options available. The decision to apply for guardianship and financial orders should always be carefully considered and subjected to rigorous critical reflection. Social workers also need to be careful not to use an application as a veiled threat to coerce or cajole a person into conforming or complying. The grounds for applying should also be person focused and not driven by institutional or community imperatives, for example, freeing up beds or moving someone off the streets.[25]

The process of applying must not be used as a threat to ensure compliance and must only be done if it is genuinely necessary. If there is no way the person can be supported to make their own decisions, social workers must still ensure that they involve the person in the process as much as possible. This requires honestly engaging with the person about what the application means and why it is necessary. Social workers must also ensure that the person understands their rights, particularly their appeal rights and rights to legal representation, and facilitate access to those rights, such as by referring to a lawyer.

This process should be culturally appropriate and responsive to any other specific needs of the person. Social workers can do simple things such as organising communication supports. Many people who are heavily medicated will have specific times of day during which they are best able to communicate, such as first thing in the morning after they wake up.

Social workers need to be aware of these issues and facilitate communication. Particularly for First Nations people, but for anyone who identifies a wish for cultural supports, social workers should ensure that someone from that person's community can assist them in the process. These are basic social work skills that become vital in this process.

Social workers also have a role in educating other professionals about human rights and supported decision-making, particularly health practitioners whose medical training may not have prepared them for the complexities of negotiating social issues. This may include reframing 'non-compliant' or 'aggressive' people as 'people who are trying to uphold their right to make their own decisions', for example. This extends into the policy advocacy role of social work, in ensuring that supported decision-making frameworks that are embedded in law are also embedded in practice. Social workers must make all use of the legal human rights protections that do exist and make sure that their colleagues do the same.

Main points

1. Historically, specific groups of people, such as those labelled with mental illness, mental impairment, cognitive disability and similar descriptors, have had decisions made for them on the basis that they are either unable to do so or on the basis that they are making 'bad' decisions.
2. This is done both voluntarily, through 'powers of attorney' or involuntarily, called 'administration' for financial matters or 'guardianship' for other matters, such as lifestyle and legal matters.
3. Powers of attorney, guardianship and administration laws are different in each jurisdiction.
4. Involuntary decision-making is referred to as *substituted decision-making*.
5. The introduction of the *Disability Convention* introduced the requirement of *supported decision-making.*
6. *Legal capacity* is the ability to make legal decisions (such as getting married or suing someone). *Mental capacity* is generally defined as the ability to do four things: understand information about the decision; retain information about the decision; use and/or weigh up information about the decision; and communicate the decision. While legal and mental capacity have traditionally been linked, they are distinct terms and should be understood separately.
7. Social workers are well positioned to facilitate supported decision-making.
8. Guardianship and financial administration orders are made by a tribunal or court and are made when the person is assessed as lacking mental capacity. They have a threshold test that must be met.

Discussion questions

1. Is supported decision-making part of the law in your jurisdiction? If so, find the relevant provision and consider how the language of supportive powers of attorney is consistent with the *Disability Convention* notion of supported, rather than substituted, decision-making.
2. Find the relevant legislation on powers of attorney in your jurisdiction. Who can be an attorney? What are the requirements?
3. Is there legislation in your jurisdiction to protect the elderly against abuse? Who are the primary perpetrators of elder abuse and what is the primary type of abuse that occurs against elders?
4. Research guardianship and administration legislation in your jurisdiction and make an assessment as to whether the language of the legislation is based on a 'best-interest' framework or a 'rights-based' framework.
5. How might the current climate of neoliberalism affect a social worker's ability to champion supported, not substituted, decision-making in practice? What are some practical strategies you can come up with to help social workers to overcome these obstacles?

Further reading

Fleur Beaupert, Linda Steele and Piers Gooding. *Disability, Rights and Law Reform in Australia* (Federation Press, 2017).

ALRC, 'Equality, Capacity and Disability in Commonwealth Laws', summary report (Australian Law Reform Commission, 2014).

R. Kokanovic et al, *Options for Supported Decision-Making to Enhance the Recovery of People Experiencing Severe Mental Health Problems* (Melbourne Social Equity Institute, 2017).

Samantha Wehbi, 'Disability Rights and Justice Activism: Lessons for Anti-Oppressive Community Organizing' in Donna Baines, *Doing Anti-Oppressive Practice: Social Justice Social Work*, 3rd ed. (Fernwood Publishing, 2017).

13.7 References

[1] UN General Assembly, Convention on the Rights of Persons with Disabilities: resolution/adopted by the General Assembly, 24 January 2007, A/RES/61/106.

[2] Sascha M. Callaghan and Christopher Ryan, 'An Evolving Revolution: Evaluating Australia's Compliance with the Convention on the Rights of Persons with Disabilities in Mental Health Law' (2016) 39 *University of New South Wales Law Journal* 596.

[3] Piers Gooding and Piers Gooding, *A New Era for Mental Health Law and Policy: Supported Decision-Making and the UN Convention on the Rights of Persons with Disabilities* (2017).
[4] Gavin Davidson et al, 'An International Comparison of Legal Frameworks for Supported and Substitute Decision-Making in Mental Health Services' (2016) 44 *International Journal of Law and Psychiatry* 30.
[5] ALRC, *Equality, Capacity and Disability in Commonwealth Laws* (Summary report, Australian Law Reform Commission, 2014) <https://www.alrc.gov.au/sites/default/files/pdfs/publications/alrc_124_summary_report_whole_pfd_.pdf>.
[6] *PJB v Melbourne Health & Anor (Patrick's Case)* [2011] VSC 327.
[7] Kevin Bell, 'Victoria's Human Rights Charter' (Law Institute of Victoria, 2011) <http://classic.austlii.edu.au/au/journals/VicJSchol/2011/24.pdf>.
[8] UN General Assembly, *Convention on the Rights of Persons with Disabilities: resolution/adopted by the General Assembly*, 24 January 2007, A/RES/61/106, art 12(3).
[9] ALRC (n 5).
[10] Reproduced from: Wanda Bennetts et al, 'The "Tricky Dance" of Advocacy: A Study of Non-Legal Mental Health Advocacy' (2018) 2018(24) *International Journal of Mental Health and Capacity Law* 12.
[11] M.B. Simmons and P.M. Gooding, 'Spot the Difference: Shared Decision-Making and Supported Decision-Making in Mental Health' [2017] *Irish Journal of Psychological Medicine* 1.
[12] R. Kokanovic et al, *Options for Supported Decision-Making to Enhance the Recovery of People Experiencing Severe Mental Health Problems* (Melbourne Social Equity Institute, 2017).
[13] C. Maylea, A. Jorgensen, S. Matta, K. Ogilvie and P. Wallin, 'Consumers' Experiences of Mental Health Advance Statements.' (2018) 7, 22 *Laws*.
[14] See, for example, the *Medical Treatment Planning and Decisions Act 2016* (Vic).
[15] Rae Kaspiew, Rachel Carson and Helen Rhoades, *Elder Abuse: Understanding Issues, Frameworks and Responses* (Australian Institute of Family Studies, 2016).
[16] See, for example, the *Powers of Attorney Act 2014* (Vic).
[17] *Guardianship Act 1987* (NSW) s 3.
[18] *Guardianship and Administration Act 1993* (SA) s 5(a).
[19] *J v Guardianship and Administration Board* [2019] TASSC 15.
[20] *Review of Guardianship and Administration Act 1995 (Tas) Final Report* (No 26, Tasmania Law Reform Institute, 2018); *A Review of Queensland's Guardianship Laws* (No 67, Queensland Law Reform Commission, 2010) <https://www.qlrc.qld.gov.au/__data/assets/pdf_file/0008/588239/qlrc-report-67-vol-1-web-with-cover.pdf>.
[21] *Powers of Attorney Act 2014* (Vic) s 103.
[22] *Powers of Attorney Act 2014* (Vic) s 91.
[23] Bennetts et al (n 10); Chris Maylea et al, *Evaluation of the Independent Mental Health Advocacy Service (IMHA)* (Social and Global Studies Centre, RMIT University, 2019) 56 <sway.office.com/GZJrEJJcVJZlGGvY>.
[24] Mental Health Advocacy Service, 'Our Approach' <https://mhas.wa.gov.au/about-us/our-approach>.
[25] Penelope Weller, 'Legal Capacity and Access to Justice: The Right to Participation in the CRPD' (2016) 5(1) *Laws* 13.

Chapter 14 MENTAL HEALTH LAW

Mental health law is an area that poses some very difficult issues for social workers. As social workers, we must work to empower the people we work with, but mental health law is designed to do just the opposite. It takes away a person's right to make their own decisions. This is justified on the basis that people who experience mental distress will sometimes lose the mental capacity to make decisions themselves, or that they will make 'bad' decisions that they will regret later.* This usually takes the form of involuntary treatment, where people are forced to take medication, or detention, where a person is kept in a hospital so they can be treated. As explored in Chapter 13, under guardianship legislation they may also have their rights to make decisions about where they live, whom they see and how they spend their money. Mental health law is different from adult guardianship law for a number of reasons, but primarily because it has therapeutic intention. It is focused on treating a person, not managing their affairs. This chapter focuses on involuntary treatment and detention that is enabled by mental health legislation, not guardianship legislation.

Mental health social work has largely uncritically accepted the need for involuntary treatment as a regrettable necessity.[1] This is largely due to the dominance of psychiatry, which argues that mental distress or strange behaviour should be viewed as a medical issue that can be treated with medical means. This biomedical model of diagnosing and treating mental health has grown to be the dominant way in which we understand mental health, although it is not without critics.[2] The United Nations has criticised this model, identifying it as one of the major obstacles to good mental health.[3] Social workers have consistently called for ways of doing social work outside this paradigm, including understanding mental distress as a genuine response to genuine issues rather than as a biological 'illness' to be 'treated'.[4]

Despite these critiques, mental health law is solidly based on a biomedical understanding of mental distress. All states and territories in Australia use a similar model for their mental health legislation, which requires a person to have a 'mental illness' and allows those people to be forced to receive 'treatment' if other criteria are also met. Treatment nearly always involves medication but can also include electroconvulsive therapy or neurosurgery. Other kinds of treatment such as psychological

---

* As discussed in Chapter 13, *decision-making capacity* is a person's ability to make decisions. It may be influenced by mental distress, alcohol, other drugs or medication. Legal capacity is the ability to make a binding legal agreement, sue someone, or make other legal decisions.

support or peer support are generally ineffective if involuntary and are not often forced on people by mental health legislation.

Involuntary treatment is a key part of mental health services in Australia, with nearly half of inpatient stays involving involuntary treatment; between 10 and 15 per cent of the people receiving public mental health treatment in the community do so involuntarily.[5] Mental health law also allows for the seclusion and restraint of people in mental health settings, despite all jurisdictions committing to reduce or eliminate these practices over a decade ago.[6] Seclusion is the practice of putting someone by themselves and preventing them from leaving. Restraint is the restriction of a person's movement. It can be *mechanical*, where a person might be strapped to a bed, *chemical,* where a person is medicated to prevent their movements, or *emotional,* where a person is coerced or threatened into not moving. Only mechanical and chemical restraint is permitted by law.

14.1 Legal frameworks

All states and territories have mental health legislation:

Table 14.1 *Mental health legislation*

Jurisdiction	Mental health legislation
NSW	*Mental Health Act 2007* (NSW)
Qld	*Mental Health Act 2016* (Qld)
SA	*Mental Health Act 2009* (SA)
Tas	*Mental Health Act 2013* (Tas)
Vic	*Mental Health Act 2014* (Vic)
WA	*Mental Health Act 2014* (WA)
ACT	*Mental Health Act 2015* (ACT)
NT	*Mental Health and Related Services Act 1998* (NT)

Each of these pieces of legislation does a similar job, ensuring that people can be treated against their will while laying out the rights they have while being involuntarily treated. These rights vary by jurisdiction and may include the right to appeal against involuntary treatment, to make complaints, to be treated with dignity and to be involved in decisions about treatment – even if the doctor actually makes the final decision. Social workers play an important part in explaining these rights to people and making sure that these rights are upheld, as discussed in due course.

In addition to the standard involuntary treatment process that will be described, there are a number of complex legal frameworks not discussed here that govern how people can be given electroconvulsive therapy or neurosurgery, and how children or people who are subject to guardianship orders can be treated. There are also legal frameworks that deal with people who commit criminal offences, such as when a person commits an offence while experiencing psychosis or when they are unable to participate in their criminal trial owing to their mental state. These are discussed in Chapter 10.

14.1.1 Treatment criteria for involuntary treatment

Most jurisdictions follow the same general process for applying mental health legislation, which is shown in Figure 14.1. A mental health practitioner, who might be a doctor, a social worker, or another allied health professional, will decide that a person needs to be assessed by a psychiatrist. In order to be assessed, they must meet a set of criteria referred to as 'assessment criteria'. In order to be treated, they must be assessed by a psychiatrist to see if they meet the 'treatment criteria'. These criteria are slightly different in different jurisdictions, but all require the person to have a 'mental illness' and that the person requires treatment to protect themselves or others from harm. There are some variations in criteria; for example, in New South Wales (NSW) the legislation makes a distinction between a 'mentally ill person' and a 'mentally disordered person'.[7] Another key difference is that in some jurisdictions, such as Queensland, Western Australia and Tasmania,[8] a person must also lack decision-making or mental capacity, whereas in other jurisdictions, such as Victoria, a person can be involuntarily treated even if they have mental capacity.[9]

There are different criteria for *assessing* a person as to *treating* a person. In general, it is a lower bar to determine if someone can be assessed against their will. Assessment orders will often be made by social workers and can be requested by courts, police, ambulance staff or family members. Assessment orders generally require that a person is taken to a hospital or other place to be assessed. Once they are assessed, a psychiatrist or a tribunal will determine if they meet the treatment criteria. As an example, the treatment criteria in Queensland are:

> a) *the person has a mental illness;*
> b) *the person does not have capacity to consent to be treated for the illness;*
> c) *because of the person's illness, the absence of involuntary treatment, or the absence of continued involuntary treatment, is likely to result in—*
>   i) *imminent serious harm to the person or others; or*
>   ii) *the person suffering serious mental or physical deterioration.*[10]

These criteria limit the purposes of mental health treatment orders. People cannot be detained just because they might harm another person – under the Queensland criteria the harm must be *likely, serious* and *imminent.* The criteria differ by jurisdiction, but nowhere can the order be made just because it is in the person's best interests or because it would make service provision to that person easier.

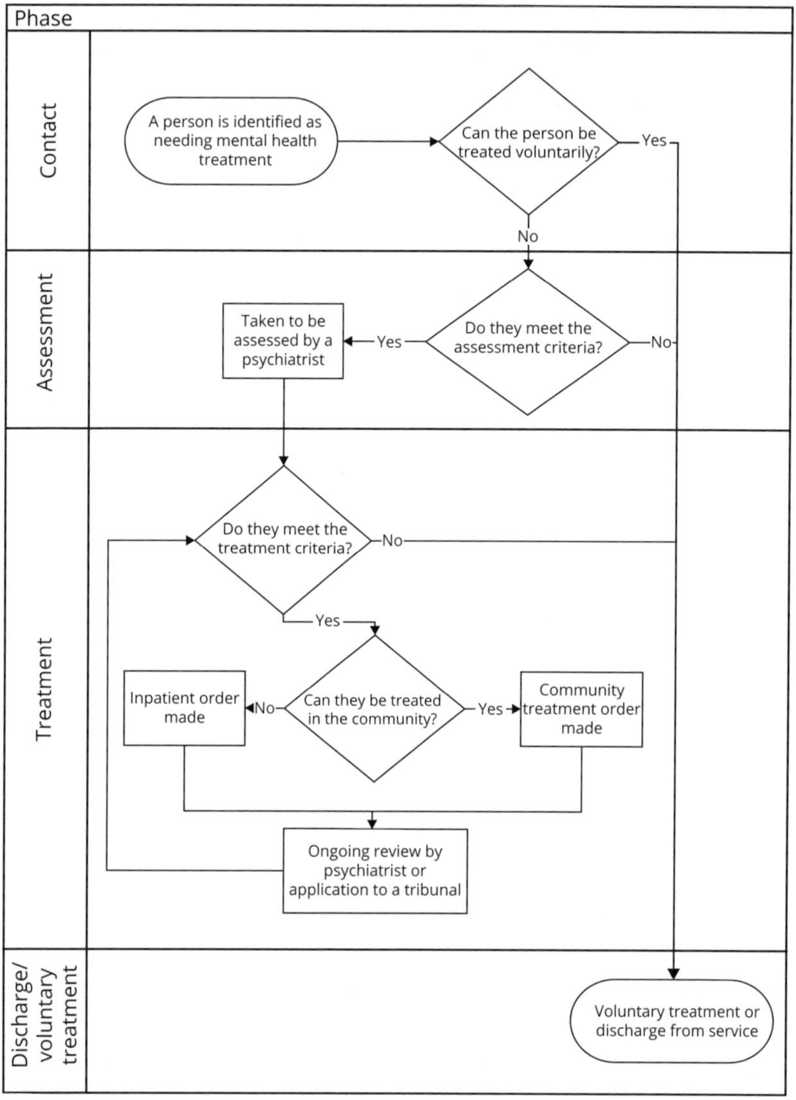

Figure 14.1 *The process of involuntary treatment*

Most jurisdictions require that people who are involuntarily treated are treated in the *least restrictive* way. This is usually interpreted to mean that if they can be treated in the community rather than the inpatient setting then they should be, or that if they can take medication orally rather than by injection then that should be what is done.

After a person has been assessed as meeting the treatment criteria by a psychiatrist, the psychiatrist can make a short-term treatment order, requiring the person to receive treatment. These orders can be for inpatient settings, requiring a person to stay in hospital, or for community settings, where a person is not detained but still required to receive treatment. If a person refuses treatment, they can be physically forced to take treatment, often by being held down and injected. If a person does not comply with a community treatment order that they may be taken by police back to the hospital and forced to take treatment there.

14.1.2 Mental health tribunals

All jurisdictions have an oversight process where a tribunal or review board will review or make treatment orders. People can apply to a tribunal to try and have their treatment order revoked, or in some jurisdictions psychiatrists must apply to the tribunal if they want to make longer-term treatment orders. The tribunal will hear evidence from the person, the treating team (including the social worker), family members and other support people, and decide if the treatment criteria still apply. Social workers can play an important role in helping people made applications to tribunals, by supporting them through the tribunal hearing and by providing important information to a tribunal so they can decide if they make an order or not.

14.1.3 Judicial guidance on mental health

Mental health cases are rarely heard in the higher courts, so there are not many decisions about mental health law to guide practice. People subject to mental health law rarely have much money to pursue expensive litigation and the courts are reluctant to limit the discretion of decision-makers. Furthermore, the higher courts move so slowly that often the person has been discharged by the time the court comes to review their case. There are a few cases that are useful guidance for social workers working in mental health, particularly when making decisions, or reminding others about their obligations in making decisions. As a starting point, Bell writes in *PBU*[11]:

> *... the right [of self determination] is not absolute and may be limited where this is justified according to the strict human rights standard ... But the starting point is that people with mental disability have the same right of self-determination as everybody else' (128).*

PBU is about when a person can be required to have electroconvulsive treatment against their will. In this case, to be forcibly administered electroconvulsive treatment the person must be shown to lack mental capacity.[12] The court found that even when electroconvulsive treatment is the clinically optimal course of treatment, the law states that only a person who lacks capacity can be treated. For social workers, this reinforces that the law is the limit of power to control another person – just because something is a good idea, or clinically appropriate, does not mean that it is within the power of a social worker or other decision-makers to do it. *PBU* states that human rights cannot be limited 'unless the contrary is demonstrably justified ... or legally demanded'.[13]

Other court decisions on mental health reinforce this, such as *Patrick's Case,*[14] *McKenna*[15] and *Kirkland-Veenstra.*[16] *Patrick's Case,* discussed in Chapter 13, also supports this idea that Patrick's human rights could only be limited when permitted by law. In McKenna, a man was discharged from an inpatient unit and subsequently killed his friend who was driving him home. The High Court found that because the psychiatrist who discharged him followed the legislation – the *Mental Health Act 1990* (NSW) – the hospital was not negligent. The High Court stated that the legislation 'required the *minimum* interference with the liberty of a mentally ill person'.[17] This meant that the duty of care owed by the doctor to prevent harm was overridden by the legislation that required minimum interference with liberty. In *Kirkland-Veenstra,* a man was in a car park in his car with the exhaust pipe connected to his car window. Police spoke to the man, who said he had changed his mind and no longer wanted to commit suicide. Police let him go home, where he did commit suicide. The man's family sued police, claiming they should have detained him under mental health legislation. The court found that as the man did not 'appear' to be mentally ill, the police had no power to detain him. All these cases reinforce the same point of law – human rights cannot be limited unless the law requires them to be.

14.2 Susie's story

The experience of being subject to involuntary treatment, seclusion and restraint have consistently been identified by consumers as dehumanising, counter-therapeutic and stigmatising.[18] Consumer advocates and peak bodies regularly call for an end to forced treatment.[19] Many people reflect on their experience of involuntary treatment and accept that it was necessary under the circumstances, but it is very rare to hear of a person enjoying the experience of forced treatment and detention. For social workers, the question should not be 'is coercion necessary?', but 'how can we reduce and eliminate the use of coercion?', and 'how can we reduce its harmful effects?' Susie's experience gives us some insight into how the experience of involuntary treatment can be mitigated by good social work practice.

My name is Susie, I am a 29-year-old woman, and I am same-sex attracted. I was born in Australia into a Chilean family and consider myself to be

Chilean. I have an undergraduate degree and am now working on my Master's degree. I have been in the public mental health system for just over ten years.

Early on I was labelled a 'problem' child and required to see counsellors and psychologists. I got nothing from these sessions at it was not until my second year of university that I sought help for my mental health. I had a panic attack in class and then poor mental health prevented me from finishing an exam. I saw a psychologist who was quite helpful; however, when I began self-harming, she suggested I seek specialist help.

I went to a handful of services; psychologists, psychiatrists and youth services, but they all told me that I had too many complex psychiatric issues for them to deal with. By this point I was highly suicidal and ready to give up. I eventually found a specialist youth mental health service. They initially told me I was not unwell enough to meet their criteria. I told them I had gone everywhere, this was my last chance, and if they didn't take me, I would surely kill myself. They reassessed me and I entered the public mental health system at age 19. I was diagnosed with Obsessive Compulsive Disorder, Anxiety, Depression and Borderline Personality Disorder. Since then I have also been diagnosed with Anorexia Nervosa.

This information is vital in understanding Susie's later experience of involuntary treatment. Note Susie's cultural background and level of education, as well as her determination to seek help on her terms. I asked Susie to share a positive experience that she had with a social worker.

Some years later, in the adult mental health system, I was allocated a great social worker who treated me as a person first and foremost. My diagnoses were only relevant when they were relevant – they did not define me. A lot of my time with her was spent on crisis management as I was regularly in and out of hospital post self-harming and suicide attempts. This was often involuntary, under the Mental Health Act. *Nevertheless, I found our time to be helpful as we focused on the positive things I had going on in my life as much as possible, such as completing my degrees, attending circus classes, and my amazing baking skills.*

I hated how my mental health was affecting my life and while in hospital I often felt unsafe being surrounded by men who were quite unwell. My social worker recognised how detrimental the hospital setting was for me and would often take me out to cafés for our appointments. It was when she did these sorts of things for me that I began to trust her, and we worked really well together. I loved how she was human. She would make cringeworthy puns, would often mix up ridiculous sayings, and would joke around. Sometimes a good laugh and a cup of coffee would be much more helpful for me than sitting in a clinic and talking about what was wrong with me.

What I appreciated about my social worker was that she never used her statutory powers to intimidate or coerce me. In fact, she created a brilliant enhanced treatment plan that reinforced my rights and helped me access treatment I needed voluntarily. The Mental Health Act *required her to involve my mother, who was then my 'carer', in my treatment, but she never did this without getting my permission first. I was only treated involuntarily and taken to hospital when I self-harmed and attempted suicide.*

Upon reflection I wonder if putting me on an order when voicing my suicidal thoughts would have prevented me from coming so close to death. Or if frequent appointments and daily phone calls were enough. I think I would have resented her had she put me on an order every time I was suicidal. There was always a constant risk that I would die. There still is. But I accepted that risk early on.

Note that Susie is not resentful of her involuntary treatment, recognising that without it she would not be around to show off her amazing baking skills. Note also her focus on what was useful and what actually helped her. This is contrasted sharply with her experience with a different social worker.

Unfortunately, I am still in the public mental health system, sometimes 'voluntarily' through coercion and other times involuntarily on a Community Treatment Order or an Inpatient Treatment Order. I prefer my case managers to be social workers; however, I've learned that not all social workers are cut out to be mental health social workers.

As part of my treatment for my Anorexia I was voluntarily going to see my GP weekly for medical observation. This became difficult over the Christmas break. My social worker said that I needed to go for a blood test on Christmas Eve. I informed her that being Chilean I celebrate Christmas on Christmas Eve and that I could not go that day, but I would be willing to do so right after Christmas. She insisted that I go and that she would send the police if I didn't. I know she had no right to do this as I was a voluntary patient.

She kept insisting, I kept refusing. Eventually she decided to call my mother, who is no longer my carer. She called all throughout the holiday period, sometimes numerous times a day, without my consent. My social worker was using the Mental Health Act *to harass me and my family so that I would do what she wanted.*

A month later I was placed on a ten-week Treatment Order. During this time, I called her when I was distressed and needed support. However, every time I expressed how I was feeling or what I was thinking she would bring up the Treatment Order and remind me that I could be put in hospital at any moment if I didn't comply. I just wanted to talk, I didn't need threats.

It is highly likely that Susie's social worker would see this as 'assertive outreach' or an appropriate response to Susie's clinical symptoms. This highlights the importance of understanding how people experience engagement with social workers, not just understanding how social work is delivered to people. Note the social worker's focus on compliance, rather than outcomes, and the way Susie feels her culture is not being taken into account.

This kind of interaction can be read both ways – Susie sees it as unhelpful and disrespectful, while others might see it as justified, claiming that Susie was not compliant and so needed assertive intervention to *prevent* the later involuntary treatment. The fact is that in this case it did not work. Susie both felt disrespected and unsupported. Good social work should be supportive and work to prevent harm.

Finally, I asked Susie to share what she thought social workers needed to know. Initially, she said, 'If only one could write "don't be a dick, it's not about you"'. She elaborates.

Users of mental health services are first and foremost people. They are not a diagnosis. Treat them as fellow human beings, and act as a human being. Be aware of your power in the relationship and never use it over them. Don't use language that can be stigmatising. Telling people it is their 'choice' to behave a certain way or to recover is devaluing. I didn't choose to have a mental illness, and I've not yet met someone who has.

In treating service users as people, it is really important that you ensure you refer to people by their preferred name and pronouns. I have found it to be highly disrespectful when workers don't bother to ask me how I would like to be called and hurtful when they continually use the wrong name despite numerous corrections.

The law is far from perfect, and organisational contexts can be very persuasive, so it is imperative that you stick to social work values when working in mental health. Subjecting a person to involuntary treatment, which can result in a person being locked in a ward for long periods of time, being restrained, secluded and subjected to violence does not reflect respect for persons, social justice or professional integrity. Question what treatment is being provided to the service user, ask them what they want, and support their treatment decisions. They are the experts of their own lives and it is their journey.

14.3 Social Work Practice

For social workers, mental health law presents an apparently insurmountable dilemma. How can social workers work in mental health settings, which are dominated by the biomedical model, and still conform with social work values and ethics? The definition of social work requires social workers to uphold human rights,[20] and yet mental health social workers will regularly infringe on these rights. We must also carefully examine the assumptions that underpin mental health law. In the treatment criteria previously outlined, there are four key assumptions about mental health: that mental illness can be treated by force, that people who are diagnosed with a mental illness are sometimes dangerous, that the risk of this dangerousness can be assessed, and that there are sometimes no less restrictive ways to avoid harm.

There are a number of things social workers can do in practice and in influencing policy to try and work through these issues. Fundamentally, the social work attitude towards mental health law should be that we never need to use it. Any use of coercion, seclusion or restraint represents a point at which the system and wider community have failed to provide the support, treatment and care that the person requires in a way that they are prepared to accept it voluntarily. In this section, rather than looking at how social workers can *use* mental health law, we will look at how we can *not use* mental health law, or how we can use mental health law to minimise trauma, stigma and other harms.

The *Practice Standards for Mental Health Social Workers* require social workers to incorporate human rights and a recovery[21] approach in their practice with involuntary clients,[22] and the *Code of Ethics* provides further guidance.[23] This amounts to just doing good social work with people who are involuntary and is an excellent starting point. As Susie's experience shows, and many studies also support, the best way to prevent the 'need' for involuntary treatment is to ensure that people get the support, treatment and care they need when they need it, and not waiting until a crisis point to force it on them.[24] This only goes part of the way to addressing the issue for two reasons: some people will find themselves in crisis no matter how good their supports, and there are better ways to support someone in crisis than causing more distress through coercion.

Before people reach crisis, social workers can assist them in crisis planning and preparation. In some jurisdictions, including Victoria and the Australian Capital Territory, the mental health legislation provides for documents called *advance statements* or *advance directives*.[25] These documents allow people to write down their preferences in the event that they are involuntarily treated, and social workers are well positioned to assist people in developing them. For example, a person might state that they prefer one medication over another, that they want (or don't want!) their family contacted, or that they have pets which require care. This allows people to have more of a say in their care and can be used as part of a broader supported decision-making process.

If and when a person is detained or involuntarily treated, social workers must assist them in exercising their rights under the legislation they are detained or treated under. These rights vary by jurisdiction but generally uphold a person's right to be treated appropriately and with dignity. For example, in South Australia, people using public mental health services have the right to a regular medical examination.[26] In Victoria, people have the right to a second psychiatric option,[27] and there is a free service for involuntary patients to access one.[28] Social workers must know these rights and how to support people to access them.

Social workers can use the *least restrictive* principle to argue that people should be able to use alternatives to involuntary treatment and that mental health and other services should provide access to alternative services. There are many alternatives with growing evidence bases, and social workers who take a human rights approach must work to ensure access to these options.[29]

Social workers must also be aware of people's appeal rights and be prepared to support them through the appeals process. This may mean helping people complete the paperwork to appeal their order, referring them to legal support, and helping them at the hearing. Access to lawyers for mental health matters varies; for example, 80 per cent of people in NSW are legally represented, compared to 16 per cent over the border in Victoria.[30] When a lawyer is not present social workers and other supports become much more important. Non-lawyers cannot act as lawyers, but they can provide information and assist people through what can be a very difficult process.

As social workers, we must also address the systemic issues. This is best done by providing good care and support and changing society to be more caring and supportive. There is no shortage of research demonstrating the success of alternative methods. [31] Unfortunately, these alternative approaches a not widely implemented, and people who use mental health services, including Susie, consistently identify difficulties in getting access to services they do require. Despite the right to health being a fundamental human right, there is no legal mechanism that ensures that people are provided with the care and support they need when they need it. Advocating for a safe, supportive and compassionate society, and for a mental health system that meets people's needs early and consistently, is the best way for social workers to address the human rights issues raised by mental health law.

Main points

1. Mental health law poses a challenging dilemma for social workers, as they attempt to balance supporting a person's right to make decisions with involuntary treatment and detention that is inherent in the mental health system.

2. The biomedical model of mental health is based on the understanding that mental illness is caused by biological malfunction. This model has been criticised by critical social workers.
3. In order for a person to be involuntarily assessed by a psychiatrist, they must meet the 'assessment criteria'. In order to be involuntarily treated, they must meet the 'treatment criteria'. While the criteria differ among jurisdictions, treatment criteria generally require a person to have a mental illness and to be need of treatment in order to prevent serious harm to self or others or serious deterioration of their physical or mental health.
4. Mental health tribunals and review boards review and make treatment orders. People can apply to the tribunal to have their treatment order revoked.
5. Involuntary treatment is consistently identified by consumers to be dehumanising, counter-therapeutic and stigmatising.
6. The best way to reduce and eliminate coercive practices is to provide adequate and timely care in a way that people want it.

Discussion questions

1. Re-read Susie's experience. How can social workers promote the human rights of people who are involuntarily treated, and what strategies can social workers use to help people advocate for reduced and eliminated use of coercion in treatment?
2. What is the recovery model of mental health, and how can it fit in with involuntary treatment?
3. Find an example of an advance statement in order to understand the scope, content and potential of an advance statement. Is an advance statement legally binding? If no, how can a social worker support a consumer in the process of understanding why the advance statement was not followed?

Further reading

Scope of Social Work Practice: Social Work in Mental Health <https: //www.aasw.asn.au/document/item/8309>.

Practice Standards for Mental Health Social Workers <https: //www.aasw.asn.au/document/item/6739>.

Noel Renouf, 'Beyond the Dominant Approach to Mental Health Practice' in Bob Pease et al, *Doing Critical Social Work: Transformative Practices for Social Justice* (Allen & Unwin, 2016).

Lisa M. Brophy et al, 'Consumers' and Their Supporters' Perspectives on Barriers and Strategies to Reducing Seclusion and Restraint in Mental

Health Settings' (21 December 2016) 40(6) *Australian Health Review* 599–604.

Christopher Maylea, 'A Rejection of Involuntary Treatment in Mental Health Social Work' (2016) *Ethics and Social Welfare*.

Murray Wright, 'Review of Seclusion, Restraint and Observation of Consumers with a Mental Illness in NSW Health Facilities' (Office of the Chief Psychiatrist, December 2017).

Michelle Funk and Natalie Drew, 'Strategies to End the Use of Seclusion, Restraint and Other Coercive Practices' (Mental Health Policy and Service Development, Department of Mental Health and Substance Abuse, World Health Organization, 2017).

Piers Gooding et al, 'Alternatives to Coercion in Mental Health Settings: A Literature Review' (Melbourne Social Equity Institute, 2018).

Felicity Callard et al, *Mental Illness, Discrimination and the Law: Fighting for Social Justice* (Wiley, 2012).

Penelope Weller, 'Mental Health Law' in Anne-Maree Farrell, John Devereux, Isabel Karpin and Penelope Weller (eds), *Health Law: Frameworks and Context*, 305–32 (Cambridge University Press, 2017).

14.4 REFERENCES

[1] Christopher Maylea, 'A Rejection of Involuntary Treatment in Mental Health Social Work' [2016] *Ethics and Social Welfare*.
[2] David Pilgrim, 'The Survival of Psychiatric Diagnosis' (2007) 65(3) *Social Science & Medicine* 536.
[3] United Nations, Report of the Special Rapporteur on the Right of Everyone to the Enjoyment of the Highest Attainable Standard of Physical and Mental Health (No A/HRC/35/21, United Nations, 2017) 5.
[4] Noel Renouf, 'Beyond the Dominant Approach to Mental Health Practice' in Bob Pease et al (eds), *Doing Critical Social Work: Transformative Practices for Social Justice* (Allen & Unwin, 2016) 123; Selma Macfarlane, 'Opening Spaces for Alternative Understandings in Mental Health Practice' in June Allan, Bob Pease and Linda Briskman (eds), *Critical Social Work: Theories and Practices for a Socially Just World* 2nd ed. (Allen & Unwin, 2009) 201.
[5] AIHW, *Mental Health Services Overview* (Australian Institute of Health and Welfare, 2018) <https://www.aihw.gov.au/reports/mental-health-services/mental-health-services-in-australia/report-contents/summary-of-mental-health-services-in-australia>.
[6] National Mental Health Working Group, *National Safety Priorities in Mental Health: A National Plan for Reducing Harm* (Department of Health and Ageing, 2005) <http://www.health.gov.au/internet/publications/publishing.nsf/Content/mental-pubs-n-safety-toc~mental-pubs-n-safety-3~mental-pubs-n-safety-3-use>.
[7] *Mental Health Act 2007* (NSW) s 13–15.

[8] *Mental Health Act 2016* (Qld) s 12, *Mental Health Act 2014* (WA) s 25, *Mental Health Act 2013* (Tas) s 40.
[9] Other than for ECT and neurosurgery: *Mental Health Act 2014* (Vic) s 5.
[10] *Mental Health Act 2016* (Qld) s 12.
[11] *PBU & NJE v Mental Health Tribunal* [2018] VSC 564.
[12] *Mental Health Act 2014* (Vic) s 96(1)(a)(i).
[13] *PBU & NJE v Mental Health Tribunal* [2018] VSC 564 [108].
[14] *PJB v Melbourne Health and Another (Patrick's Case)* [2011] VSC 327.
[15] *Hunter and New England Local Health District v McKenna* [2014] HCA 44.
[16] *Kirkland-Veenstra v Stuart* [2008] VSCA 32.
[17] *Hunter and New England Local Health District v McKenna* [2014] HCA 44 [31].
[18] Lisa M. Brophy et al, 'Consumers' and Their Supporters' Perspectives on Barriers and Strategies to Reducing Seclusion and Restraint in Mental Health Settings' (2016) 40(6) *Australian Health Review* 599; Murray Wright, *Review of Seclusion, Restraint and Observation of Consumers with a Mental Illness in NSW Health Facilities* (Office of the Chief Psychiatrist, December 2017) <http://www.health.nsw.gov.au/patients/mentalhealth/Documents/report-seclusion-restraint-observation.pdf>; Michelle Funk and Natalie Drew, *Strategies to End the Use of Seclusion, Restraint and Other Coercive Practices* (Mental Health Policy and Service Development, Department of Mental Health and Substance Abuse, World Health Organization, 2017) <http://apps.who.int/iris/bitstream/handle/10665/254809/WHO-MSD-MHP-17.9-eng.pdf;jsessionid=ACF2753CFF93E2A04E30596CA03B0BE2?sequence=1>.
[19] See, for example, the Victorian Mental Illness Awareness Council <www.vmiac.org.au>.
[20] AASW, *Code of Ethics* (Australian Association of Social Workers, 2010).
[21] Patricia Deegan, 'Recovery as a Journey of the Heart' (1996) 19(3) *Psychiatric Rehabilitation Journal* 91.
[22] AASW, *Practice Standards for Mental Health Social Workers* (Australian Association of Social Workers, 2014) <https://www.aasw.asn.au/document/item/6739>.
[23] AASW (n 20).
[24] Michael H. Allen et al, 'What Do Consumers Say They Want and Need during a Psychiatric Emergency?' (2003) 9(1) *Journal of Psychiatric Practice* 39; Vikram Patel and Kamaldeep Bhui, 'Unchaining People with Mental Disorders: Medication Is Not the Solution' (2018) 212(1) *The British Journal of Psychiatry* 6; Renata Kokanović et al, 'Supported Decision-Making from the Perspectives of Mental Health Service Users, Family Members Supporting Them and Mental Health Practitioners' (2018) 52(9) *Australian & New Zealand Journal of Psychiatry* 826.
[25] C. Maylea, A. Jorgensen, S. Matta, K. Ogilvie and P. Wallin, 'Consumers' Experiences of Mental Health Advance Statements.' (2018) 7, 22 *Laws*.
[26] *Mental Health Act 2009* (SA) s 7(1)(d).
[27] *Mental Health Act 2014* (Vic) s 79.
[28] Second Psychiatric Opinion Service <www.secondopinion.org.au>.
[29] For example, Open Dialog is increasingly seen as a viable human rights aligned alternative to coercion in mental health settings: Sebastian von Peter et al, 'Open Dialogue as a Human Rights-Aligned Approach' (2019) 10 *Frontiers in Psychiatry* <https://www.frontiersin.org/articles/10.3389/fpsyt.2019.00387/full>; For a detailed review of alternatives to coercion see Piers Gooding et al, *Alternatives to Coercion in Mental Health Settings: A Literature Review* (Melbourne Social Equity Institute, 2018) <www.socialequity.unimelb.edu.au>.

[30] NSW Mental Health Review Tribunal, 'Annual Report 2016–17' (2017) <https://www.mhrt.nsw.gov.au/files/mhrt/pdf/MHRT%20Annual%20Report%20Final%202016%2017.pdf>; Victorian Mental Health Tribunal, *Annual Report 2016–2017* (Mental Health Tribunal, 2017) 52 <https://www.mht.vic.gov.au/forms-and-publication/mental-health-tribunal-annual-reports-2/>.

[31] Gooding et al (n 29).

Chapter 15 REFUGEE AND ASYLUM LAW

Asher Hirsch and Chris Maylea

Asher Hirsch is a lawyer, academic and Senior Policy Officer at the Refugee Council of Australia. His PhD is in refugee and human rights law, and he is the author of over 40 works on the topic, including peer-reviewed papers, book chapters and online articles. He worked with the Human Rights Law Centre on the case of M68/2015 v Minister for Immigration and Border Protection[1] *and has been funded by the European Union to investigate refugee and human rights issues.*

In other decades and in other countries there would be little need for a distinct chapter on refugee or asylum law for social workers. There is little need, for example, for social workers to have a detailed understanding of general migration law. People of refugee background and people seeking asylum would still require social work services, but the law would not be such a significant factor in this process. Unfortunately, contemporary Australian politics has created an environment in which people seeking asylum and people of refugee background are actively persecuted by the law. Social workers cannot ethically practise with people of refugee background or people seeking asylum* without engaging with and challenging oppressive legal regimes wherever they exist, and cannot work effectively with people unless they understand the legal processes that they are subject to.

It must first be acknowledged that Australia has one of the best resettlement programs in the world. For people who come via the approved government processes, services and support are provided, people are given a pathway to citizenship and overall their human rights are well maintained. Social workers often work with these people. This chapter will outline the legal process for this group, but if this legal process was our only concern there would be no need for an entire chapter on the topic. The other group, people who are eligible to seek asylum in Australia but who are denied or detained by the Australian government while seeking asylum, are the main focus of this chapter.

---

* A note on terminology. Our preferred way to refer to people seeking asylum and people of refugee background is to refer to them as people, but refugee has a specific legal meaning as discussed below, so the term 'refugee' is used when referring to that legal category.

This chapter has been written with every effort to stay accurate for as long as possible, but as with any area of the law it is subject to change. Refugee law is especially fluid owing to its contested and politicised nature in the Australian policy context. More so than with most other areas of law, social workers will need to do their own research and stay up to date with developments as they emerge.

15.1 Refugee Convention

The starting point in understanding refugee law is that anyone who meets the criteria is eligible to seek asylum in countries that have signed the *Convention Relating to the Status of Refugees 1951 (Refugee Convention).*[2] The *Refugee Convention* is a United Nations convention that Australia signed in 1954. This is the international law that Australia (and all other signatories) is required to follow in relation to people seeking asylum and people of refugee background. All Australian law and policy should comply with the *Refugee Convention*, but as discussed in this chapter, it sometimes does not.

There are many reasons why nation states such as Australia are hesitant to comply with their obligations under the *Refugee Convention*. The *Convention* was originally conceived in response to refugee movements following the Second World War and the failure of states to respond to Jewish refugees escaping the Holocaust.* Now, with 65 million forcibly displaced people, including 25.4 million refugees, destination countries in the West are increasingly reluctant to honour their obligations. Conservative politicians warn of being 'swamped' by people looking for a better life. Even in 2000, 50 years after the drafting of the *Refugee Convention*, it was clear that signatories did not see it as suitable for the context of the time:

> *While the Convention-based asylum system may have operated well enough until the end of the Cold War, it was not designed with today's mass refugee outflows or migratory movements in mind.*[3]

Since then, mass refugee outflows and migratory movements have only continued, and continue to dominate policy debate in the West. Despite this, Australia is a signatory to the *Refugee Convention* and is obliged to comply with it.

---

* While the *Refugee Convention* was originally written only for people fleeing Europe before 1951, the *Protocol Relating to the Status of Refugees* removed this limitation, thereby making the *Refugee Convention* apply to all people who meet the above definition. Australia is a signatory to both the *Refugee Convention* and the *Protocol.*

15.1.1 Definition of a refugee under the *Convention*

Article 1(A) of the *Refugee Convention* defines a refugee as someone who:

> *owing to **well-founded fear** of being **persecuted** for reasons of **race, religion, nationality,** membership of a particular **social group** or **political opinion,** is outside the country of his nationality and is unable or, owing to such fear, is unwilling to avail himself of the protection of that country; or who, not having a nationality and being outside the country of his former habitual residence as a result of such events, is unable or, owing to such fear, is unwilling to return it.*

The key elements of this definition are that a refugee is someone who fears persecution based on one of the five grounds above and cannot return to their country. This is important as people who do not fit these categories are not legally refugees, such as people fleeing climate change events or natural disasters. A person must also be outside their country to be considered a refugee – those still remaining but who have had to flee internally are referred to as 'internally displaced persons'.

Box 15.1 *Who is a refugee?*

- *well-founded fear*
- *persecuted for*
  - *race*
  - *religion*
  - *nationality*
  - *social group*
  - *political opinion*
- *outside the country of nationality*
- *not protected by their county*

15.1.2 Refugee, asylum seeker or migrant?

Refugees are in a distinct legal category compared to other migrants. While migrants may choose to move for economic, social or family reasons, they can often return home. Refugees cannot return because they fear violence, death threats or other forms of persecution.

A person seeking asylum is someone who has sought protection as a refugee, but whose claim for refugee status has not yet been assessed. Every refugee was once a person seeking asylum. Under international law, a person is a refugee as soon as they meet the definition of refugee, whether or not their claim has been assessed. If they are found to be refugees, then they are 'recognised refugees'.

15.1.3 Non-refoulement

A key principle of the *Refugee Convention* is the *non-refoulement* provision.[4] This means that countries who are signatories to the *Refugee Convention* cannot return a refugee to a place where they will face harm. They are also not allowed to return refugees to another country if there is a risk that that country may subsequently return the person to harm.

In order to ensure that refugees are not returned to harm, countries must assess a person's asylum claim. Until they have undergone a fair and accurate assessment of their claims, a refugee (or someone claiming to be a refugee) must not be returned to their country, or another country where they may face harm. Only if they are found not to be a refugee, and have no other risks to their safety, they may be returned.

Australia is breaching this provision when it returns people by boat, such as the policy of 'turnbacks' to Indonesia, Sri Lanka and Vietnam. It also may be breaching international law when it returns an asylum seeker before they have had a proper chance to submit their refugee claims or has not properly considered them. This is also a concern for people going through 'fast-track processes',[5] where people seeking asylum may not have a proper chance to have their claim assessed.

15.1.4 Non-penalisation for mode of entry

Because refugees often have to flee for their lives, and they may not have the required documents to enter regularly (such as a passport and a visa), refugees may often have to enter a country without permission. Article 31 of the *Refugee Convention* recognises this by prohibiting countries from penalising refugees because of how they entered the country, even if they did so without authorisation.

Because of this provision, it is incorrect to refer to refugees or people seeking asylum as illegal immigrants. They have committed no crime by entering without a visa or passport. However, the Australian government continues to refer to refugees and people seeking asylum who entered by boat as Illegal Maritime Arrivals.

Australia also breaches this provision with its mandatory detention policy (discussed later in this chapter). By requiring all arrivals without a visa to be detained, Australia is penalising refugees based on their mode of arrival or lack of documentation.

15.1.5 Durable solutions

The United Nations High Commissioner for Refugees (UNHCR), the UN Refugee Agency, considers that there are three 'durable solutions' for refugees around the world: voluntary repatriation, local integration and resettlement.[6]

Voluntary repatriation

Voluntary repatriation is where a refugee voluntary agrees to go home, often because the war or persecution has ended. UNHCR and other governments and organisations are often involved in supporting refugees to return home. This is different from *refoulement* as it is a voluntary process.

Local integration

Local integration refers to supporting refugees to settle and integrate into the country they had fled to. This involves ensuring safety, protection and rights for refugees in their host country. Ideally, local integration will result in naturalisation (citizenship) for refugees in the host country.

However, over 85 per cent of refugees are living in developing countries neighbouring the conflict they have fled from. These countries have not signed the *Refugee Convention* and do not provide basic rights for refugees living there. While many are allowed to remain, either in refugee camps or in the community, they are often denied the right to work, education, healthcare and other social rights. They rely on aid agencies and international organisations for support. As such, local integration is not a reality for most refugees.

Resettlement

Resettlement is the transfer of refugees to a country that has agreed to take them and ultimately grant them permanent settlement. Resettlement is not an obligation under the *Refugee Convention* and is instead a voluntary act by countries to help a small number of refugees. Resettlement remains out of reach for most refugees, with less than 1 per cent of refugees receiving resettlement each year.

Resettlement is often referred by Australian politicians as 'the right way to come to Australia', and that people seeking asylum, such as by boat, are queue jumpers.[7] However, if there was a queue, it would take over 200 years for all refugees to be resettled.[8] Instead, the most vulnerable are recommended for resettlement by UNHCR, after which states decide whether or not to accept them. While resettlement is a positive contribution to refugee protection, it is a very small number of people, and should not be used to undermine another person's right to seek asylum.

Because the three durable solutions are not an option for most refugees, many people must take matters into their own hands and seek asylum by entering a country that has promised safety through the signing of the *Refugee Convention.* For people coming to Australia, that means coming by plane or by boat.

15.2 Refugee pathways to Australia

There are two main pathways for refugees to get protection in Australia. First, Australia runs a resettlement program of about 16,000 places a year, where it takes refugees referred by UNHCR or proposed by a person in Australia.[9] Resettled refugees are given one of four permanent visas set out below. This is known as the 'offshore' program.

The second pathway is to reach Australian territory and then apply for asylum. Because Australia has signed the *Refugee Convention,* it must not return people seeking asylum to harm and must assess their claims. Most refugees through the onshore program arrive via aeroplane with a valid visa, usually a tourist, student or another similar visa. If they are found to be a refugee after being assessed they are given a permanent visa.

The politicisation of the 'refugee issue' has led to many changes in the law, meaning that people who arrived at different times by different modes, for example by boat or by plane, have different legal statuses under Australian law. Until 2013, refugees who arrived by boat were also assessed in Australia and could be given permanent visas. In 2013, then Prime Minister Kevin Rudd announced that refugees who arrive by boat will never be settled in Australia, and instead will be sent to offshore detention centres on the tiny island country of Nauru or Manus Island in Papua New Guinea.*

For people who arrived in Australia by boat between 2012 and 2013, before the new laws were introduced, they are required to go through a less comprehensive refugee assessment procedure known as the 'fast-track process'. If they are found to be a refugee after going through this process, they are not entitled to a permanent visa and can only receive a temporary visa.

The other way refugees may come to Australia is through family reunion, where a family member already in Australia sponsors a close relative. While there is significant demand for family reunion, there are very limited visas, with many visas costing thousands of dollars.[10] This prolonged separation can contribute to mental health problems for the separated family and hinders people's successful settlement in Australia.[11]

15.3 Migration Act

The primary legislation governing migration in Australia is the *Migration Act 1958* (Cth). This Act, and the related regulations and procedures set out a comprehensive and complex set of rules regarding all migration-related issues. The following section will focus on how the *Migration Act* applies to refugees.

* The Manus Island detention facility was closed in 2017.

15.3.1 Definitions

Section 5H of the *Migration Act* provides the definition of a refugee under Australian law. The *Migration Act* follows similar wording to the *Refugee Convention* but has a couple of important distinctions. Firstly, when considering whether a person is a refugee, section 5J requires that the person seeking asylum demonstrate that there is a 'real chance' that they would face persecution in 'all areas' of their home country. This means that a person will not be considered a refugee if they can move to another part of the country that may be safe. This is a controversial provision, as conflict areas may often change or persecution may spread to other areas of the country.

Further, a person will not be considered to be a refugee under Australian law if they can modify their behaviour so to avoid persecution in their home country, other than a 'characteristic that is fundamental to the person's identity or conscience'.[12] For example, if a person can change their career to avoid persecution they will not be considered a refugee under Australian law. The Australian legal definition of a refugee is narrower than the international legal definition.

15.3.2 Visa types

Australia is the only country in the world to have a mandatory visa regime, meaning that every person who is not a citizen must hold a valid visa or face mandatory detention. The *Migration Act* sets out a number of different visa classes for a variety of purposes. Visas can be categorised as either permanent or temporary visas. Permanent visas allow a person to remain in Australia for their entire life (unless their visa is cancelled for a serious criminal offence). Temporary visas have a limited time someone can stay in Australia. Before their temporary visa expires they need to leave Australia or apply for another visa.

Most people coming through the offshore resettlement program have a permanent visa, allowing them to settle in Australia and make it their home. The permanent visas through the offshore program are:

- Refugee Visa for people whom the United Nations High Commissioner for Refugees (UNHCR) has referred to Australia for assistance
- In-Country Special Humanitarian Visa for people who are still living in their country and have been unable to leave
- Emergency Rescue Visa, which gives priority processing for people who are in immediate danger
- Woman at Risk Visa for women who do not have the protection of a partner or a relative and are in danger of victimisation.

People found to be refugees after arriving in Australia by aeroplane are also given a Permanent Protection Visa. Refugees who arrived by boat before 2012 were also given these visas. However, after legislative changes in 2014,[13] refugees who arrived by boat between 2012 and 2013 are now only entitled to a three-year Temporary Protection Visa or a five-year Safe Haven Enterprise Visa. After these visas expire they must apply again for protection.

People seeking asylum may also be given a bridging visa while they wait for an outcome on their refugee application. Bridging visas may have certain restrictions, such as no work rights or no study rights. Bridging visas may also have very short expiry dates, which, when they expire, may leave people with no visa and at risk of detention.

Box 15.2 *Changes to disability eligibility*

Until 2012, the Migration Act *discriminated against refugees with a disability. The* Migration Act *and regulations are exempt from the* Disability Discrimination Act 1992 (Cth), *allowing the government to discriminate against people with a disability in the area of migration. To receive a visa through the offshore program, a person must meet the health requirements set out in Public Interest Criteria 4007. People with a disability were considered to be a cost to the health system or provision of community services, and therefore were excluded from resettlement.*

In 2012, changes were made to the migration policies that provided that a person applying for resettlement can receive a health waiver, even if they are likely to place significant costs on Australian healthcare or community services. This has resulted in more people with a disability coming to Australia through the offshore resettlement program. However, settlement services and disability services have not kept up with this increase and government policies have not provided additional support to address the additional needs of this group.[14]

15.3.3 Mandatory detention

Since 1992 Australia has been the only country to impose mandatory indefinite detention for all non-citizens without a visa.[15] There are no time limits for how long a person can be detained, leading to indefinite and arbitrary detention.

Box 15.3 *Al-Kateb*

The case of Al-Kateb v Godwin & Ors *(2004) 219 CLR 562 held that indefinite detention is not unlawful under the* Australian Constitution *if it is for an administrative purpose. Al-Kateb was a stateless Palestinian who had failed in his bid for refugee status. However, as he had no country to return to he was held indefinitely in immigration detention until he could be removed to another country. The High Court held that since his detention was for an administrative purpose (i.e. to remove him from the country), he could be held indefinitely.*

Immigration detention centres have been found to be in violation of international law.[16] The Australian Human Rights Commission has found that indefinite detention causes significant mental health problems, with particular concerns for detained children.[17] The United Nations has repeatedly called for Australia to end the practice of mandatory indefinite detention.[18]

15.3.4 Community detention

An alternative to closed immigration detention is community detention. This means that a person can be required to reside at a certain residence, rather than an immigration detention centre. People released on community detention may have certain restrictions, such as a curfew, and are normally required to stay at a residence that is paid for by the government. However, as a person is still technically in 'detention', they have no visa and cannot work or study (unless they are school-aged children).

Community detention is a positive alternative to closed immigration detention, but still has a number of restrictions. Often, while people are glad to be out of detention, the ongoing limbo and uncertainty can also affect a person's well-being.

In addition to community detention, people seeking asylum awaiting an outcome on their refugee application may also be granted a bridging visa as outlined above. This may have a few more rights associated with it, such as work rights, but a person is then required to find their own accommodation and generally support themselves. People in community detention or a bridging visa may receive a small allowance through the Status Resolution Support Service (SRSS), discussed below.

15.3.5 Asylum application process

People seeking asylum who arrive in Australia must make an application for refugee status, known as a protection application. The process is very onerous and requires a detailed explanation of a person's history and reason for fleeing their country. The application must also be written in English. For this reason, many people need legal assistance; however, there is often limited support from free community legal centres.

The process can take a number of months, or even years, to complete. This is often due to delays on the part of the officials processing the application, rather than the time taken to consider the application. While people are awaiting a decision, they are either held in immigration detention or released into the community through community detention or a bridging visa.

The application process first requires a completed form with a written statement from the person about the reasons they fled their country and why they fear returning. This is considered by the Department of Home Affairs, who then usually invite the applicant for an interview, which usually goes through the person's claim in detail and can often be difficult and emotional for the applicant. If they are successful they will be granted their relevant visa.

If they are rejected at this stage they can seek a review. For those who arrived by boat between 2012 and 2013, they can only seek a review through the Immigration Assessment Authority (IAA). This is known as the fast-track process and has a very limited review process that may not consider the application in detail. The IAA does not have to interview the applicant again and it is difficult to provide further information to the IAA. Often they make a decision 'on the papers', which means that they do not consider any new information and simply reassess the documents and original interview. This provides a risk that a refugee may be denied a protection visa and sent back to harm.

If a person arrived with a valid visa, such as by aeroplane, they are able to seek a review of their first rejection through the Migration and Refugee Division of the Administrative Appeals Tribunal (AAT). This process involves an entirely new assessment and provides a hearing for the applicant to put their case before a tribunal member.

If a person is rejected again, either after an IAA or AAT decision, they are able to seek review through the federal courts. However, this review is not a review of whether the decision was correct, but rather whether the correct procedure was followed and if the decision-maker followed the law. As such, there are limited grounds to seek review through the federal courts.

Often once a person receives a negative decision at the IAA or AAT, they will be detained or may be allowed to remain in the community but without any work rights or income support. The Australian government does not provide any support to people who have been rejected after the IAA or AAT, even if they are seeking review in the courts. This is often to pressure people to return home.

15.3.6 Offshore processing

As mentioned above, people seeking asylum who arrived by boat after June 2013 are sent to offshore detention centres in Nauru and (previously) Manus Island, Papua New Guinea. The *Migration Act* provides a mechanism for regional processing, where people seeking asylum may be sent to third countries to be detained and have their claims processed.[19] Under current policy, those sent to offshore detention will never be resettled in Australia, even if determined to be refugees. Instead, they are given the option of resettling in Nauru, Papua New Guinea or a third country. In 2017, the detention centre on Manus Island closed following a decision of the Papua New Guinea Supreme Court on the basis that it breached the right to personal liberty in the Papua New Guinean Constitution. Numerous United Nations bodies, non-governmental organisations and government inquiries have found that offshore processing breaches international law and causes significant physical and mental health problems for people sent there.[20]

This policy is ostensibly to prevent people who are seeking asylum from drowning at sea on their way to Australia. This is a noble aim, but other than the United States,[21] no other country that has signed the *Refugee Convention* has a policy of offshore processing, boat turnbacks or mandatory detention. Whatever the justification, these policies intentionally prevent people from exercising their human right to seek asylum. Australia violates the human rights of people seeking asylum and makes the experience unnecessarily traumatic so as to deter other people from exercising their right to seek asylum.

15.4 Australian Citizenship Act 2007

People of refugee background on a permanent visa are able to live in Australia for their entire life. Generally, people on a permanent visa have the same rights and access to services as other Australians. However, many feel they are not at the end of their asylum journey until they find security and safety through obtaining Australian citizenship. Citizenship provides people of refugee background with the safety they need to settle and heal and gives them the security to build and imagine their new lives. For this reason, most people of refugee background and humanitarian entrants are eager to apply for citizenship as soon as they can, and prize it highly. The *Refugee Convention* also requires Australia to 'as far as possible facilitate the assimilation and naturalisation of refugees'.[22]

The *Australian Citizenship Act 2007* (Cth) sets out the law regarding Australian Citizenship. People of refugee background who are permanent citizens are able to receive citizenship if they have resided in Australia for the last four years and have held a permanent visa for at least 12 months. Applicants also have to sit a basic citizenship test and make a pledge of commitment, usually at a public citizenship ceremony. However, the Australian government has been making citizenship harder to achieve for people of refugee background, including by delaying and freezing applications, making security and identity assessments more difficult, and attempting to change the law to require four years on a permanent visa and passing a high-level English language test.

Consider Arif's story as an example of how social workers can be more or less useful when working with people seeking asylum or who come from refugee backgrounds.

15.5 Arif's story

My name is Arif. I am from Afghanistan. I came to Australia in 2011 as an asylum seeker on a boat. I went to high school in Melbourne and later graduated from RMIT University with a Commerce degree. I am currently working in the ACT Treasury as a Graduate Analyst. I have used social services in various forms, from my time in immigration detention to community-based detention and then as a 'free' person, and from numerous organisations with varying level of control and mandate.

Prior to coming to Australia, I had never experienced or received direct services from social workers – or if I did, I didn't realise it. During my initial years in Australia, it was fairly a new experience for me. At the time, I didn't even know that it was 'community service' and that there exists such a thing. That is one reason that I had a low expectation from social and case workers. I was already very thankful to them for merely existing, overlooking the fact that it was their obligation to provide services or to work for my best interests.

Due to my lack of awareness of rights or needs, I didn't ask for anything specific beyond essentials such as when we needed to go for shopping during our time in the community detention. I also wouldn't proactively express my interests that would otherwise enable social workers to provide me personalised support. This led to a very unproductive relationship with one of my social or case workers from a settlement service.

I had been assigned a caseworker immediately after my release from community detention who was supposed to support me with integration and settlement. However, I never actually met her and the very few interactions that we had were over the phone. She never asked for my needs beyond essentials, which in this case included provision of furniture and household items. I wasn't asked where my interests lay and what I wanted to do, nor was I referred to youth or active community programs which would have helped me with integration. She did not even mention the programs available run by her own organisation. It was a very typical client-organisation relationship devoid of emotion or empathy. They didn't attempt to understand what my background and experience was and what my needs would be based on that. In short, I wasn't proactively questioned to find the best way of supporting me.

At that time (this is my first year out of immigration detention), I was fortunate enough that I had also been assigned another caseworker from Department of Health and Human Services (DHHS) in their Refugee Minor Program (RMP). She would regularly meet me, ask me about my school and needs there and, where needed, speak to my teachers and provide me all material and emotional support. During our conversation she would ask me about my interests and regularly sent me programs that local organisations were running in the area which were of benefit to me. For example, through our conversations, she recognised that I would be interested in youth leadership programs so she had me registered for those that were run by the local Council. She was also aware that I had a carer so she would frequently get in touch with him and make sure that he was aware of his responsibilities. My DHHS social worker also had good relationship with and knowledge of programs being run by other community organisations that were operating in the area such as a youth organisation where I later got my first paid internship.

I do believe that where I am today is partly due to those early efforts to keep me focused and the support that I received.

Arif's experience speaks for itself. The contrast between the engaged worker and the unengaged worker highlights how good social work can result in improved outcomes. Neither social worker required a highly developed understanding of the law, but they did need to understand his situation and what he was entitled to. In the refugee and asylum-seeking context, doing good social work requires specific skills and knowledge, as discussed in the following section.

15.6 Social Work Practice

Social workers in all fields will encounter people of refugee background, although it will be much less common to work with people actively seeking asylum. Social workers will also be involved in settlement programs, in asylum seeker case management and working in detention.

15.6.1 Generic social work practice

The refugee experience can be traumatic and destabilising, and many people face additional discrimination and stigma on arrival.[23] For these reasons, social workers will see people in mental health services because of trauma that took place in their country of origin, or because of their transition experience or their settlement experience. Newly arrived people may lack support networks or find it difficult to navigate the service system, requiring additional supports. Most people, particularly those who come via the official resettlement program, will have little contact with the law.

Sometimes cultural differences can lead to contact with the legal system. Adjusting to the Australian cultural context can be difficult for all migrants and particularly for people of refugee background, even after they have become citizens. Polygamy, female genital mutilation, child brides and youth gangs tend to fill headlines, but these cases are not characteristic of the refugee community as a whole. People born outside Australia are half as likely to commit crimes than people born in Australia, although some migrant groups are overrepresented in some crimes.[24] Even so, social workers will need a good understanding of laws around sexual interactions, family violence and gender relations so they can support people in their compliance with them.

The law becomes more relevant when working with people who have not obtained citizenship. Some visa types restrict the rights, entitlements or services available to the visa holder. This is particularly true of work rights and rights to welfare entitlements. Social workers must be very careful when supporting people who are moving along the precarious road to permanent residency. For example, a social worker working for an employment service might note that a person had begun work. If this information was documented and reported, it might result in the person's visa being cancelled. The various rights and entitlements are too complex to detail here and may have changed by the time this chapter is published, so social workers must ensure that they find out on a case-by-case basis what restrictions apply to people they work with.

The process of having a claim for asylum processed can be highly stressful and distressing. There is no comprehensive data on timelines, but a single decision may take many months to be made and appeals processes can take months and years, even with the fast-tracking process.[25] Social workers will need to ensure that people are supported in whatever they require and with a compassionate understanding of the experiences that have led people to seek asylum in Australia.

15.6.2 Specific services

There are a range of services targeted specifically at supporting people of refugee background and other newly arrived migrants. These are in addition to the mainstream services that are available to everyone and include:

- Adult Migrant English Program (AMEP)
- The Humanitarian Settlement Program (HSP)
- The Settlement Engagement and Transition Support Program (SETS)
- Translating and Interpreting Service (TIS).

Many mainstream services will also have supports designed for people of refugee background and other newly arrived migrants, such as specialised school programs or counselling for survivors of torture.

Some people who have applied for asylum and are living in the community on bridging visas or who are in community detention may be eligible for case management, temporary accommodation and income support under the Status Resolution Support Services (SRSS) Program. This program is aimed at supporting people until their visa issues are resolved –

either by the granting of a different visa or deportation. Income support for people on SRSS is less than Newstart (typically 89 per cent), and while most will have access to Medicare some will not. Most people waiting to have their claims for asylum processed will not be eligible for financial assistance at university, and if they choose to study rather than work they might have their financial support cut. This has left many people excluded from higher education.[26] Increasingly, supports such as SRSS are becoming more restricted, forcing people to return to their countries of origin and potential harm.[27]

15.6.3 Detention and compliance roles

Social workers may also work in detention settings or in the community with people who are subject to visa restrictions. This can include casework roles working directly for the government or they may be working for other contracted organisations. These roles are different from parole or mental health compliance roles, as they do not usually have anything to do with the person's legal process to seek asylum. They may have some responsibility for ensuring that people comply with their visa conditions.

These roles are very restricted in their ability to advocate publicly, but they may find ways to assist the people they are working with to advocate for themselves. They can also assist people in their legal processes, for example by helping them collect evidence to support their claims for asylum or by linking them with a lawyer. Working in these environments requires a very well-developed understanding of the law.

For example, a social worker might know that under Australian law a person can be returned to their country of origin if they can be safe in some parts of it – perhaps outside the main cities. A good social worker will also know that a person cannot be sent back if they cannot access services they need in those areas, such a mental health services. This social worker might arrange for evidence from the person's mental health clinician to be provided to their lawyer to support this line of argument. In this way, this social worker could make the difference between a person being returned to persecution or staying in Australia.

15.7 Conclusion

Refugee law in Australia is complex, rapidly changing and highly political. A core element of this area of law is a deterrence framework, where refugees are punished based on the way they arrived in Australia. This is not only a violation of human rights, but a policy to deter others from exercising their right to seek asylum. Social workers working in Australia's refugee support and asylum seeker processing system can respond in four ways: they can be complicit in the human rights abuses perpetrated by the system; they can retreat and refuse to work in the system; they can advocate through whistleblowing, policy reform and litigation; or they can act subversively and reduce the harm caused by the system.[28] The first of these two are not ethically viable; social workers cannot ignore human rights violations. This leaves only the options of advocacy and subversion, which are addressed in Chapters 16 and 17.

Main points

1. Seeking asylum is a human right.
2. Australia is in violation of its human rights obligations in denying the right to seek asylum.
3. A refugee is a person who:
   a. Has a well-founded fear
   b. of persecution for
      i. race
      ii. religion
      iii. nationality
      iv. social group
      v. political opinion
   c. is outside the country of his nationality
   d. is not protected by their county.
4. Australia is the only country to impose mandatory indefinite detention for all non-citizens without a visa.
5. Social workers work at many points in the refugee support system or the asylum seeker processing system.
6. Social workers cannot ignore human rights violations.

Discussion questions

1. What is missing from the definition of a refugee? What kind of people are not protected?
2. What are alternatives to the current system? What could be done to fix it?
3. Re-read Arif's story. What could social workers have done better to support him?
4. What should social workers do in the refugee support and asylum seeker processing sector? How can we act ethically?

Further reading

Linda Briskman and Jane Doe, 'Social Work in Dark Places: Clash of Values in Offshore Immigration Detention' (2016) 35(4) *Social Alternatives* 73.

Christopher Maylea and Asher Hirsch, 'Social Workers as Collaborators? The Ethics of Working Within Australia's Asylum System' (3 April 2018) 12(2) *Ethics and Social Welfare* 160–78.

Marjorie Quinn, June Allan, Bob Pease and Linda Briskman, 'Towards Anti-Racist and Culturally Affirming Practices', in *Critical Social Work: Theories and Practices for a Socially Just World* (Allen and Unwin, 2009).

Jane McAdam and Fiona Chong. *Refugee Rights and Policy Wrongs: A Frank, up-to-Date Guide by Experts* (UNSW Press, 2019).

Madeline Gleeson, *Offshore: Behind the Wire on Manus and Nauru* (NewSouth Publishing, 2016).

Asher Lazarus Hirsch, 'The Borders Beyond the Border: Australia's Extraterritorial Migration Controls' (1 September 2017) 36(3) *Refugee Survey Quarterly* 48–80.

James C. Hathaway, *The Rights of Refugees under International Law* (Cambridge University Press, 2005).

Guy S. Goodwin-Gill and Jane McAdam, *The Refugee in International Law* (Oxford University Press, 2007).

15.8 REFERENCES

[1] *M68/2015 v Minister for Immigration and Border Protection* [2016] HCA 1.
[2] UN General Assembly, Convention Relating to the Status of Refugees, 28 July 1951, United Nations, Treaty Series, vol. 189, p. 137.
[3] Adrienne Millbank, *The Problem with the 1951 Refugee Convention* (Research Paper No 5 2000–01, Parliament of Australia, 2000) <https://www.aph.gov.au/About_Parliament/Parliamentary_Departments/Parliamentary_Library/pubs/rp/rp0001/01RP05>.
[4] UN General Assembly, Convention Relating to the Status of Refugees, 28 July 1951, United Nations, Treaty Series, vol. 189, p. 137, art 33.
[5] Department of Home Affairs, 'Subclass 790 Safe Haven Enterprise Visa' (2019) <https://immi.homeaffairs.gov.au/visas/getting-a-visa/visa-listing/safe-haven-enterprise-790#About>.
[6] Core Group on Durable Solutions, *Framework for Durable Solutions for Refugees and Persons of Concern* (United Nations High Commissioner for Refugees, May 2003) 179 <https://academic.oup.com/rsq/article-lookup/doi/10.1093/rsq/23.1.179>.
[7] Anne Pedersen and Lisa K. Hartley, 'Can We Make a Difference? Prejudice Towards Asylum Seekers in Australia and the Effectiveness of Antiprejudice Interventions' (2015) 9(1) *Journal of Pacific Rim Psychology* 1.
[8] Janet Phillips, *Asylum Seekers and Refugees: What Are the Facts?* (Parliament of Australia, 2015) <https://www.aph.gov.au/about_parliament/parliamentary_departments/parliamentary_library/pubs/rp/rp1415/asylumfacts#_Toc413067442>.
[9] Ibid.
[10] Department of Home Affairs, 'Subclass 115 Remaining Relative Visa' (2019) <https://immi.homeaffairs.gov.au/visas/getting-a-visa/visa-listing/remaining-relative-115>.
[11] Laura Simich and Lisa Andermann, *Refuge and Resilience Promoting Resilience and Mental Health among Resettled Refugees and Forced Migrants* (Springer, 2014).
[12] *Migration Act 1958* (Cth) 5J(3)(a).

[13] *Migration and Maritime Powers Legislation Amendment (Resolving the Asylum Legacy Caseload) Act 2014* (Cth).
[14] A. Hirsch et al, 'The Changing Face of Disability and Refugee Services and Policy in Australia: Implications for Social Work' (2019) 2(1) *Social Work and Policy Studies: Social Justice, Practice and Theory* 1.
[15] *Migration Act 1958* (Cth) s 189.
[16] Azadeh Dastyari, 'Detention of Australia's Asylum Seekers in Nauru: Is Deprivation of Liberty by Any Other Name Just as Unlawful' (2015) 38 *UNSWLJ* 669; Linda Briskman and Jane Doe, 'Social Work in Dark Places: Clash of Values in Offshore Immigration Detention' (2016) 35(4) *Social Alternatives* 73.
[17] *The Forgotten Children: National Inquiry into Children in Immigration Detention 2014* (Australian Human Rights Commission, 2014) 553 <https://www.mja.com.au/journal/2015/202/11/forgotten-children-national-inquiry-children-immigration-detention-2014>.
[18] *Concluding Observations on the Sixth Periodic Report of Australia* (No CCPR/C/AUS/CO/6, United Nations Human Rights Committee, 2017).
[19] *Migration Act 1958* (Cth) ss 198AA–198AJ.
[20] Amy Nethery and Rosa Holman, 'Secrecy and Human Rights Abuse in Australia's Offshore Immigration Detention Centres' [2016] *The International Journal of Human Rights* 1; RCoA, *State Of The Nation: Refugees And People Seeking Asylum In Australia* (Refugee Council of Australia, 2017) <http://www.refugeecouncil.org.au/publications/reports/state-nation-2017/>; Amnesty International, *Island of Despair: Australia's 'Processing' of Refugee on Nauru* (2016) <https://static.amnesty.org.au/wp-content/uploads/2016/10/ISLAND-OF-DESPAIR-FINAL.pdf>; *Concluding Observations on the Sixth Periodic Report of Australia* (n 18).
[21] Dastyari (n 16).
[22] UN General Assembly, *Convention Relating to the Status of Refugees*, 28 July 1951, United Nations, Treaty Series, vol. 189, p. 137, art 34.
[23] RCoA (n 20).
[24] Joint Standing Committee on Migration, *Inquiry into Migrant Settlement Outcomes* (text, Parliament of Australia, 2017) <https://www.aph.gov.au/Parliamentary_Business/Committees/Joint/Migration/settlementoutcomes/Report/section?id=committees%2Freportjnt%2F024098%2F25141>.
[25] Refugee Council of Australia, *Fast Tracking Statistics* (Refugee Council of Australia, 16 February 2019) <https://www.refugeecouncil.org.au/fast-tracking-statistics/>.
[26] Asher Hirsch and Chris Maylea, 'Education Denied: People Seeking Asylum and Refugees Trapped in Limbo' (2016) 14(55) *New Community* 19.
[27] *Starving Them out: Destitution of People Seeking Asylum in Australia* (Refugee Council of Australia, 2018) <https://www.refugeecouncil.org.au/starving-them-out/>.
[28] Christopher Maylea and Asher Hirsch, 'Social Workers as Collaborators? The Ethics of Working Within Australia's Asylum System' (2018) 12(2) *Ethics and Social Welfare* 160.

Chapter 16 ETHICAL SOCIAL WORK AROUND THE LAW

16.1 INTRODUCTION

Key figures in the historical narrative of human rights and social justice, including figures such as Rosa Parks, Martin Luther King, Jr. and Mahatma Gandhi, who actively and intentionally acted outside the law, are rarely mentioned in standard social work texts.[1] Despite this, social work has been described as a 'dissenting profession' that demands social workers challenge social issues and correct human rights violations.[2]

Social workers are required by the *Code of Ethics* to uphold human rights, 'even though employers' policies or official orders may not be compatible'.[3] As discussed in Chapter 4, what it means to be ethical is a fairly subjective question, but whatever ethical basis social workers adopt for practice will inevitably come into conflict with the restrictions laid down by law and policy. As highlighted throughout this book, the legal system is fraught with human rights violations and overloaded with socioeconomic disadvantage and discrimination.

Social work education and practice focus on the skills required to work in the system and on the skills needed to change it, but much less attention is given to how social workers can effectively work in a system that will take time to change. Policy and practice are widely divergent and social workers often appear to have little power to influence either. Social workers must help people navigate the coercive system and resist becoming agents of coercion themselves, while also looking after themselves. Ethical social work practice is often inconsistent with the law, policy and organisational restrictions, so social workers will inevitably face the dilemma of complying and acting inconsistently, with their values or not complying and acting outside the law. This chapter considers two ways social workers might ethically act around the edges of the law: through hidden, subversive practices and whistleblowing.

In order to understand why this is so important, social workers must tune into their own moral distress and ontological anxiety.

16.2 MORAL DISTRESS AND ONTOLOGICAL ANXIETY

Moral distress is the experience of knowing the right course of action to take but, owing to social, organisational, legal or other restrictions, being unable to do so.[4] There is also distress associated with *not* knowing the right course of action to take, but knowing that the current course of action is not the right one.[5] Taylor calls this inability to work in alignment with values 'ontological guilt', and contrasts it to 'ontological anxiety'. Ontology is a person's worldview, their way of understanding the world and the nature of being. A person's ontology will directly inform their values, how they relate to the world and how they think the world should be.

Ontological guilt is the experience of acting in contravention with values. Ontological anxiety is the healthy anxiety felt when acting in accordance with values but outside the confines of the law or the requirements of the social work role. Taylor writes that:

> *... ontological anxiety is the price of living authentically. By contrast, choosing the more comfortable, non-anxiety-provoking course of action will, in the short term, result in feeling safer but in the long term lead to the more malignant state of 'ontological guilt'.*[6]

Subversive social work is one way in which social workers can act in alignment with their values, embracing ontological anxiety and delivering the social work that people need. This comes with its own anxiety. A worker in one study said:

> *I think about it. Have I crossed the line, have I not crossed the line? It comes up a lot. It does.*[7]

Moral injury, including 'perpetrating, failing to prevent, bearing witness to, or learning about acts that transgress deeply held moral beliefs and expectations',[8] has been linked to post-traumatic stress symptoms, depression, suicidality, anxiety and hostility.[9] Social workers will have to negotiate this for themselves, balancing their own well-being with that of people they work with. Social workers must resist being enfeebled by neoliberalism or risk management paradigms and so fail in supporting the people they work with. The alternative is that social workers will be paralysed by moral distress and burnout, leaving only those who are content to comply remaining in the profession. For those who hope to remain on the long march towards social justice, subversion provides one opportunity to embrace ontological anxiety.

16.3 Subversive Practice in Social Work

Briskman and Zion argue that subversive practices are one way to resolve the dilemma of upholding human rights in systems that routinely violate them,[10] but subversion can also help social workers resolve moral distress and retain their humanity in inhumane environments. Subversion is not a new idea. Moreau, often referred to as the 'father' of structural social work, wrote in 1990:

> *It is not easy to turn a blind eye to discriminatory policies of social agencies and the State to ally oneself with clients when their interests go against the agency's. It calls for the worker to develop 'functional noncapitulation strategies' ... The worker must be comfortable with conflict, be ready to exercise diplomacy, and be capable of resorting to what Mispelblom ... has called silent or low-key practices.*[11]

This is distinct from the need for social change, which is widely accepted as part of social work practice and is discussed in Chapter 17. It is also distinct from whistleblowing or other 'in the open' practices aimed at promoting intervention discussed later in this chapter. Subversive social work is what we do while we are working for social change and when intervention is not forthcoming.[12]

This does not mean that subversion does not contribute to social change, but that it will not in itself change the system. It may highlight the problems within the system and undermine it while contributing to a sense that the system can be changed. Portelli and Eizadirad write:

> *The objective of subversion is to stand up to injustice and inequitable practices as a means of rupturing the status quo, in the process preventing and/or reducing harm to self, others, and members of the community, and harnessing hope for change and opening up of new possibilities. At the core of subversion is an understanding that everyday decisions and actions have consequences far beyond the surface level and that they impact others in numerous ways.*[13]

Subversive social work is poorly defined and poorly theorised but is a central part of social work practice. It might be referred to as subversion,[14] or as 'functional noncapitulation strategies',[15] 'positive deviant social work',[16] covert practices[17] or (my favourite) 'isolated acts of banditry'.[18] For this chapter, subversive social work is defined as:

> *... intentionally small-scale practice behaviours of caring resistance that social workers engage in to support vulnerable groups, using practices that are aligned with their own ethics, but falling outside the professional, procedural, or even legal boundaries of their roles.*[19]

Subversion can take a variety of forms, from small-scale everyday acts to broader, system-level subversions. This is not just damaging the system for the sake of it, but undertaken to bring an ethic of care into a system devoid of compassion.

At the most basic level, simply displaying compassion in systems that are designed to be punitive can subvert the intentions of that system. Employment service providers, for example, are designed to be punitive and to force people off benefits and into work. Nguyen and Velayutham argue that frontline workers in employment service provision can enact more compassionate policy and contradict the punitive intent of the system.[20] Social workers may simply choose not to hear when a person shares news of their new cash-in-hand job, which may jeopardise their disability payments.[21]

Social workers in one study described these acts as 'being creative' with policies, filling in forms, feigning ignorance and 'massaging the truth'.[22] These actions may result in organisational censure but are unlikely to be unlawful or criminal. Even quite seriously subversive actions, such as when social workers were accused of running an organised scheme of marrying people seeking asylum to circumvent off-shore detention (see Box 16.1), may not be strictly illegal. Often, the repercussions will be limited to a professional reprimand, but when practice strays outside the law, the implications can be more serious.

Box 16.1 *Manus at first sight*

In 2016 the then Immigration Minister, Peter Dutton, claimed to have uncovered a spectacular example of subversive social work. He claimed, on radio and in the federal parliament, that there was an organised scheme by social workers on Manus Island to circumvent the asylum seeker processing system by marrying people seeking asylum and bringing them to Australia on spousal visas.[23] *In an interview with Dutton, radio host Ray Hadley put it in these terms:*

> *... social workers over there who go you know, I guess deliberately employed there, thinking I'm going to get to Manus Island, I'll show this Dutton character, he can't stop us and I'll get there and I'll marry this person and therefore they come here under the spousal visa.*[24]

There is no concrete evidence of this occurring, but it provides an interesting case of subversive social work and the law. If all six social workers genuinely fell in love and married six asylum seekers, there is no law broken. They may have breached employment contracts or violated ethical standards by engaging in sexual relationships with people they worked with, but little more. Dutton cited the age gap between the person seeking asylum and the social worker as evidence that this was not a case of true love:

> *... in some cases I'm aware that there are literally decades difference in age between the male and the female social worker and this is a problem'.* [25]

If it was an organised scheme, and the marriages were not genuine, then this may constitute criminal fraud under section 234 of the Migration Act 1958 *(Cth). This carries a maximum ten-year prison sentence.*

If true, this is either a remarkably subversive action in pursuit of an individual's human rights or a heart-warming story of true love blossoming on the rockiest of ground. Or both!

16.4 Subversive Social Work and the Law

Social workers are already intentionally breaking the law in practice but are understandably not forthcoming with details. While research on this topic is limited, those studies which have gone looking for subversive practice have consistently found it. A child protection worker in one study told researchers:

> *We try to make accommodations for whatever the [parents] need. We may be doing some things that violate the rules or the law. It happens. Believe me it happens. We put ourselves on the line. Whatever it takes.*[26]

Sometimes social workers will be forced by one law to break another. A study into the decision-making process of workers in the asylum seeker processing system in Finland identified this issue, where the law required the worker to terminate services to people, which resulted in them becoming homeless:

> *There are these regulations on negligence. So, if you throw a person out of here, and they don't have a place to stay and it's −30 Celsius outside, you will certainly be guilty according to another law.*[27]

Social workers may stray over this line in a number of areas. Sometimes this will be intentional, when social workers know the law and decide not to follow it; other times the law will not be clear, allowing the social worker plausible deniability if they are caught. As discussed in Chapter 6, the law is often unclear when it comes to social work practice, but social workers should be clear about when it is not clear. Understanding the law is essential to breaking it properly, as the consequences can be significant, including serious fines and imprisonment.

Often, the subversive practice will be not doing something. For example, as discussed in Chapter 6, social workers working in Victorian prisons are required by the *Corrections Act 1986* (Vic) to report anything that might 'reasonably be thought to jeopardize the security of the prison or the welfare of the prisoners'.[28] What should a social worker do if they see someone with a contraband item such as a digital music player? What if the social worker knows that a person loves listening to music and that listening to music is therapeutic for them? What if the social worker brings them the music player? That is a criminal offence, for which the social worker might join the prisoner in prison.[29]

Box 16.2 *Bye, Daddy!*

A social worker had been supporting a woman and her children who were staying in a women's refuge. They were separated from a dog that the woman claimed belonged to her, but as part of the power and control tactics, the perpetrator would not let her dog go with her, saying that the dog was his and registered in his name. The perpetrator was a manufacturer of illicit drugs and had security cameras all around the exterior and interior of the home. Police had gone to the home as they were looking for the perpetrator on a drug-related matter, and the social worker explained to the police that she needed to visit the property to retrieve some belongings for the woman.

When she got to the property with the police, she searched for the dog and found him, in the social worker's words, 'really high', on the floor in the drug lab. The social worker picked up the dog, and on noticing a camera in the ceiling, held the dog up to the camera and said, 'Bye, Daddy'. The dog was reunited with his family at the refuge (which was very rare in that it was companion animal-friendly), and they were all able to be rehomed together.

This all seems fine until you realise that the social worker used the police to help her commit a burglary.

(Thanks to Melissa Laing for this example.)

There are endless ways in which the law and subversive actions can interact. For example, people subject to involuntary mental health treatment sometimes request to view their clinical files. Sometimes this request is allowed by the mental health service but often it is not. Under section 191 of the *Mental Health Act 2014* (Vic) a mental health service must 'give a person who is the subject of a proceeding access to any documents in its possession in connection with the proceeding at least 48 hours before the hearing'. A social worker who knows of this requirement might share this with a person who wanted to view their file. The person might then request a hearing for their order to be revoked so they can have access to their file, then cancel the hearing after they had read it. This is not unlawful, but is certainly a subversive use of the law.*

* This is, for the avoidance of doubt, not something I would ever do or have ever done. As a solicitor, as per rule 3.1 of the *Legal Profession Uniform Law Australian Solicitors' Conduct Rules 2015*, my 'duty to the court and the administration of justice is paramount and prevails to the extent of inconsistency with any other duty'. Social workers who are not also solicitors, however, are not bound by this duty.

Similarly, it might be possible to stretch around the boundaries of the law. For example, there are allegations that social workers on Nauru provided mobile phones to people detained in offshore detention.[30] This is probably not exactly breaking the law but is clearly not aligned with the spirit of the obligations of silence the law imposes in that context.

The Australian Association of Social Workers (AASW) *Code of Ethics* requires social workers to 'act in accordance with the law' but also recognises that the law may be in conflict with social work ethics.[31] The AASW directs social workers in this dilemma to the AASW Ethics Consultation Service, but the reality is that often the social worker will need to make their own decision about what to do.

16.5 Getting Subversion Right

Social workers who act outside legal or organisational policies to assist people they work with take significant risks, not just to themselves but in sometimes unpredictable ways. They risk immediate professional sanction and legal repercussions. Social workers who intend to act ethically must be aware of the legal limits on their roles so that if they overstep them they are able to weigh the potential outcome. If all the ethical social workers lose their jobs because they act subversively, there will be no ethical social workers left.

Social workers acting subversively may also, by the nature of subversive action, be acting without direct guidance or oversight. For all social workers, but particularly for new social workers, this is a very dangerous space to be in. Social workers must always ensure they have good supervision, but if they are acting subversively they may need to seek supervision outside their line management structure or outside their organisation.

Box 16.3 *A new lease*

I worked some years ago as a youth homelessness worker. I worked with a young woman, a 16-year-old single parent with three children. Child protection had removed her children and would not support their return until she had appropriate long-term accommodation. She could not afford a big enough house in private rental, and Centrelink would not give her the parenting payment until she had her children back in her care. The local community housing provider would not give her a house big enough until she had the children back in her care. She was stuck, while her children were growing up without their mother.

In my role as a youth homelessness worker I had 'allocation rights' to three transitional properties. This meant young people could stay in these properties until I had supported them into other accommodation. Without notifying my manager, I moved her into one of these transitional properties, which had four bedrooms. I knew that child protection would not support the return of her children until she had permanent accommodation, so when I was organising the paperwork I ticked the box for an ongoing lease. A lease is a legal document, and once in she could not be evicted unless she broke the terms of the lease.

She moved in and child protection begrudgingly supported the return of her children. I faced no repercussions, as I changed jobs soon after. She stayed in that house for years. A great outcome, except that we lost that transitional property, so no other young people could use it. This may have meant that dozens of young people and their children stayed homeless, denied the chance offered by a transitional housing property. I would do it again, but I still do not know if it was worth it in the long run.

There is also a real risk that social workers will believe that their values are 'good' or 'correct' and use that belief as an excuse for highly unethical practices. This also requires good supervision to keep in check, but there is a good chance that social workers who engage unreflexively in subversion will lack the insight required to seek out supervision when required. This demands social work educators and senior practitioners to engage with subversive social work as a practice modality so that social workers are equipped for practice. Ultimately, the responsibility for subversive actions will lie with the social worker who undertakes them.

Box 16.4 *Nola*

In 1973, in the Northern Territory, child protection social worker John Tomlinson returned Nola, a seven-year-old First Nations girl to her birth mother without departmental approval.[32] *Nola had been placed with a white foster family who had lobbied the department for her to stay with them. Tomlinson's view was that Nola's parents were legally entitled to have her returned. Not trusting that the dispute would be fairly settled in the Northern Territory Supreme Court, Tomlinson organised for her be returned without approval.*

With the benefit of hindsight, we can see this as a courageous action, albeit one that carried significant risk. Tomlinson reports that Nola returned to her community and country and was happy to be with her family. Tomlinson faced professional consequences and little changed in the system itself, which continued to place First Nations children with white families.

Above all, social workers should not see subversion as an end in itself. It is not even a means to an end. It is just what we do to minimise the harm the system can inflict while we work to change the system itself. A social worker in Sweden shared this:

> *Although I am working in this system, I am willing to cross the boundaries, even breaking the laws in order to help people. But it should not be a parallel activity that can continue forever without changing the structures.*[33]

There are many ways to work to change the structures, as discussed in Chapter 17, but some of them are less legal than others.

16.6 Whistleblowing

Whistleblowing is the practice of reporting wrongdoing in the workplace, usually outside of standard processes and outside of the ordinary chain of command.[34] Whistleblowing is necessary because social workers will be legally bound from sharing certain information about their organisation outside their organisation (see Chapter 6). This may be through employment contracts, in which case social workers can lose their jobs, or through legislative restrictions, which can have more serious penalties including imprisonment. Raymond, Beddoe and Staniforth argue that whistleblowing should have a special place in social work:

> *Whistleblowing in social work should perhaps be viewed as a special form of advocacy, as it is often about exposing unethical or other harmful behaviour on behalf of service users.*[35]

Whistleblowing will not always be acting outside the law. The AASW *Code of Ethics* requires social workers to report such issues, and social workers are advised by the *Code of Ethics* 'to ascertain what, if any, whistleblower protection options are provided in their state or territory'.[36] This is, unfortunately, much more difficult than it sounds, with different protections for whistleblowers in each jurisdiction and different laws for the Commonwealth public service, state and territory public services, and the private sector. Differences include what is permitted to be reported and how it is protected, such as if the whistleblower is allowed to stay anonymous. Often, social workers will be able to blow the whistle lawfully and will be enabled by whistleblower legislation.

Table 16.1 *Whistleblower protection legislation*

State or territory	Relevant legislation
Cth	*Public Interest Disclosure Act 2013* (Cth) *Treasury Laws Amendment (Enhancing Whistleblower Protections) Act 2019* (Cth)
ACT	*Public Interest Disclosure Act 2012* (ACT)
NSW	*Public Interest Disclosures Act 1994* (NSW)
NT	*Public Interest Disclosure Act 2008* (NT)
Qld	*Public Interest Disclosure Act 2010* (Qld)
SA	*Whistleblowers Protection Act 1993* (SA)
Tas	*Public Interest Disclosures Act 2002* (Tas)
Vic	*Protected Disclosure Act 2012* (Vic)
WA	*Public Interest Disclosure Act 2003* (WA)

Even when following legal processes, there can be significant consequences for whistleblowers, including bullying, exclusion in the workplace and carer impacts.[37] Social workers need to be aware of these consequences and weigh up their decision. When blowing the whistle outside legal protections, the consequences can be even more severe.

Box 16.5 *Saving the children*

In 2015, a group of Save the Children workers, including child protection social workers, had their employment terminated and were referred to the Federal Police. They had been working in the offshore detention facility on Nauru and were accused of breaching section 70 of the Crimes Act 1914 *(Cth), which dealt with the unauthorised disclosure of information.*

One of the social workers, Viktoria Vibhakar, described that when she had started work on Nauru she had been required to sign a legal document detailing her obligations of silence:

> *One of the first things I got, which was the most striking, was a deed of confidentiality, which was a couple pages and it basically said, you cannot say anything about what goes on in this facility and if you do, you are liable for two years in jail for each disclosure.*[38]

The human rights abuses in offshore detention in Nauru are well documented by numerous sources, including the United Nations. Later, Vibhakar told a Senate Committee that:

> *As a social worker, an important part of my ethical responsibility is to report child abuse as well as to report inadequate institutional responses to abuse that leave children at continued risk of harm. While I was employed*

> *at the Nauru detention facility, children and their families experienced physical and sexual assault, as well as extensive mental harm, as a result of their detainment. This harm could have been prevented.*[39]

A review exonerated the group,[40] *and the federal government eventually paid them $1 million in compensation.*[41] *They were never prosecuted, but the experience was by all accounts very difficult and distressing:*

> *Social worker Poppy Browne said the allegations 'absolutely destroyed' her. 'This experience impacted every part of me – my personal life, my professional capacities, my relationships and my daily functioning'.*[42]

Beyond the implications for the individuals involved, this treatment of social workers who speak out must have an overall chilling effect on other social workers who are considering blowing the whistle.

In 2019, four years after the social workers had their contracts terminated, the federal government bowed to community pressure and removed all children from Nauru.

16.7 Conclusion

Ultimately, even if acting legally, social workers acting subversively or blowing the whistle should anticipate some ramifications, even if only to be tagged as a troublemaker or a rule breaker within their organisation. Dominelli argues that social workers must 'be prepared for controversy that jeopardizes livelihoods, including their own, accepting that practising anti-oppressively is not without risk'.[43] Yu asks:

> *What form does social work practice take within regimes that brazenly allow or instigate the violation of human rights and welfare? What defines legitimate acting in such contexts? In state systems where injustice is institutionally sanctioned and legitimate avenues for dissent are systematically curtained, where does professional practice begin and end?*[44]

These are questions social workers must answer with their ethics, not the law.

Main points

1. Social workers will sometimes be forced into situations where their ethics collide with the law.
2. Subversive practice is risky, both for the social worker and the person they are supporting, but may be the only option left available, or may be justified in its own right.
3. Whistleblowing is protected in some circumstances and not in others, but even when done legally it can carry risks.

Discussion questions

1. Would you give up your job, to blow the whistle? Would you go to gaol? For how long? For what sort of issue?
2. Re-read Box 16.2 – Bye, Daddy! What sentence could that social worker have faced? What do you think might have happened if she had been caught?
3. Would you go to prison to share issues that it appears the general public doesn't care about? What if you have children, or if you care for your elderly parent?
4. What examples of subversive practice can you think of from your practice? How have you justified them?
5. What impact might laws that criminalise whistleblowing have on democracy? Think about the example of the social workers on Nauru.

Further reading

Nilan Yu and Deena Mandell (eds), *Subversive Action: Extralegal Practices for Social Justice* (Wilfrid Laurier University Press, 2015).

Sally Raymond, Liz Beddoe and Barbara Staniforth, 'Social Workers Experiences with Whistleblowing: To Speak or Not to Speak?' (25 September 2017) 29(3) *Aotearoa New Zealand Social Work* 17–29.

John Portelli and Ardavan Eizadirad, 'Subversion in Education: Common Misunderstandings and Myths' (2018) 9(1) *International Journal of Critical Pedagogy* 53–72.

Christopher Maylea and Asher Hirsch, 'Social Workers as Collaborators? The Ethics of Working Within Australia's Asylum System' (3 April 2018) 12(2) *Ethics and Social Welfare* 160–78.

Melissa Laing and Chris Maylea, 'A Conceptual Framework for Taking Subversive Social Work into the Classroom' (2018) 20(2) *Advances in Social Work and Welfare Education* 23–30.

16.8 References

[1] Nilan Yu and Deena Mandell, 'Social Work and Salt Making' in Nilan Yu and Deena Mandell (eds), *Subversive Action: Extralegal Practices for Social Justice* (Wilfrid Laurier University Press, 2015) 1.

[2] Patricia Fronek and Polly Chester, 'Moral Outrage: Social Workers in the Third Space' (2016) 10(2) *Ethics and Social Welfare* 163.

[3] AASW, *Code of Ethics* (Australian Association of Social Workers, 2010) 33.

[4] A. Jameton, 'Dilemmas of Moral Distress: Moral Responsibility and Nursing Practice' (1993) 4(4) *AWHONN's clinical issues in perinatal and women's health nursing* 542.

[5] Carina Fourie, 'Who Is Experiencing What Kind of Moral Distress? Distinctions for Moving from a Narrow to a Broad Definition of Moral Distress' (2017) 19(6) *AMA Journal of Ethics* 578.

[6] Melissa Floyd Taylor, 'Professional Dissonance' (2007) 77(1) *Smith College Studies in Social Work* 89, 94.

[7] Mimi Abramovitz, 'The Largely Untold Story of Welfare Reform and the Human Services' (2005) 50(2) *Social Work* 175, 182.

[8] Brett T. Litz et al, 'Moral Injury and Moral Repair in War Veterans: A Preliminary Model and Intervention Strategy' (2009) 29(8) *Clinical Psychology Review* 695, 700.

[9] Victoria Williamson, Sharon A.M. Stevelink and Neil Greenberg, 'Occupational Moral Injury and Mental Health: Systematic Review and Meta-Analysis' (2018) 212(6) *The British Journal of Psychiatry* 339.

[10] Linda Briskman and Deborah Zion, 'Dual Loyalties and Impossible Dilemmas: Health Care in Immigration Detention' (2014) 7(3) *Public Health Ethics* 277.

[11] Maurice J. Moreau, 'Empowerment through Advocacy and Consciousness-Raising: Implications of a Structural Approach to Social Work' (1990) 17(2) *Journal of Sociology and Social Welfare* 53.

[12] For a discussion on the relationship between small scale resistance and social change see: Patricia Ewick and Susan Silbey, 'Narrating Social Structure: Stories of Resistance to Legal Authority' (2003) 108(6) *American Journal of Sociology* 1328.

[13] John Portelli and Ardavan Eizadirad, 'Subversion in Education: Common Misunderstandings and Myths' (2018) 9(1) *International Journal of Critical Pedagogy* 53.

[14] Briskman and Zion (n 10); John Wallace and Bob Pease, 'Neoliberalism and Australian Social Work: Accommodation or Resistance?' (2011) 11(2) *Journal of Social Work* 132; Christopher Maylea and Asher Hirsch, 'Social Workers as Collaborators? The Ethics of Working Within Australia's Asylum System' (2018) 12(2) *Ethics and Social Welfare* 160; Ann Carrington, 'Feminism under Siege: Critical Reflections on the Impact of Neoliberalism and Managerialism on Feminist Practice' in Bob Pease et al (eds), *Doing Critical Social Work: Transformative Practices for Social Justice* (Allen & Unwin, 2016) 226 <https://www.allenandunwin.com/browse/books/academic-professional/social-work/Doing-Critical-Social-Work-Edited-by-Bob-Pease-Sophie-Goldingay-Norah-Hosken-and-Sharlene-Nipperess-9781760110840>; Magdalena Mostowska, '"We Shouldn't but We Do…": Framing the Strategies for Helping Homeless EU Migrants in Copenhagen and Dublin' [2014] *British Journal of Social Work* bcu043.

[15] Moreau (n 11).

[16] Malcolm Carey and Victoria Foster, 'Introducing "Deviant" Social Work: Contextualising the Limits of Radical Social Work Whilst Understanding (Fragmented) Resistance within the Social Work Labour Process' (2011) 41(3) *British Journal of Social Work* 576.

[17] Marshall Fine and Eli Teram, 'Overt and Covert Ways of Responding to Moral Injustices in Social Work Practice: Heroes and Mild-Mannered Social Work Bipeds' (2013) 43(7) *The British Journal of Social Work* 1312; Lyndal Greenslade, Donna

McAuliffe and Lesley Chenoweth, 'Social Workers' Experiences of Covert Workplace Activism' (2015) 68(4) *Australian Social Work* 422.
[18] B Jordan, *Social Work in an Unjust Society* (Harvester Wheatsheaf, 1990).
[19] Melissa Laing and Chris Maylea, 'A Conceptual Framework for Taking Subversive Social Work into the Classroom' (2018) 20(2) *Advances in Social Work and Welfare Education* 23.
[20] Tran Nguyen and Selvaraj Velayutham, 'Street-level Discretion, Emotional Labour and Welfare Frontline Staff at the Australian Employment Service Providers' (2018) 0(0) *Australian Journal of Social Issues* 1.
[21] Fine and Teram (n 17).
[22] Lyndal Greenslade, 'Social Work Activism: Resistance at the Frontier' (PhD Doctorate, Griffith University, 2013) 130 <https://www120.secure.griffith.edu.au/rch/items/d7fdcf64-505f-cda1-5269-2068451b8859/1/>.
[23] Peter Dutton, 'Questions without Notice: Asylum Seekers' (Hansard - Australian Parliament, 8 November 2016) <http://parlinfo.aph.gov.au/parlInfo/search/display/display.w3p;query=Id%3A%22chamber%2Fhansardr%2F35853536-eb47-48bb-9a4e-8044d466345a%2F0080%22>.
[24] Peter Dutton, 'Minister - Interview with Ray Hadley, Radio 2GB-4BC November 2016' <http://www.minister.border.gov.au/peterdutton/2016/Pages/interview-ray-hadley,-radio-2GB-4BC-nov-2016.aspx>.
[25] Ibid.
[26] Abramovitz (n 7) 182.
[27] Ida Okkonen and Tuomo Takala, 'Managers' Moral Struggle: A Case Study on Ethical Dilemmas and Ethical Decision-Making in the Context of Immigration' (2019) 0(0) *Ethics and Social Welfare* 1.
[28] *Corrections Act 1986* s 14.
[29] *Corrections Act 1986* s 32.
[30] Philip Moss, *Review into Recent Allegations Relating to Conditions and Circumstances at the Regional Processing Centre in Nauru* (Department of Immigration and Border Protection, 6 February 2015).
[31] AASW (n 3) 14.
[32] John Tomlinson, 'Challenging State Aggression against Indigenous Australians' in Nilan Yu and Deena Mandell (eds), *Subversive Action: Extralegal Practices for Social Justice* (Wilfrid Laurier University Press, 2015) 1.
[33] Jessica H Jönsson, 'Local Reactions to Global Problems: Undocumented Immigrants and Social Work' [2014] *British Journal of Social Work* i48 <http://bjsw.oxfordjournals.org/content/early/2014/05/14/bjsw.bcu042>.
[34] Angie Ash, *Whistleblowing and Ethics in Health and Social Care* (Jessica Kingsley Publishers, 2016).
[35] Sally Raymond, Liz Beddoe and Barbara Staniforth, 'Social Workers' Experiences with Whistleblowing: To Speak or Not to Speak?' (2017) 29(3) *Aotearoa New Zealand Social Work* 17, 18.
[36] AASW (n 3) 32.
[37] Raymond, Beddoe and Staniforth (n 35) 20.
[38] David Greene, Steve Inskpeek and Viktoria Vibhakar, 'Ex-Aid Worker: Abuse Of Refugee Children On Nauru Was Mostly Ignored', *Parallels* (NPR.org, 24 August 2016) <https://www.npr.org/sections/parallels/2016/08/24/491170178/ex-aid-worker-abuse-of-refugee-children-on-nauru-was-ignored>.
[39] Viktoria Vibhakar, *Commonwealth Government's Responsibilities Relating to the Management and Operation of the Nauru Regional Processing Centre* (Senate Committee, 9 June 2015) <http://parlinfo.aph.gov.au/parlInfo/search/display/display.w3p;query=Id%3A%22committees%2Fcommsen%2Fcf736b90-95c1-47c2-8f8e-1562423baa0e%2F0003%22>.

[40] Moss (n 30).
[41] Michael Koziol, 'Immigration Department Pays $1 Million Compensation to Save the Children Workers Fired from Nauru', *The Sydney Morning Herald* (online at 31 January 2017) <http://www.smh.com.au/federal-politics/political-news/immigration-department-pays-1-million-compensation-to-save-the-children-workers-fired-from-nauru-20170131-gu27nm.html>.
[42] Adam Morton, 'Save the Children Staff Accused and Deported from Nauru Demand an Explanation', *The Sydney Morning Herald* (4 October 2015) <http://www.smh.com.au/federal-politics/political-news/save-the-children-staff-accused-and-deported-from-nauru-demand-an-explanation-20151002-gk0g64.html>.
[43] Lena Dominelli, 'Anti-Oppressive Practice' in *Ethics and Value Perspectives in Social Work* (Palgrave Macmillan, 2010) 165.
[44] Yu, Nilan, 'Rights, Justice, the Law, and Extralegal Action' in Nilan Yu and Deena Mandell (eds), *Subversive Action: Extralegal Practices for Social Justice* (Wilfrid Laurier University Press, 2015) 1, 8.

Chapter 17 CHANGING THE LEGAL SYSTEM

Social workers cannot be complicit in environments and practices that inhibit social justice and violate human rights and still call themselves social workers – unless they are also working to challenge and change those environments and practices.[1] Where the law inhibits social justice and violates human rights, social workers have an obligation to change the law. This is not merely a matter of professional identity, although it is that too. Social workers have a fundamental obligation to the people they work with to examine the structural and social determinants of social problems.[2]

The legal system also reflects and shapes society at large, so it forms a key part of macro-social work practice. There are many ways in which social workers will engage in policy reform, social issue advocacy and other, non-legal aspects of reform, but these will also often have legal aspects. We cannot legislate away family violence, child abuse, mental distress or discrimination, but the law can play a key role in protecting people and in progressing social change. Any attempt to change the law will need to include broader social and political advocacy as it is often not possible to separate legal and political reform. Even formal law reform processes such as are described in this chapter need to be instigated by a politician. Any government or organisational policy relies on the government or organisation having the legal power to make the policy and all policy must conform with legislation and with the Constitution. This all means that social workers who work in policy settings or want to influence policy need a good understanding of the law to be able to make intelligent and useful contributions to policy reform.

There are many resources that can assist social workers with broader policy advocacy, activism and social reform. Which of these will be useful will depend largely on the motivation and political orientation of the social worker, from the conflict focused leftist *Rules for Radicals*,[3] to the conservative *Atlas Shrugged*.[4] Some resources provide practical guidance, guiding social workers in getting media attention, forming alliances, developing clear policy goals and applying political pressure. Others provide principles for informing activist practice.[5] Whatever the aims of social change, social workers will need to influence legal reform to achieve them. This chapter focuses on how the law can be used in policy and social reform, and how the law can be changed using two specific examples: formal law reform process and public interest litigation. Both these examples must be considered in the context of our democratic process, while the final section looks at radical law reform outside the democratic process.

17.1 Democracy and law reform

Australia's democratic system of government means that Australian laws are supposed to reflect the will of the people, and to some extent this is true. Laws often change to reflect changing social attitudes. The change to legally allow same-sex marriage is a good example of this. Following decades of campaigning and a national plebiscite, the Australian Parliament passed the *Marriage Amendment (Definition and Religious Freedoms) Act 2017* (Cth). It is also a good example of democracy not working, in that for many years the majority of Australians supported same-sex marriage and yet the law did not change until 2017. Between 2004 and 2017, 22 bills to legalise same-sex marriage were introduced and none of them passed into law.

Other examples, such as adult guardianship law reform, are so fringe that the great majority of voters will never take them into account when voting. This is probably not such a bad thing, because the majority of voters would not be able to make an informed decision about such issues.

Other times, politics trumps democracy. Depending on their political persuasion, social workers might look to the rise of populist demagogues both locally and overseas, at both ends of the political spectrum, for evidence that parliamentary democracy and social justice are not always aligned. The way some politicians use fearmongering and othering tactics, such as with people seeking asylum or other migrants, can shift public opinion and undermine democratic processes. As discussed in Chapter 10, the criminal legal system does not seem to reduce reoffending, but neither side of politics can afford to look weak on crime and so both regularly campaign on being tough on law and order. Similarly, democracy has proven spectacularly incapable of dealing with major issues that sit beyond the election cycle. Buchan writes:

> *We carry on as if we are in the normal course of events. Elections come and go; governments form and fall; the banal mendacity of public discourse washes over us like a fetid tide from which it seems we are unwilling to lift ourselves. Yet these are not normal times. It is our fate to live on the cusp of an abnormal course of events.*[6]

Buchan is writing of the inability of democracy to address climate change, but the same argument applies to the inability of democracy to address any social issue that requires consensus and cooperative action. Other failures of democracy include the influence of lobbyists, the focus on swing voters and marginal seats, corruption and the ability of the majority to oppress the minority. Social workers must be attuned to these issues with our political system when working to change the law. Any of the work social workers do to galvanise public opinion or bring political attention to an issue will have to navigate this context, which will sometimes mean taking alternative approaches to law reform.

17.2 Formal law reform

Each jurisdiction has a law reform agency, variously referred to as a commission, institute or council.[7] These bodies take issues referred to them from the government and go through a structured process to work out how the law should change, shown in Figure 17.1. This process will vary by jurisdiction, but usually the attorney general, who is a member of the cabinet, refers an issue to the law reform agency. They will consult with a wide variety of people, including people who will be impacted by any changes in the law, experts including academics, peak bodies and lobby groups. They will release an 'issues paper' that identifies the issues that need to be discussed, then take formal submissions. Usually, anyone can make a submission. For issues that impact on their practice, social workers should consider making submissions at this point. Following this, the law reform agency will usually release a discussion paper, which is a more detailed look at the issues, including what other people have submitted. Another round of submissions usually follows this. The agency will then formulate recommendations, which will go in a report and be given to the government. The government is then left to decide if it will implement those recommendations or not.

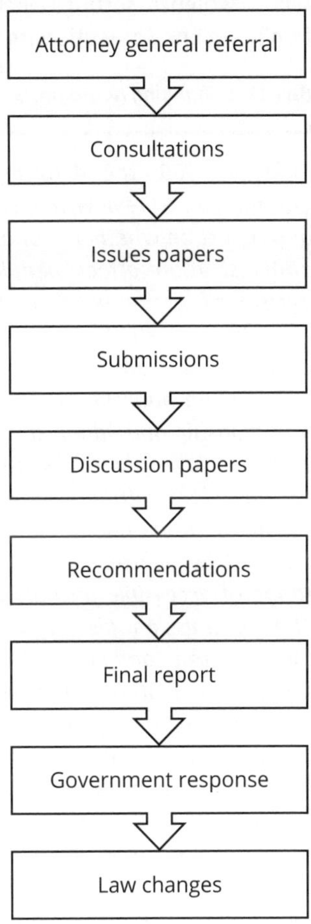

Figure 17.1 *Formal law reform process*

There is a similar process for royal commissions. These are a bit different in that once started they cannot be stopped by the government.[8] They are independent of the government and tend to be a bit more inquisitorial and can compel people to give testimony. Commissions of inquiry are similar to royal commissions but are used for less significant issues and tend to have more limited powers. Sometimes, royal commissions can lead to positive law reform. The Royal Commission into Aboriginal Deaths in Custody, for example, resulted in significant legal reform that halved the rate at which First Nations people die in custody,[9] albeit often too little and too late.[10] Similarly, the Victorian government has committed to implementing all 227 of the recommendations from the Royal Commission into Family Violence and has set up a website so the public can track its progress.[11] The Australian Association of Social Workers (AASW) and many social workers made submissions to that Royal Commission, and the recommendations include changes to the way social workers are trained and employed in family violence settings, including that 'all funded services must require family violence practitioners to hold a social work or equivalent degree'.[12]

Box 17.1 *Changing guardianship laws*

In May 2009, the Attorney-General asked the Victorian Law Reform Commission to review the Guardianship and Administration Act 1986 *(Vic) and report on whether changes were needed. Laws about guardianship and administration affect people who have someone appointed to make decisions for them because their decision-making capacity is impaired.*

In January 2010, the Commission published an information paper that explained the operation of the laws in Victoria. In February 2011, the Commission published a consultation paper that described how Victoria's guardianship and administration laws currently operate, outlined problems with the current laws, discussed laws in other jurisdictions and put forward options for reform. This reference required extensive community consultation to understand the day-to-day realities of community members affected by guardianship laws. The Commission published materials in a range of accessible formats to encourage broad community participation. The Commission also conducted significant community consultation in metropolitan and regional areas. Many individuals and community organisations attended consultations and made submissions to the review over two-and-a-half years. The Commission also established two expert advisory committees.

The final report was tabled in Parliament on 18 April 2012. It included 440 recommendations to modernise, clarify and simplify guardianship laws to better meet the needs of Victoria's changing population. The report, consultation paper and other documents can be downloaded from the Victorian Law Reform Commission website.

Implementation

- *1 May 2018 –* Guardianship and Administration Bill 2018 *moved a second time. Further work and consideration of VLRC recommendations is required before it will pass (Council, Second Reading, Mr Jennings).*
- *1 September 2015 – Powers of attorney in Victoria changed with the commencement of the* Powers of Attorney Act 2014, *which implements many of the Committee's recommendations.*

The Bill allows for the appointment of a support person to assist those with impaired decision-making abilities (Recommendation 47).

(Reproduced with permission from the Victorian Law Reform Commission[13])

A third formal law reform process is a parliamentary inquiry. Parliamentary inquiries are conducted by members of parliament, often by standing committees. They also consider an issue in depth and then report back to parliament. An example is the Inquiry into laws governing termination of pregnancy in Queensland. The *Abortion Law Reform (Woman's Right to Choose) Amendment Bill 2016* (Qld) was tabled in the Queensland Parliament in 2016. At the time, abortion was criminalised under the *Criminal Code 1899* (Qld). Rather than vote on the bill immediately, it was referred to the Health, Communities, Disability Services and Domestic and Family Violence Prevention Committee for consideration.[14] This committee is comprised of members of the Queensland Parliament. They conducted public hearings and received 1400 submissions on the issue, then recommended that the bill not be passed. The bill was withdrawn and not voted on, and the issue was referred to the Queensland Law Reform Commission, which received 1200 submissions and released a report in 2018.[15] This report recommended that a different bill, the *Termination of Pregnancy Bill 2018* (Qld) should be introduced. This was then passed into law as the *Termination of Pregnancy Act 2018* (Qld) in December 2018. All of this occurred in the context of political demonstrations on both sides, abortion law reform across the country and influence from international human rights law.[16]

Other bodies might also conduct inquiries that follow a similar process, such as ombudsmen, coroners, anti-corruption bodies and government departments. Most law reform processes have specific 'terms of reference' that outline and restrict what they can and cannot do. A good example is the *National Disability Insurance Scheme Act 2013* (Cth), which enabled the National Disability Insurance Scheme. This was passed in response to an inquiry by the Australian Productivity Commission,[17] albeit following decades of lobbying to get the political will to examine the issue.

Social workers can use these formal processes to influence law reform. They can call for inquiries or commissions to be established, they can influence terms of reference and they can make submissions in response to issues papers and discussion papers, and they can hold governments to account to ensure they follow up on the recommendations. The AASW has developed a guide for social workers to make submissions in law and policy reform processes.[18] Submissions will be most persuasive when they are research- and evidence-based, so social workers can develop that evidence themselves through research projects or in partnership with research organisations such as universities.

Social workers can also help lawyers and policy workers in this process. This might include community organising, providing links between formal policy bodies and activists. One function social workers often play is in supporting people who have used services to speak about their experience, either in formal law reform agencies or in the media. This is a tricky process, as people may experience retraumatisation and other distress from publicly sharing their stories. With this in mind, social workers should always be alert to ways they can maximise the voices of people they work with in reforming laws that impact on them, particularly their human rights.

These formal processes work well in situations where the government wants to fix the issue and where the issue can be fixed by changing legislation. When this is not the case other strategies will be required to bring the government's attention to the issue. There are other situations, such as offshore detention of people seeking asylum, where the government has intentionally designed the law to be draconian and are unlikely to want to change it.

17.3 Public interest litigation

Social workers do not have a tradition of public interest litigation, although there are some examples from the United States.[19] Public interest litigation, sometimes referred to as strategic litigation or strategic legal advocacy, is the process of taking a case to court not necessarily with the intention of winning that specific case, but of getting the law changed. It seeks to benefit the wider community, not just the person in that specific case.

There are a number of reasons why public interest litigation is a valuable tool. Sometimes, public interest litigation is useful for clarifying a point of law or getting decision-makers to understand a point of law, rather than having a law overturned. Other times it might be aimed at getting the High Court to make a decision that will apply to all the other courts, or it might be a constitutional challenge to the authority of government. Sometimes public interest litigation is just about drawing attention to an issue by pushing it through the courts. To illustrate what this looks like in practice, consider four examples of public interest litigation.

In *Roach v Electoral Commissioner*,[20] the Commonwealth government introduced legislation to prevent all sentenced prisoners from voting. Vicki Lee Roach, a Yuin woman from Victoria who was serving a prison sentence for robbing a milk bar, challenged the legislation, represented by a former judge. The High Court found that a blanket ban on prisoners voting was unconstitutional but found that previous legislation banning prisoners serving a sentence of three years or longer did not breach the constitution. Vicki Lee Roach did not benefit from this outcome as she was serving a six-year sentence, but thousands of other prisoners on shorter sentences were given this right. This case is also mentioned in Chapter 9.

Innes v Rail Corporation NSW is another good example of this process at work.[21] Graeme Innes was the Commonwealth Disability Discrimination Commissioner and is blind. He sued the Rail Corporation New South Wales (NSW) for failing to provide audible 'next stop' announcements, claiming that this failure amounted to unlawful discrimination and a breach of the *Disability Discrimination Act 1992* (Cth). The Federal Magistrates' Court found that failure to make the announcements was indirect discrimination and awarded Mr Innes $10,000.* As a result, the train company agreed to ensure that all trains would carry 'next stop' announcements – a win for the 100,000 blind and vision-impaired people living in NSW. There are similar cases for wheelchair accessible buses,[22] wheelchair accessible taxis,[23] and air travel.[24]

PBU & NJE v Mental Health Tribunal[25] is a case that was heard before the Victorian Supreme Court. PBU and NJE were both ordered to have electroconvulsive treatment (ECT) by the Victorian Mental Health Tribunal and by the Victorian Civil and Administrative Tribunal. The Supreme Court found that in both cases the tribunals had incorrectly applied the law, particularly regarding a person's capacity to consent to or refuse treatment. This case was not just about getting ECT overturned for these two people, although that was certainly part of it. The aim for the lawyers who ran the case was to get the tribunals to focus more on rights and less on best interests. This was a strategic move. The lawyer who ran the case said:

> *The decision provides clear guidance that mental health patients have the same fundamental human rights as everyone else in the community, and decisions about their treatment must be made in accordance with those rights.*[26]

Public interest litigation can sometimes be undermined if the other party does not want the law to be clarified. This occurred in *Masterton v DHHS*,[27] where Masterton wanted to challenge Centrelink's 'robodebt' scheme. Robodebt is the name given to a Centrelink process that automatically

* The total remuneration for the Disability Discrimination Commissioner in 2016 was $339,460, so $10,000 is not a significant sum.

sends people invoices for debts they owe, which has been widely criticised for raising debts that do not actually exist.[28] Rather than risk losing the case and having the robodebt scheme revoked, the government just cancelled Masterton's debt. This meant that there was no case to answer – without a debt Masterton could no longer contest her debt in court and challenge the scheme. This case is ongoing at the time of writing, with Masterton's lawyers arguing that the case should be heard anyway. This highlights the slightly perverse nature of public interest litigation, as Masterton has won the case but nonetheless wants to go to court.

Social workers will not be running public interest litigation as that will be done by lawyers, but social workers can assist in the process and should understand how it works. Social workers can work closely with lawyers to identify people who may be interested in participating in public interest litigation. Finding the right person for the right issue can be really difficult. They need to be a good example of why the law needs to be changed or clarified, they need to have a strong legal case and they need to be prepared not to settle before the case gets to judgment. They also need to be at a point in their lives where being involved in litigation will not be harmful to them, or they need to be prepared for the challenges, which can include a loss of privacy and public humiliation, with no sure chance of winning. There is no point in running public interest litigation if the person at the centre of the case is going to accept a settlement or withdraw halfway through the process, which they have every right to do. Social workers can help in supporting people so that they are able to get through what can be a very difficult process, especially if they are not anonymous and are able to be identified by the media.

Box 17.2 highlights how social workers can use strategic litigation to effect legal change.

Box 17.2 *An open secret*

In 2015 a group for more than 40 health and welfare workers published an open letter in defiance of new secrecy laws in the Australian Border Force Act 2015 *(Cth). This letter detailed human rights violations and other abuses in the asylum seeker processing system. The new laws meant that 'entrusted persons' sharing 'protected information' would be subject to two years imprisonment. The group, including social workers, doctors, nurses, teachers and other humanitarian workers, called on the government to prosecute:*

> *We are aware that in publishing this letter we may be prosecuted under the Australian Border Force Act and we challenge the Department to prosecute so that these issues may be discussed in open court and in the full view of the Australian public.*[29]

This was a strategic attempt to get the government to prosecute. The government did not prosecute, but also did not change the legislation. Subsequently, an advocacy group called Doctors for Refugees launched a High Court challenge to the legislation, claiming it infringed on the right of political communication in the Constitution. This case had some chance of succeeding, but it was far from being a sure thing. Under political pressure, the federal government backed down anyway.

The government exempted health practitioners (but not social workers or other professionals) from the legislation. Because the High Court challenge had been about doctors, the Doctors for Refugees case was withdrawn. In 2017, under more political pressure, the government passed the Australian Border Force Amendment (Protected Information) Bill 2017 *(Cth), which meant that 'protected information' was limited to issues of national security, defence, international relations or sensitive personal or commercial matters. The law is still unclear, but this means that social workers may be able to speak more freely about human rights violations in offshore detention and other immigration facilities without risking imprisonment. Since then, more workers, including social workers, have spoken out about issues with government contractors supporting asylum seekers.*[30]

Box 17.2 is a good example of a combination of public interest litigation and other policy advocacy combining to bring legal change. The government did not prosecute the group who published their open letter, and the subsequent litigation by Doctors for Refugees was not successful in court, but the law was changed anyway.

17.4 Radical Social Reform and the Law

Sometimes, social change can be achieved from within, as shown above using democratic processes, formal law reform or public interest litigation. Other social change is not possible within the current system and would require a complete reorganisation of society and a refutation of its core systems, including the legal system. Take, for example, Foucault's arguments that courts and prisons – the whole judicial and penal systems – should be dismantled:

> *... the revolution can only take place via the radial elimination of the judicial apparatus, and anything which could reintroduce the penal apparatus, anything which could reintroduce its ideology and enable this ideology to surreptitiously creep back into popular practices, must be banished.*[31]

Depending on the ethical and values framework that social workers adopt, they will inevitably come up against an issue that is not only not solvable within the current legal system, but one that is actively caused by it. For social workers who agree with Foucault's analysis of power in the legal system, it is really very difficult to see how that legal system could be used to fix itself. The legal system arose as a way of settling disputes about property, of maintaining power over others and asserting personal rights. It has become much more than that, but at its core it is a mechanism for maintaining the status quo. For social workers who see social problems as arising from property ownership, power imbalances and personal rights, the legal system will always be more part of the problem than part of the solution. Despite a generally high level of adherence to the rule of law (see Chapter 2), we have consistently seen that the law has not prevented human rights violations (see Chapter 9). In the areas of disability (Chapter 13), mental health (Chapter 14) and refugee and asylum seeker responses (Chapter 15), the law not only fails to prevent human rights violations but actively upholds and legitimises human rights violations as key elements of the legal system. This is never more the case than when considering violations of the rights of First Nations people and communities (see Chapter 12). Fanon, speaking to revolutionaries and potential revolutionaries across what we now call the Global South, argues that decolonisation cannot occur without violence, and that violence – lawlessness – is necessary to achieve the liberation of colonialised peoples.[32]

This revolutionary response is not without its own risks. With this kind of social change, a social change outside the legal system, both Foucault and Fanon warn that the mechanism of revolutionary social change can lead to a reproduction of the exploitative forces that were what the revolution was trying to address in the first place. Fanon writes:

> *The militant who faces the colonialist war machine with the bare minimum of arms realizes that while he is breaking down colonial oppression he is building up yet another system of exploitation. This discovery is unpleasant, bitter, and sickening: and yet everything seemed so simple before.*[33]

How much change is necessary or possible and how that change might be achieved are necessarily points of disagreement across the political spectrum. Ultimately, whether you choose to overthrow the system in a bloody coup or if you choose to collude with the status quo and are first up against the wall when the revolution comes will be largely a matter of taste. At the very least, social workers will need to look beyond the law for answers to social problems and will need to determine if those social problems can be addressed using the law, within the law or if they demand a step outside the law.

This idea of social work without the law, or of radical social reform beyond the law or outside the law, brings us to the very edge of the topic that is 'law for social work', and seems as such an appropriate place to end this book.

17.5 Conclusion

Social workers are mandated to engage in social reform, which means they must engage with legal reform. All of the topics discussed in this book demonstrate the power of the law to protect people and the potential of the law to harm people. Social workers must harness the law, shape it, change it and perhaps overthrow it to uphold human rights and to work towards social justice. This is only one step in the long march towards social justice, but it is one that social workers must take.

Main points

1. Social workers must challenge environments and practices that violate human rights and impede social justice. This includes the legal system.
2. Australia's democratic system of government is set up in a way that should allow laws to adapt to shifting social values and attitudes.
3. Each Australian jurisdiction has a law reform body.
4. Royal commissions are independent of the government, are more inquisitorial and once started, they cannot be stopped by the government.
5. Social workers can make submissions in law and policy reform processes in order to create change.
6. Public interest litigation is the process of taking a case to court for the purpose of getting the law changed, clarifying a point of law, getting decision-makers to understand a point of law or drawing attention to an issue. While social workers will not run these cases, they can assist in the process.

Discussion questions

1. What is the name of the law reform body in your jurisdiction? Remember, it may be called a commission, an institute or a council. What are they currently working on? What are their recent reports relevant to social work?
2. Review some royal commissions that took place over the last ten years. Were their recommendations generally followed? Are they useful?
3. *Roach v Electoral Commissioner*, *Innes v Rail Corporation NSW* and *PBU & NJE v Mental Health Tribunal* are all examples of public interest litigation. Can you find other examples where public interest litigation has been used to create change?

Further reading

Donna Baines, 'Bridging the Practice-Activism Divide: Advocacy, Organising and Social Movements'. In Donna Baines, *Doing Anti-Oppressive Practice: Social Justice Social Work* 3rd ed. (Fernwood Publishing, 2017).

Bruce Buchan, 'The Mandate of the Dead' (2019) 234 (Autumn) *Overland* <https://overland.org.au/2019/06/the-mandate-of-the-dead/>.

17.6 REFERENCES

[1] Christopher Maylea and Asher Hirsch, 'Social Workers as Collaborators? The Ethics of Working Within Australia's Asylum System' (2018) 12(2) *Ethics and Social Welfare* 160.
[2] Jonathan P. Beckett, 'The Changing Nature of Social Work' (2018) 61(6) *International Social Work* 968.
[3] Ayn Rand and Leonard Peikoff, *Atlas Shrugged: 35th Anniversary Edition* (Dutton Adult, 1992).
[4] Ibid.
[5] Donna Baines, *Doing Anti-Oppressive Practice: Social Justice Social Work* (Fernwood Pub., 2011); Jessica Morrison, 'Taking It to the Streets: Critical Social Work's Relationship with Activism' in Bob Pease et al (eds), *Doing Critical Social Work: Transformative Practices for Social Justice* (Allen & Unwin, 2016) 286; Lena Dominelli, 'Anti-Oppressive Practice' in *Ethics and Value Perspectives in Social Work* (Palgrave Macmillan, 2010).
[6] Bruce Buchan, 'The Mandate of the Dead' (2019) 234 (Autumn) *Overland* <https://overland.org.au/2019/06/the-mandate-of-the-dead/>.
[7] 'Australian Law Reform Agencies', *Australian Law Reform Commission* (22 June 2018) <https://www.alrc.gov.au/links/australian-law-refom>.
[8] *Royal Commission Act 1902* (Cth).
[9] Alexandra Gannoni and Samantha Bricknell, *National Deaths in Custody Program: Deaths in Custody in Australia 2016–17* (Text, Australian Institute of Criminology, 21 February 2019) <https://aic.gov.au/publications/sr/sr13>.
[10] Royal Commission into Aboriginal Deaths in Custody (Australian Government Publishing Service, 1991) <http://www.austlii.edu.au/au/other/IndigLRes/rciadic/>.
[11] Victorian Government, 'Ending Family Violence: Victoria's 10 Year Plan for Change' (2019) <http://www.vic.gov.au/familyviolence>.
[12] Marcia Neave, Patricia Faulkner and Tony Nicholson, *Royal Commission into Family Violence Report* (Royal Commission into Family Violence, 2016) 102.
[13] Victorian Law Reform Commission, 'Guardianship' (2019) <https://www.lawreform.vic.gov.au/all-projects/guardianship>.
[14] *Abortion Law Reform (Woman's Right to Choose) Amendment Bill 2016 and Inquiry into Laws Governing Termination of Pregnancy in Queensland* (No 24, Health, Communities, Disability Services and Domestic and Family Violence Prevention Committee, August 2016) <https://www.parliament.qld.gov.au/documents/tableOffice/TabledPapers/2016/5516T1337.pdf>.
[15] *Review of Termination of Pregnancy Laws* (Queensland Law Reform Commission, 2018).
[16] Tom Gotsis and Laura Ismay, *Abortion Law a National Perspective* (NSW Parliamentary Research Service, 2017) <https://www.parliament.nsw.gov.au/researchpapers/Pages/Abortion-law-a-national-perspective.aspx>.

[17] Australia and Productivity Commission, *Disability Care and Support: Productivity Commission Inquiry Report*, vol 1 (Productivity Commission, 2011).
[18] AASW, *AASW Policy & Advocacy How to Develop a Policy Submission* (Australian Association of Social Workers) <https://www.aasw.asn.au/document/item/8708>.
[19] Paul A. Levy, 'Social Work Roles in Law Reform Litigation' (1991) 36(5) *Social Work* 434.
[20] *Roach v Electoral Commissioner* [2007] HCA 43.
[21] *Innes v Rail Corporation NSW* [2013] FMC 36.
[22] *Haraksin v Murrays Australia Limited (No 2)* [2013] FCA 217.
[23] *Killeen v Combined Communications Network Pty Ltd* [2011] FCA 27.
[24] *Corcoran v Virgin Blue Airlines Pty Ltd* [2008] FCA 864.
[25] *PBU & NJE v Mental Health Tribunal* [2018] VSC 564.
[26] McLachlan, Hamish, 'Landmark Judgment Strengthens Patients' Rights in Compulsory Electroconvulsive Treatment Cases', Victoria Legal Aid (Text, 31 October 2018) <https://www.legalaid.vic.gov.au/about-us/news/landmark-judgment-strengthens-patients-rights-in-compulsory-electroconvulsive-treatment-cases>.
[27] This is an ongoing case (2019), so does not have a proper court report to cite. See *Masterton v Secretary, Department of Human Services* (Federal Court, VID73/2019, 04-Feb-2019).
[28] Luke Henriques-Gomes, 'Centrelink Drops Woman's Robodebt after She Mounts Court Challenge', *The Guardian* (online at 4 May 2019) <https://www.theguardian.com/australia-news/2019/may/05/centrelink-drops-womans-robodebt-after-she-mounts-court-challenge>.
[29] 'Letter to Prime Minister Tony Abbott' Letter from John-Paul Sanggaran et al, 1 July 2015 <https://www.scribd.com/document/270132364/Letter-to-Prime-Minister-Tony-Abbott>.
[30] Alexandra Blucher and Natalie Whiting, '"Cook the Books": Workers Told to Falsify Documents to Prepare for Audit', *ABC News* (online at 5 May 2019) <https://www.abc.net.au/news/2019-05-05/refugee-caseworkers-in-png-told-to-falsify-reports-for-australia/11062160>.
[31] Michel Foucault, *Power/Knowledge: Selected Interviews and Other Writings, 1972–1977*, ed. Colin Gordon (Pantheon Books, 1980) 16.
[32] Frantz Fanon, *The Wretched of the Earth*, tr. Richard Philcox, reprint ed. (Grove Press, 2005).
[33] Ibid 145.

Table of Authorities

Note: Page numbers followed by 'n' refer to notes.

Cases

A

B

C

D

E

G

Statutes

International Law

Index

Note: Page numbers followed by 'n' refer to notes.